AF766191

EUROPEAN
UNION

CYBER SECURITY STRTEGY AND PROGRAMS HANDBOOK

VOLUME 1

STRATEGIC INFORMTION AND REGULATIONS

International Business Publications, USA
Washington DC, USA

EUROPEAN UNION

CYBER SECURITY STRTEGY AND PROGRAMS HANDBOOK

VOLUME 1 STRATEGIC INFORMTION AND REGULATIONS

UPDATED ANNUALLY

We express our sincere appreciation to all EU Central Bank and other government agencies and international organizations which provided information and other materials for this handbook This handbook is based on information obtained free of charge from the European Bank sources and other European financial organizations. No modification to the information have been made

Cover Design: International Business Publications, USA

International Business Publications, USA. ***has used its best efforts in collecting, analyzing and preparing data, information and materials for this unique handbook. Due to the dynamic nature and fast development of the economy and business environment, we cannot warrant that all information herein is complete and accurate. IBP does not assume and hereby disclaim any liability to any person for any loss or damage caused by possible errors or omissions in the handbook.***
This handbook is for individual use only. Use this handbook for any other purpose, included but not limited to reproducing and storing in a retrieval system by any means, electronic, photocopying or using the addresses or other information contained in this handbook for any commercial purposes requires a special written permission from the publisher.

2018 Edition Updated Reprint International Business Publications, USA
ISBN 1-5775-1343-6

For additional analytical, business and investment opportunities information,
please contact Global Investment & Business Center, USA
at (703) 370-8082. Fax: (703) 370-8083. E-mail: ibpusa3@gmail.com
Global Business and Investment Info Databank - www.ibpus.com

Printed in the USA

For additional analytical, business and investment opportunities information,
please contact Global Investment & Business Center, USA
at (703) 370-8082. Fax: (703) 370-8083. E-mail: ibpusa3@gmail.com
Global Business and Investment Info Databank - www.ibpus.com

EUROPEAN
UNION
NATIONAL CYBER SECURITY STRTEGY AND PROGRAMS HANDBOOK
VOLUME 1
STRATEGIC INFORMTION AND REGULATIONS

EUROPEAN UNION STRATEGIC INFORMATION **8**
BASIC INFORMATION 8
COUNTRIES *10*
History *11*
A United States of Europe? *12*
The Treaties *12*
Governing System *14*
Governing Institutions *15*
Codecision Procedure *15*
European Parliament *15*
European Council *16*
Council of the European Union *16*
Agencies and Other Bodies *17*
European Commission *17*
European Economic and Social Committee *18*
Committee of the Regions *18*
European Court of Justice (ECJ) *18*
Culture *19*
Education and Training *20*
eEurope *20*
Employment and Social Policy *20*
Energy *21*
Environment *21*
Foreign Aid *22*
Foreign Policy *22*
Human Rights *22*
Justice and Home Affairs: Free Movement, Counterterrorism and Internal Security *23*
Regional Development *24*
Research and Technological Development (R&TD) *24*
Telecommunications *25*
Trade *25*
Transport *25*
BUILDING THE NEW EUROPE: THE EU AND ITS NEIGHBORS 26
Toward EU Membership *26*
Future European Union Enlargement *28*
Cyprus, Malta, and Turkey *30*
Norway and Switzerland *30*
Croatia *30*

PHARE, TACIS, CARDS ... 31
Russia and Its Neighbors ... 31
Projecting Stability in Southeast Europe ... 32
Mediterranean and Middle East Countries ... 32

ECONOMIC, TRADE AND MONETARY UNION OF THE EUROPEAN UNION ... 34

History of the EMU ... 34
Stage One: 1 July 1990 to 31 December 1993 ... 35
Stage Two: 1 January 1994 to 31 December 1998 ... 35
Stage Three: 1 January 1999 and continuing ... 35

CYBER SECURITY STANDARDS - STRATEGIC INFORMATION AND DEVELOPMENTS ... 36

INTERNATIONAL CYBERCRIME - IMPORTNT DEFINITIONS ... 36
Intrusive Offences ... 36
Content-related offences ... 36
Copyright and trademark-related offences ... 37
Computer-related offences ... 37
Combination offences ... 37
Threats ... 37
International trends ... 38
INTERNATIONAL LEGISLATIVE RESPONSES AND COOPERATION ... 39
International responses ... 39
Regional responses ... 40
Voluntary industry response ... 41
CONVENTION ON CYBERCRIME ... 41
Objectives ... 41
Accession by the United States ... 42
Accession by other non-European states ... 43
INTERNATIONAL PROGRAMS AND PROGECTS IN CYBER CRIME PREVENTION ... 43
Strategic Priorities for the Cooperation against Cybercrime ... 43
DIRECTIVE ON PRIVACY AND ELECTRONIC COMMUNICATIONS ... 52
Subject and Scope ... 52
Main provisions ... 52
Data retention and other issues ... 52
Unsolicited e-mail and other messages ... 53
Cookies ... 53

EU CYBER SECURITY STRATEGY - IMPORTANT DEVELOPMENTS AND REGULTIONS.. 55

Definition of computer-related crime ... 55
Legislative and non-legislative proposals ... 55
Common EU Cyber Crime Crime Strategy ... 56
New measures ... 57
EU Cybersecurity plan to protect open internet and online freedom and opportunity ... 57
EU COUNTRIES Competent Authorities ... 59

EU CYBER SPACE DEVELOPMENT STRATEGY ... 61

PILLAR I: DIGITAL SINGLE MARKET ... 61
Action 1: Simplifying pan-European licensing for online works ... 61
Action 2: Preserving orphan works and out of print works ... 61
Action 3: Open up public data resources for re-use ... 62
Action 4: Wide stakeholder debate on further measures to stimulate a European online content market ... 63
Action 5: Simplifying the distribution of creative content ... 64
Action 6: Protecting intellectual property rights online ... 65

Action 7: Fix a date for migration to Single European Payment & eInvoicing 65
Action 8: Revision of the eSignature directive 66
Action 9: Updating the eCommerce Directive 67
Action 10: Member States to implement laws to support the digital single market 68
Action 11: Member States to transpose the VAT Directive 69
Action 12: Review the EU data protection rules 69
Action 13: Complementing the Consumer Rights Directive 70
Action 14: Explore the possibilities for Alternative Dispute Resolution 71
Action 15: Consult the stakeholders on collective redress 71
Action 16: Code of EU online rights 72
Action 17: Stakeholder platform for EU online trustmarks 73
Action 18: Harmonisation of numbering regimes 73
Action 19: Spectrum Policy plan 75
Action 20: Investigate the cost of non-Europe in the telecoms market 75
Action 101: Look for durable solutions for voice and data roaming by 2012. 76
Action 102: Key Transformative Action 1: Copyright – the way forward 76
Action 103: Adopt and implement the key digital single market proposals of the Digital Agenda 77
Action 104: Follow up on eCommerce Action Plan, Green Paper on payments 78
Action 105: Guidelines to correctly implement EU rules on consumer information requirements 78
Action 106: VAT reform - align tax rates for digital content and similar physical goods 79
Action 107: Proposals to strengthen the data industry in Europe 80
Action 108: Green paper on a converged audiovisual world 81
PILLAR II: INTEROPERABILITY & STANDARDS 82
Action 21: Propose legislation on ICT interoperability 82
Action 22: Promote standard-setting rules 83
Action 23: Provide guidance on ICT standardisation and public procurement 84
Action 24: Adopt a European Interoperability Strategy and Framework 86
Action 25: Identify and assess means of requesting significant market players to licence information about their products or services 87
Action 26: MS to implement European Interoperability Framework 88
Action 27: Member States to implement Malmö and Granada declarations 88
PILLAR III: TRUST & SECURITY 89
Action 28: Reinforced Network and Information Security Policy 89
Action 29: Combat cyber-attacks against information systems 90
Action 30: Establish a European cybercrime platform 91
Action 31: Analyse the usefulness of creating a European cybercrime centre 91
Action 32: Strengthen the fight against cybercrime and cyber-attacks at international level 92
Action 33: Support EU-wide cyber-security preparedness 93
Action 34: Explore the extension of security breach notification provisions 94
Action 35: Guidance on implementation of Telecoms rules on privacy 95
Action 36: Support reporting of illegal content online and awareness campaigns on online safety for children 95
Action 37: Foster self-regulation in the use of online services 99
Action 38: Member States to establish pan-European Computer Emergency Response Teams 100
Action 39: Member States to carry out cyber-attack simulations 101
Action 40: Member States to implement harmful content alert hotlines 101
Action 41: Member States to set up national alert platforms 103
Action 123: Proposal for Directive on network and information security 104
Action 124: EU Cyber-security strategy 105
Action 125 Expand the Global Alliance against Child Sexual Abuse Online 106
CYBERSECURITY STRATEGY OF THE EUROPEAN UNION: AN OPEN, SAFE AND SECURE CYBERSPACE 108
1. INTRODUCTION 108
2. STRATEGIC PRIORITIES AND ACTIONS 110
3. ROLES AND RESPONSIBILITIES 124

4. CONCLUSION AND FOLLOW-UP ... 127
PROPOSAL FOR A COUNCIL FRAMEWORK DECISION ON ATTACKS AGAINST INFORMATION SYSTEMS ... 128
1. INTRODUCTION ... 128
2. LEGAL BASIS ... 134
3. THE FRAMEWORK DECISION: ARTICLES ... 135

BASIC INTERNATIONAL AND EU OFFICIAL MATERIALS ... 149

CODE OF EU ONLINE RIGHTS ... 149
Rights & Principles applicable when you access and use online services ... 149
Rights & Principles applicable when you buy goods or services online ... 152
THE CONVENTION ON CYBERCRIME ... 158
Preamble ... 158
Chapter I – Use of terms ... 159
Chapter II – Measures to be taken at the national level ... 160
Chapter III – International co-operation ... 169
Chapter IV – Final provisions ... 176
DIRECTIVE ON PRIVACY AND ELECTRONIC COMMUNICATIONS ... 180
Article 2 Definitions ... 188
Article 3 Services concerned ... 189
Article 4 Security ... 189
Article 5 Confidentiality of the communications ... 190
Article 6 Traffic data ... 190
Article 7 Itemised billing ... 191
Article 8 Presentation and restriction of calling and connected line identification ... 191
Article 9 Location data other than traffic data ... 191
Article 10 Exceptions ... 192
Article 11 Automatic call forwarding ... 192
Article 12 Directories of subscribers ... 192
Article 13 Unsolicited communications ... 193
Article 14 Technical features and standardisation ... 193
Article 15 Application of certain provisions of Directive 95/46/EC ... 194
Article 16 Transitional arrangements ... 194
Article 17 Transposition ... 194
Article 18 Review ... 194
Article 19 Repeal ... 195
Article 20 Entry into force ... 195
DIRECTIVE OF THE EUROPEAN PARLIAMENT AND OF THE COUNCIL CONCERNING MEASURES TO ENSURE A HIGH COMMON LEVEL OF NETWORK AND INFORMATION SECURITY ACROSS THE UNION ... 195
EXPLANATORY MEMORANDUM ... 195
2. RESULTS OF CONSULTATIONS WITH THE INTERESTED PARTIES AND IMPACT ASSESSMENTS ... 199
3. LEGAL ELEMENTS OF THE PROPOSAL ... 200
4. BUDGETARY IMPLICATIONS ... 202
CHAPTER I GENERAL PROVISIONS ... 208
CHAPTER II NATIONAL FRAMEWORKS ON NETWORK AND INFORMATION SECURITY ... 210
CHAPTER III COOPERATION BETWEEN COMPETENT AUTHORITIES ... 212
CHAPTER IV SECURITY OF THE NETWORKS AND INFORMATION SYSTEMS OF PUBLIC ADMINISTRATIONS AND MARKET OPERATORS ... 215
CHAPTER V FINAL PROVISIONS ... 216
ANNEX I Requirements and tasks of the Computer Emergency Response Team (CERT) ... 218
ANNEX II List of market operators Referred to in Article 3(8) a) : ... 219
EUROPEAN UNION AGENCY FOR NETWORK AND INFORMATION SECURITY (ENISA) ... 226
SECTION 1 SCOPE OBJECTIVES AND TASKS ... 237
SECTION 2 ORGANISATION ... 240

For additional analytical, business and investment opportunities information, please contact Global Investment & Business Center, USA at (703) 370-8082. Fax: (703) 370-8083. E-mail: ibpusa3@gmail.com Global Business and Investment Info Databank - www.ibpus.com

SECTION 3 OPERATION ... *245*
SECTION 4 FINANCIAL PROVISIONS ... *247*
SECTION 5 STAFF ... *249*
SECTION 6 GENERAL PROVISIONS ... *250*
SECTION 7 FINAL PROVISIONS ... *252*

SUPPLEMENTS ... 254

EU CYBER SECRURITY PROGRAMS COORDINATORS IN MEMBER COUNTRIES ... 254
CYBER ATTACK THREAT TRENDS ... 257
TOP CYBER THREATS ... 257
1 Drive-By Downloads ... *257*
2 Malicious Code: Worms/Trojans ... *258*
3 Code Injection ... *259*
4 Exploit Kits ... *260*
5 Botnets ... *261*
6 Physical Damage/Theft/Loss of media ... *261*
7 Identity Theft/Fraud ... *262*
8 Denial of Service ... *263*
9 Phishing ... *264*
10 Spam ... *265*
11 Rogueware/Ransomware/Scareware ... *265*
12 Data Breaches (Compromising Confidential Information) ... *266*
13 Information leakage ... *267*
14 Targeted Attacks ... *268*
15 Watering hole attacks ... *269*
16 Visualising changes in the current threat landscape ... *269*
BASIC TITLES ON EUROPEAN UNION (EU) ... 271

EUROPEAN UNION STRATEGIC INFORMATION

BASIC INFORMATION

Capital	Brussels (de facto) 50°51′N 4°21′E
Largest cities	Paris and London
Official languages	24 languages
Official scripts	• Latin • Greek • Cyrillic
Religion	• 71.6% Christianity ○ 45.3% Roman Catholic ○ 11.1% Protestant ○ 9.6% Eastern Orthodox ○ 5.6% other Christian • 24% No religion • 1.8% Muslim • 2.6% other faiths
Demonym	European
Type	Political and economic union
Member states	28 states
Government	Supranational and intergovernmental
• President of the European Council	Donald Tusk
• President of the European Parliament	Antonio Tajani
• President of the European Commission	Jean-Claude Juncker
Legislature	• Council of the EU • European Parliament
Formation	
• Treaty of Rome	1 January 1958
• Treaty of Maastricht	1 November 1993
• Treaty of Lisbon	1 December 2009
• Last polity admitted	1 July 2013
Area	
• Total	4,475,757 km^2 (1,728,099 sq mi)
• Water (%)	3.08
Population	
• 2018 estimate	▲512,596,403
• Density	117.3/km^2 (303.8/sq mi)
GDP (PPP)	2018 estimate
• Total	$22.0 trillion (2nd)
• Per capita	$43,074
GDP (nominal)	2018 estimate
• Total	$19.7 trillion (2nd)
• Per capita	$38,370
Gini (2016)	▼ 30.8 medium
HDI (2017)	▲ 0.899

	very high
Currency	Euro (EUR; €; Eurozone) 10 others
Time zone	UTC to UTC+2 (• WET • CET • EET)
• Summer (DST)	UTC+1 to UTC+3 (• WEST • CEST • EEST) (see also Summer Time in Europe) Note: with the exception of the Canary Islands and Madeira, the outermost regions observe different time zones not shown
Date format	dd/mm/yyyy (AD/CE) See also: Date and time notation in Europe
Internet TLD	.eu[f]
Website	europa.eu

The **European Union** (**EU**) is an economic and political union of 28 member states that are located primarily in Europe. The EU operates through a system of supranational independent institutions and intergovernmental negotiated decisions by the member states. Institutions of the EU include the European Commission, the Council of the European Union, the European Council, the Court of Justice of the European Union, the European Central Bank, the Court of Auditors, and the European Parliament. The European Parliament is elected every five years by EU citizens. The EU's *de facto* capital is Brussels.

The EU traces its origins from the European Coal and Steel Community (ECSC) and the European Economic Community (EEC), formed by the Inner Six countries in 1951 and 1958, respectively. In the intervening years the community and its successors have grown in size by the accession of new member states and in power by the addition of policy areas to its remit. The Maastricht Treaty established the European Union under its current name in 1993. The latest major amendment to the constitutional basis of the EU, the Treaty of Lisbon, came into force in 2009.

The EU has developed a single market through a standardised system of laws that apply in all member states. Within the Schengen Area (which includes 22 EU and 4 non-EU states) passport controls have been abolished. EU policies aim to ensure the free movement of people, goods, services, and capital, enact legislation in justice and home affairs, and maintain common policies on trade, agriculture, fisheries, and regional development.

The eurozone, a monetary union, was established in 1999 and came into full force in 2002. It is currently composed of 18 member states. Through the Common Foreign and Security Policy the EU has developed a role in external relations and defence. Permanent diplomatic missions have been established around the world. The EU is represented at the United Nations, the WTO, the G8, and the G-20.

With a combined population of over 500 million inhabitants, or 7.3% of the world population, the EU in 2012 generated a nominal gross domestic product (GDP) of 16.584 trillion US dollars, constituting approximately 23% of global nominal GDP and 20% when measured in terms of purchasing power parity, which is the largest nominal GDP and GDP PPP in the world. The EU was the recipient of the 2012 Nobel Peace Prize

The European Union is a unique, treaty-based, institutional framework that defines and manages economic and political cooperation among its fifteen European member countries. The Union is the latest stage in a process of integration begun in the 1950s by six countries—Belgium, France, Germany, Italy, Luxembourg, and the Netherlands—whose leaders signed the original treaties establishing various forms of European integration.

These treaties gave life to the novel concept that, by creating communities of shared sovereignty in matters of coal and steel production, trade, and nuclear energy, another war in Europe would be unthinkable. While common EU policies have evolved in a number of other sectors since then, the fundamental goal of the Union remains the same: to create an ever-closer union among the peoples of Europe.

COUNTRIES

Country name	Capital	Accession	Population	Area (km²)	GDP (PPP) (millions of US$)	GDP per cap. (PPP)	Languages
Austria	Vienna	1995	8,792,500	83,855	437,582	49,869	German
Belgium	Brussels	Founder	11,365,834	30,528	534,230	46,553	Dutch French German
Bulgaria	Sofia	2007	7,101,859	110,994	55,824	21,686	Bulgarian
Croatia	Zagreb	2013	4,154,213	56,594	57,073	24,423	Croatian
Cyprus	Nicosia	2004	854,802	9,251	23,263	37,023	Greek Turkish
Czech Republic	Prague	2004	10,467,628	78,866	205,270	35,512	Czech
Denmark	Copenhagen	1973	5,743,947	43,075	342,362	49,883	Danish
Estonia	Tallinn	2004	1,315,635	45,227	26,506	31,749	Estonian
Finland	Helsinki	1995	5,577,282	338,424	272,649	44,333	Finnish Swedish
France	Paris	Founder	67,024,633	632,833	2,833,687	43,761	French
Germany	Berlin	Founder	82,437,641	357,021	3,874,437	50,425	German
Greece	Athens	1981	10,757,293	131,990	237,970	27,737	Greek
Hungary	Budapest	2004	9,797,561	93,030	136,989	29,473	Hungarian
Ireland	Dublin	1973	4,774,833	70,273	250,814	75,538	Irish English
Italy	Rome	Founder	61,219,113	301,338	2,147,744	38,140	Italian
Latvia	Riga	2004	1,950,116	64,589	31,972	27,644	Latvian
Lithuania	Vilnius	2004	2,847,904	65,200	48,288	32,299	Lithuanian
Luxembourg	Luxembourg	Founder	589,370	2,586.4	65,683	106,374	French German Luxembourgish
Malta	Valletta	2004	440,433	316	10,514	41,945	Maltese English
Netherlands	Amsterdam	Founder	17,220,721	41,543	880,716	53,635	Dutch Frisian

Country name	Capital	Accession	Population	Area (km²)	GDP (PPP) (millions of US$)	GDP per cap. (PPP)	Languages
Poland	Warsaw	2004	37,972,964	312,685	547,894	29,521	Polish
Portugal	Lisbon	1986	10,309,573	92,390	229,948	30,416	Portuguese
Romania	Bucharest	2007	19,638,309	238,391	199,093	24,508	Romanian
Slovakia	Bratislava	2004	5,435,343	49,035	99,869	33,025	Slovak
Slovenia	Ljubljana	2004	2,065,895	20,273	49,570	34,407	Slovene
Spain	Madrid	1986	46,528,966	504,030	1,406,538	38,286	Spanish Galician Catalan Basque
Sweden	Stockholm	1995	10,080,000	449,964	570,591	51,475	Swedish
United Kingdom	London	1973	65,808,573	243,610	2,950,039	44,118	English Welsh Scottish Gaelic

HISTORY

Economic integration was launched in the wake of World War II, as a devastated Western Europe sought to rebuild its economy. On May 9, 1950, French Foreign Minister Robert Schuman announced a plan, conceived by French businessman-turned-advisor, Jean Monnet, that proposed pooling European coal and steel production under a common authority. While contributing to economic recovery, this plan would also control the raw materials of war.

The Schuman Declaration was regarded as the first step toward achieving a united Europe—an ideal that in the past had been pursued only by force. Belgium, the Federal Republic of Germany, Italy, Luxembourg, and the Netherlands accepted the French proposal and signed the European Coal and Steel Community (ECSC) Treaty in Paris on April 18, 1951. The Six set up the ECSC High Authority, to which member governments transferred portions of their sovereign powers. Coal and steel trade among the Six increased by 129 percent over the next five years.

Encouraged by this success, the Six pursued integration in the military and political fields. When these efforts were derailed, European leaders decided to continue the unification of Europe on the economic front alone. A historic meeting in Messina, Italy, in June 1955, launched the negotiation of two treaties to establish:

- A European Economic Community (EEC) to merge separate national markets into a single market that would ensure the free movement of goods, people, capital, and services with a wide range of common economic policies; and
- A European Atomic Energy Community (EAEC or EURATOM) to further the use of nuclear energy for peaceful purposes.

The Six signed the treaties on March 25, 1957, in Rome. Often referred to as the "Rome Treaties," they came into force in January 1958.

Membership: Who can join the EU?

Union membership is open to any European country with a stable democratic government, a good human rights record, a properly functioning market economy, and sound macroeconomic policies. Candidates must also have the capacity to fulfill and to implement existing EU laws and policies (known as the *acquis communautaire*) .

Four enlargements have taken place: Denmark, Ireland, and the United Kingdom joined the original six European Community members (Belgium, France, Germany, Italy, Luxembourg, Netherlands) in 1973. Greece joined in 1981, followed by Spain and Portugal in 1986. Austria, Finland, and Sweden acceded to the European Union on January 1, 1995. Norway had also negotiated and signed an accession treaty in 1994, but Norwegian voters narrowly rejected membership in a referendum.

Although it was not officially an enlargement, the five Laender of the former German Democratic Republic entered the Union as part of a united Germany on October 3, 1990. A fifth enlargement of the European Union to more than twenty-five member states is in progress. For more on the latest enlargement, see Chapter Six.

A UNITED STATES OF EUROPE?

The Union is often compared to the United States, and there are some similarities. Member countries have agreed to pool some of their sovereign powers for the sake of unity, just as American states did to create a federal republic. In the fields where such pooling of national sovereignty has occurred—for example, in trade and agriculture—the Union negotiates directly with the United States and other countries. Twelve member states have also pooled their sovereignty in the area of monetary policy by joining the Economic and Monetary Union. (See Chapter Three) .

But there are also many differences. EU member states retain their sovereign powers in such fields as security and defense, although they now can take joint action in certain foreign and security policy areas. The development of a European Security and Defense Policy and Rapid Reaction Force (see Chapter Seven) are important steps in this effort.

While the US federal model continues to inspire the search for political unity, Europe is constructing its own model for unification, ensuring respect for the historical, cultural, and linguistic diversity of the European nations. Following the signing of the Treaty of Nice, European leaders engaged in the "Debate on the Future of the European Union" (http://europa.eu.int/futurum/index_en.htm) to exchange their visions prior to the 2004 EU Intergovernmental Conference (IGC) .

THE TREATIES

The European Union does not yet have a formal constitution. A Constitutional Convention to discuss this issue (http://european-convention.eu.int/Static.asp?lang=EN&Content=Introduction) was organized recently. Instead, the European Union was built by means of a series of treaties that represent binding commitments by the member states signing them. Member states negotiate these treaties through intergovernmental conferences, or "IGCs," that culminate in a summit chaired by the member state holding the Council presidency.

This process began with three separate treaties dating from the 1950s: the European Coal and Steel Community (ECSC) , the European Atomic Energy Community (EURATOM) and the European Economic Community (EEC) . In 1967, they collectively became known as the European Communities.

The Treaty on European Union, signed in Maastricht, Netherlands, and in effect since November 1993, was a major overhaul of the founding treaties. Maastricht provided a blueprint to achieve Economic and Monetary Union (EMU) , further developed the Union's inherent political dimension through the new Common Foreign and Security Policy (CFSP) , and expanded cooperation in judicial and policing matters.

It created the "three pillar" European Union that exists today (see below) .

Pillar One incorporated the three founding treaties now forming the "European Community" and set out the institutional requirements for EMU. It also provided for expanded Community action in certain areas, such as the environment, research, education, and training.

Pillar Two established the CFSP, which makes it possible for the Union to take joint action in foreign and security affairs.

Pillar Three created the Justice and Home Affairs (JHA) policy, dealing with asylum, immigration, judicial cooperation in civil and criminal matters, and customs and police cooperation against terrorism, drug trafficking, and fraud.

The CFSP and JHA operate by intergovernmental cooperation, rather than by the Community institutions that operate Pillar One. Maastricht also created European citizenship and strengthened the European Parliament's legislative role in certain areas.

THE TREATY OF AMSTERDAM

The Treaty of Amsterdam, which took effect in 1999, continued the reforms of the Maastricht Treaty and began to streamline the EU's institutions ahead of the next enlargement. Many institutional questions were postponed to the Intergovernmental Conference launched at the Helsinki European Council Summit in December 1999 and resulting in the Treaty of Nice.

The Amsterdam Treaty strengthened the CFSP and the EU's ability to undertake joint foreign policy actions. More decisions could be reached by qualified majority instead of unanimity, as required by Maastricht, and member states became able to abstain from a vote or an action without impeding the majority. The Union also appointed Javier Solana as High Representative for CFSP and established a new policy unit.

THE TREATY OF NICE

The Treaty of Nice, signed in Nice, France, in December 2000, entered into force on February 1, 2003. It addressed a number of institutional questions remaining after the Treaty of Amsterdam. Most of the institutional aspects of the Treaty of Nice will not take effect until 2005.

Its most important purpose is to prepare the EU institutions for enlargement to as many as twenty-eight member states. Measures in the Treaty of Nice include:

- Extension of qualified majority voting and reweighting of votes within the Council (see chart in Chapter Two) ;
- Extending the use of "enhanced cooperation" to allow groups of at least eight member states to proceed with policy initiatives;

- Redistribution of seats within the European Parliament in preparation for new members (see chart in Chapter Two) ; and

- Reconfiguring the College of Commissioners and strengthening the European Commission presidency.

The *Declaration on the Future of the Union,* annexed to the Treaty of Nice, called for a deeper and wider debate about the future of Europe and the structure of the European Union. The "European Convention" and the "Debate on the Future of the European Union" have provided the groundwork for the 2004 Intergovernmental Conference (IGC) to consider:

- More clearly defining the competences of the Union and its member states, based on the principle of subsidiarity;

- Measures to simplify the treaties;

- The role of national parliaments in the European construction; and

- The legal status of the *Charter of Fundamental Rights.*

Looking Ahead

Through the search for "ever closer union," the European Union has consolidated economic prosperity and democracy in Western Europe and helped bring stability to Central and Eastern Europe. Increasingly, the EU must deal with the challenges of globalization in the twenty-first century. The Treaty of Nice and the 2004 IGC are important developments, but they should be seen in this broad, evolutionary context.

GOVERNING SYSTEM

As the treaties summarized in Chapter One indicate, the EU system is inherently evolutionary, adapting to changing political and economic circumstances.

Unlike the United States, the EU is founded on international treaties among sovereign nations rather than a constitution. (A Constitutional Convention to discuss this issue was organized recently.) The power to enact laws that are directly binding on all EU citizens throughout the EU territory also distinguishes the Union from international organizations. This governing system differs from all previous national and international models.

In areas falling under Pillar One of the EU (as described in Chapter One) , member states have relinquished part of their national sovereignty to the EU institutions. This has led to descriptions of the Union as a supranational entity, with many decisions made and final authority residing at the EU level. In these areas the member states work together, in their collective interest, through the EU institutions to administer their sovereign powers jointly.

Under Pillars Two and Three, member states have agreed to cooperate but retain much more discretion over their participation, including the right to veto certain measures. Here the EU has been described as an intergovernmental entity, with EU policies administered largely by the member states themselves, rather than through the EU institutions.

The Union also operates according to the principle of "subsidiarity"—or devolution, as it is known in the US, which characterizes most federal systems. Under this principle, the Union is granted jurisdiction only over those policies that cannot be handled effectively at the national or lower levels of government.

GOVERNING INSTITUTIONS

The European Union is governed by five institutions: European Parliament, Council of the European Union, European Commission, European Court of Justice, and European Court of Auditors. In addition, the heads of state and government and the Commission president meet at least twice a year in European Council (see below) summits to provide overall strategy and political direction. The European Central Bank is responsible for monetary policy and managing the euro in the Economic and Monetary Union.

These institutions embody the supranational and intergovernmental aspects of the EU.

CODECISION PROCEDURE

The Maastricht Treaty gave the European Parliament the power of "codecision" with the Council in a limited number of areas such as research, health, and culture. It left the Council with the last say on a significant number of other policies but still substantially increased the Parliament's power. Before Maastricht, the Parliament could amend the Council's draft legislation (the so-called cooperation procedure) , offer its opinion through the "consultation" procedure, or withhold its "assent" to Council decisions in certain areas (residence rights, the structural and cohesion funds, treaties of accession, and others) .

The Amsterdam Treaty increased Parliament's responsibilities by making the codecision procedure the general rule, furthered by the Treaty of Nice. If the Council and Parliament cannot agree, a special Conciliation Committee is formed. Even if the Committee agrees to a joint text, Parliament may still reject the proposed act by an absolute majority of its members.

The "cooperation" procedure will survive only within the confines of Economic and Monetary Union. The "assent" procedure will be required in cases such as applications for membership of the Union and certain major international agreements.

For more on changes made by the Treaty of Nice, please consult Memo/03/23.

For additional information on EU decision-making, please see the description and chart on the Europa website under "Institutions" (http://europa.eu.int/institutions/decision-making/index_en.htm) and/or a similar section on the Council of Ministers website (http://ue.eu.int/codec/en/index.htm) .

EUROPEAN PARLIAMENT

The European Parliament (EP) comprises 626 members, directly elected in EU-wide elections for five-year terms. The president of the Parliament is elected for a two-and-a-half year term. Though they are elected on a national basis, members of the European Parliament (MEPs) form political rather than national groups based on party affiliation.

The legislative role of the European Parliament has been strengthened over the years. Although the EP cannot enact laws like national parliaments, the Maastricht Treaty provided for a codecision procedure that empowers Parliament to veto legislation in certain policy areas and to

For additional analytical, business and investment opportunities information, please contact Global Investment & Business Center, USA at (703) 370-8082. Fax: (703) 370-8083. E-mail: ibpusa3@gmail.com Global Business and Investment Info Databank - www.ibpus.com

confer with the Council in a "conciliation committee" to iron out differences in their respective drafts of legislation. The Amsterdam Treaty extended the number of policy areas in which Parliament can exercise these powers. The Treaty of Nice also extended the codecision powers of the Parliament and, for the first time, established a statute for political parties at the European level. It also increased (with the next Parliamentary term) the maximum number of seats to 732 and modified their distribution to make room for the elected representatives of future new members

The Parliament acts as the EU's public forum. It can question the Commission and the Council; amend or reject the EU budget; and dismiss the entire Commission through a vote of censure, a power it has never used. However, pressure from the Parliament led to a critical report and the Commission's collective resignation in March 1999. Parliament now also has the power to confirm a newly appointed Commission and to hold hearings on individual Commissioners. It cannot reject individual nominees, only the full Commission. Since Maastricht, Parliament has an appointed ombudsman to address allegations of maladministration in EU institutions and agencies. The Parliament holds plenary sessions in Strasbourg and Brussels. Its twenty committees, which prepare the work for plenary meetings, and its political groups usually meet in Brussels.

EUROPEAN COUNCIL

The European Council brings together heads of state and government and the president of the Commission. It meets at least twice a year at the end of each EU member state's six-month presidency. The Single European Act (SEA) of 1986 formalized the European Council, which was not foreseen in the original EC treaties. The Nice European Council decided that, from 2002 on, one European Council meeting per presidency would be held in Brussels. Following the accession of ten new member states in 2004, all European Council meetings are held there, reinforcing its status as "the capital of Europe."

COUNCIL OF THE EUROPEAN UNION

The Council of the European Union enacts EU laws, acting on proposals submitted by the Commission.

Comprising ministers from each member state, the Council strikes a balance between national and Union interests. Different ministers participate in the Council according to the subject under discussion. Agricultural ministers, for instance, discuss farm prices in the Agriculture Council, and economic and finance ministers discuss monetary affairs in the ECOFIN Council.

The ministers for foreign affairs provide overall coordination in the General Affairs and External Relations Council (GAERC) . They are also responsible for foreign policy in the framework of the Common Foreign and Security Policy. Each government acts as president of the Council for six months in rotation. The Council is assisted by a Committee of Permanent Representatives (COREPER) , comprising member state officials holding ambassadorial rank, and a secretariat with a staff of about 2,000.

The Council makes most decisions by qualified majority vote (QMV) , with the Treaty of Nice extending QMV to twenty-nine new policy areas. With the Treaty of Nice, QMV requires support by a majority of member states, representing at least 62 percent of the EU population. The voting threshold for QMV also rose with Nice from 71.3 percent for fifteen members—eventually to become 73.9 percent in an EU of twenty-seven members

Unanimity is still required for areas like amendments to the treaties, taxation, the launch of a new common policy, or the admission of a new member state.

In the area of CFSP, the Amsterdam Treaty provided that as many as one-third of member states could "constructively abstain" from a decision while allowing the others to act together on behalf of the EU. Member states that "constructively abstain" were not able to take any action that impeded the decision made by the majority. Amsterdam also provided for qualified majority voting in implementing basic political decisions.

The Treaty of Nice made the procedure of "enhanced cooperation" among member states even more flexible. A minimum of eight member states may choose to cooperate in certain areas, provided that participation is open to all and they do not infringe upon the rights of other member states.

AGENCIES AND OTHER BODIES

- ***Committee of European Securities Regulators*** **(CESR)** (Paris, France)
- ***Community Plant Variety Office*** **(CPVO)** (Angers, France) .
- ***European Agency for Reconstruction*** **(EAR)** (Thessaloniki, Greece) .
- ***European Agency for Safety and Health at Work*** **(OSHA)** *(*Bilbao, Spain) .
- ***European Agency for the Evaluation of Medicinal Products*** **(EMEA**) (London, UK) .
- ***European Aviation Safety Agency*** **(EASA)** (Brussels, Belgium) .
- ***European Center for the Development of Vocational Training*** **(CEDEFOP)** (Thessaloniki, Greece) .
- ***European Environment Agency*** **(EEA)** (Copenhagen, Denmark) —a repository of environmental data.
- ***European Food Safety Authority (EFSA)*** (Brussels, Belgium)
- ***European Foundation for the Improvement of Living and Working Conditions*** **(E.FOUND)** *(*Dublin, Ireland) .
- ***European Judicial Network*** **(EUROJUST – EJN)** (Brussels, Belgium) .
- ***European Maritime Safety Agency*** **(EMSA)** (Brussels, Belgium) .
- ***European Monitoring Center for Drugs and Drug Addiction (*****EMCDDA*****)*** (Lisbon, Portugal) .
- ***European Monitoring Center on Racism and Xenophobia (*****EUMC*****)*** (Vienna, Austria) .
- ***European Police Office*** **(EUROPOL*)*** (The Hague, The Netherlands) —for police coordination among EU member states.
- ***European Training Foundation*** **(ETF)** (Turin, Italy) .
- ***European Union Institute for Security Studies (EUISS)*** (Paris, France) .
- ***European Union Satellite Centre (EUSC)*** (Madrid, Spain) .
- ***The Food and Veterinary Office*** **(FVO)** (Dunsany, Ireland) .
- ***Humanitarian Aid Office*** **(ECHO)** (Brussels, Belguim)
- ***Office of Harmonization in the Internal Market*** **(OHIM)** (Alicante, Spain) —trademarks and designs.
- ***Translation Center for the Bodies of the European Union*** **(CDT)** (Luxembourg) .

EUROPEAN COMMISSION

The Commission is the policy engine. It proposes legislation, is responsible for administration, and ensures that the provisions of the treaties and the decisions of the institutions are properly implemented. It has investigative powers and can take legal action against persons, companies, or member states that violate EU rules. It manages the budget and represents the Union in international trade negotiations and other issues within its jurisdiction.

The twenty commissioners are appointed for five-year terms in line with the European Parliament, which approves the appointment of the Commission as a body. The commissioners act in the Union's interest, independently of the national governments that nominated them. Each is assigned one or more policy areas and is assisted by a small cabinet or team of aides. The Commission's administrative staff, based mainly in Brussels, numbers more than 22,000, divided among more than thirty "Directorates-General" and other administrative services. Given the number of EU official languages (accommodating all member state principal languages) , more than 8 percent of the Commission staff are translators and interpreters.

Under the Treaty of Nice, the composition of the College of Commissioners was altered and the powers of the Commission president strengthened. The five largest states gave up their right to name a second commissioner as of 2005, and new member states name one commissioner until the EU reaches twenty-seven members. At that point, the total number of commissioners will be set at a lower number, with appointments made by rotation among member states in a manner to be determined by a unanimous Council vote. The president will be selected by the European Council according to the qualified majority voting procedure, rather than by unanimity as pre-Nice. He or she will have greater control of the structure and allocation of responsibilities within the College of Commissioners and can request a commissioner's resignation. Up to two vice presidents are appointed from among the commissioners.

EUROPEAN ECONOMIC AND SOCIAL COMMITTEE

The European Economic and Social Committee (ESC) was established by the EEC Treaty to fulfill a role as an advisory institution. It is based in Brussels and consists of representatives of labor, employers, agriculture, consumers, and professional associations.

COMMITTEE OF THE REGIONS

The Committee of the Regions (COR) was also established as a consultative body by the Maastricht Treaty and is comprised of representatives of regional and local bodies. It is based in Brussels.

EUROPEAN COURT OF JUSTICE (ECJ)

LEGISLATION

Legislation takes different forms, depending on the objectives to be achieved.

Regulations are binding in their entirety, self-executing, directly applicable, and obligatory throughout the EU territory. They can be compared to US federal laws.

Directives are binding in terms of the results to be achieved and are addressed to the member states, which are free to choose the best forms and methods of implementation.

Decisions are binding in their entirety upon those to whom they are addressed—member states and natural and/or legal persons.

Recommendations and **Opinions** are not binding.

The European Court of Justice, sitting in Luxembourg, is the Community's "Supreme Court." It ensures that the treaties are interpreted and applied correctly by other EU institutions and by the member states. The Court comprises one judge from each member state, appointed for renewable terms of six years. Judgments of the Court in the field of EC law are binding on EU institutions, member states, national courts, companies, and private citizens, and they overrule those of national courts.

Since 1989 a Court of First Instance, also consisting of one judge per member state, has assisted the European Court of Justice.

Under the Treaty of Nice, the Court of First Instance became the common law judge for all direct actions (particularly proceedings against a decision: Article 230 of the Treaty Establishing the European Community) , action for failure to act (Article 232 of the Treaty Establishing the European Community) , action for damages (Article 235 of the Treaty Establishing the European Community) , with the exception of those that will be attributed to a specialized chamber and those the statute reserves for the Court of Justice itself.

The Court of Justice retains responsibility for other proceedings (particularly action for failure to fulfill obligations: Article 226 of the Treaty Establishing the European Community) , but the statute can entrust to the Court of First Instance categories of proceedings other than those listed in Article 225 of the Treaty Establishing the European Community.

The idea is to maintain within the Court of Justice, as the jurisdictional supreme body of the European Union, disputes concerning essential issues. The Court of Justice, which is responsible for ensuring uniform application of EU law within the European Union, in principle retains competence for investigating questions referred for a preliminary ruling; however, pursuant to Article 225 of the Treaty Establishing the European Community, the statute may entrust to the Court of First Instance the responsibility for preliminary rulings in certain specific matters.

For additional information on the changes in the EU judicial system wrought by the Treaty of Nice, please consult Memo/03/23.

EUROPEAN COURT OF AUDITORS (ECA)

The European Court of Auditors, based in Luxembourg, is responsible for the sound financial management of the EU budget. It has extensive powers to examine the legality of receipts and expenditures.

European Central Bank (ECB)

The European System of Central Banks (ESCB) and the European Central Bank in Frankfurt are responsible for monetary policy and the euro

CULTURE

One of Europe's greatest assets is its cultural diversity, which will never become an area for harmonization among the member states. The Maastricht Treaty gave the EU a role to play in bringing "the common cultural heritage to the fore" while respecting national and regional diversity. The completion of the single market, however, does require some measures related to

For additional analytical, business and investment opportunities information, please contact Global Investment & Business Center, USA at (703) 370-8082. Fax: (703) 370-8083. E-mail: ibpusa3@gmail.com Global Business and Investment Info Databank - www.ibpus.com

creative endeavor, particularly as regards cross-frontier television, copyright, and the free movement of cultural goods and services.

EDUCATION AND TRAINING

Education and training play a central role in building a highly skilled workforce for a more competitive Europe. While responsibility for academic systems and curricula rests with the member states, the EU has two large-scale education programs to promote cooperation among them. Socrates, with a budget of $1.7 billion for 2000-2006, provides for cross-border mobility of students and teachers; promotion of foreign language competence; and mutual recognition of diplomas, periods of study, and other qualifications.

Leonardo, with a budget of $1.06 billion for 2000-2006, aims to improve the quality of vocational training; promote exchanges; and promote wider use of information age resources.

EEUROPE

The EU's eEurope initiative, launched in March 2000, aims to maximize access to the Internet, create a digitally literate Europe, and spark an entrepreneurial culture—all while avoiding a digital divide and reinforcing social inclusion and cohesion. Making the European Union the most competitive and dynamic knowledge-based economy in the world is a major EU priority. The number of EU households connected to the Internet rose from 18.3 percent in March 2000 to 36.1 percent in June 2001 and 40.4% in June 2002.

EMPLOYMENT AND SOCIAL POLICY

Since the 1957 founding of the Union, the standard of living of Europe's citizens has doubled. However, unemployment remained high in some member states as Europe's economies prepared to launch the euro and begin a new enlargement. To pave the way for a more coordinated European strategy, the 1997 Amsterdam Treaty introduced a new chapter on employment that made job creation a formal goal of the Union. European Councils, beginning particularly with Lisbon in March 2000, expanded this goal to encompass specific measures to alleviate unemployment—including preparations for the shift to a digital, knowledge-based economy. According to the EU's *Employment In Europe, 2002 Report,* high-tech and knowledge-intensive sectors have driven job creation. These sectors contributed approximately 90 percent of total job creation between 1995 and 2001. The unemployment rate in the EU fell from 8.2 percent in 2000 to 7.6 percent in 2002.

With the removal of barriers within the Union, the drive to complete the single market was accompanied by social legislation guaranteeing workers a certain standard of health and safety in all member states and facilitating vocational training and retraining. A Social Protocol was added to the Maastricht Treaty which led to legislation on the European Works Councils, equal rights for part-time and full-time workers, and parental leave for men as well as for women. The Social Protocol was incorporated into the Amsterdam Treaty, giving the Union a greater role in social legislation and providing fresh impetus to initiatives in the social policy area.

The March 2000 Lisbon European Council launched an annual meeting on the economy, and it highlighted the essential linkage between Europe's economic strength and its social model: the

Lisbon Strategy. Subsequently, the December 2000 Nice Council adopted the Social Policy Agenda (2000-2005) , which seeks to modernize the European social model, invest in people, and combat social exclusion (poverty) . The agenda includes job creation that profits from the new working environment and the potential of the knowledge-based economy; modern and improved social protection (the social safety net) ; social inclusion, gender equality, reinforced fundamental rights; and preparations for enlargement.

ENERGY

Although not a full-fledged common policy, the founding treaties provided for certain common activities in the field of energy, such as promoting energy research under the EU's Research and Technological Development (R&TD) policy, and supporting the establishment of a Trans-European Network (TEN) for energy. In recent years, however, security of the EU's energy supply and protection of the environment have become priorities. The Union is working to establish a single energy market as a means to ensure a supply of energy to all consumers at affordable prices, while respecting both the environment and sustainable development. Policies have focused on the liberalization of the electricity and gas markets within the EU and the facilitation of cross-border transit of both these energy sources. Renewable energy resources are playing an important role in the diversification of energy sources and environmental protection.

The Union was instrumental in the creation of the European Energy Charter, which was signed by fifty-one nations in the Netherlands in 1991. The mission of the Energy Charter process is to strive toward open, efficient, sustainable, and secure energy markets and to promote a constructive climate conducive to energy interdependence based on trust among nations.

ENVIRONMENT

The EU's environment policy was officially launched in 1972 and incorporated into the EEC Treaty by the Single European Act (SEA) (1986) . The EU has developed a substantial body of environmental law to protect against water, air, and noise pollution and to control risks related to chemicals, biotechnology, and nuclear energy within the Union. These are supplemented by multiannual action programs, the most recent of which—the Sixth Environmental Action Program (2001-2010) —concentrates on four priority areas: climate change, nature and biodiversity, environment and health, and natural resources and waste.

A European Environment Agency (EEA) was set up in 1993 in Copenhagen to provide reliable scientific data and evaluations for those involved in implementing and developing European environment policy. The Agency is open to participation from other European countries.

The EU is an important actor in international initiatives on the environment. It is party to the Montreal Protocol on Ozone Depletion, the Basel Convention on Toxic Waste, and most recently the Kyoto Protocol on Climate Change. The EU continues its ongoing efforts to secure the entry into force of the Kyoto Protocol and to work hard to reach the agreed-upon Kyoto targets. The EU-US June 2001 summit issued a statement reflecting divergent EU-US views: *"We disagree on the Kyoto Protocol and its ratification, but we are determined to work together in all relevant fora to address climate change…."* Climate change negotiators meeting in Bonn in late July 2001 agreed on implementation rules for the Kyoto Protocol and funding for developing countries. In Marrakech in November 2001, the Seventh Conference of the Parties to the Convention on Climate Change ended with an agreement on operational rules to fight climate change.

For additional analytical, business and investment opportunities information, please contact Global Investment & Business Center, USA at (703) 370-8082. Fax: (703) 370-8083. E-mail: ibpusa3@gmail.com Global Business and Investment Info Databank - www.ibpus.com

The European Union and its member and states—being strong advocates of renewable energies and having experienced significant benefits from the setting of targets and timetables—with fifty-one other nations, launched in 2002 the Johannesburg Coalition on Renewable Energy: a "coalition of the like-minded countries on the way forward on Renewable Energies."

Sustainable development, a fundamental objective under the EU treaties, dictates that the economic, social, and environmental effects of all policies should be examined in a coordinated way and considered in decision-making. It means meeting the needs of the present generation without compromising those of future generations. According to the June 2001 Göteborg summit, *"Getting prices right so that they better reflect the true costs to society of different activities would provide a better incentive for consumers and producers in everyday decisions about which goods and services to make or buy."*

FOREIGN AID

The European Union, many of whose member states are former colonial powers, has been active in development cooperation since the beginning. The Cotonou Convention (formerly the Lomé Conventions) with seventy-seven former African, Caribbean, and Pacific colonies is a prime example of the EU's generous aid and trade relationships with developing countries. The goals of EU development policy were formally set out in the Maastricht Treaty. They are: fostering sustainable economic and social development in developing countries; promoting their smooth and gradual integration into the world economy; fighting poverty and HIV/AIDS; and helping to consolidate democracy, the rule of law, and respect for human rights.

Today, the EU has cooperative agreements with most developing countries and is a leading donor of emergency and humanitarian aid (through the Humanitarian Aid Office, ECHO) .

FOREIGN POLICY

The Common Foreign and Security Policy (CFSP) was established by the Maastricht Treaty in 1993. For a fuller description, see Chapter Seven.

HUMAN RIGHTS

The Treaty on European Union (Article 6) explicitly affirms the EU's commitment to respect the rule of law and fundamental and human rights as guaranteed by the 1950 European Convention for the Protection of Human Rights and Fundamental Freedoms (Council of Europe) .

Death Penalty. All EU member states have banned the death penalty—all adhere to the European Convention for the Protection of Human and Fundamental Rights, which, according to Protocol 6, Article 1, abolishes the death penalty. Nearly all EU applicant countries (not including Turkey) have ratified this Protocol and prohibit the death penalty. The European Union is opposed to the death penalty in all cases and has consistently called for its abolition in countries that condone capital punishment.

External Actions. Respect for human rights and fundamental freedoms is a general objective of the Common Foreign and Security Policy (CFSP) . Many of the EU's external agreements include a section on "political dialogue" dealing with the rule of law, democratization, and human rights. The EU publicly condemns human rights violations wherever they occur, appealing to the countries concerned to end such violations and pressuring the authorities in question.

For additional analytical, business and investment opportunities information, please contact Global Investment & Business Center, USA at (703) 370-8082. Fax: (703) 370-8083. E-mail: ibpusa3@gmail.com Global Business and Investment Info Databank - www.ibpus.com

Charter of Fundamental Rights of the European Union. The *Charter* is a basis for continued integration in Europe. It raises the status of rights in the areas of human dignity, freedom, equality, solidarity, citizenship, and justice to the level of fundamental rights for all citizens.

The 2004 Intergovernmental Conference has been charged with determining the ultimate legal status of the *Charter,* which was not originally legally binding. Romano Prodi, President of the European Commission, announced that he would like to see the *Charter* incorporated into the EU's treaties to make it legally binding "as soon as possible." The European Parliament passed resolutions that support the incorporation of the *Charter* into the treaties.

JUSTICE AND HOME AFFAIRS: FREE MOVEMENT, COUNTERTERRORISM AND INTERNAL SECURITY

The Justice and Home Affairs policy (JHA) , established by the Maastricht Treaty and strengthened by the Amsterdam Treaty, had as its objective establishing by May 1, 2004 (five years after the Amsterdam Treaty went into effect) , the free movement of European citizens and non-EU nationals throughout the EU, while guaranteeing public security by combating all forms of organized crime and terrorism. Home Affairs cooperation focuses mainly on policy toward non-EU countries in matters of asylum and immigration. Justice involves coordinated measures to combat the trafficking of drugs, arms, and human beings; large-scale international fraud; and other international crime.

The European Police Office (EUROPOL) was established as the EU law enforcement organization to handle criminal intelligence. Once the EUROPOL Convention was ratified by all member states, EUROPOL became fully operational in July 1999 and serves essentially as a police coordination center for the collection, analysis, and dissemination of information. EUROPOL deals with an expanding range of criminal issues when two or more member states are affected.

The Amsterdam Treaty helped make the JHA policy more effective by incorporating the Schengen Agreement into the EU framework. Schengen was concluded in 1990 by Belgium, France, Germany, Luxembourg, and the Netherlands to enable them to remove internal border controls on people without compromising public security. All EU member states except the United Kingdom and Ireland have since joined the Schengen area.

In the wake of the September 11, 2001, terrorist attacks, the EU has made the concerted fight against terrorism a top priority. Within ten days of the attack, the EU acted to establish an EU-wide list defining acts of terrorism and their commensurate penalties. Additionally, the EU adopted a European arrest warrant to replace the traditional extradition procedures among member states. This warrant allows wanted persons to be handed over directly from one judicial authority to another. Yet another measure improved EUROPOL's operation and created a special unit dedicated to counterterrorism.

The US and the EU have resolved to work together to combat terrorism. The September 20, 2001, EU-US Ministerial statement declares, *"The nature of our democratic societies makes it*

For additional analytical, business and investment opportunities information, please contact Global Investment & Business Center, USA at (703) 370-8082. Fax: (703) 370-8083. E-mail: ibpusa3@gmail.com Global Business and Investment Info Databank - www.ibpus.com

imperative to protect our citizens from terrorist acts, while at the same time protecting their individual liberties, due process, and the rule of law. The US and the EU are committed to enhancing security measures, legislation, and enforcement."

REGIONAL DEVELOPMENT

Reducing the social and economic disparities among the regions has always been an EU objective—one that has new relevance considering EU enlargement toward Central and Eastern Europe (see Chapter Six) . A Cohesion Fund was set up by the Maastricht Treaty to reduce economic disparities among the EU and Spain, Greece, Portugal, and Ireland. Cohesion funding for the four eligible EU member states is $16.6 billion for the period 2000-2006.

The four Structural Funds benefit all the member states and consist of three older funds set up in the 1970s—the European Social Fund (ESF) , the European Regional Development Fund (ERDF) , and the Guidance section of the European Agricultural Guidance and Guarantee Fund (EAGGF) —plus the newer Financial Instrument for Fisheries Guidance (FIFG) . These funds cofinance projects in areas affected by economic distress or industrial decline. Funding for the period 2000-2006 is $179 billion.

ISPA (Instrument for Structural Policies for Pre-Accession Programs) was created to assist the applicant countries in Central and Eastern Europe with investment projects in transport and the environment. For each year during the period 2000-2006, $920 million is budgeted.

RESEARCH AND TECHNOLOGICAL DEVELOPMENT (R&TD)

A real "European area of research" is beginning to take shape on the European continent, fueled in large part by the accomplishments of the Research and Technological Development (R&TD) framework programs that have been in place since the early 1980s. Formally designated by the Maastricht Treaty as the EU's main R&TD instrument, the framework programs set out the Union's principal scientific and technological objectives. These programs aim to promote cooperation among partners in different countries by funding transnational work and promoting coordination among scientific and technological facilities.

The $16.1 billion Sixth Framework Program (2003-2006) constitutes part of the European Research Area initiative and represents a deliberate break with past programs in terms of ambition, scope, and implementing instruments. The goal is to achieve greater focus on questions of European importance and a better integration of research efforts based on an enhanced partnership among European researchers. This latest program also provides for independent research in the nuclear field as well as comparable efforts to be undertaken by the Joint Research Center (JRC) .

The Joint Research Center, the EU's scientific and technical research laboratory, is an integral part of the European Commission. It provides the scientific advice and technical know-how to support EU policies. Another framework program supports the JRC's efforts in the areas of food safety and health, environment and sustainable development, technology foresight, metrology, combating fraud, monitoring/prediction of natural disasters, and data security.

The Fifth Framework Program (1998 to 2002) concentrated on research in four main areas: quality of life and living resources; the information society; competitive and sustainable growth; and preserving the ecosystem. The Fifth Framework Program was also open to the then-EU membership candidates.

The original Community's involvement in R&TD was once confined to coal, steel, and nuclear energy. The Single European Act of 1986 provided specific legal powers in this field that has become crucial to the Union's industrial competitiveness. The Union participates in EUREKA, a Europe-wide venture aimed at developing new high-tech products in response to market demand.

The EU also cooperates with its European neighbors, as well as with the United States and Japan, on a variety of other R&TD projects. The EU-US Agreement on Science and Technology Cooperation was signed in December 1997. An implementation agreement covering scientific co-operation between the US and the EU in the field of environmental research was forged in 2001.

TELECOMMUNICATIONS

A liberalized telecommunications environment is essential for Europe's economic growth and transition to the information society. The European Union fully liberalized telecommunications, voice telephony, and infrastructure on January 1, 1998, and played a key role in the conclusion of the WTO basic telecommunications agreement, which took effect in February 1998. Since the EU's liberalization process began, there has been tremendous growth in new technologies and services, including mobile phones, the Internet, and electronic commerce.

Several key indicators demonstrate impressive progress: more than one-third of the EU population is now using the Internet (40.4 percent) . The gap with the US remains, but it is narrowing. Mobile phone use in Europe is growing at an even faster rate. According to the International Telecommunication Union's *2002 World Telecommunication Indicators*, 76 percent of the EU population subscribed to mobile phones, compared to 45.8 percent in the US.

TRADE

EU member states agree to share sovereignty with the Union in matters of external trade. On trade, the European Commission negotiates on behalf of the Union under a mandate agreed to by the member states. When agreement is reached, the Council of Ministers and the European Parliament must give their approval. The European Commission and the Council of the European Union adjust the common customs tariff, guide export policy, and decide on trade protection measures where necessary. The EU has played a leading role within the General Agreement on Tariffs and Trade (GATT) and its successor, the World Trade Organization (WTO) .

TRANSPORT

Because of the importance of transport to the free movement of goods, the 1992 single market program introduced market-opening legislation—applicable EU-wide for all modes of transport. Considerable progress has been achieved in the deregulation of road, air, and maritime services; better access to the market; and the application of competition rules. Legislation has been introduced that addresses the needs of the rail sector. A primary objective of transport policy is to establish "sustainable mobility." This means organizing transport so as to make optimum use of energy consumption and transport times, routes, and conditions.

BUILDING THE NEW EUROPE: THE EU AND ITS NEIGHBORS

As new member countries joined in the seventies, eighties, and nineties, the European Union grew from six to fifteen member countries in its first four decades. Looking ahead, the Union expects to grow to nearly thirty member countries in the immediate future and will include more than a half-billion people. For the first time in history, nearly all the people of Europe will be joined in a single Union by free and democratic consent. The European Union is also forging stronger relations with its neighbors to the east, west, and south, whether or not they will eventually join the Union. The goal is to improve prosperity, political stability, security, and respect for democracy, the rule of law, and human rights in the European region as a whole. The final architecture of Europe is not yet set, nor is the European Union the only entity helping to shape the new Europe. But the EU plays a pivotal role in shaping post-cold war Europe. As it continues to deepen and widen, the Union will likely play an ever more prominent role on the continent in the twenty-first century.

TOWARD EU MEMBERSHIP

June 1989: Western Economic Summit (G7) asks European Commission to coordinate all Western aid to develop democracy and market economies in Central and Eastern Europe. Commission also launches PHARE, the world's largest grant program for the region.

December 1991: Europe Agreements (association agreements, paving way to free trade and eventual full EU membership) signed with Poland, Hungary, and Czechoslovakia. Agreements with Bulgaria, Romania, Estonia, Latvia, Lithuania, and Slovenia follow.

December 1992: Separate Europe Agreements signed with Czech Republic and Slovakia, following breakup of Czechoslovakia. This brings to ten the number of EU membership applicants from Central and Eastern Europe (CE 10) .

For additional analytical, business and investment opportunities information, please contact Global Investment & Business Center, USA at (703) 370-8082. Fax: (703) 370-8083. E-mail: ibpusa3@gmail.com Global Business and Investment Info Databank - www.ibpus.com

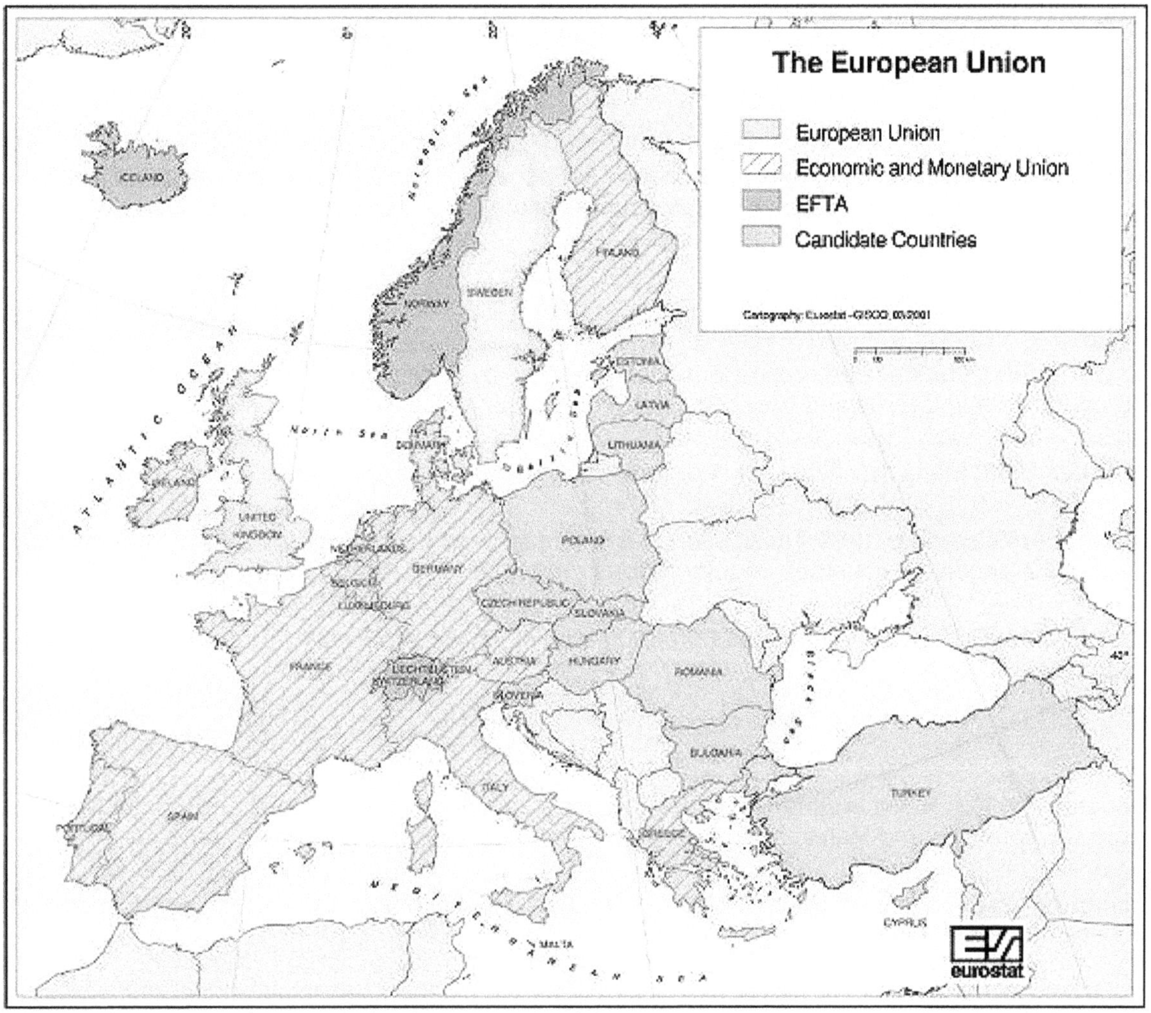

June 1993: Copenhagen summit pledges membership for eligible applicants (demonstrating stable democracy, respect for human rights, rule of law, functioning market economy, readiness for obligations of EU membership) .

December 1994: Essen summit adopts "pre-accession strategy" to intensify efforts to prepare CE 10 for membership. Pre-accession package sets up a structured dialogue, improves market access, and directs more PHARE funds to support investment projects.

May 1995: Commission White Paper outlines measures to bring laws, standards, and product certification systems in CE 10 into conformity with EU single market.

July 1997: Commission releases Agenda 2000, with opinions on the readiness of each of the candidates and recommendations for internal EU reforms and expenditures.

December 1997: Luxembourg summit decides on accession strategy based on Agenda 2000, including launching actual negotiations and convening a European conference among all candidate countries on pan-European issues.

March 1998: European conference launched, followed by formal opening of negotiations with five CE countries and Cyprus and accession partnerships for all CE 10.

October 1998: Malta reactivates its membership application, frozen since 1996.

November/December 1998: Publication of first annual reports on progress toward accession by each of the candidate countries; regular reports endorsed by Vienna Council.

March 1999: Berlin Council adopts 2000-2006 funding, including pre-accession and accession-related expenditure.

December 1999: Helsinki summit decides to open negotiations on EU membership with five more CE countries and Malta and to treat Turkey as a candidate on the same terms as others.

December 2000: Treaty of Nice embodies the necessary reforms to EU institutions to prepare for EU enlargement.

June 2001: Göteborg summit declares intention to complete negotiations with a first group of applicants, provided they are ready, in time to allow them to participate as EU members in the June 2004 European Parliament elections.

December 2002: Copenhagen summit declares that Cyprus, Czech Republic, Estonia, Hungary, Latvia, Lithuania, Malta, Poland, Slovak Republic, and Slovenia will become EU members by May 1, 2004.

April 2003: Treaty of Accession for ten new members (above) signed in Athens, Greece.

May 2004: Ten new members join the European Union.

2007: Following the conclusions of the European Council in Brussels and depending on further progress in complying with the membership criteria, the EU hopes to welcome Bulgaria and Romania as members of the European Union.

FUTURE EUROPEAN UNION ENLARGEMENT

In March 1998 the EU opened talks on full membership with six countries: Cyprus, the Czech Republic, Estonia, Hungary, Poland, and Slovenia. Two years later, in February 2000, negotiations began with six other applicant countries: Bulgaria, Latvia, Lithuania, Malta, Romania, and Slovakia. At the Helsinki European Council in December 1999, when this decision was made, it was also decided to grant Turkey full candidate status (see below) . Joining a highly integrated Union is inherently complex, and most of the applicant countries were compelled to make far-reaching economic, political, and social adjustments following the end of Communism. Negotiations with each applicant proceed on their own merits and as quickly as possible. As decided by the Copenhagen European Council in December 2002, as of May 1, 2004, the European Union has ten new members: Cyprus, Czech Republic, Estonia, Hungary, Latvia, Lithuania, Malta, Poland, Slovak Republic, and Slovenia. This brings EU membership to twenty-five nations in time for the next elections to the European Parliament in June 2004. The accession treaty, signed in Athens in April 2003, was first to be ratified in each of the ten candidate countries and in each of the then-fifteen EU member states before the ten states became formal EU members in 2004.

US Secretary of State Colin Powell, on the occasion of the signing of the 2003 Treaty of Accession, said: *"The embrace of ten new members attests to the European Union's institutional strength and to its confidence in itself. It also testifies to the essential role the Union plays as a force for democracy, prosperity and a force for stability throughout Europe and well beyond Europe."*

Following the conclusions of the European Council in Brussels and depending on further progress in complying with the membership criteria, the EU hopes to welcome Bulgaria and Romania as members of the European Union in 2007.

Agenda 2000 reinforced the pre-accession strategy under which candidate countries received increased aid, participated in certain EU programs, and adapted to EU procedures in anticipation of membership. EU and member state aid to Central and Eastern Europe alone totaled $85 billion for the period 1990-1999. In today's dollars, this is approximately equivalent to the $13.2 billion in US Marshall Plan aid for the reconstruction of Europe after World War II. This process continues for Bulgaria and Romania, slated for EU membership in 2007—according, again, to the December 2002 Copenhagen European Council. Turkey's accession position has been strengthened.

In July 1997, the Commission completed an exhaustive review of the state of readiness of the applicant countries for full membership, publishing its findings in a three-volume report, known as *Agenda 2000: For a Stronger and Wider Union*. At the time, the Commission concluded that none of the ten Central and East European applicants was ready for full membership under criteria adopted at the 1993 Copenhagen European Council, but five were sufficiently advanced along the path to open negotiations.

In addition, Cyprus (see below) was offered negotiations in this round.

The purpose of Agenda 2000 was twofold: to prepare the candidate countries for membership and to prepare the EU and its institutions for the biggest and most challenging enlargement in its history. After two years of intensive debate, EU leaders meeting in Berlin in March 1999 approved the Agenda 2000 strategy. This included reforms of the Common Agricultural Policy (CAP) , the Structural Funds, the EU decision-making procedures, and a financial package totaling $230 billion for the years 2000-2006 for the Central and East European applicants in preparation for the enlargement. Pre-accession financial assistance to Cyprus and Malta extended through 2004.

CYPRUS, MALTA, AND TURKEY

Negotiations with Cyprus for EU membership began in March 1998, along with five countries from Central and Eastern Europe. The European Council had decided in 1995 that the next phase of EU enlargement would include Cyprus and Malta. The EU wanted representatives of both communities in Cyprus to take part in the accession negotiations and hoped that the negotiations would contribute to efforts under United Nations auspices to resolve the dispute dividing the island. However, given the still-divided status of Cyprus at the time, the December 2002 Copenhagen summit stated: *"The European Council has decided that, in the absence of a settlement, the application of the acquis to the northern part of the island shall be suspended, until the Council decides unanimously otherwise, on the basis of a proposal by the Commission. Meanwhile, the Council invites the Commission, in consultation with the government of Cyprus, to consider ways of promoting economic development of the northern part of Cyprus and bringing it closer to the Union."*

Although the EU has decided that Turkey does not yet meet all the criteria for full membership of the Union, it has frequently reaffirmed Turkey's eligibility for EU membership. Turkey applied for full membership in 1987. But the Commission recommended an alternate path, including steadily closer economic relations—a strategy that both sides are implementing. Since 1995, the EU and Turkey have been joined in a customs union that provides for enhanced economic cooperation. Pre-accession financial assistance, comparable to that available to other candidate countries, is being provided to Turkey. In August 1999, following a devastating earthquake in Turkey, the EU responded immediately with humanitarian assistance.

At the December 1999 Helsinki European Council, Turkey was declared a candidate on the same terms as the twelve other then-applicants. An Accession Partnership with Turkey was adopted in March 2001. As a candidate country, Turkey benefits from a pre-accession strategy and partnership with the EU that aims to stimulate and support its political and economic reforms. A closer political dialogue with the Union is sought as well. The timing of Turkey's accession depends upon its progress toward meeting the membership criteria, which are equally stringent for all candidate nations. The December 2002 Copenhagen European Council stated: *"The Union encourages Turkey to pursue energetically its reform process. If the European Council in December 2004, on the basis of a report and a recommendation from the Commission, decides that Turkey fulfils the Copenhagen political criteria, the European Union will open accession negotiations with Turkey without delay."*

NORWAY AND SWITZERLAND

In referenda, Norway decided against EU membership in 1973 and 1994. Switzerland has applied for EU membership in the past, though not actively pursued it. One day perhaps both may reactivate their applications.

CROATIA

On February 21, 2003, Croatia presented its application for EU membership. European Commission President Romano Prodi said at the time: *"This is a powerful signal of hope in future development, stability and growth and for peaceful coexistence throughout the region. It shows that this region, which is an integral part of Europe, is resolved to set behind it forever the dramas and traumas of its recent past. Only once the Balkan countries are members can the Union's enlargement and Europe's reorganisation be considered complete, and only then will the founding fathers' vision of peace and prosperity have come true, perhaps even beyond their wildest dreams."*

PHARE, TACIS, CARDS

PHARE (Originally launched in 1989 as Action Plan for Coordinated Aid to Poland and Hungary for Economic Reconstruction; also means "beacon" in French) is an EU grants program to help the countries of Central and Eastern Europe rejoin the mainstream of European development through membership of the European Union. It acts as a powerful catalyst by unlocking funds for important projects from other donors through studies, capital grants, guarantee schemes, and credit lines. It also invests directly in infrastructure, which will account for more PHARE funds as integration progresses. By 1999, PHARE, the world's largest grant assistance effort for Central and Eastern Europe, committed some $11 billion to programs promoting private sector development; effective food production, processing and distribution; modern energy, transport, and telecommunications infrastructures; nuclear safety and environment; public administration reform; and university education under the TEMPUS (Trans-European Mobility Scheme for University Students) program. For the period 2000-2006, PHARE committed some $10 billion.

TACIS (Technical Assistance to the Commonwealth of Independent States) provides grant finance for the transfer of know-how to twelve countries of the former Soviet Union and Mongolia. It fosters the development of market economies and democratic societies. It is the largest program of its kind operating in the region, and has launched more than 3,000 projects since its inception in 1991. Between 1991 and 2001, TACIS provided $2,624.41 billion in assistance. The TACIS budget for 2000-2006 is $2.9 billion.

CARDS (Community Assistance for Reconstruction, Development, and Stabilization) provides assistance to Albania, Bosnia and Herzegovina, Croatia, the Federal Republic of Yugoslavia, and the Former Yugoslav Republic of Macedonia. It is the successor to OBNOVA (which it repealed) and PHARE for these countries. It establishes a single legal framework for assistance to these countries to help them participate in the stabilization and association process. Program funding for 2000-2006 is $4.3 billion.

RUSSIA AND ITS NEIGHBORS

The EU is forging a network of far-reaching partnerships with countries of the former Soviet Union and is at the forefront of international efforts to support them in carrying out political and economic reforms. Accordingly, the EU has concluded Partnership and Cooperation Agreements (PCAs) with Russia, Armenia, Azerbaijan, Belarus, Georgia, Kazakhstan, Kyrgyz Republic, Moldova, Turkmenistan, Ukraine, and Uzbekistan. All but the two PCAs with Belarus and Turkmenistan have entered into force. (No PCA is envisioned yet with Tajikistan, given its present instability.) These agreements provide for political, economic, and trade relations and lay the basis for cooperation in the social, financial, scientific, technological, and cultural fields. The Partnership and Cooperation Agreement with Russia entered into force in December 1997. The first Cooperation Council under the new agreement was held in January 1998, yielding agreement on a comprehensive work plan for the short and medium terms. Summits with the

Russian Federation are held at approximately six-month intervals, as are meetings of the Cooperation Council.

The PCA with Russia provides for talks on the possibility of free trade as part of the EU's vision of liberalizing trade throughout the continent. Building on the PCA, the European Council adopted a common strategy toward Russia in June 1999, which brings greater focus to the EU's political and economic actions.

The EU is the major trading partner for Russia and most of the newly independent states, accounting for 40 to 50 percent of their global trade. In 2001, EU imports from Russia totaled $42.9 billion, versus $6.3 billion for the US, while EU exports to Russia totaled $25.2 billion, versus $2.7 billion for the US.

The EU continues to support democracy and economic reform in Central and Eastern Europe through PHARE, which is the largest technical assistance program in the region. By 1999, some $11 billion had been committed for projects related to government and private sector reform. For the period 2000-2006, PHARE committed some $10 billion. Since 1991, TACIS has also provided aid to twelve countries of the former Soviet Union, plus Mongolia

PROJECTING STABILITY IN SOUTHEAST EUROPE

As a product of the reconstruction and reconciliation that followed World War II, the EU is a model for Southeast Europe (SEE) . For more than a decade, the EU has been helping countries in the region to rebuild their economies and rejoin the mainstream of European development.

Following the September 2000 elections in Yugoslavia, which brought to power a democratically elected coalition with a reform mandate, the EU provided emergency aid for the winter, totaling $184 million, and convened together with the World Bank an international donors conference in June 2001 at which $1.2 billion was pledged for the reconstruction of Yugoslavia.

To promote long-term peace and prosperity in Southeast Europe, the EU is pursuing a two-pronged strategy including: a regional approach aimed at building cooperation among the five former Yugoslav republics plus Albania; and a long-term Stabilization and Association Process, to which the EU committed itself at the Zagreb summit with the countries of the region in November 2000. The EU hopes to draw these countries closer to the EU through Stabilization and Association Agreements (SAA) . These aim at developing existing trade ties, reforming political and economic institutions in the SEE countries, and preparing them for eventual EU membership. Croatia applied for EU membership on February 21, 2003. The June 21, 2003, EU Western Balkans Summit participants confirmed the EU intention of extending membership to these nations and resolved to meet periodically to review progress.

MEDITERRANEAN AND MIDDLE EAST COUNTRIES

Euro-Mediterranean Partnership

Algeria
Cyprus*
Egypt
Israel
Jordan
Lebanon
Libya (observer status)
Malta*

Morocco
Palestinian Authority
Syria
Tunisia
Turkey*

*Applicant Countries for EU Membership

ECONOMIC, TRADE AND MONETARY UNION OF THE EUROPEAN UNION

In economics, a monetary union is a situation where several countries have agreed to share a single currency among them. The European **Economic and Monetary Union** (EMU) consists of three stages coordinating economic policy and culminating with the adoption of the euro, the EU's single currency. All member states of the European Union participate in the EMU. Thirteen member states of the European Union have entered the third stage and have adopted the euro as their currency. The United Kingdom, Denmark and Sweden have not accepted the third stage and the three EU members still use their own currency today.

Under the Copenhagen criteria, it is a condition of entry for states acceding to the EU that they be able to fulfil the requirements for monetary union within a given period of time. The 10 new countries that acceded to the European Union in 2004 all intend to join third stage of the EMU in the next ten years, though the precise timing depends on various economic factors. Similarly, those countries who are currently negotiating for entry will also take the euro as their currency in the years following their accession. (See Enlargement of the European Union.)

Prior to adopting the euro, a member state has to have its currency in the European Exchange Rate Mechanism (ERM II) for two years. Cyprus, Denmark, Estonia, Latvia, Lithuania, Malta, and Slovakia are the current participants in the exchange rate mechanism. EMU is sometimes misinterpreted to mean **European Monetary Union**.

HISTORY OF THE EMU

First ideas of an economic and monetary union in Europe were raised well before establishing the European Communities. For example, already in the League of Nations, Gustav Stresemann asked in 1929 for a European currency (Link) against the background of an increased economic division due to a number of new nation states in Europe after WWI.

A first attempt to create an economic and monetary union between the members of the European Communities goes back to an initiative by the European Commission in 1969, which set out the need for "greater co-ordination of economic policies and monetary cooperation"(Barre Report) , which was followed by the decision of the Heads of State or Government at their summit meeting in The Hague in 1969 to draw up a plan by stages with a view to creating an economic and monetary union by the end of the 1970s.

On the basis of various previous proposals, an expert group chaired by Luxembourg's Prime Minister and Finance Minister, Pierre Werner, presented in October 1970 the first commonly agreed blueprint to create an economic and monetary union in three stages (Werner plan) . The project experienced serious setbacks from the crises arising from the non-convertibility of the US dollar into gold in August 1971 and from rising oil prices in 1972.

The debate on EMU was fully re-launched at the Hanover Summit in June 1988, when an ad hoc committee of the central bank governors of the twelve member states, chaired by the President of the European Commission, Jacques Delors, was asked to propose a new timetable with clear, practical and realistic steps for creating an economic and monetary union.
The Delors report of 1989 set out a plan to introduce the EMU in three stages and it included the creation of institutions like the European System of Central Banks (ESCB) , which would become responsible for formulating and implementing monetary policy.

The three stages for the implementation of the EMU were the following:

For additional analytical, business and investment opportunities information, please contact Global Investment & Business Center, USA at (703) 370-8082. Fax: (703) 370-8083. E-mail: ibpusa3@gmail.com Global Business and Investment Info Databank - www.ibpus.com

STAGE ONE: 1 JULY 1990 TO 31 DECEMBER 1993

- On 1 July 1990, exchange controls were abolished, thus capital movements were completely liberalised in the EEC.
- The Treaty of Maastricht in 1992 establishes the completion of the EMU as a formal objective and sets a number of economic convergence criteria, concerning the inflation rate, public finances, interest rates and exchange rate stability.
- The treaty enters into force on the 1 November 1993.

STAGE TWO: 1 JANUARY 1994 TO 31 DECEMBER 1998

- The European Monetary Institute is established as the forerunner of the European Central Bank, with the task of strengthening monetary cooperation between the member states and their national banks, as well as supervising ECU banknotes.
- On 16 December 1995, details such as the name of the new currency (the euro) as well as the duration of the transition periods are decided.
- On 16-17 June 1997, the European Council decides at Amsterdam to adopt the Stability and Growth Pact, designed to ensure budgetary discipline after creation of the euro, and a new exchange rate mechanism (ERM II) is set up to provide stability between the euro and the national currencies of countries that haven't yet entered the eurozone.
- On 3 May 1998, at the European Council in Brussels, the 11 initial countries that will participate in the third stage from 1 January 1999 are selected.
- On 1 June 1998, the European Central Bank (ECB) is created, and in 31 December 1998, the conversion rates between the 11 participating national currencies and the euro are established.

STAGE THREE: 1 JANUARY 1999 AND CONTINUING

- From the start of 1999, the euro is now a real currency, and a single monetary policy is introduced under the authority of the ECB. A three-year transition period begins before the introduction of actual euro notes and coins, but legally the national currencies have already ceased to exist.
- On 1 January 2001, Greece joins the third stage of the EMU.
- The euro notes and coins are finally introduced in January 2002.
- On 1 January 2007, Slovenia joins the third stage of the EMU.

CYBER SECURITY STANDARDS - STRATEGIC INFORMATION AND DEVELOPMENTS

INTERNATIONAL CYBERCRIME - IMPORTNT DEFINITIONS

There is no commonly agreed single definition of “cybercrime”. Broadly speaking, it refers to illegal internet-mediated activities that often take place in global electronic networks. Cybercrime is "international" or "transnational" – there are ‘no cyber-borders between countries'. **International cybercrimes** often challenge the effectiveness of domestic and international law and law enforcement. Because existing laws in many countries are not tailored to deal with cybercrime, criminals increasingly conduct crimes on the Internet in order to take advantages of the less severe punishments or difficulties of being traced. No matter in developing or developed countries, governments and industries have gradually realized the colossal threats of cybercrime on economic and political security and public interests. However, complexity in types and forms of cybercrime increases the difficulty to fight back. In this sense, fighting cybercrime calls for international cooperation. Various organizations and governments have already made joint efforts in establishing global standards of legislation and law enforcement both on a regional and on an international scale. U.S.-China's cooperation is one of the most striking progress recently because they are the top two source countries of cybercrime.

Information and communication technology (ICT) plays an important role in helping ensure interoperability and security based on global standards. General countermeasures have been adopted in cracking down cybercrime, such as legal measures in perfecting legislation and technical measures in tracking down crimes over the network, Internet content control, using public or private proxy and computer forensics, encryption and plausible deniability, etc. Due to the heterogeneity of law enforcement and technical countermeasures of different countries, this article will mainly focus on legislative and regulatory initiatives of international cooperation

In terms of cybercrime, we may often associate it with various forms of Internet attacks, such as hacking, Trojans, malware (keyloggers) , botnet, Denial-of-Service (DoS) , spoofing, phishing, and vishing. Though cybercrime encompasses a broad range of illegal activities, it can be generally divided into five categories:

INTRUSIVE OFFENCES

Illegal Access: “Hacking” is one of the major forms of offences that refers to unlawful access to a computer system.

Data Espionage: Offenders can intercept communications between users (such as e-mails) by targeting communication infrastructure such as fixed lines or wireless, and any Internet service (e.g., e-mail servers, chat or VoIP communications) .

Data Interference: Offenders can violate the integrity of data and interfere with them by deleting, suppressing, or altering data and restricting access to them.

CONTENT-RELATED OFFENCES

Pornographic Material (**Child-Pornography**) : Sexually related content was among the first content to be commercially distributed over the Internet.

For additional analytical, business and investment opportunities information, please contact Global Investment & Business Center, USA at (703) 370-8082. Fax: (703) 370-8083. E-mail: ibpusa3@gmail.com Global Business and Investment Info Databank - www.ibpus.com

Racism, Hate Speech, Glorification of Violence: Radical groups use mass communication systems such as the Internet to spread propaganda.

Religious Offences: A growing number of websites present material that is in some countries covered by provisions related to religious offences, e.g., anti-religious written statements.

Spam: Offenders send out millions of e-mails to users, often containing advertisements for products and services.

COPYRIGHT AND TRADEMARK-RELATED OFFENCES

Common copyright offences: cyber piracy, software piracy, piracy of music or movies.

Trademark violations: A well-known aspect of global trade. The most serious offences include phishing and domain or name-related offences, such as cybersquatting.

COMPUTER-RELATED OFFENCES

Fraud: online auction fraud, advance fee fraud, credit card fraud, Internet banking

Forgery: manipulation of digital documents.

Identity theft: It refers to stealing private information including Social Security Numbers (SSN) , passport numbers, Date of birth, addresses, phone numbers, and passwords for non-financial and financial accounts.

COMBINATION OFFENCES

Cyberterrorism: The main purposes of it are propaganda, information gathering, preparation of real-world attacks, publication of training material, communication, terrorist financing and attacks against critical infrastructure.

Cyberwarfare: It describes the use of ICTs in conducting warfare using the Internet.

Cyberlaundering: Conducting crime through the use of virtual currencies, online casinos and etc.

THREATS

Similar to conventional crime, economic benefits, power, revenge, adventure, ideology and lust are the core driving forces of cybercrime. Major threats caused by those motivations can be categorized as following:

Economic security, reputation and social trust are severely challenged by cyber fraud, counterfeiting, impersonation and concealment of identity, extortion, electronic money laundering, piracy and tax evasion.

Public interest and national security/integrity can be threatened by dissemination of offensive material —e.g., pornographic, defamatory or inflammatory/intrusive communication— cyber stalking/harassment, Child pornography and paedophilia, electronic vandalism/terrorism.

For additional analytical, business and investment opportunities information, please contact Global Investment & Business Center, USA at (703) 370-8082. Fax: (703) 370-8083. E-mail: ibpusa3@gmail.com Global Business and Investment Info Databank - www.ibpus.com

Privacy, domestic and even diplomatic information security are harmed by unauthorized access and misuse of ICT, denial of services, and illegal interception of communication.

Domestic, as well as international security are threatened by cybercrime due to its transnational characteristic. No single country can really handle this big issue on their own. It is imperative for us to collaborate and defend cybercrime on a global scale.

INTERNATIONAL TRENDS

As more and more criminals are aware of potentially large economic gains that can be achieved with cybercrime, they tend to switch from simple adventure and vandalism to more targeted attacks, especially platforms where valuable information highly concentrates, such as computer, mobile devices and the Cloud. There are several emerging international trends of cybercrime.

- **Platform switch**: Cybercrime is switching its battle ground from Windows-system PCs to other platforms, including mobile phones, tablet computers, and VoIP. Because a significant threshold in vulnerabilities has been reached. PC vendors are building better security into their products by providing faster updates, patches and user alert to potential flaws. Besides, global mobile devices' penetration—from smart phones to tablet PCs—accessing the Internet by 2013 will surpass 1 billion, creating more opportunities for cybercrime. The massively successful banking Trojan, Zeus is already being adapted for the mobile platform. Smishing, or SMS phishing, is another method cyber criminals are using to exploit mobile devices, which users download after falling prey to a social engineering ploy, is designed to defeat the SMS-based two-factor authentication most banks use to confirm online funds transfers by customers. VoIP systems are being used to support vishing (telephone-based phishing) schemes, which are now growing in popularity.

- **Social engineering** scams: It refers to a non-technical kind of intrusion, in the form of e-mails or social networking chats, that relies heavily on human interaction and often involves fooling potential victims into downloading malware or leaking personal data. Social engineering is nevertheless highly effective for attacking well-protected computer systems with the exploitation of trust. Social networking becomes an increasingly important tool for cyber criminals to recruit money mules to assist their money laundering operations around the globe. Spammers are not only spoofing social networking messages to persuade targets to click on links in emails — they are taking advantage of users' trust of their social networking connections to attract new victims.

- **Highly targeted**: The newest twist in "hypertargeting" is malware that is meant to disrupt industrial systems — such as the Stuxnet network worm, which exploits zero-day vulnerabilities in Microsoft. The first known copy of the worm was discovered in a plant in Germany. A subsequent variant led to a widespread global outbreak.

- **Dissemination and use of malware**: malware generally takes the form of a virus, a worm, a Trojan horse, or spyware. In 2009, the majority of malware connects to host Web sites registered in the U.S.A. (51.4%) , with China second (17.2%) , and Spain third (15.7%) . A primary means of malware dissemination is email. It is truly international in scope.

- **Intellectual property theft (IP theft)** : It is estimated that 90% of the software, DVDs, and CDs sold in some countries are counterfeit, and that the total global trade in counterfeit goods is more than $600 billion a year. In the USA alone, IP theft costs businesses an estimated $250 billion annually, and 750,000 jobs.

INTERNATIONAL LEGISLATIVE RESPONSES AND COOPERATION

INTERNATIONAL RESPONSES

G8

Group of Eight (G8) is made up of the heads of eight industrialized countries: the U.S., the United Kingdom, Russia, France, Italy, Japan, Germany, and Canada.

In 1997, G8 released a Ministers' Communiqué that includes an action plan and principles to combat cybercrime and protect data and systems from unauthorized impairment. G8 also mandates that all law enforcement personnel must be trained and equipped to address cybercrime, and designates all member countries to have a point of contact on a 24 hours a day/7 days a week basis.

United Nations

In 1990 the UN General Assembly adopted a resolution dealing with computer crime legislation. In 2000 the UN GA adopted a resolution on combating the criminal misuse of information technology. In 2002 the UN GA adopted a second resolution on the criminal misuse of information technology.

ITU

The International Telecommunication Union (ITU) , as a specialized agency within the United Nations, plays a leading role in the standardization and development of telecommunications and cybersecurity issues. The ITU was the lead agency of the World Summit on the Information Society (WSIS) .

In 2003, Geneva Declaration of Principles and the Geneva Plan of Action were released, which highlights the importance of measures in the fight against cybercrime.

In 2005, the Tunis Commitment and the Tunis Agenda were adopted for the Information Society.

Council of Europe

Council of Europe is an international organisation focusing on the development of human rights and democracy in its 47 European member states.

In 2001, the Convention on Cybercrime, the first international convention aimed at Internet criminal behaviors, was co-drafted by the Council of Europe with the addition of USA, Canada, and Japan and signed by its 46 member states. But only 25 countries ratified later. It aims at providing the basis of an effective legal framework for fighting cybercrime, through harmonization of cybercriminal offences qualification, provision for laws empowering law enforcement and enabling international cooperation.

For additional analytical, business and investment opportunities information, please contact Global Investment & Business Center, USA at (703) 370-8082. Fax: (703) 370-8083. E-mail: ibpusa3@gmail.com Global Business and Investment Info Databank - www.ibpus.com

REGIONAL RESPONSES

APEC

Asia-Pacific Economic Cooperation (APEC) is an international forum that seeks to promote promoting open trade and practical economic cooperation in the Asia-Pacific Region. In 2002, APEC issued Cybersecurity Strategy which is included in the Shanghai Declaration. The strategy outlined six areas for co-operation among member economies including legal developments, information sharing and co-operation, security and technical guidelines, public awareness, and training and education.

OECD

The Organisation for Economic Co-operation and Development (OECD) is an international economic organisation of 34 countries founded in 1961 to stimulate economic progress and world trade.

In 1990, the Information, Computer and Communications Policy (ICCP) Committee created an Expert Group to develop a set of guidelines for information security that was drafted until 1992 and then adopted by the OECD Council. In 2002, OECD announced the completion of "Guidelines for the Security of Information Systems and Networks: Towards a Culture of Security".

European Union

In 2001, the European Commission published a communication titled "Creating a Safer Information Society by Improving the Security of Information Infrastructures and Combating Computer-related Crime".

In 2002, EU presented a proposal for a "Framework Decision on Attacks against Information Systems". The Framework Decision takes note of Convention on Cybercrime, but concentrates on the harmonisation of substantive criminal law provisions that are designed to protect infrastructure elements.

Commonwealth

In 2002, the Commonwealth of Nations presented a model law on cybercrime that provides a legal framework to harmonise legislation within the Commonwealth and enable international cooperation. The model law was intentionally drafted in accordance with the Convention on Cybercrime.

ECOWAS

The Economic Community of West African States (ECOWAS) is a regional group of west African Countries founded in 1975 it has fifteen member states. In 2009, ECOWAS adopted the Directive on Fighting Cybercrime in ECOWAS that provides a legal framework for the member states, which includes substantive criminal law as well as procedural law.

GCC

In 2007, the Arab League and Gulf Cooperation Council (GCC) recommended at a conference seeking a joint approach that takes into consideration international standards.

VOLUNTARY INDUSTRY RESPONSE

During the past few years, public-private partnerships have emerged as a promising approach for tackling cybersecurity issues around the globe. Executive branch agencies (e.g., the Federal Trade Commission in US) , regulatory agencies (e.g., Australian Communications and Media Authority) , separate agencies (e.g., ENISA in the EU) and industry (e.g., MAAWG, ...) are all involved in partnership.

In 2004, the London Action Plan was founded, which aims at promoting international spam enforcement cooperation and address spam related problems, such as online fraud and deception, phishing, and dissemination of viruses

CONVENTION ON CYBERCRIME

Signed	23 November 2001
Location	Budapest
Effective	1 July 2004
Condition	Ratification by 3 Council of Europe States
Signatories	50
Parties	41
Depositary	Secretary General of the Council of Europe

The **Convention on Cybercrime**, also known as the **Budapest Convention on Cybercrime** or the **Budapest Convention**, is the first international treaty seeking to address Internet and computer crime by harmonizing national laws, improving investigative techniques, and increasing cooperation among nations. It was drawn up by the Council of Europe in Strasbourg, France, with the active participation of the Council of Europe's observer states Canada and Japan.

The Convention and its Explanatory Report was adopted by the Committee of Ministers of the Council of Europe at its 109th Session on 8 November 2001. It was opened for signature in Budapest, on 23 November 2001 and it entered into force on 1 July 2004. As of November 2013, 41 states have ratified the convention, while a further 11 states had signed the convention but not ratified it.

On 1 March 2006 the Additional Protocol to the Convention on Cybercrime came into force. Those States that have ratified the additional protocol are required to criminalize the dissemination of racist and xenophobic material through computer systems, as well as threats and insults motivates by racism or xenophobia

OBJECTIVES

The Convention is the first international treaty on crimes committed via the Internet and other computer networks, dealing particularly with infringements of copyright, computer-related fraud, child pornography, hate crimes, and violations of network security. It also contains a series of powers and procedures such as the search of computer networks and lawful interception.

For additional analytical, business and investment opportunities information, please contact Global Investment & Business Center, USA at (703) 370-8082. Fax: (703) 370-8083. E-mail: ibpusa3@gmail.com Global Business and Investment Info Databank - www.ibpus.com

Its main objective, set out in the preamble, is to pursue a common criminal policy aimed at the protection of society against cybercrime, especially by adopting appropriate legislation and fostering international cooperation.

The Convention aims principally at:

- Harmonising the domestic criminal substantive law elements of offences and connected provisions in the area of cyber-crime
- Providing for domestic criminal procedural law powers necessary for the investigation and prosecution of such offences as well as other offences committed by means of a computer system or evidence in relation to which is in electronic form
- Setting up a fast and effective regime of international cooperation

The following offences are defined by the Convention: illegal access, illegal interception, data interference, system interference, misuse of devices, computer-related forgery, computer-related fraud, offences related to child pornography, and offences related to copyright and neighbouring rights.

It also sets out such procedural law issues as expedited preservation of stored data, expedited preservation and partial disclosure of traffic data, production order, search and seizure of computer data, real-time collection of traffic data, and interception of content data. In addition, the Convention contains a provision on a specific type of transborder access to stored computer data which does not require mutual assistance (with consent or where publicly available) and provides for the setting up of a 24/7 network for ensuring speedy assistance among the Signatory Parties.

The Convention is the product of four years of work by European and international experts. It has been supplemented by an Additional Protocol making any publication of racist and xenophobic propaganda via computer networks a criminal offence. Currently, cyber terrorism is also studied in the framework of the Convention.

ACCESSION BY THE UNITED STATES

Its ratification by the United States Senate by unanimous consent in August 2006 was both praised and condemned. The United States became the 16th nation to ratify the convention. The Convention entered into force in the United States on 1 January 2007.

"While balancing civil liberty and privacy concerns, this treaty encourages the sharing of critical electronic evidence among foreign countries so that law enforcement can more effectively investigate and combat these crimes", said Senate Majority Leader Bill Frist.

"The Convention includes a list of crimes that each signatory state must transpose into their own law. It requires the criminalization of such activities as hacking (including the production, sale, or distribution of hacking tools) and offenses relating to child pornography, and expands criminal liability for intellectual property violations. It also requires each signatory state to implement certain procedural mechanisms within their laws. For example, law enforcement authorities must be granted the power to compel an Internet service provider to monitor a person's activities online in real time. Finally, the Convention requires signatory states to provide international cooperation to the widest extent possible for investigations and proceedings concerning criminal offenses related to computer systems and data, or for the collection of evidence in electronic form of a criminal offense. Law enforcement agencies will have to assist police from other participating countries to cooperate with their mutual assistance requests".

Although a common legal framework would eliminate jurisdictional hurdles to facilitate the law enforcement of borderless cyber crimes, a complete realization of a common legal framework may not be possible. Transposing Convention provisions into domestic law is difficult especially if it requires the incorporation of substantive expansions that run counter to constitutional principles. For instance, the United States may not be able to criminalize all the offenses relating to child pornography that are stated in the Convention, specifically the ban on virtual child pornography, because of its First Amendment's free speech principles. Under Article 9(2) (c) of the Convention, a ban on child pornography includes any "realistic images representing a minor engaged in sexually explicit conduct". According to the Convention, the United States would have to adopt this ban on virtual child pornography as well, however, the U.S. Supreme Court, in *Ashcroft v. Free Speech Coalition*, struck down as unconstitutional a provision of the CPPA that prohibited "any visual depiction" that "is, or appears to be, of a minor engaging in sexually explicit conduct". In response to the rejection, the U.S. Congress enacted the PROTECT Act to amend the provision, limiting the ban to any visual depiction "that is, or is indistinguishable from, that of a minor engaging in sexually explicit conduct". 18 U.S.C

The United States will not become a Party to the Additional Protocol to the Convention on Cybercrime.

ACCESSION BY OTHER NON-EUROPEAN STATES

The Convention was signed by Canada, Japan, the United States, and the Republic of South Africa on 23 November 2001, in Budapest. As of November 2013, the non-European states that have ratified the treaty are Australia, Dominican Republic, Japan, Mauritius, and the United States.

On October 21, 2013, The Foreign Ministry of Colombia through a press release, stated the Council of Europe invited Colombia to adhere to the "Convention of Budapest". Colombia has not acceded to the convention

INTERNATIONAL PROGRAMS AND PROGECTS IN CYBER CRIME PREVENTION

STRATEGIC PRIORITIES FOR THE COOPERATION AGAINST CYBERCRIME[1]

DECLARATION ON STRATEGIC PRIORITIES FOR COOPERATION AGAINST CYBERCRIME

We, representatives of Ministries of Interior and Security,
Ministries of Justice and Offices of Prosecutor's General
of States participating in the CyberCrime@EAP project of the
Eastern Partnership Facility

* Meeting at this regional Conference on Strategic Priorities on Cybercrime held in Kyiv, from 30 to 31 October 2013, in cooperation with the Council of Europe and the European Union;

* Taking note of the Joint Declaration on Eastern Partnership Justice and Home Affairs adopted by Ministers responsible for justice and home affairs of European Union Member States and States participating in the Eastern Partnership (Luxembourg, 8 October 2013) which stresses,

[1] in the Eastern Partnership Region Adopted at the Conference on Strategic Priorities under the CyberCrime@EAP project Kyiv, Ukraine, 31 October 2013 Data Protection and Cybercrime Division Council of Europe Kyiv, Ukraine, 31 October 2013

inter alia, the importance of enhancing cooperation against cybercrime through effective application of the standards of the Budapest Convention on Cybercrime;

* Conscious of the benefits of information and communication technologies that are transforming our societies;

* Concerned by the risk of cybercrime that adversely affects confidence and trust in information technologies as well as the rights and safety of individuals, including in particular children;

* Recognising the positive obligation of governments to protect individuals against cybercrime;

* Mindful of the need to respect fundamental rights and freedoms, including the protection of individuals with regarding to the processing of personal data, when protecting society against crime;

* Considering the need for cooperation between public and private sectors for the prevention and control of cybercrime and the protection of computer systems;

* Believing that effective measures against cybercrime require efficient regional and international cooperation;

* Underlining the value of the Budapest Convention on Cybercrime as a guideline for domestic legislation and a framework for international cooperation;

* Noting with appreciation the increasing importance paid by the European Union to cybersecurity and action against cybercrime;

* Considering, in particular, that partnerships should be sought between the European Cybercrime Centre (EC3) at Europol and our law enforcement authorities;

* Grateful for the support provided by the European Union and the Council of Europe through the CyberCrime@EAP regional project;

* Building on the progress made and on the action on cybercrime already taken in the States of the region, while noting that further efforts are required;

We endorse the strategic priorities for cooperation against cybercrime presented at this conference and we are committed to

* Pursue cybercrime strategies to ensure an effective criminal justice response to offences against and by means of computers as well as to any offence involving electronic evidence;

* Adopt complete and effective legislation on cybercrime that meets human rights and rule of law requirements;

* Strengthen specialised law enforcement units and the specialisation of prosecution services with respect to cybercrime and electronic evidence;

* Implement sustainable law enforcement training strategies;

* Support the training of judges and prosecutors on cybercrime and electronic evidence;

For additional analytical, business and investment opportunities information, please contact Global Investment & Business Center, USA at (703) 370-8082. Fax: (703) 370-8083. E-mail: ibpusa3@gmail.com Global Business and Investment Info Databank - www.ibpus.com

* Pursue comprehensive strategies to protect children against online sexual exploitation and sexual abuse in line with the Lanzarote Convention;

* Promote financial investigations and the prevention and control of fraud and money laundering on the Internet;

* Strengthen cooperation with the private sector, in particular between law enforcement authorities and Internet service providers;

* Engage in efficient regional and international cooperation;

* Share our experience with other regions of the world to support capacity building against cybercrime;

* Promote adherence to the Budapest Convention on Cybercrime at the global level.

Declaration adopted by acclamation in

Kyiv, Ukraine, 31 October 2013

1. STRATEGIC PRIORITY: CYBERCRIME POLICIES AND STRATEGIES

As societies are transformed by information and communication technology, the security of ICT has become a policy priority of many governments. This is reflected in adoption of cybersecurity strategies by many governments with a primary focus on the protection of critical information infrastructure. However, governments also have the positive obligation to protect people and their rights against cybercrime and to bring offenders to justice.

Governments may therefore consider the preparation of specific cybercrime strategies or to enhance cybercrime components within cybersecurity strategies or policies.

Relevant authorities may consider the following actions:

* Pursue cybercrime policies or strategies with the objective of ensuring an effective criminal justice response to offences against and by means of computers as well as to any offence involving electronic evidence. Consider as elements of such policies or strategies preventive measures, legislation, specialised law enforcement units and prosecution services, interagency cooperation, law enforcement and judicial training, public/private cooperation, effective international cooperation, financial investigations and the prevention of fraud and money laundering, and the protection of children against sexual violence.

* Ensure that human rights and rule of law requirements are met when taking measures against cybercrime.

* Establish online platforms for public reporting on cybercrime. This should provide a better understanding of cybercrime threats and trends and facilitate criminal justice action. Such platforms may also be used for public information and threat alerts.

* Create awareness and promote preventive measures at all levels.

For additional analytical, business and investment opportunities information, please contact Global Investment & Business Center, USA at (703) 370-8082. Fax: (703) 370-8083. E-mail: ibpusa3@gmail.com Global Business and Investment Info Databank - www.ibpus.com

* Engage in public/private cooperation, including in particular in the cooperation between law enforcement authorities and Internet Service Providers.

* Engage in international cooperation to the widest extent possible. This includes making full use of the existing bi- and multilateral and regional agreements, in particular the Budapest Convention on Cybercrime. Measures and training to accelerate mutual legal assistance should be implemented. Governments (Parties and Observers to the Convention) should actively participate in the work of the Cybercrime Convention Committee (T-CY) and should engage in cooperation with the European Cybercrime Centre (EC3) and other initiatives of the European Union.

* Evaluate on a regular basis the effectiveness of the criminal justice response to cybercrime and maintain statistics. Such analyses would help determine and improve the performance of criminal justice action and allocate resources in an efficient manner.

2. STRATEGIC PRIORITY: A COMPLETE AND EFFECTIVE LEGAL BASIS FOR CRIMINAL JUSTICE ACTION

Adequate legislation is the basis for criminal justice measures on cybercrime and the use of electronic evidence in criminal proceedings. States participating in the CyberCrime@EAP project have made much progress in bringing their legislation in line with the Budapest Convention as well as related Council of Europe and European Union standards on data protection, on the protection of children against sexual violence or on crime proceeds and money laundering.1 However, further strengthening is required and often legislation has yet to stand the test of practice. This is particularly true for specific procedural law powers.

1 See for example Council of Europe Convention for the Protection of Individuals with regard to Automatic Processing of Personal Data (ETS 108), the "Lanzarote Convention" on the Sexual Exploitation and Sexual Abuse of Children (CETS 201), Convention on the Laundering, Search, Seizure and Confiscation of Proceeds from Crime and the Financing of Terrorism (CETS 198).

The adoption of complete and effective legislation that meets human rights and rule of law requirements should be a strategic priority.

Relevant authorities should consider the following actions:

* Further improve procedural law provisions to secure electronic evidence by law enforcement. This should include laws and implementing regulations on the use of the expedited preservation provisions of the Budapest Convention (follow up to assessment by Cybercrime Convention Committee), but also other rules on access to data held by private sector entities.

* Evaluate the effectiveness of legislation. The application in practice of legislation and regulations should be evaluated on a regular basis. Statistical data on cases investigated, prosecuted and adjudicated should be maintained and the procedures applied should be documented.

* Ensure that law enforcement powers are subject to conditions and safeguards in line with Article 15 Budapest Convention. This should include judicial oversight of intrusive powers but also respect of principles of proportionality and necessity.

* Strengthen data protection legislation in line with international and European standards. Governments are encouraged to ensure that their national data protection legislation complies with the principles of the Council of Europe's data protection convention ETS 108 and to participate in the Convention's current modernisation process. The same applies to the future

data protection standards of the European Union. This will facilitate the transborder sharing of data also for law enforcement purposes.

* Complete legislation and take preventive and protective measures on the protection of children against online sexual violence. While many provisions of the Lanzarote Convention have been implemented, in some States or areas issues such as "possession of child pornography", "knowingly obtaining access" and "grooming" still need to be addressed.

* Adapt legislation on financial investigation, the confiscation of crime proceeds and on money laundering and the financing of terrorism to the online environment. Rules and regulations should in particular allow for swift domestic and international information exchange.

3. Strategic priority: Specialised cybercrime units

Cybercrime and electronic evidence require a specialised response by criminal justice authorities. Law enforcement authorities and prosecution services need to be able to investigate and prosecute offences against computer data and systems, offences by means of computers as well as electronic evidence in relation to any crime. In all States participating in the CyberCrime@EAP project, the creation or strengthening of police-type cybercrime units is in progress and the specialisation of prosecutors is under consideration in some. This process should be pursued. It is essential to understand that technology changes day by day and that the workload of cybercrime and forensic units is increasing constantly. The resourcing (staff, equipment, software) and maintenance of specialised skills and the adaptation of such units to emerging requirements is a continued challenge.

The continued strengthening of specialised cybercrime units should be strategic priority.

Relevant authorities should consider the following actions:

* Establish – where this has not yet been done – specialised cybercrime units within the criminal police. The exact set up and functions should be the result of a careful analysis of needs and be based on law.

* Enhance the specialisation of prosecutors. Consider the establishment of specialised prosecution units or, alternatively, of a group of specialised prosecutors to guide or assist other prosecutors in cases involving cybercrime and electronic evidence.

* Review the functions and resourcing of specialised units on a regular basis. This should allow to adjustments and thus to meet new challenges and increasing demands.

* Facilitate cooperation and exchange of good practices between specialised units at regional and international levels.

* Improve procedures for cybercrime investigations and the handling of electronic evidence. Examine and consider implementation of national and international standards and good practices in this respect. Consider making use of the Guide on Electronic Evidence developed under the CyberCrime@IPA project in cooperation with experts of the Eastern Partnership region.

4. Strategic priority: Law enforcement training

Law enforcement authorities need to be able not only to investigate offences against and by means of computer systems but also deal with electronic evidence in relation to any type of

For additional analytical, business and investment opportunities information, please contact Global Investment & Business Center, USA at (703) 370-8082. Fax: (703) 370-8083. E-mail: ibpusa3@gmail.com Global Business and Investment Info Databank - www.ibpus.com

crime. With the exponential growth in the use of information technologies by society, law enforcement challenges have increased equally. All law enforcement officers – from first responders to highly specialised computer forensic investigators – need to be enabled to deal with cybercrime and electronic evidence at their respective levels. Elements of law enforcement training strategies have been identified, but consistent training strategies have not yet been adopted.

The preparation and implementation of sustainable training strategies to train law enforcement officers at the appropriate level should be a strategic priority.

Relevant authorities should consider the following actions:

* Implementation of a domestic law enforcement training strategy. The objective should be to ensure that law enforcement agencies have the skills and competencies necessary to investigate cybercrime, secure electronic evidence, carry out computer forensic analysis for criminal proceedings, assist other agencies and contribute to network security. Investment in such training is justified given the reliance of society on information technologies and associated risks.

* Include rules and protocols on the handling of electronic evidence in all levels of national training. It is important to recognise that electronic evidence impacts on all criminal activities and training in recognising and dealing with electronic evidence is needed by all law enforcement operatives and not only those in specialised units. This training could be based on the Guide on Electronic Evidence developed under the CyberCrime@IPA project.

* Consider the introduction of individual training plans for specialist investigators. The changes in technology and the manner in which criminal abuse that technology mean that there is a need for an appropriate number of highly trained personnel that are competent and able to conduct investigations and or digital evidence examinations at the highest level. It will also enhance their status within the criminal justice system.

* Consider the implementation of procedures to ensure best value for the investment in cybercrime training. Cybercrime and computer forensics training is very expensive. In order to ensure that an adequate return is received for the investment, States should ensure that staff are appointed to and remain in posts that reflect the level of knowledge and skills they have. To this end, training and human resource strategies need to be complimentary.

5. STRATEGIC PRIORITY: JUDICIAL TRAINING

As – in addition to offences against and by means of computers – an increasing number of other types of offences involve evidence on computer systems or other storage devices, eventually all judges and prosecutors need to be prepared to deal with electronic evidence. A clear need for systematic and sustainable training for judges and prosecutors has been identified in all States participating in the CyberCrime@EAP project.

Enabling all judges and prosecutors to prosecute and adjudicate cybercrime and make use of electronic evidence in criminal proceedings should remain a strategic priority.

Relevant authorities should consider the following actions:

* Adapt existing training materials and train trainers. Training concepts and materials have already been developed by the Council of Europe and could be adapted to the needs of domestic training institutions. Trainers should be trained in the delivery of the materials.

For additional analytical, business and investment opportunities information, please contact Global Investment & Business Center, USA at (703) 370-8082. Fax: (703) 370-8083. E-mail: ibpusa3@gmail.com Global Business and Investment Info Databank - www.ibpus.com

* Mainstream judicial training on cybercrime and electronic evidence. Domestic institutions for the training of judges and prosecutors should integrate basic and advanced training modules on cybercrime and electronic evidence in their regular training curricula for initial and in-service training.

* Introduce measures to ensure that judicial training on cybercrime and electronic evidence is compulsory. It has been apparent during the project that training for judges and prosecutors is voluntary in most project areas. This led to many instances where participants only attended training for very short periods of courses and did not benefit fully from the training that was delivered.

* Introduce training records for individual judges and prosecutors. In order to ensure that best use is made of the training delivered to judges and prosecutors, it is advisable that a record is kept of all training received by individuals so as to inform requirements for further specialised training and to ensure the right people are trained and their skills utilised appropriately.

6. Strategic priority: Financial investigations and prevention and control of fraud and money laundering on the Internet

Most crime involving the Internet and other information technologies is aimed at generating economic profit through different types of fraud and other forms of economic and serious crime. Large amounts of crime proceeds are thus generated and are circulating on the Internet.

Therefore, financial investigations targeting the search, seizure and confiscation of crime proceeds and measures for the prevention of fraud and for the prevention and control of money laundering on the Internet should become a strategic priority.

Governments should consider the following actions:

* Establish an online platform for public reporting on fraud on the Internet and on cybercrime in general. The use of standardised reporting templates will allow for a better analysis of threats and trends, of criminal operations and organisations, and of patterns of money flows and money laundering. This will facilitate measures by criminal justice authorities and financial intelligence units to prosecute offenders and to seize and confiscate crime proceeds. The platform should also serve preventive functions (public awareness and education, threat alerts, tools and advice). The more domestic platforms are harmonised with those of other States, the easier it will facilitate regional and international analyses and action.

* Promote pro-active parallel financial investigations when investigating cybercrime or offences involving information technologies/the Internet. This requires increased interagency cooperation between authorities responsible for cybercrime and for financial investigations as well as financial intelligence units. Joint training may facilitate such interagency cooperation.

* Create trusted fora (domestic and regional) for public/private information sharing on cyber threats regarding the financial sector. Domestic fora should be available to key stakeholders (such as financial sector representatives, Internet service providers, cybercrime units, financial intelligence units, Computer Security Incident Response Teams). Their purpose is to identify threats, trends, tools and solutions to protect the financial sector against cybercrime. The regional forum should consist of the fora established at domestic levels.

* Establish the legal framework for the seizure and confiscation of crime proceeds and digital assets as well as for the prevention of money laundering on the Internet. This should include

digital assets, such as e-money and virtual currencies. Rules, regulations and procedures for anti-money laundering should also apply to Internet-based payment systems.

* Exploit opportunities for more efficient international cooperation. Linking anti-money laundering measures and financial investigations with cybercrime investigations and computer forensics offers added possibilities for international cooperation. Governments should make use of the opportunities available under the Budapest Convention on Cybercrime, the Convention on the Laundering, Search, Seizure and Confiscation of Proceeds from Crime and the Financing of Terrorism (CETS 198) of the Council of Europe and the revised 40 Recommendations of the Financial Action Task Force (FATF). Consideration should furthermore be given to the findings of the MONEYVAL typology study on criminal money flows on the Internet of March 2012.2

2 http://www.coe.int/t/DGHL/cooperation/economiccrime/cybercrime/Documents/Reports-Presentations/MONEYVAL_2012_6_Reptyp_flows_en.pdf

7. Strategic priority: Cooperation between law enforcement and Internet service providers

Cooperation between law enforcement agencies and Internet service providers (ISPs) and other private sector entities is essential for protecting the rights of Internet users and for protecting them against crime. Effective investigations of cybercrime are often not possible without the cooperation of ISPs. However, such cooperation needs to take into account the different roles of law enforcement and of ISPs as well as the privacy rights of users.

Enhanced law enforcement/ISP cooperation and public/private sharing of information in line with data protection regulations should become a strategic priority.

Governments should consider the following actions:

* Establish clear rules and procedures at the domestic level for law enforcement access to data held by ISPs and other private sector entities in line with data protection regulations. A clear legal basis in line with the procedural law provisions and the safeguards and conditions of the Budapest Convention on Cybercrime will help meet human rights and rule of law requirements. Guidelines3 adopted at the Octopus Conference of the Council of Europe in 2008 may help law enforcement and ISPs organise and structure their cooperation. Governments should facilitate the use of the expedited preservation provisions (Articles 16, 17, 29 and 30) of the Budapest Convention taking into account the results of the assessments by the Cybercrime Convention Committee.4

3
http://www.coe.int/t/dghl/cooperation/economiccrime/cybercrime/Documents/LEA_ISP/default_en.asp .

4 Assessment report adopted by the T-CY in December 2012
http://www.coe.int/t/DGHL/cooperation/economiccrime/cybercrime/TCY2013/TCYreports/TCY_2012_10_Assess_report_v30_public.pdf

* Foster a culture of cooperation between law enforcement and ISPs. Memoranda of understanding between law enforcement and Internet Service Providers are a fundamental tool in this respect. Regional coordination of such MOUs would facilitate the ability of law enforcement authorities to conduct investigations across regional borders, with the knowledge that comparable standards have been adopted in other States. MOUs combined with clear rules and procedures

For additional analytical, business and investment opportunities information, please contact Global Investment & Business Center, USA at (703) 370-8082. Fax: (703) 370-8083. E-mail: ibpusa3@gmail.com Global Business and Investment Info Databank - www.ibpus.com

may also facilitate the cooperation with multi-national ISPs and other private sector entities including in the disclosure of data stored in foreign jurisdiction or on cloud servers that are managed by these ISPs.

* Facilitate private/public information sharing across borders. Private sector entities hold large amounts of data on cybersecurity incidents. The transborder sharing of such data would help improve the security of the information infrastructure as well as investigate offenders. Governments should consider legislation and the conclusion of agreements allowing for private/public information sharing and encourage the development of guidelines to facilitate the sharing of information intra- and transborder, including procedural, technical, legal and data protection safeguards.

8. Strategic priority: More efficient regional and international cooperation

Cybercrime and electronic evidence are transnational by nature, thus requiring efficient international cooperation. Immediate action is required to secure electronic evidence in foreign jurisdictions and to obtain the disclosure of such evidence. However, the inefficiency of international cooperation, in particular of mutual legal assistance, is still considered among the main obstacles preventing effective action against cybercrime.

Rendering international cooperation on cybercrime and electronic evidence more efficient should be a strategic priority.

Governments should consider the following actions:

* Exploit the possibilities of the Budapest Convention on Cybercrime and other bilateral, regional and international agreements on cooperation in criminal matters. This includes making full use of Articles 23 to 35 of the Budapest Convention in relation to police-to-police and judicial cooperation, including legislative adjustments and improved procedures. Governments (parties and observers to the Convention) should fully participate in the 2013 assessment of the international cooperation provisions of the Budapest Convention that is being undertaken by the Cybercrime Convention Committee (T-CY) and any follow up resulting from this assessment. They should follow up to the T-CY assessment of 2012 and promote the use of Articles 29 and 30 of the Budapest Convention regarding international preservation requests.

* Provide for training and sharing of good practices. Authorities for police and judicial cooperation should engage in domestic, regional and international training and the sharing of good practices. This should facilitate cooperation based on trust.

* Evaluate the effectiveness of international cooperation. Ministries of Justice and of Interior and Prosecution Services should collect statistical data on international cooperation requests regarding cybercrime and electronic evidence, including the type of assistance requests, the timeliness of responses and the procedures used. This should help identify good practices and remove obstacles to cooperation. They may engage with regional partners in an analysis of the issues adversely affecting international cooperation.

* Strengthen the effectiveness of 24/7 points of contact. Such contact points have been established in all States in line with Article 35 Budapest Convention, but their role needs to be enhanced and they may need to become more pro-active and fully functional.

* Compile statistics on and review the effectiveness of 24/7 contact points and other forms of international cooperation on a regular basis.

For additional analytical, business and investment opportunities information, please contact Global Investment & Business Center, USA at (703) 370-8082. Fax: (703) 370-8083. E-mail: ibpusa3@gmail.com
Global Business and Investment Info Databank - www.ibpus.com

DIRECTIVE ON PRIVACY AND ELECTRONIC COMMUNICATIONS

Directive **2002/58** on Privacy and Electronic Communications, otherwise known as **E-Privacy Directive**, is an EU directive on data protection and privacy in the digital age. It presents a continuation of earlier efforts, most directly the Data Protection Directive. It deals with the regulation of a number of important issues such as confidentiality of information, treatment of traffic data, spam and cookies. This Directive has been amended by Directive 2009/136, which introduces several changes, especially in what concerns cookies, that are now subject to prior consent.

SUBJECT AND SCOPE

The Electronic Privacy Directive has been drafted specifically to address the requirements of new digital technologies and ease the advance of electronic communications services. The Directive complements the Data Protection Directive and applies to all matters which are not specifically covered by that Directive. In particular, the subject of the Directive is the "right to privacy in the electronic communication sector" and free movement of data, communication equipment and services.

The Directive does not apply to Titles V and VI (Second and Third Pillars constituting the European Union) . Likewise, it does not apply to issues concerning public security and defence, state security and criminal law. At present, the interception of data is covered by the new EU Data Retention Directive the purpose of which is to amend E-Privacy Directive.

Contrary to Data Protection Directive, which specifically addresses only individuals, Article 1(2) makes it clear that E-Privacy Directive also applies to legal persons.

MAIN PROVISIONS

The first general obligation in the Directive is to provide security of services. The addressees are providers of electronic communications services. This obligation also includes the duty to inform the subscribers whenever there is a particular risk, such as a virus or other malware attack.

The second general obligation is for the confidentiality of information to be maintained. The addressees are Member States, who should prohibit listening, tapping, storage or other kinds of interception or surveillance of communication and "related traffic", unless the users have given their consent or conditions of Article 15(1) have been fulfilled.

DATA RETENTION AND OTHER ISSUES

The directive obliges the providers of services to erase or anonymize the traffic data processed when no longer needed, unless the conditions from Article 15 have been fulfilled. Retention is allowed for billing purposes but only as long as the statute of limitations allows the payment to be lawfully pursued. Data may be retained upon a user's consent for marketing and value-added services. For both previous uses, the data subject must be informed why and for how long the data is being processed.

Subscribers have the right to non-itemised billing. Likewise, the users must be able to opt out of calling-line identification.

Where data relating to location of users or other traffic can be processed, Article 9 provides that this will only be permitted if such data is anonymized, where users have given consent, or for provision of value-added services. Like in the previous case, users must be informed beforehand of the character of information collected and have the option to opt out.

UNSOLICITED E-MAIL AND OTHER MESSAGES

Article 13 prohibits the use of email addresses for marketing purposes. The Directive establishes the opt-in regime, where unsolicited emails may be sent only with prior agreement of the recipient. A natural or legal person who initially collects address data in the context of the sale of a product or service, has the right to use it for commercial purposes provided the customers have a prior opportunity to reject such communication, either where it was initially collected or subsequently. Member States have the obligation to ensure that unsolicited communication will be prohibited, except in circumstances given in Article 13.

Two categories of emails (or communication in general) will also be excluded from the scope of the prohibition. The first is the exception for existing customer relationships and the second for marketing of similar products and services. The sending of unsolicited text messages, either in the form of SMS messages, push mail messages or any similar format designed for consumer portable devices (mobile phones, PDAs) also falls under the prohibition of Article 13.

COOKIES

The Directive provision applicable to cookies is Article 5(3) . Recital 25 of the Preamble recognizes the importance and usefulness of cookies for the functioning of modern Internet and directly relates Article 5(3) to them but Recital 24 also warns of the danger that such instruments may present to privacy. The change in the law does not affect all types of cookies. For cookies that are deemed to be 'strictly necessary for the delivery of a service requested by the user' the consent of the user is not needed. An example of a 'strictly necessary' cookie is when you press 'add to basket' or 'continue to checkout' when shopping online. It is important that the browser remembers information from a previous web page in order to complete a successful transaction.

The article is technology neutral, not naming any specific technological means which may be used to store data, but applies to any information that a website causes to stored in a user's browser. This reflects the EU legislator's desire to leave the regime of the directive open to future technological developments.

The addressees of the obligation are Member States, who must ensure that the use of electronic communications networks to store information in a visitor's browser is only allowed if the user is provided with "clear and comprehensive information", in accordance with Data Protection Directive, about the purposes of the storage of, or access to, that information; and has given his or her consent.

The regime so set-up can be described as opt-in, effectively meaning that the consumer must give his or her consent before cookies or any other form of data is stored in their browser. The UK Regulations allow for consent to be signified by future browser settings, which have yet to be

For additional analytical, business and investment opportunities information, please contact Global Investment & Business Center, USA at (703) 370-8082. Fax: (703) 370-8083. E-mail: ibpusa3@gmail.com Global Business and Investment Info Databank - www.ibpus.com

introduced but which must be capable of presenting enough information so that a user can give their informed consent and indicating to a target website that consent has been obtained. Initial consent can be carried over into repeated content requests to a website. The Directive does not give any guidelines as to what may constitute an opt-out, but requires that cookies, other than those "strictly necessary for the delivery of a service requested by the user" are not to be placed without user consent.

EU CYBER SECURITY STRATEGY - IMPORTANT DEVELOPMENTS AND REGULTIONS

The development of new information and communication technologies is radically changing our economy and society. The success of the information society is crucial for Europe's growth, competitiveness and employment opportunities. That is why the Commission adopted the eEurope initiative in December 1999 to ensure that the EU can reap the full benefits. The general action plan on the eEurope initiative, approved by the Feira European Council in June 2000, highlights the importance of network security and the fight against cybercrime.

At the same time the growing importance of information and communication infrastructure opens up new opportunities for criminal activities. The European Union has therefore taken a number of steps to fight harmful and illegal content on the Internet, protect intellectual property and personal data, promote electronic commerce and tighten up the security of transactions:

The action programme on organised crime, adopted by the Council (Justice and Home Affairs) in May 1997 and endorsed by the Amsterdam European Council, called on the Commission to carry out a study on computer-related crime. The Commission presented the study (known as the "COMCRIME study") in April 1998.

The Tampere European Council acknowledged that high-tech crime should be included in efforts to reach agreement on common definitions and penalties for a number of criminal offences.

Initial measures have been adopted under the Union's strategy for combating high-tech crime

DEFINITION OF COMPUTER-RELATED CRIME

The communication addresses computer crime in its broadest sense as any crime involving the use of information technology. The terms "computer crime," "computer-related crime," "high-tech crime" and "cybercrime" share the same meaning in that they describe a) the use of information and communication networks that are free from geographical constraints and b) the circulation of intangible and volatile data.

The main offences covered by existing European and national legislation are:

privacy offences: illegal collection, storage, modification, disclosure or dissemination of personal data;

content-related offences: the dissemination of pornography, in particular child pornography, racist statements and information inciting violence;

economic crimes, unauthorised access and sabotage: offences relating to unauthorised access to systems (e.g. hacking, computer sabotage and distribution of viruses, computer espionage, computer forgery, and computer fraud) ;

intellectual property offences: violations of the legal protection of computer programs and databases, copyright and related rights.

LEGISLATIVE AND NON-LEGISLATIVE PROPOSALS

Legislative measures aimed at approximating national provisions on cybercrime need to be backed up by non-legislative measures such as:

the creation of specialised national units (law enforcement and judicial authorities) ;

continuous, specialised training for police and judicial authority staff;

the creation of a harmonised set of rules for police and judicial record-keeping and appropriate tools for statistical analysis of computer crime;

the establishment of a European forum to foster cooperation between the various players;

encouragement for direct action by industry against computer-related crime;

EU-funded research and technological development (RTD) projects.

The Commission will present legislative proposals on:

approximating Member States' laws on child pornography offences;

approximating substantive criminal law in the field of high-tech crime;

applying the principle of mutual recognition to pre-trial orders associated with cybercrime investigations involving more than one Member State.

Planned non-legislative measures include:

creation of a European forum bringing together law enforcement agencies, service providers, network operators, consumer groups and data protection authorities with the aim of stepping up cooperation at EU level;

further action to promote security and trust in the context of the eEurope initiative, the Internet Action Plan, the Information Society Technologies (IST) Programme and the next framework programme for RTD;

launch of further projects under existing programmes to support the training of staff;

financing of measures aimed at improving the content and usability of the database of Member States' national laws provided by the COMCRIME study.

COMMON EU CYBER CRIME CRIME STRATEGY

Crime on the internet is increasing rapidly. Computer viruses, network breaches, and cyber-crime can lead to substantial financial losses, erode trust in online services and cause major damage to the EU's economy.

Unless more is done to protect critical digital networks, public safety and national security could also come under threat. It's a global problem calling for a common approach – online criminals can attack from anywhere.

Around 38% of European internet users have changed their behaviour because of cyber-security concerns: 18% are less likely to buy goods online and 15% are less likely to use online banking according to a recent survey

To reverse this trend the Commission has launched acomprehensive strategy to defend the EU's digital networks and protect consumers from cyber-crime. A common approach would help make critical networks more resilient to attack and drastically reduce online crime.

Getting other countries onboard would also increase security in the EU and protect citizens. EU countries would work more closely together to promote cyber-security globally by advocating the application of existing international laws in cyberspace and helping other nations become more cyber-secure.

NEW MEASURES

In line with this strategy the Commission is alsoproposing EU countries, internet providers and vulnerable business sectors take steps to secure critical digital networks.

All EU governments would become responsible for preventing and responding to threats to digital networks. All would have to meet common standards on cyber-security and increase cooperation in combating cyber-crime.

E-commerce service providers and businesses in the energy, transport, banking and healthcare sectors would have to improve network security. Current EU law requiring the reporting of online security incidents would be extended to cover all major internet services and public administrations.

For example, under current law, regular telecoms providers have to report security incidents while voice-over-IP (VOIP) services, like internet telephone calls such as Skype, do not. The new measures would close such loopholes by requiring VOIP services to also report incidents.

EU CYBERSECURITY PLAN TO PROTECT OPEN INTERNET AND ONLINE FREEDOM AND OPPORTUNITY

The European Commission, together with the High Representative of the Union for Foreign Affairs and Security Policy, has published a cybersecurity strategy alongside a Commission proposed directive on network and information security (NIS) .

The cybersecurity strategy – "An Open, Safe and Secure Cyberspace" - represents the EU's comprehensive vision on how best to prevent and respond to cyber disruptions and attacks. This is to further European values of freedom and democracy and ensure the digital economy can safely grow. Specific actions are aimed at enhancing cyber resilience of information systems, reducing cybercrime and strengthening EU international cyber-security policy and cyber defence.

The strategy articulates the EU's vision of cyber-security in terms of five priorities:

Achieving cyber resilience

Drastically reducing cybercrime

Developing cyber defence policy and capabilities related to the Common Security and Defence Policy (CSDP)

DEVELOPING THE INDUSTRIAL AND TECHNOLOGICAL RESOURCES FOR CYBER-SECURITY

Establishing a coherent international cyberspace policy for the European Union and promoting core EU values

The EU international cyberspace policy promotes the respect of EU core values, defines norms for responsible behaviour, advocates the application of existing international laws in cyberspace, while assisting countries outside the EU with cyber-security capacity-building, and promoting international cooperation in cyber issues.

The EU has made key advances in better protecting citizens from online crimes, including establishing a European Cybercrime Centre (IP/13/13) , proposing legislation on attacks against information systems (IP/10/1239) and the launch of a Global Alliance to fight child sexual abuse online (IP/12/1308) . The Strategy also aims at developing and funding a network of national Cybercrime Centers of Excellence to facilitate training and capacity building.

The proposed NIS Directive is a key component of the overall strategy and would require all Member States, key internet enablers and critical infrastructure operators such as e-commerce platforms and social networks and operators in energy, transport, banking and healthcare services to ensure a secure and trustworthy digital environment throughout the EU. The proposed Directive lays down measures including:

(a) Member State must adopt a NIS strategy and designate a national NIS competent authority with adequate financial and human resources to prevent, handle and respond to NIS risks and incidents;

(b) Creating a cooperation mechanism among Member States and the Commission to share early warnings on risks and incidents through a secure infrastructure, cooperate and organise regular peer reviews;

(c) Operators of critical infrastructures in some sectors (financial services, transport, energy, health) , enablers of information society services (notably: app stores e-commerce platforms, Internet payment, cloud computing, search engines, social networks) and public administrations must adopt risk management practices and report major security incidents on their core services.

Neelie Kroes, European Commission Vice-President for the Digital Agenda said:

"The more people rely on the internet the more people rely on it to be secure. A secure internet protects our freedoms and rights and our ability to do business. It's time to take coordinated action - the cost of not acting is much higher than the cost of acting."

Catherine Ashton, High Representative of the Union for Foreign Affairs and Security Policy/Vice-President of the Commission said:

"For cyberspace to remain open and free, the same norms, principles and values that the EU upholds offline, should also apply online. Fundamental rights, democracy and the rule of law need to be protected in cyberspace. The EU works with its international partners as well as civil society and the private sector to promote these rights globally."

For additional analytical, business and investment opportunities information, please contact Global Investment & Business Center, USA at (703) 370-8082. Fax: (703) 370-8083. E-mail: ibpusa3@gmail.com Global Business and Investment Info Databank - www.ibpus.com

Cecilia Malmström, EU Commissioner for Home Affairs said:

"The Strategy highlights our concrete actions to drastically reduce cybercrime. Many EU countries are lacking the necessary tools to track down and fight online organised crime. All Member States should set up effective national cybercrime units that can benefit from the expertise and the support of the European Cybercrime Centre EC3."

Cyber-security incidents are increasing in frequency and magnitude, becoming more complex and know no borders. These incidents can cause major damage to safety and the economy. Efforts to prevent, cooperate and be more transparent about cyber incidents must improve.

Previous efforts by the European Commission and individual Member States have been too fragmented to deal with this growing challenge.

FACTS ABOUT CYBERSECURITY TODAY

There are an estimated 150,000 computer viruses in circulation every day and 148,000 computers compromised daily.

According to the World Economic Forum, there is an estimated 10% likelihood of a major critical information infrastructure breakdown in the coming decade, which could cause damages of $250 billion.

Cybercrime causes a good share of cyber-security incidents, Symantec estimates that cybercrime victims worldwide lose around €290 billion each year, while a McAfee study put cybercrime profits at €750 billion a year.

The 2012 Eurobarometer poll on cyber security found that 38 % of EU internet users have changed their behaviour because of these cyber-security concerns: 18 % are less likely to buy goods online and 15 % are less likely to use online banking. It also shows that 74% of the respondents agreed that the risk of becoming a victim has increased, 12% have already experienced online fraud and 89% avoid disclosing personal information.

According to the public consultation on NIS, 56.8% of respondents had experienced over the past year NIS incidents with a serious impact on their activities. Meanwhile, Eurostat figures show that, by January 2012, only 26% of enterprises in the EU had a formally defined ICT security policy.

EU COUNTRIES COMPETENT AUTHORITIES

COUNTRY	TYPE OF AUTHORITY	NAME OF THE AUTHORITY
Austria	NRA + DPA	Data Protection Commission (DSK) Austrian Regulatory Authority for Broadcasting and Telecommunications (RTR)
Belgium	NRA	http://www.ibpt.be/en
Bulgaria	DPA	Commission for personal data protection (CPDP)
Croatia	NRA	Croatian Post and electronic communications Agency

Cyprus	DPA + NRA	Office for Personal Data Protection Office of the Commissioner of Electronic Communications and Postal Regulation (OCECPR)
Czech republic	DPA	Office for Personal Data Protection (OPDP)
Denmark	NRA	Danish Business Authority
Estonia	DPA	Estonian Data Protection Inspectorate
Finland	NRA	Finnish Communications Regulatory Authority
France	DPA	Commission Nationale de l'Informatique et des Libertés (CNIL)
Germany	DPA + NRA	The Federal Commissioner for Data Protection and Freedom of Information (BfDI) The Federal Network Agency for Electricity, Gas, Telecommunications, Post and Railway (BNetzA)
Greece	DPA + NRA	Hellenic Data Protection Authority (HDPA) Hellenic Authority for Communication Security and Privacy (ADAE)
Hungary	NRA	National Media and Infocommunications Authority (NMHH) / Article 4.
Ireland	DPA	Office of the Data Protection Commissioner
Italy	DPA	Garante per la protezione dei dati personali
Latvia	DPA	Data State Inspectorate
Lithuania	DPA	State Data Protection Inspectorate
Luxembourg	DPA	Commission nationale pour la protection des données (CNPD)
Malta	DPA	Office of the Information and Data Protection Commissioner (IDPC)
Netherlands	NRA + DPA	Dutch Data Protection Authority Authority for Consumers and Markets
Poland	DPA	The Inspector General for the Protection of Personal Data (GIODO)
Portugal	DPA	Comissão Nacional de Protecção de Dados
Romania	DPA	National Supervisory Authority for Personal Data Processing
Slovakia	NRA	Telecommunications Regulatory Authority of the Slovak Republic
Slovenia	DPA + NRA	Information Commissioner Post and Electronic Communications Agency of the Republic of Slovenia
Spain	DPA	Agencia Española de Protección de Datos
Sweden	NRA	Swedish Post and Telecom Authority (PTS)
UK	DPA	Information Commissioner's Office (ICO)

EU CYBER SPACE DEVELOPMENT STRATEGY[2]

PILLAR I: DIGITAL SINGLE MARKET

Too many barriers still block the free flow of online services and entertainment across national borders. The Digital Agenda will update EU Single Market rules for the digital era. The aims are to boost the music download business, establish a single area for online payments, and further protect EU consumers in cyberspace.

ACTION 1: SIMPLIFYING PAN-EUROPEAN LICENSING FOR ONLINE WORKS

The proposal for a Directive on collective management of copyright and related rights and multi-territorial licensing was adopted by the European Commission on 11 July 2012. The action aimed at simplifying copyright clearance, management and cross-border licensing by enhancing the governance, transparency and pan European licensing for (online) rights management by proposing a framework Directive on collective rights management by 2010.

Online platforms are an easy way to distribute and exchange all kinds of creative content: music, films, pictures and more. Consumers have high expectations – they want to access content of their choice anytime and on a range of devices. But Europe lacks unified markets for online content. It can be difficult, for example, for a Maltese consumer to download or stream from a German website.

Consumers do not have access to diverse European content, and creators are losing revenue because of the illegal markets which spring up to bridge the gaps.

Often, the difficulties with accessing content online are due to licensing issues. Industry-led changes combined with the improvement of legal framework will enable innovative and consumer-friendly content distribution across Europe.

The Commission proposed legislation on collective rights management in July 2012 and is working with the European Parliament and the Council to ensure its swift adoption. A structured stakeholder dialogue "Licences for Europe" took place in 2013 with the objective of identifying practical industry-led solutions to ensure that copyright management stays fit for purpose in the digital world.

The Commission will complete its on-going review of the EU copyright framework, based on market studies and impact assessment and legal drafting work, with a view to a decision in 2014 whether to table the resulting legislative reform proposals.

ACTION 2: PRESERVING ORPHAN WORKS AND OUT OF PRINT WORKS

Create a legal framework to facilitate the digitisation and dissemination of cultural works in Europe by proposing a Directive on orphan works by 2010, to conduct a dialogue with stakeholders with a view to further measures on out-of-print works, complemented by rights information databases.

What is the problem? Legal difficulties block online access to copyrighted cultural works.

[2] Digital Agenda for Europe: Communication from the Commission (26/08/2010)

For additional analytical, business and investment opportunities information, please contact Global Investment & Business Center, USA at (703) 370-8082. Fax: (703) 370-8083. E-mail: ibpusa3@gmail.com Global Business and Investment Info Databank - www.ibpus.com

Millions of copyrighted cultural works lie unexploited in libraries and museums throughout Europe. This includes orphan works, where the copyright owner cannot be traced which makes approval for digitalisation and online distribution impossible to obtain. The same difficulties apply to out-of-print material which constitutes some 70% of publishers' collections.

We need clear, Europe-wide rules and an agreed legal framework to enable further digitisation and dissemination of our cultural resources – literary, musical and artistic. These are crucial for the European digital libraries initiative and for the future Europeana – Europe's digital library – which aims to place Europe's vast cultural resources at the disposal of all Europeans.

The Commission Directive on orphan works was adopted by the European Parliament in September 2012.

The Commission will assist Member States in the transposition of the directive.

Together with stakeholders, the Commission drew up conclusions of the ARROW project and launched a follow-up measure ARROW+ which also covers audiovisual works.

The Commission continues work on the framework of a stakeholders' forum on the digitisation of out-of-print works

ACTION 3: OPEN UP PUBLIC DATA RESOURCES FOR RE-USE

By 2012, review the Directive on re-Use of Public Sector Information, notably its scope and principles on charging for access and use.

What is the problem? Turning public data to business opportunities

Public authorities produce large amounts of data that could become the raw material for new, innovative cross-border applications and services e Examples of products and services based on the re-use of public sector information (PSI) are GPS, weather forecasts, financial and insurance services.

PSI is the single largest source of information in Europe. Its estimated market value is €32 billion. Re-used, this public data could generate new businesses and jobs and give consumers more choice and more value for money.

Why is EU action needed? To unlock the public data potential across Europe

Often the use of this information is restricted to governments or public bodies. Governments could stimulate content markets by making public sector information more widely available for re-use on transparent and effective terms.

What has the Commission done so far?

A Directive was adopted in 2003 which lays down basic principles of availability, transparency and cost limits to ensure a level playing field for commercial re-users of public sector information.

A proposal for a revision of the Directive was adopted on 12 December 2011. The main changes that the Commission is proposing are:

Introducing the general rule that all documents held by public sector bodies will be re-usable for both commercial and non-commercial purposes, unless covered by the exceptions provided for in the Directive

Including libraries, museums and archives under the Directive for the first time

Establishing that public bodies shall in principle not be allowed to charge more than costs triggered by the individual request for data (marginal costs) ;

Introducing regulatory oversight over how public authorities handle requests for re-use and in particular the fees they charge;

Calling on Member States to use commonly-used machine-readable formats so as not to create technical barriers for re-use.

The proposal is now being examined by the legislator, i.e. by the Council and by the European Parliament. The date of adoption of the revised Directive is expected at the earliest in the spring of 2013.

What will the European Commission do?

Set up a data portal website as a single access point for the information that it holds, encouraging other EU institutions, agencies and bodies to use this access portal for their documents.

Work with Member States on a pan-European umbrella portal for all information held by the EU, the Member States, regional and local governments.

Continue supporting open data initiatives, notably through funding provided by the CIP ICT Policy Support Programme and the future Connecting Europe Facility (CEF) .

Ongoing actions:

Awareness-raising and promotional activities through seminars and workshops organised by Member States and stakeholders,

Networking across Europe and in a wider international context (with Member States, PSI Alliance, national industrial associations, PSI platform, software developers and open data communities) to further stimulate action and monitor progress towards a stronger and more transparent environment.

ACTION 4: WIDE STAKEHOLDER DEBATE ON FURTHER MEASURES TO STIMULATE A EUROPEAN ONLINE CONTENT MARKET

After an extensive stakeholder dialogue, report by 2012 on the need for additional measures beyond collective rights management allowing EU citizens, online content services providers and right-holders to benefit from the full potential of the digital internal market, including measures to promote cross-border and pan-European licenses, without excluding or favouring at this stage any possible legal option.

What is the problem? Europe lacks unified and efficient markets in creative content sectors, Europe's copyright framework is falling behind digital developments.

The Commission has identified a range of specific issues to be addressed, including cross-border portability of content, user-generated content, data- and text-mining, private copy levies, access to audiovisual works and cultural heritage.

The Commission will also look into mitigating the effects of territoriality in the single market; agreeing appropriate levels of harmonisation, limitations and exceptions to copyright in the digital age; and improving the legitimacy of enforcement in the context of wider copyright reform.

Why is EU action needed? To create a true digital single market

Unlocking this part of the digital single market would help Europe's economic recovery, one of the key aims of the EU 2020 strategy.

What will the European Commission do?

In 2013

The Commission will pursue two parallel tracks of action:
A structured stakeholder dialogue to explore the potential and limits of innovative licensing and technological solutions in making EU copyright law and practice fit for the digital age.
Market studies, impact assessment and legal drafting work with a view to a decision in 2014 whether to table legislative reform proposals.

Replace with reference to KTA in DSM chapter of review

ACTION 5: SIMPLIFYING THE DISTRIBUTION OF CREATIVE CONTENT

Issue a Green Paper addressing the opportunities and challenges of online distribution of audiovisual works and other creative content by 2010.

What is the problem? The market and consumers are not getting the most out of digital distribution

European audiovisual markets are very fragmented, preventing market players from realizing economies of scale and becoming viable global competitors. Consumers often don't have a chance to see valuable TV programs or films originating across the border.

Why is EU action needed? To promote the sector EU wide

Digital distribution of audiovisual content is cheaper and quicker than traditional distribution systems and allows authors and content-providers to reach new and larger audiences. This is a fast-developing market in Europe which will have a huge impact on the traditional content production and distribution structures.

What will the European Commission do?

The European Commission will:

For additional analytical, business and investment opportunities information, please contact Global Investment & Business Center, USA at (703) 370-8082. Fax: (703) 370-8083. E-mail: ibpusa3@gmail.com
Global Business and Investment Info Databank - www.ibpus.com

In 2013:

Report on the issue of digital distribution - based on the Audiovisual Green Paper (July 2011) and subsequent stakeholder consultation – in the context of the on-going review of the copyright framework.

ACTION 6: PROTECTING INTELLECTUAL PROPERTY RIGHTS ONLINE

On the basis of the review of the Directive on the enforcement of intellectual property rights, and following extensive stakeholder dialogue, report by 2012 on the need for additional measures to reinforce the protection against persistent violations of intellectual property rights in the online environment, consistent with the guarantees provided in the Telecoms Framework and fundamental rights on data protection and privacy.

What is the problem? Balancing copyright owner and consumer rights online

The development of the digital economy is creating opportunities, but also new challenges in the area of protection of Intellectual Property Rights. We need to strike the right balance between protection of Intellectual Property Rights and the general public's access to content and knowledge as well as fundamental rights.

Why is EU action needed? To develop the EU's digital single market

Legislation might not even be necessary. Mass copyright infringements in the internet could be reduced if consumers have the possibility to access content legally and at a reasonable price. Moreover, piracy could be tackled through better cooperation among the different players in the creative content value chain, such as right-holders and intermediaries.

What will the Commission do?

In 2013:

The Commission will provide an assessment based particularly on the public consultation on the civil enforcement of intellectual property rights carried out from November 2012 to March 2013. Specifically, the Commission will consider how to improve the effectiveness and efficiency of enforcement while underpinning its legitimacy.

ACTION 7: FIX A DATE FOR MIGRATION TO SINGLE EUROPEAN PAYMENT & EINVOICING

Ensure the completion of the Single Euro Payment Area (SEPA) , if necessary, by binding legal measures fixing an end date for migration before 2010 and facilitate the emergence of an interoperable European e-invoicing framework through a Communication on e-invoicing and by establishing a multi-stakeholder forum.

What is the problem? Need for the single market in payments

A fully implemented Single European Payment Area (SEPA) could generate net benefits of € 123 billion over six years for the market as a whole. Pan-European payment instruments, such as SEPA credit transfers and direct debits, reduce the costs of payments, increase competition and make cross-border payments as easy as domestic ones.

.... and cost- saving thanks to e-invoicing

For additional analytical, business and investment opportunities information, please contact Global Investment & Business Center, USA at (703) 370-8082. Fax: (703) 370-8083. E-mail: ibpusa3@gmail.com Global Business and Investment Info Databank - www.ibpus.com

Replacing paper invoices by e-invoices across the EU could lead to roughly € 240 billion in savings over a six-year period, according to studies. On the basis of these savings, the Commission wants e-invoicing to become the predominant method of invoicing in Europe by 2020. In the case of the public sector, a preliminary estimate indicates that in the next few years, savings of approximately €1 billion per year could potentially be achieved if all invoices were submitted in electronic format.

Why is EU action needed?

Migration towards internal market in payment and electronic invoicing needs to take place at European level in order to streamline both internal and cross-border transactions online. To this end, the Commission has already taken several actions:

What has the Commission done so far and what are the next steps?

Internal market in payments

The Commission proposed the Regulation setting EU-wide end-dates for the migration of old national credit transfers and direct debits to pan-European SEPA instruments by 1st of February 2014. The regulation entered into force in March 2012. More detailed information can be found here.

The Commission's work on payments has been pursued with Green Paper on an integrated European market for card, internet and mobile payments, which opened a public consultation. More details on the Green Paper can be found here.

As a result, the Commission announced specific follow-up actions to the Green Paper which will be proposed by the 2nd quarter of 2013. These are:
Review Payment Services Directive (directive 2007/64/EC)
A legislative initiative on multilateral interchange fees

eInvoicing

For legal aspects related to VAT and e-invoicing, see action 11.

The Communication of 2nd December 2010 on e-invoicing defines a set of tangible actions to facilitate the uptake of e-invoices in Europe. In particular, the Commission called on Member States to set up national multi-stakeholder fora on e-invoicing and easier and established a multi-stakeholder forum at European level.

The last meeting of the European multi-stakeholder forum took place in September 2012..More information about the work of the group can be found here.

In Single Market Act II the Commission announces an additional action on e-invoicing which aims at making it a standard mode of invoicing in public procurement

ACTION 8: REVISION OF THE ESIGNATURE DIRECTIVE

DAE Action 8 on the revision of the eSignature Directive has been merged with DAE Action 83 on mutual recognition of electronic identification to provide a comprehensive and predictable legal framework in view of boosting user empowerment, convenience and trust in the digital world. As indicated in the Digital Agenda Progress Report 2011, these actions will encourage innovation and competition as well as making it easier for small e-business players to access the scale economies of the electronic market place.

What is the Problem? Need to eliminate barriers to cross-border electronic services

There is no comprehensive EU cross-border and cross-sector framework for secure, trustworthy and easy-to-use electronic transactions that encompasses electronic identification and trust services. At EU level, a legal framework exists only for e-signatures (Directive 1999/93/EC) but not for e-identification (eID) nor for other trust services.

eID technologies and trust services (including eSignatures) are essential for all kinds of online transactions. However, barriers to cross-border secure electronic services exist and need to be eliminated in order to enable citizens and business to fully benefit from the digital single market.

Why is the EU action required? Open the door to new business opportunities

Boosting trust and confidence in the digital world as well as user convenience are essential prerequisites to stimulate further use and development of the digital single market. Accessing cross-border online services will favour travelling, working and studying across the Union. This will offer new business opportunities for providers of trust services and products as set out in the Europe 2020 strategy.

What has the Commission proposed?

The Commission proposed a holistic and comprehensive legal framework which includes consistent and coherent provisions on electronic identification and trust services in order to overcome the deficiencies of the current eSignatures Directive and to provide legal measures on cross-border mutual recognition and acceptance of national eIDs thereby contributing to making Europeans enjoy all the convenience and benefits of the online world.

The Commission adopted the proposal for a Regulation on electronic identification and trust services for electronic transactions in the internal market on 4th June 2012

The proposal contributes to unlocking the potential offered by the internet revolution. It provides a trustworthy, secure and predictable environment that enables the development of cross-border secure services and business opportunities. This will ensure that enterprises and citizens fully enjoy the opportunities provided by the digital economy in order to achieve a digital single market.

ACTION 9: UPDATING THE ECOMMERCE DIRECTIVE

Consult stakeholders about the impact of the e-commerce directive on Digital Single Market.by the end of 2010.

What is the problem? EU online markets are fragmented.

The Digital Agenda for Europe set targets for e-commerce: 50% of the population should be buying online by 2015, 20% should buy cross – border and 33% of SME's should conduct online purchases by this date. To date, e-commerce remains insufficiently developed in the EU. Consumers and businesses have difficulties accessing online shops and offering their services in other EU countries.

Why is EU action needed? To modernise the legal framework for a Digital Single Market

A genuine Digital Single Market would generate new types of growth. The hitherto unrealised potential is enormous and would benefit all territories and sectors of the European Union.

The Digital Single Market is far from achieving its full potential; the cost of the failure to complete it is expected to be at least 4.1% of GDP between now and 2020, i.e. EUR 500 billion or EUR 1000 per citizen.

What has the Commission done so far and what are the next steps?

The Commission , after conducting a public consultation, decided that an update of the e-Commerce directive was not necessary and adopted the e-Commerce Communication in January 2012. The Communication contains 16 actions aimed at doubling the volume of e-commerce in Europe by 2015.

The Commission will implement the action plan announced in the e-commerce communication, notably
propose actions to streamline postal delivery, after having consulted with stakeholders
adopt a horizontal initiative on notice-and-action
propose initiatives in the area of card, electronic and mobile payments (see action 8
propose an overall strategy on internet security in Europe aimed at better protection against cyber attacks in the EU

ACTION 10: MEMBER STATES TO IMPLEMENT LAWS TO SUPPORT THE DIGITAL SINGLE MARKET

Member States to implement swiftly and coherently the key Directives supporting the digital single market, including the Services Directive, Unfair Commercial Practices Directive and the Telecoms Framework and to ensure the implementation of the provisions of the Audiovisual Media Services Directive.

What is the problem? Fragmented digital single market

Europe's telecoms and audiovisual markets are partitioned by Member State. To remedy the situation, the Member States need to fully implement key EU Directives on the creation of the digital single market. National legislation also needs to be coordinated to make sure that audiovisual content can circulate freely. This is the aim of the Audiovisual Media Services (AVMS) Directive.

Why is EU action needed? Building the legal framework for a digital single market

It is important that the key Directives are implemented timely and consistently in order reinforce the digital single market. The Commission is monitoring the implementation process in Member States and has provided guidance on some of the key implementation issues.

What has the Commission done so far and what are the next steps?

The Commission has taken the necessary steps to set-up an autonomous Office of the Body of European Regulators (BEREC) , so that BEREC is able to operate efficiently and facilitate cooperation between national regulatory authorities and the Commission in promoting the digital single market. The BEREC Office became autonomous in September 2011.
Monitor the transposition of telecoms legislation, given that national measures were due by 25 May 2011. The Commission has started to address any transposition problems swiftly and, at first

stage, has taken action in those cases where transposition has not taken place by the due date. Assess the status and effect of implementation in the Digital Agenda Scoreboard, for example such an assessment was included in the first Digital Agenda Scoreboard published in May 2012. Monitor the transposition of the AVMS Directive, given that national measures were due by 19 December 2009. All Member states have in the meantime notified their transposition measures, and requests for clarification were sent to all Member States. Open issues were subsequently clarified in bilateral meetings with the Member States, or Member States made commitments to change their legislation. Five Member States have already brought their legislation into compliance with the AVMS Directive while in some cases infringement actions were started (BE and UK) . With regard to the 20 remaining Member States the assessment or the monitoring of the commitments is on-going. Give guidance to Member States through the Contact Committee and the Working Group of the EU Regulatory Authorities responsible for Audiovisual Media Services.

Consult broadly with stakeholders. In 2013 the Commission published a Green Paper on Preparing for a Fully Converged Audiovisual World: Growth, Creation and Values. This launched a public consultation and will allow to gather also feedback on issues related to the digital single market.

ACTION 11: MEMBER STATES TO TRANSPOSE THE VAT DIRECTIVE

Member States should transpose by 2013 the VAT Directive ensuring equal treatment for eInvoicing with paper invoices.

What is the problem? Different national VAT rules for paper and electronic invoices

Member States have adopted various domestic rules which govern the validity and acceptability of eInvoices within their own countries. This makes it difficult to use eInvoicing across the EU.

Compared to paper invoices, eInvoices offer huge advantages for companies. They can be processed more quickly and cheaply as there are no postal delays or costs. The mass adoption of e-invoicing within the EU could generate savings of around € 240 billion over a six-year period.

Why is EU action needed? To extend the benefits of eInvoicing to cross-border transactions

The European market for electronic payments and eInvoicing is still fragmented (see also action 7) . Only in an integrated payment market will it be possible for enterprises and consumers to rely on safe and efficient online payment methods.

What has the Commission done so far?

On 13 July 2010 the Council adopted a Directive (2010/45/EU amending Directive 2006/112/EC) which sets out new VAT rules for e-invoicing and removes the obstacles to the uptake of e-invoicing by creating equal treatment between paper and e-invoices, while also ensuring that no additional requirements are imposed on paper invoices.

What will Member States do?

Member States are obliged to transpose this Directive into national law by 1st January 2013.

ACTION 12: REVIEW THE EU DATA PROTECTION RULES

Review the EU data protection regulatory framework to strengthen individual rights and tackle emerging challenges from globalisation and new technologies.

For additional analytical, business and investment opportunities information, please contact Global Investment & Business Center, USA at (703) 370-8082. Fax: (703) 370-8083. E-mail: ibpusa3@gmail.com Global Business and Investment Info Databank - www.ibpus.com

What is the problem? Data protection rules vary and are difficult to understand

EU citizens have the right to the protection of their personal data and of their privacy in the online world. However, these rights are encoded in many different laws and are not always easy to grasp, while national approaches to data protection rules can vary widely across the EU.

Why is EU action needed? Lack of trust means less online business

This lack of clarity in online privacy rules triggers a lack of trust among consumers, which slows down the growth of Europe's online economy. Worries about payment security privacy concerns and trust were some of the top reasons for not making online purchases in a survey of people who did not shop online in 2009. Recent surveys and independent studies confirm that privacy concerns continue to grow among the public.

What has the Commission done so far and what are the next steps?

The European Commission (DG JUST in lead) has reviewed the existing EU data protection framework. On 25 January 2012 the Commission proposed a data protection Regulation with the aim of modernizing the legal framework and enhancing the trust and confidence of European consumers.

In 2010 & 2011:
The Commission consulted the public and stakeholders, adopted a Commission Communication on renewing the EU data protection rules.

In 2012:
The Commission adopted a data protection Regulation to strengthen online privacy rights and boost Europe's digital economy.
The Commission is currently working with the Parliament and Council towards final adoption of the Regulation.

ACTION 13: COMPLEMENTING THE CONSUMER RIGHTS DIRECTIVE

An optional contract law instrument should complement the Consumer Rights Directive to overcome the fragmentation of contract law, in particular as regards the online environment.

What is the problem? Varying national contractual rules hamper the single market

Every EU Member State has its own contractual rules and often, the provisions in force differ from one country to another. This is a serious challenge to the smooth functioning of the internal market. For instance, businesses trading across borders may face high legal costs when their contracts are subject to foreign consumer law. Those costs are passed on to consumers who will eventually have to pay higher prices.

Why is EU action needed? Legal uncertainty strangling cross-border e-commerce

Divergent rules mean that some companies could decide not to enter foreign markets because of the high compliance costs. Businesses then lose out in market reach and consumers end up with less choice. The full potential of cross-border e-commerce therefore remains unfulfilled.

What has the Commission done so far and what are the next steps?

The Commission adopted a legislative proposal in October 2011 for a Common European Sales Law to complement the EU Consumer Rights Directive. The Consumer Rights Directive was adopted by the European Parliament and the Council. The next steps will be the following:

For additional analytical, business and investment opportunities information, please contact Global Investment & Business Center, USA at (703) 370-8082. Fax: (703) 370-8083. E-mail: ibpusa3@gmail.com Global Business and Investment Info Databank - www.ibpus.com

Transposition of the new rules into the national laws by 13 December 2013.
The rules will be applied in all Member States at the latest by 13 June 2014.

The proposal for Common European Sales Law, which provides a set of rules the buyer and seller can agree to use, will help break down trade barriers and will benefit consumers by providing increased choice and a high level of protection. It will offer a single set of rules for cross-border contracts in all 27 EU countries.

ACTION 14: EXPLORE THE POSSIBILITIES FOR ALTERNATIVE DISPUTE RESOLUTION

Explore initiatives on consumer Alternative Dispute Resolution in the EU with a view to adopting a legislative proposal by the end of 2011 and proposing an EU-wide Online Dispute Resolution system for cross-border eCommerce transactions by 2012.

What is the problem? Difficult to resolve online cross-border shopping disputes

In 2009, only 8% of EU consumers bought goods and services online from a provider from another Member State. This could be down to a lack of trust in online cross-border shopping. About 70% of consumers also think it would be harder to resolve problems when shopping from another Member State. Consumers need reassurance that if things go wrong they can obtain redress, despite the involvement of different jurisdictions.

Alternative Dispute Resolution (both off- and on-line) is an out-of-court mechanism, usually involving a third party, which helps solve problems when the two parties to a dispute cannot agree. ADR can offer cheap, simple and quick redress for consumers and is also a vital tool for maintaining business reputation.

Why is EU action needed? To bolster current ADR schemes

Today, more than 750 ADR schemes exist in EU Member States, but ADR has not yet reached its full potential. Why? Firstly, there are both sectoral and geographical gaps in ADR coverage. Secondly, consumers and businesses often do not know about those schemes. Thirdly, not all businesses are ready to engage in the ADR process.

What has the Commission done so far and what are the next steps?

In November 2011, The Commission issued a package setting a framework for Alternative Dispute Resolution processes at the EU level and creating an EU-wide online dispute resolution system for the e-commerce transactions. The legislative process is finalised. On 22 April 2013, the package was adopted by Council after Parliament's 1st reading, awaiting signature and subsequent publication.

ACTION 15: CONSULT THE STAKEHOLDERS ON COLLECTIVE REDRESS

Identify a coherent European approach to collective redress, based on stakeholder consultation.

What is the problem? Giving EU consumers to access to "collective redress"

Illegal online behaviour by a single trader can seriously damage the interests of a large number of consumers. But enforcement of rights in the digital environment can be difficult for consumers. Uncertainty and perceived difficulty to access redress is an important factor undermining confidence in electronic commerce. Mechanisms of "collective redress" could be considered to remedy the shortcomings of the current situation.

However, the majority of stakeholders underline the fact that, until more consensus is reached on the remit of the issues and the solutions to be proposed, regulating this field is not appropriate.

This action is related to the initiative on Alternative Dispute Resolution (Action 14) .

What has the Commission done so far?

In 2013, the Commission adopted a package on collective redress: a Communication that reports the main views expressed in the public consultation and reflects the position of the Commission on some central issues regarding collective redress. It is accompanied by a Commission Recommendation, which recommends that all Member States of the European Union have national collective redress systems based on a number of common European principles. The Recommendation advocates a horizontal approach, and its content therefore also applies to the field of competition law, an area for which specific rules – justified by the specificities of competition law – are included in a proposal Directive on certain rules governing actions for damages under national law for infringements of the competition law provisions of the Member States and of the European Union . While the Recommendation encourages all Member States to follow the principles suggested therein, the proposed Directive leaves it to Member States whether or not to introduce collective redress actions in the context of the private enforcement of competition law.

ACTION 16: CODE OF EU ONLINE RIGHTS

What is the problem? Lack of consumer trust

The Digital Agenda for Europe acknowledges the importance of building digital confidence and the difficulty for citizens to be fully aware and understand their existing rights in the digital environment. Today, consumers do not entirely trust cyberspace. Consequently, they are often afraid to take advantage of online services. Consumers will not shop online if they feel their rights are not protected.

Why is EU action needed? To increase confidence in the Digital Single Market

It is necessary to increase consumers' awareness about their protection when acceding and using online services. This will encourage consumers to conduct more activity online and will also contribute to the virtuous cycle of the digital economy, the results of which in terms of growth, jobs and innovation would be largely self-reinforcing.

Digital Agenda for Europe – Action 16 concerns the issuing of a Code of EU Online Rights by 2012 summarising the existing digital user rights in the EU in a clear and accessible way. The Code has been published in December 2012.

The objective of the Code of EU Online Rights is to enable citizens and consumers to find simple, codified explanations of their rights and obligations, set out in a transparent and understandable way.

Under European Union legislation, citizens in the EU already enjoy a series of rights that are relevant to the digital environment, such as freedom of expression and information, protection of personal data and privacy, requirements for transparency and universal functional internet services and a minimum quality of service. However, these rights are scattered across various laws and due to the complexity of the legal framework many online consumers might not be aware of them.

For additional analytical, business and investment opportunities information, please contact Global Investment & Business Center, USA at (703) 370-8082. Fax: (703) 370-8083. E-mail: ibpusa3@gmail.com Global Business and Investment Info Databank - www.ibpus.com

This is precisely the reason for establishing this Code: to make citizens aware of their minimum rights and the principles recognised in EU law when going online, being online, and when buying and consuming services online.

ACTION 17: STAKEHOLDER PLATFORM FOR EU ONLINE TRUSTMARKS

Create a stakeholder platform by 2012 for EU online trustmarks, notably for retail websites.

What is the problem? Online trustmarks have good, but limited impact

In some countries, there exist trustmarks and trustmark providers that inform consumers whether the website complies with a certain set of rules. The trustmarks can be certified according to a national certification scheme and the certification process can be supervised by the competent authority. In some cases the trustmarks are based on mutual agreements between the retailer and the trustmark provider without any official certification scheme. The aim of trustmarks is to guarantee the quality and security of the online transaction. Trustmarks can boost consumer confidence in cyberspace.

However, trustmark schemes are often unknown to consumers and especially unknown outside a consumer's home country. As a result, EU citizens can find it difficult to identify reputable e-merchants in other EU markets and are therefore reluctant to shop online from another country;

Why is EU action needed? To develop EU trustmarks for EU-wide trust

The Commission is exploring the usefulness and benefits of the EU-wide trustmark schemes to reassure consumers on the reliability of accredited traders.

The Commission will also encourage the establishment of pan-EU price-comparison websites. If certified by reliable trustmark, such sites would help consumers to make informed decisions, when using online retail services. Consumers would benefit from the knowledge that the price comparison site and the listed merchants are accredited and trustworthy. They would find out about shopping opportunities outside their home market and know which foreign sites to trust.

What has the Commission done so farand what are the next steps?
The Commission conducted a comparative study on trustmark schemes in EU Member States and discussed the issue at the Digital Agenda Assembly 2012..
The Commission will further elaborate different policy options for EU-wide trustmark schemes and the effectiveness of cooperation platforms in the governance of such trustmark systems

ACTION 18: HARMONISATION OF NUMBERING REGIMES

Harmonisation of a numbering space for businesses. New rules for harmonising EU-wide telephone numbers by 2011.

What is the problem?

After a public consultation it was decided that further harmonisation of the numbering space for businesses was not necessary. Nevertheless, EU-wide phone are needed for services of social value. The most commonly known EU-wide phone numbers are: EU's emergency number 112 and the 116 harmonised numbers for services of social value, including missing children hotline 116 000. As of December 2012, the majority of assigned 116 numbers are still not operational, and the 116 000 service is not yet operational in all Member States.

DAE envisaged that "improved harmonisation of national numbering regimes on the basis of the current framework could help European manufacturers and retailers by enabling sales, after-sales and customer enquiry services over a single Europe-wide number, while the better functioning of socially useful numbers (e.g. 116 numbers used for hotlines for missing children) will benefit citizens".

Why is the EU action required?

Thanks to the deployment of the Europe-wide 112 emergency number, anyone can phone emergency services in any Member State without having to remember 27 different national emergency telephone numbers. The common 116 000 hotlines for missing children are becoming operational throughout the EU as well.

Also the work is on-going to link e-Call system with the emergency 112 number.
In the case of crash, an eCall-equipped car will automatically call emergency centre.

However, experience shows that even the existing harmonised numbers still face considerable implementation difficulties. As regards the introduction of new numbers (short numbers or ETNS) , while they may offer potential for business as well as public services, a closer analysis of the tendencies and developments in the numbering area as well in the market, supported also by the results of a public consultation carried out in this respect, has shown that the introduction of new numbers at this stage would not seem appropriate.

What has the Commission done so far and what are the next steps?

In 2011:
The Commission held a public consultation on the future harmonisation of numbering resources for the provision of business services between 6 December 2010 and 28 February 2011.
Report on the state of implementation on 112 and launch of Key Performance Indicators
Eurobarometer survey on 112 measuring the awareness on 112
In February 2012, Vice-President Neelie Kroes launched an initiative to promote 112 with transport companies
The eligibility criteria of 116 candidate numbers has been revised and tightened, expert meetings to coordinate the application for candidate numbers were organised.
The Commission organized a High Level Conference on to missing children
Report on the state of implementation, including 112 and the 116 numbering range was prepared.

In 2012:
Report on implementation of 112 and survey on the awareness of 112
Launch of initiatives to promote 112
Launch of specialized website for the 116 numbers
Continued monitoring the transposition of enhanced requirements
In May 2012, the Commission encouraged a coalition of telecommunications operators (via GSM Association) to increase and streamline publicity for 116 000 services in 14 Member States (over 250 million citizens) . 2012 actions include web publicity, text messages and informing subscribers through their bills. Vice-Presidents Kroes and Reding jointly called Member States that did not render operational its 116 000 hotline to take action.
DG JUST provided funding for 116 000 operators via its Daphne Programme
Eurobarometer survey was carried to assess awareness and public support in the Member States

In 2013:
Follow up to the contribution of telecom operators
Update to the 116 website

ACTION 19: SPECTRUM POLICY PLAN

Coordinate the technical and regulatory conditions applying to spectrum use and, where necessary, harmonise spectrum bands so that consumers would be able to use the same electronic devices across the EU.

What is the problem? Not all electronic devices work across the EU

The management of radio spectrum in the EU remains an area of Member State competence - one reason why some electronic devices may not work everywhere in the EU. However, this is a pre-condition for the development of pan-EU services enabling better quality of life for EU citizens and more growth and jobs in the EU internal market.

Why is the EU action required? Common EU radio waves

In order to make sure that all EU citizens benefit from wireless innovations, radio waves for electronic devices must be common across the EU. Consumers and businesses already benefit from harmonised spectrum usage for many products and applications, such as GSM or Wi-Fi. By implementing the Radio Spectrum Policy Programme (RSPP) , the EU can further support consumers and businesses in using and developing cross-border services to benefit from the Single Market. Moreover, global competition is growing in terms of wireless equipment, so spectrum coordination at EU level is increasingly urgent.

What will the Commission do?

In the framework of the RSPP, the European Commission is working towards the harmonisation of spectrum management rules and is pursuing a targeted action plan focussing on the development of wireless communication networks and services for the benefit of EU consumers and businesses.

ACTION 20: INVESTIGATE THE COST OF NON-EUROPE IN THE TELECOMS MARKET

Conduct an investigation into the cost of non-Europe in telecommunication markets to take further measures to reinforce the benefits of the Single Market by 2011.

Why is EU action required? Reinforce Telecoms Single Market

Tackling market and regulatory fragmentation at EU level and building a fully-fledged Single Market for electronic communications is one of the main goals of the Digital Agenda.

What are the main findings of the investigation into the cost of non-Europe in telecoms??

On 27 February 2012, the Commission released the results of a one year investigation into the cost of non-Europe in electronic communications conducted by a team of international consultants and academics.

The findings show that the annual gains which would result from the building of a fully-fledged internal market amount to up to 0.9% of GDP, or up to 110 billion Euros, per year. These gains could be achieved by means of easier entries on more competitive markets and through a better exploitation of economies of scale.

The main obstacles to the single market which have been identified are the lack of EU standards for interoperability, the heterogeneity in the implementation of EU telecoms rules and the current design of the institutional arrangements which support the functioning of market regulation at national and EU levels

For additional analytical, business and investment opportunities information, please contact Global Investment & Business Center, USA at (703) 370-8082. Fax: (703) 370-8083. E-mail: ibpusa3@gmail.com Global Business and Investment Info Databank - www.ibpus.com

What will the Commission do next?

In the face of these findings, and considering as well that Europe's global competitiveness increasingly depends on its ability to tap into the potential of its single market for electronic communication networks and services, the Commission will publicly engage in 2013 with stakeholders as the ways to move forward.

ACTION 101: LOOK FOR DURABLE SOLUTIONS FOR VOICE AND DATA ROAMING BY 2012.

Single market for telecoms services – the difference between roaming and national tariffs should approach zero by 2015.

What is the problem? A lack of internal market in telecoms services

The differences in national mobile charges and roaming charges illustrate the lack of internal market in telecoms services. There should be no difference between the costs of providing roaming services and domestic mobile services. There is no justification in a competitive market for charging customers considerably higher prices for roaming services.

Why is EU action necessary?

All Europeans need to benefit from an internal market for roaming. One of the Commission's priorities is to create an internal market for roaming services and eliminate the excessive charges.

What has the European Commission done so far and what are the next steps?

In 2012:
Completed the legislative process with the Council and the EP so that the revised Regulation entered into force as of 1 July 2012.
Adopted detailed technical implementation rules for the separate sale of regulated retail roaming services.
Work, together with BEREC, on implementing provisions that stems from the newly proposed rules (wholesale access, facility for separate sale of roaming services) .

In 2013:
Establish a cooperation platform for the implementation of decoupling obligation, so that separate sale of roaming services is made possible by 1 July 2014 in a coordinated manner

ACTION 102: KEY TRANSFORMATIVE ACTION 1: COPYRIGHT – THE WAY FORWARD

Completing the on-going review of the Copyright Framework, including legal drafting work, with a view to a decision in 2014 whether to table legislative reform proposals and seeking the resolution of copyright-related issues where rapid progress is needed via a structured stakeholder dialogue in 2013.

What is the problem?

Online there are new ways of providing, creating and distributing content, and new ways to generate value. The emergence of new business models that use the internet to deliver content represents both a challenge and an opportunity for the creative industries, authors and artists. The nature of activities of non-commercial users of copyrighted works (heritage institutions, researchers) is also changing rapidly. Yet copyright framework and licensing practices are not keeping up with these developments.

Why is EU action required?

The digital economy has been a major driver of growth in the past two decades, and is expected to grow seven times faster than overall EU GDP in coming years. The aim of the European Commission is to ensure that copyright and licensing stay fit for purpose in this new digital context.

What has the Commission done so far?

On 18 December 2012 the Commission adopted a Communication "on Content in the Digital Single Market". It sets out two parallel tracks of action.

A structured stakeholder dialogue, "Licences for Europe" has been established, with the aim to deliver rapid progress to bringing content online through practical industry-led solutions in these 4 areas: (i) cross-border access and the portability of services; (ii) user-generated content and licensing for small-scale users; (iii) online accessibility of films in the EU; and (iv) promoting efficient text and data mining for scientific research purposes.

What will the Commission do?

In parallel, the Commission is working on the completion of the on-going review of the EU copyright framework, based on market studies and impact assessment and legal drafting work, with a view to a decision in 2014 whether to table the resulting legislative reform proposals.

ACTION 103: ADOPT AND IMPLEMENT THE KEY DIGITAL SINGLE MARKET PROPOSALS OF THE DIGITAL AGENDA

Adopt and implement the key digital single market proposals of the Digital Agenda

What is the problem?

The internet is borderless, but online markets, both globally and in the EU, are still separated by multiple barriers affecting access to online services and content.

Why is EU action required?

The creation of attractive online content and services and its free circulation inside the EU and across its borders are fundamental to stimulate the virtuous cycle of demand. Persistent fragmentation of digital single market is stifling Europe's competitiveness in the digital economy. Despite the body of key single market legislation on intellectual property, data protection, eCommerce, transactions in the digital environment are still too complex, with inconsistent implementation of the rules across Member States. Consumers and businesses are still faced with considerable uncertainty about their rights and legal protection when doing business on line.

What has the Commission done so far?

The Commission adopted key legal proposals from Digital Agenda 2010:
Framework Directive on collective rights management (Action 1 DAE 2010)
Orphan Works Directive (Action 2, DAE 2010)
Regulation on data protection (Action 12, DAE 2010)

The Commission decided not to review the e-commerce directive; however, it took a number of measures in the context of e-commerce action plan adopted in January 2012.

What will the Commission do?

The Commission will assist the European Parliament and the Council in legislative process. The Commission will monitor transposition of key directives and implementation of the regulation on data protection by the Member States

ACTION 104: FOLLOW UP ON ECOMMERCE ACTION PLAN, GREEN PAPER ON PAYMENTS

What is the problem?

EU payment market suffers from a number of drawbacks. The costs of acceptance of cards, as the most common payment instrument online are high, payments markets are still fragmented, in some cases the industry has not yet agreed on a set of technical standards for the whole of the EU. The markets are not as dynamic and innovative as they should. There are many new technologies, such as using electronic wallets or smartphone at the point of sale. However – except in a few EU countries – it is difficult for these services to enter cross-border market for payments.

Why is EU action required?

The traditional approach to the payments, which combined regulation, self-regulation and competition enforcement, has brought concrete results. At the core lies the Single Euro Payments Area, a project run by the banking sector. The body in charge of SEPA – the European Payments Council – has achieved a lot since it was set up in 2002, but after ten years the project needs to be reinvigorated. (Action 7, DAE 2010)

The Commission needs to update the current legal framework in the area of payments to reflect market developments, ensure level playing field for innovative payment service providers as well as consumer's convenience and security. Standardisation and interoperability issues need to addressed by appropriate fora.

What has the Commission done so far?

The Commission's work on payments has been pursued with Green Paper on an integrated European market for card, internet and mobile payments, which opened a public consultation. The Commission enquired stakeholders on a number of issues related to: innovative payment service providers, costs of payments for consumers and merchants, standardisation and interoperability.

In Single Market Act II, the Commission announced legislative actions as a follow up to the Green Paper:
Review Payment Services Directive (directive 2007/64/EC)
A legislative initiative on multilateral interchange fees

What will the Commission do?

The Commission will adopt the proposals in the 2nd quarter of 2013.

ACTION 105: GUIDELINES TO CORRECTLY IMPLEMENT EU RULES ON CONSUMER INFORMATION REQUIREMENTS

Guidelines to correctly implement EU rules on consumer information requirements

What is the problem?

After the adoption on of the Consumer Rights Directive, proper enforcement must be secured in key sectors.

Why is EU action required?

The Digital Area is a particularly sensitive area for consumer, where despite the freedom and empowerment opportunities offered by the Internet, in certain limited cases, the consumers might end up being even more vulnerable than in the physical world.

What has the Commission done so far?

The Directive on Consumer Rights, which was published on 22 November 2011, aims at achieving a real business-to-consumer (B2C) internal market, striking the right balance between a high level of consumer protection and the competitiveness of enterprises.

What will the Commission do?

To ensure that consumer information requirements in the digital area are applied consistently, the Commission will develop guidelines by 2014 to help enforcers correctly implement EU rules and the newly adopted Consumer Rights Directive. Concerted action will be taken by

the Commission and national authorities to combat unfair practices in the sector, such as those related to the misleading advertising of internet broadband speed.

ACTION 106: VAT REFORM - ALIGN TAX RATES FOR DIGITAL CONTENT AND SIMILAR PHYSICAL GOODS

DAE (section 2.1.1) states "Public authorities should play their part in promoting markets for online content. The challenges of convergence should be addressed in all reviews of public policy, including tax matters."

What is the problem?

The VAT Directive, as it currently stands, obliges MS to apply a standard rate of at least 15% and provides for the optional application of a reduced rate, set no lower than 5%, to an exhaustive list of supplies contained in Annexe III to the VAT Directive. All electronically supplied services are excluded from the scope of reduced VAT rates. These services are therefore taxed at the standard rate. Electronically services supplied to final consumers within the EU by an EU established supplier are subject to VAT in the MS of establishment of the supplier.

Why is EU action required?

It has major importance to ensure the consistency of VAT rates on cultural products online and offline. For the time being there is a discrimination against online services as they are subject to higher VAT rates than equivalent goods or services of traditional supports. Normally all cultural products and services should be subject to the same (reduced) tax treatment, whether they appear online or offline. The EC's DAE pays particular attention to these issues and promotes their convergence in order to support a widespread development and utilisation of the Internet and related goods and services.

What has the Commission done so far?

The Commission launched a work to elaborate a new VAT system which is to enter into force on 1. January 2015. The Commission presented a Green Paper in 2010, it conducted a public consultation early 2011 and published a Communication in Dec. 2011. Its third guiding principle states that "similar goods and services should be subject to the same VAT rate". The New VAT system will contain two such elements which are important from the point of view of online media products (eBook, online newspaper and magazine) . First, from 1 January 2015, the supply of these products will be taxed at the VAT rate of the MS where the consumer is established. It means that the risk of distortions of competition and relocation will disappear. Second, the alignment of VAT rates applied to printed and online media products was proposed but its details are still undecided. TAXUD organised a public consultation on this issue. The summary report of the outcome was published. DG CONNECT organised a VAT expert seminar on the impacts of alignment of VAT rates applied to offline and online media products on 8 March (the proceeding is on G1 website) . Moreover, TAXUD commissioned a study on the economic rationality of reduced VAT rates.

What will the Commission do?

On the basis of the outcomes of the public consultation and the study TAXUD will elaborate a proposal on the new structure of VAT rates. The whole proposal on the "New VAT" will be presented by the end of 2013. EP and the Council have to agree by the end of 2014. It requires unanimity in the Council. CONNECT will closely follow the preparation of the legislative proposal, will remain in constant collaboration with TAXUD (e.g. CIS) and will prepare a guidebook on the VAT rules for eBook traders.

ACTION 107: PROPOSALS TO STRENGTHEN THE DATA INDUSTRY IN EUROPE

What is the problem?

Public sector information remains an underexploited resource and further steps are needed to unlock its full potential, especially in the light of an incoherent approach to PSI re-use within and across the Member States.

The need for guidance in the field of PSI re-use, in particular with regard to licensing and charging, was one of the main requests formulated during an extensive public consultation that fed into the Impact Assessment for the revision of the PSI Directive.

Such soft law measures were deemed necessary to promote best practice in re-use of government data across the EU and to connect exemplary public sector bodies with those that have not yet made their data available for re-use.

Why is EU action required?

Recital 18 of the draft revised Directive on of the re-use of public sector information (PSI Directive) (adoption expected in Q2 2013) , which itself is a part of a wider Open Data Strategy, calls upon the Commission to issue guidelines in order to help the Member States in implementing the legal provisions in a consistent way.

The guidelines are therefore a necessary element of the strategy that further includes legislative measures, support to R&D on data, development of European data-portals and other actions designed to facilitate EU-wide access to PSI and to stimulate the creation of information products based on PSI re-use.

What has the Commission done so far?

In parallel to updating the legal framework on the re-use of PSI, the Commission has been in close contact with the Member States in the framework of an expert group (PSI Group) which meets regularly to discuss issues directly linked to the re-use of public sector information and to promote the exchange of best practices in this field.

What will the Commission do?

The Commission, in line with its commitment formulated in the recitals of the revised PSI Directive, will issue a series of guidelines on recommended standard licenses, datasets and charging for the re-use of documents, after consulting interested parties.

ACTION 108: GREEN PAPER ON A CONVERGED AUDIOVISUAL WORLD

Green Paper - Preparing for a Fully Converged Audiovisual World: Growth, Creation and Values

Europeans want to be informed on data security breaches

Broadcast media and the Internet are converging, especially in the audiovisual area, in a way increasingly visible to citizens.

Illustrations include TV sets with internet connectivity ("connected TV") , films and TV shows watched over tablets, game consoles or smartphones, and on-demand services viewed on computers.

Familiar twentieth-century consumption patterns (notably linear broadcasting viewed on TV sets) are evolving profoundly; consumers are increasingly pro-active and some even creating their own content..

This changing media landscape offers many opportunities for players across the audiovisual value chain. At the same time it raises new challenges, like the conditions for dynamic EU businesses to deal with international competition; how to protect European values (including for media freedom and pluralism) ; and user interests (e.g. protecting minors, accessibility for users with disabilities) ; and how to promote the right technological environment.

Why is EU action required?

The area impacted is subject to harmonisation at EU level and this new reality is already being discussed in several EU countries and in the European Parliament. Views differ on how to respond. Some parties call for immediate changes to rules and regulations; some remain satisfied with the status quo for the time being, while others point to self and co-regulation. It was therefore time to gather broad stakeholder feedback in a structured manner to prepare for possible follow up action.

What has the Commission done so far?

The Commission has launched a public consultation to explore what this convergence of technology and content could mean for Europe's economic growth and innovation, cultural diversity, and consumers.

What will the Commission do?

The consultation does not presuppose any specific outcome. Nonetheless, in the medium to long term it may have an impact on a number of legal instruments, including the Audiovisual Media Services Directive (AVMSD) . The Commission will prepare proposals for follow up actions (not necessarily only legislative) after the consultation has been closed and duly assessed.

PILLAR II: INTEROPERABILITY & STANDARDS

The internet is a great example of interoperability – numerous devices and applications working together anywhere in the world. Europe must ensure that new IT devices, applications, data repositories and services interact seamlessly anywhere – just like the internet. The Digital Agenda identifies improved standard-setting procedures and increased interoperability as the keys to success. (Interoperability & Standards analysis and data)

ACTION 21: PROPOSE LEGISLATION ON ICT INTEROPERABILITY

As part of the review of EU standardisation policy, propose legal measures on ICT interoperability to reform the rules on implementation of ICT standards in Europe.

What is the problem? Fragmentation of EU-produced technologies and services

Digital devices, applications and services should interact seamlessly anywhere, anytime.

However, this is far from being the case in Europe. The fragmentation of the potential market for EU-produced technologies and services hampers growth in Europe's ICT sector.

Why is EU action required? EU-wide standards ensure interoperability

Better Europe-wide standards would enhance interoperability and ensure that digital applications and devices work across borders. ICT standards issued by leading fora and consortia cannot currently be referenced in public procurement, EU policies and legislation. One simple example is the protocol that you are probably using to access this page on the web. These problems will be addressed in the reform of the EU standardization framework, which is essential to keep pace with fast-moving international technology market.

What has the Commission done until now?

On 1st June 2011 the European Commission adopted a reform package to strengthen the system of standard-setting in Europe.

Following its adoption by the Council on 4 October 2012, the Regulation (EU) No 1025/2012 of the European Parliament and of the Council of 25 October 2012 on European standardisation was published in the Official Journal of the European Union in the series L 316.

What will the Commission do?

The European Commission will provide ICT expertise where necessary to support the implementation of the legislative package.

The European Commission is chairing the "European Multi-Stakeholder Platform on ICT Standardisation" which has the role to advise the Commission on matters relating to the implementation of standardisation policy in the ICT field. This will make it easier to use those technical specifications, which are mainly those regulating the technical implementation of the Internet, for example in public procurement.

As a result, public authorities will have fewer constraints in the selection of their vendors and consumers will have a broader choice of products at a lower price.

Furthermore, the European Commission will identify and execute appropriate standardization actions in the context of the Framework Programme for Research and Innovation, as well as in regulatory actions and in public policies.

ACTION 22: PROMOTE STANDARD-SETTING RULES

Promote appropriate rules for essential intellectual property rights and licensing conditions in standard-setting, in particular through guidelines by 2011.

What is the problem?

Standard-setting can give rise to restrictive effects on competition by potentially restricting price competition and limiting or controlling production, markets, innovation or technical development.

Why is the EU action required?

First, if companies were to engage in anti-competitive discussions in the context of standard-setting, this could reduce or eliminate price competition in the markets concerned, thereby facilitating a collusive outcome on the market.

Second, standards that set detailed technical specifications for a product or service may limit technical development and innovation. While a standard is being developed, alternative technologies can compete for inclusion in the standard. Once one technology has been chosen and the standard has been set, competing technologies and companies may face a barrier to entry and may potentially be excluded from the market.

Third, standardisation may lead to anti-competitive results by preventing certain companies from obtaining effective access to the results of the standard-setting process.

What has the Commission done up to now?

The European Commission has adopted and published the "Revised rules for the assessment of horizontal cooperation agreements under EU competition law", December 2010, including the Communication from the Commission "Guidelines on the applicability of article 101 of the treaty on the functioning of the European Union to horizontal cooperation agreements".

The European Commission is for example together with European Patent Office organising conferences on Intellectual Property rights in ICT standardisation:

22 November 2011: The public authorities and international perspective: how to increase transparency and predictability

18 April 2012: Transparency and Predictability of Licensing in ICT through Patent Pools

22 November 2012: Implementing FRAND standards in Open Source: Business as usual or mission impossible

What will the Commission do?

Promote appropriate rules for essential intellectual property rights and licensing conditions in standard-setting, in particular through guidelines by 2011.

What is the problem?

Standard-setting can give rise to restrictive effects on competition by potentially restricting price competition and limiting or controlling production, markets, innovation or technical development.

Why is the EU action required?

First, if companies were to engage in anti-competitive discussions in the context of standard-setting, this could reduce or eliminate price competition in the markets concerned, thereby facilitating a collusive outcome on the market.

Second, standards that set detailed technical specifications for a product or service may limit technical development and innovation. While a standard is being developed, alternative technologies can compete for inclusion in the standard. Once one technology has been chosen and the standard has been set, competing technologies and companies may face a barrier to entry and may potentially be excluded from the market.

Third, standardisation may lead to anti-competitive results by preventing certain companies from obtaining effective access to the results of the standard-setting process.

What has the Commission done up to now?

The European Commission has adopted and published the "Revised rules for the assessment of horizontal cooperation agreements under EU competition law", December 2010, including the Communication from the Commission "Guidelines on the applicability of article 101 of the treaty on the functioning of the European Union to horizontal cooperation agreements".

The European Commission is for example together with European Patent Office organising conferences on Intellectual Property rights in ICT standardisation:

22 November 2011: The public authorities and international perspective: how to increase transparency and predictability

18 April 2012: Transparency and Predictability of Licensing in ICT through Patent Pools

22 November 2012: Implementing FRAND standards in Open Source: Business as usual or mission impossible

What will the Commission do?

The European Commission will follow the impact of the guidelines carefully by continuing interacting with the stakeholders.The European Commission will follow the impact of the guidelines carefully by continuing interacting with the stakeholders.

ACTION 23: PROVIDE GUIDANCE ON ICT STANDARDISATION AND PUBLIC PROCUREMENT

Issue a Communication to provide guidance on the link between ICT standardisation and public procurement to help public authorities use standards.

What is the problem? Vary specifications for tenders on public procurement

Public authorities should make the best use of available standards when commissioning hardware, software and IT services from external suppliers. Yet, the practices of public authorities across the EU vary greatly when it comes to writing tender specifications for public procurement. In some cases, public authorities find themselves unintentionally locked into particular IT solutions for decades, simply because they failed to draft sufficiently flexible tender specifications allowing for open choices in technological evolution.

Why is EU action required? Public authorities lose out

The Commission has drawn up detailed guidelines on how to make best use of ICT standards in tender specifications. For instance, public authorities should select standards which can be implemented by all interested suppliers, allowing for more competition and reducing the risk of lock-in. (See also action 26.)

What has the Commission done?

More specifically, the European Commission has:

In 2011:

Conducted a pan-European study assessing the public procurement practices in the EU, through an on-line survey for public procurers and ICT suppliers.

On 12 December 2011, there was a workshop on ICT Procurement in Brussels. This workshop formed part of the work undertaken by Europe Economics to develop guidelines to assist public procurers in purchasing ICT that is based on standards.

In 2012:

A web consultation took place on the draft guidelines and the socio-economic impact of using the guidelines was established.

In 2013:

Adopted the Communication on standardisation and public procurement.

Make sure that the guidelines are practically applicable by all public procurers of ICT goods and services.

ACTION 24: ADOPT A EUROPEAN INTEROPERABILITY STRATEGY AND FRAMEWORK

Promote interoperability by adopting in 2010 a European Interoperability Strategy and European Interoperability Framework

What is the problem? No standard-setting

Europe does not yet reap the maximum benefits from interoperability. Weaknesses in standard-setting, public procurement and coordination between European public authorities prevent digital services and devices working across borders as well as they should.

Why is the EU action required? Get greater interoperability throughout the EU

When establishing National Public Services, there is a risk that different Member States opt for solutions which are incompatible with one another. New electronic barriers, so-called "e-barriers", emerge - impeding the proper functioning of the internal market. Member States and the Commission should do more to pre-empt the emergence of these new e-barriers and the resulting market fragmentation by getting greater interoperability of public IT systems throughout the EU.

What has the Commission done?

In December 2010, The Commission adopted a Communication "Towards interoperability for European public services" to promote interoperability between public administrations. The Communication included two annexes: the European Interoperability Strategy and the European Interoperability Framework. See also other actions under this pillar (21, 22, 23, 25 26 and 27).

ACTION 25: IDENTIFY AND ASSESS MEANS OF REQUESTING SIGNIFICANT MARKET PLAYERS TO LICENCE INFORMATION ABOUT THEIR PRODUCTS OR SERVICES

Examine the feasibility of measures that could lead significant market players to license interoperability information.

What is the problem?

Companies in the ICT sector that achieve wide market penetration of their products or applications may not easily make available information that would allow other products to interoperate with them. If their products are incompatible with those of other brands, users feel locked into one company's product range, for fear that any new product they purchase will not be compatible with their existing ones.

Why is EU action required?

Companies should easily provide interoperability information about their products. With this information available, smaller enterprises have the opportunity to develop compatible products or applications. . The end result will be an extremely competitive market and a happy consumer.

What has the Commission done up to now?

A Public Consultation on the Access to Interoperability Information of Digital Products and Services closed in June 2012. It addressed owners and potential users of interoperability information not covered by standards.

What will the Commission do?

Following the public consultation, the Commission is exploring legislative and non-legislative measures for facilitating access to and licensing of interoperability information. The results are expected tobe issued in early 2013.

ACTION 26: MS TO IMPLEMENT EUROPEAN INTEROPERABILITY FRAMEWORK

Member States should apply the European Interoperability Framework at national level by 2013.

What is the problem? No internal virtual market due to interoperability problems

In the virtual world barriers against the internal market are raising, mainly due to interoperability issues.

Why is EU action needed? European Commission encouraging Member States to adopt interoperability laws

At the end of 2010 the Commission adopted a communication on the "European Interoperability Framework". The next step is: Member States adopting a national interoperability framework, in line with the European one. To this end, the programme "Interoperability Solutions for European Public Administrations" will be monitoring the progress within the Member States, while in parallel will implement the European Framework.

What has the Commission done?

In 2010 the Commission adopted the European Interoperability Strategy and a European Interoperability Framework (EIF) as annexes of the Communication "Towards interoperability for European public services". By 2013 Member States should align their national interoperability frameworks to the EIF. (See action 24).

What will the Commission do?

The Commission will assist Member States through supporting actions, including awareness raising and exchange of information on national interoperability frameworks.

It has launched a study on the needs and costs benefits of cross-border services and the existing barrier. The results of the first CIP ICT PSP Large Scale Pilots are being deployed across Member States. Details of their deployment are available on the DAE implementation web site. http://www.daeimplementation.eu/dae_actions.php?action_n=26

ACTION 27: MEMBER STATES TO IMPLEMENT MALMÖ AND GRANADA DECLARATIONS

Member States should implement commitments on interoperability and standards in the Malmö and Granada Declarations by 2013.

The Malmö Declaration commits EU public administrations to promote open standard to ease the path for the new products. It also commits to align national interoperability frameworks with applicable European frameworks.

The Granada Declaration complements the Malmö Declaration on eGovernment by encouraging the development of more efficient interoperable public services that promotes the re-use of public sector information, increase the efficiency of government and lead to a measurable reduction in administrative burdens on citizens and businesses as well as contribute to a low-carbon economy.

What is the problem? Absence of common standards

Europe does not yet reap the maximum benefits from interoperability. Weaknesses in standard-setting, public procurement and coordination between European public authorities prevent digital services and devices working across borders as well as they should.

Why is the EU action required? Guidance for standardisation

This action is the "umbrella" action for the Interoperability and Standards Pillar of the Digital Agenda. See other actions of the same pillar.

What has the Commission done?

The European Commission published draft guidelines on the selection of standards and specifications and the socio-economic impact of using them.

PILLAR III: TRUST & SECURITY

ACTION 28: REINFORCED NETWORK AND INFORMATION SECURITY POLICY

The Commission will reinforce the Network and Information Security Policy and will modernise European Network and Information Security Agency (ENISA) , and measures allowing faster reactions in the event of cyber-attacks, including a CERT for the EU institutions.

What is the problem? Networks are not secure

The internet has become a critical information infrastructure, encompassing IT systems and networks across the globe. It must be resilient and secure against all sorts of threats.

Why is EU action required? EU helps Member States to cooperate

Strong cooperation between EU governments, public bodies and private companies is necessary to improve information exchange and to ensure that security problems are addressed quickly and effectively.

The European Network Information and Security Agency (ENISA) serves as a focal point for this exchange and cooperation. An enhanced ENISA is expected to have a significant positive economic impact, as the current costs associated with network and information security breaches are considerable and are still growing.

For additional analytical, business and investment opportunities information, please contact Global Investment & Business Center, USA at (703) 370-8082. Fax: (703) 370-8083. E-mail: ibpusa3@gmail.com Global Business and Investment Info Databank - www.ibpus.com

To react to threats in real-time conditions, a well-functioning and wider network of Computer Emergency Response Teams (CERTs) should also be established in Europe, including for European institutions (see Action 38 for more information on CERTs) .

What has the Commission done so far?

In 2012:

Conducted a public consultation on improving network and information security in the EU.

Established CERT-EU, a Computer Emergency Response Team for the EU institutions, on a permanent basis.

In 2013:

Presented in February 2013 a proposal, together with the High Representative of the Union for Foreign Affairs and Security Policy, for a 'Cyber security Strategy of the European Union' (action 124 of the Digital Agenda Review package) .

Presented in February 2013 a legislative proposal on enhanced network and information security across the Union (action 123 of the Digital Agenda Review package) .

Secured ENISA's future – in April 2013 the European Parliament voted to extend ENISA's mandate by seven years.

What will the Commission do now?

Work with the European Parliament and Council on adoption of its cyber security proposals.

Ensure that CERTs become operational

ACTION 29: COMBAT CYBER-ATTACKS AGAINST INFORMATION SYSTEMS

Present measures, including legislative initiatives, to combat cyber-attacks against information systems by 2010, and related rules on jurisdiction in cyberspace at European and international levels by 2013.

What is the problem? Growing number of cyber-attacks on information systems

Attacks against information systems are a growing threat, and there is an increasing concern about the potential for terrorist or politically motivated attacks against information systems which form part of the critical infrastructures of Member States and the Union.

Why is EU action required? Strengthen security of citizens and businesses

This action requires Member States to amend their criminal laws regarding attacks against information systems. The main aim is to provide EU law enforcement authorities with enhanced tools to fight cybercrime. The new proposed Directive on Attacks against Information Systems will update the current level of protection and take account of new developments. It will include provisions for use of specific software ('Botnets') as a method of committing cybercrimes making it a criminal offence and also increasing the maximum penalty for offenders. The initiative will strengthen security of citizens and businesses and is expected to have a positive economic impact, as the current costs to business of countering cyber-attacks and repairing post-attack damage are very considerable and rising continually.

What will the Commission do?

In 2013:

Expects final adoption of the Directive since negotiations on the compromise text have now been concluded. The Directive's adoption is awaiting agreement from the European Parliament.

ACTION 30: ESTABLISH A EUROPEAN CYBERCRIME PLATFORM

Establish a European cybercrime platform by 2012.

What is the problem? Wide range of cybercrime

IT networks and end users' terminals are vulnerable to a wide range of threats, not least related to malicious activities, which could undermine citizens' trust in electronic communications and in turn prevent a wider uptake of ICTs. Cybercrime is an increasingly growing trend, and the lack of collecting, reporting and/or sharing data and statistics on offences might widen the disruptive potential of those malicious activities.

Why is EU action required? Fight cybercrime throughout the EU

Europol, in cooperation with the European Commission, was invited to integrate all relevant EU national platforms into a single "cybercrime alert platform". The European alert platform would function as a centre for collection and storage of information about Internet-related offences and for compilation of regular statistical reports on cybercrime. The European Cybercrime Platform is expected to be a major element of the European Cyber Crime Centre (action 31) .

What has the Commission done so far?

Launched in January 2013 a European Cybercrime Centre (EC3) to provide more efficient channels for Member States to share cybercrime-related information.

What will the Commission do now?

Ensure that EC3 delivers in line with the vision outlined in the 2012 Communication.

ACTION 31: ANALYSE THE USEFULNESS OF CREATING A EUROPEAN CYBERCRIME CENTRE

Examine the feasibility by 2011 to create a European cybercrime centre.

What is the problem? Cyber threats

As digital technology increasingly becomes an integral part of our lives, the potential impact of ICT-related criminal threats multiplies in scope and sophistication. Given the interconnectedness of electronic networks and systems, any criminal activity could have relevance for more than one jurisdiction; this calls for an enhanced and close cooperation between relevant authorities (i.e. law enforcement agencies, judicial authorities, police) .

Why is EU action required? Fight cybercrime at European level

The Commission conducted a study to investigate the pros and cons of creating a pan-European cybercrime centre. The study considered the aim, scope and possible financing of the centre. This initiative is strongly linked with action 30 and action 41.

Following on from the feasibility study, the Commission set up a pan-European cybercrime centre (EC3) in January 2013 within Europol. The centre will be the focal point in the fight against cybercrime, providing operational support to Member States, becoming an information hub for cybercrime-related information; reaching out to industry and the research community; cooperating with CEPOL for more targeted training for police, prosecutors and judges; producing threat assessments and trend forecasts and developing forensic digital tools to collect evidence of cybercrime that can be used in courts to try suspects.

What has the Commission done so far?

Issued in 2012 a Communication calling for the establishment of a European Cybercrime Centre (EC3) within Europol.

Launched in January 2013 the European Cybercrime Centre (EC3) in Europol.

What will the Commission do?

Ensure that EC3 delivers in line with the vision outlined in the 2012 Communication.

ACTION 32: STRENGTHEN THE FIGHT AGAINST CYBERCRIME AND CYBER-ATTACKS AT INTERNATIONAL LEVEL

Work with global stakeholders notably to strengthen global risk management in the digital and in the physical sphere and conduct internationally coordinated targeted actions against computer-based crime and security attack.

What is the problem? The challenges ahead are neither specific to the European Union (EU) , nor can they be overcome by the EU on its own. The pervasiveness of ICT and of the Internet allows more efficient, effective and economic communication, coordination and cooperation among stakeholders and results in a vibrant ecosystem of innovation in all fields of life. However, threats can now originate from anywhere in the world and, due to global interconnectedness, impact any part of the world.

Why is EU action required? To fight effectively against these threats and to address global interdependencies, we need stronger cooperation among Member States and the private sector at national, European and international level.

What are the Commission's plans?

2 main strands of action:

Within the EU: creation of a European Forum for Member States to stimulate discussion between national public authorities, especially about better integration of national risk management policies and of a European Public-Private Partnership for Resilience to engage the private sector in increasing the level of security of our digital environment.

International cooperation: consolidate EU-US relations, and explore cooperation with other strategic partners, around the Commission plan to improve the resilience and stability of Internet & discuss how to leverage public private partnerships to guarantee the security and resilience of global communication and information networks.

What has the Commission done so far?

In 2010:

continued policy dialogue and exchange of information practices with the US, and participated in Cyberstorm III exercise as an observer.

In 2011:

promoted the development of globally-agreed principles for the stability and resilience of the Internet by establishing strategic international partnerships with key third countries, as well as by promoting the discussion in international fora.

a joint EU-US table-top cyber exercise (Cyber Atlantic 2011) took place.

In 2012:

The 1st European Cyber Security Month, initiated by the Commission and supported by ENISA, was organised by eight European countries.

What will the Commission do now?

In 2013:

The European Cyber Security Month initiative will be enlarged to include more Member States and the private sector with the aim of a synchronised EU-US cyber security month in 2014.

The European Cybercrime Centre (EC3) will cooperate with international partners such as non-EU Member States with whom Europol has signed a cooperation agreement as well as with the Interpol's Global Complex for Innovation which is about to be set up in in Singapore.

ACTION 33: SUPPORT EU-WIDE CYBER-SECURITY PREPAREDNESS

Support EU-wide cyber-security preparedness exercises.

What is the problem? Europeans will not use technology they do not trust.

Users must be safe and secure when they connect online but online identity theft and fraud are growing. Attacks are becoming more and more sophisticated (trojans, botnets, etc.) and often motivated by financial purposes. They can also be politically motivated as shown by the cyber-attacks that targeted Estonia, Lithuania and Georgia.

For additional analytical, business and investment opportunities information, please contact Global Investment & Business Center, USA at (703) 370-8082. Fax: (703) 370-8083. E-mail: ibpusa3@gmail.com Global Business and Investment Info Databank - www.ibpus.com

Why is EU action required? Security is a shared responsibility.

With the support of the EU, all the Member States are responsible for organising and conducting the first EU-wide cyber-security preparedness exercise, but ENISA will coordinate and facilitate the organisation. The aim is to build trust; increase the understanding on how cyber-incidents are handled; understand how key actors work and depend on each other in each Member State and promote mutual support between the Member States. This action is closely linked to action 39.

What has the Commission done?

In 2011:

Adopted a Communication on Critical Information Infrastructure Protection 'Achievements and next steps: towards global cyber-security'

Ensured financial support for pan-European cyber security exercises

In 2012:

ENISA and European Commission supported Members States in the organisation of the second pan-European cyber exercise - Cyber Europe 2012 (See also action 39) .

What will the Commission do?

In 2013:

Support discussions on the future involvement of the EU in international/global cyber security exercises and evaluate the state of Network and Information System (NIS) health in Europe

ACTION 34: EXPLORE THE EXTENSION OF SECURITY BREACH NOTIFICATION PROVISIONS

Explore the extension of security breach notification provisions, as part of the modernisation of the EU personal data protection regulatory framework.

What is the problem? Europeans want to be informed on data security breaches

According to surveys, 84% of Europeans would wish to be informed if their personal data was lost, stolen or altered. That is one reason why data security breaches are high on the EU agenda.

Why is EU action required? EU can provide rules

The current review of the EU data protection framework will include an extension of the obligation to notify data security breaches, which would be an important move towards improving data security. For legislative aspects, see more under Action 12.

The draft Commission proposals reviewing the EU data protection framework contain provisions setting forth requirements to notify personal data breaches to supervisory authorities and individuals alike

What has the Commission done?

In January 2012 the Commission set out its proposals on reviewing the EU data protection regulatory framework to ensure the extension of security breach notification provisions to all data controllers (this action is a component of action 12) .

ACTION 35: GUIDANCE ON IMPLEMENTATION OF TELECOMS RULES ON PRIVACY

Give guidance by 2011 for the implementation of new Telecoms Framework with regard to the protection of individuals' privacy and personal data.

What is the problem ? Implementation of new ePrivacy rules

The EU telecoms reform package adopted on 25 November 2009 brings several changes to the Directive on privacy and electronic communications and strengthens rules on access to users' terminal equipment applicable to malware, spyware and cookies. By 25 May 2011, EU Member States had to implement the new EU telecoms rules.

Why is EU action needed ? EU can provide guidance

In as much as there is a risk of incorrect and/or inconsistent implementation across the EU the Commission should give guidance in order to achieve effective protection of ePrivacy rights and legal certainty for industry.

This action is closely linked with the Digital Agenda action 34, action 12 and action 10.

What has the Commission done? What will the Commission do?

In October 2010, guidance was provided to the Member States on the implementation of Article 5(3) of the ePrivacy Directive via the Communications Committee (Working document COCOM10-34) .This document was made available to the wider public on 21 December 2010. It leaves room for industry self-regulatory solutions.

The Commission has also hosted roundtables to discuss an EU level self-regulatory initiative proposed by the advertising and media industry. In addition, Member States were asked in October 2011 to inform the Commission how they have implemented the rules, how they enforce them, including via self-regulatory schemes. The Commission will continue to monitor the process.

Infringements have meanwhile been launched against those Member States which had not fully transposed the revised telecom rules, including amendments to Article 5(3) of the ePrivacy Directive.

ACTION 36: SUPPORT REPORTING OF ILLEGAL CONTENT ONLINE AND AWARENESS CAMPAIGNS ON ONLINE SAFETY FOR CHILDREN

Support reporting points for illegal content online (hotlines) and awareness campaigns on online safety for children run at national level and enhance pan-European cooperation and sharing of best practice in this field.

What is the problem? Children are not safe online

Internet has become one of the main distribution channels for material (images, films, audio files etc) depicting sexual abuse of children. Internet Watch Foundation confirmed 1.316 child abuse domains in 2009. The content is becoming worse over years: 44% of the images reported to the largest hotline depict the rape or torture of a child; 70% of the victims are under the age of 10.

More and more European children go online via mobile phones and game consoles. More than 50% of 13-16 year olds go online from their bedroom and more than half of 9-16 year olds have a social networking profile. At the same time, young people are a vulnerable group as they do not always see the risks of their online actions such as sharing personal information online or talking to people they have never met in real life.

Why is EU action required? Collective fight against the illegal content online

Online distribution of child abuse material is a global problem – abuse takes place and is uploaded in one place, the hosting might be in another country, and downloading happens all over the world - this international dimension makes it harder to detect and combat. Therefore, a collective effort supported by the EU would increase the effectiveness of fighting illegal content online.

These issues are still relatively new and require fast reaction. Despite cultural differences, the risks for children are similar all over the EU. Therefore sharing of best practice experiences in the field of awareness raising among countries is necessary to achieve large scale results in the short term.

What has the Commission done so far?

Launched in May 2012, the European strategy for a better internet for children to give children the digital skills and tools they need to fully and safely benefit from being online around the following main goals:

Stimulate the production of creative and educational online content for children as well as promoting positive online experiences for young children

Scaling up awareness and empowerment including teaching of digital literacy and online safety in all EU schools

Create a safe environment for children through age-appropriate privacy settings, wider use of parental controls and age rating and content classification

Combat child sexual abuse material online and child sexual exploitation

Safer Internet Day, 5 February 2013 was celebrated in more than 100 countries worldwide under the theme "Online Rights and Responsibilities" and the slogan "Connect with respect" reaching out to more than 10 million people and more than 16,000 schools. For more information: http://www.saferinternetday.org

Continued to support the network of Safer Internet Centres with enhanced focus on promotion of positive online experience, youth participation and special attention to vulnerable children. Safer Internet Centres are present in all the Member States (plus Iceland, Norway and Russia) running hotlines, awareness centres and helplines to provide information and support to children, parents and educators on the safe use of new online technologies.

Single, comprehensive web portal to provide visibility for awareness activities, helplines and hotlines: www.saferintenet.eu (INHOPE&INSAFE) and www.safetinternet.org (INSAFE)

Organisation of Safer Internet Forum 2012 (international conference with more than 300 participants including Pan-European Youth Panel and Teachers/parents Panel meetings)

Multilingual resources for young users and teens by INSAFE

Collection through online platform of statistics about the awareness raising, helpline and hotline activities and the results of the Safer Internet Centres across Europe:

INHOPE annual report for 2011

For additional analytical, business and investment opportunities information, please contact Global Investment & Business Center, USA at (703) 370-8082. Fax: (703) 370-8083. E-mail: ibpusa3@gmail.com Global Business and Investment Info Databank - www.ibpus.com

Safer Internet centres statistics for 2012

Monitor the implementation of "notice and take down" of child abuse images: Hotlines have been supported to facilitate reporting of online child pornography, actions have been taken to improve N&TD and get better statistics on timelines and on where such content is hosted. The time span needed between reporting child sexual abuse content on the internet and taking it down has been further reduced.

Strengthen cooperation of Child Sexual Abuse investigators between Member States: contribution to the Global Alliance against Child Sexual Abuse online

Encourage sharing investigation tools (software tools etc.) between Member States: launch of a new project to enhance law enforcement agencies' identification and analysis of child pornography

International co-operation

Signature of Joint EU/US Declaration, committing to make the Internet a safer and better place for children by European Commission Vice President for the Digital Agenda Neelie Kroes and the U.S. Secretary of Homeland Security Janet Napolitano

Participation in IGF 2012 in Baku with a workshop on child online protection

Participation of Russia in the INSAFE and INHOPE networks

What will the Commission do in 2013:

Collect and disseminate information about the awareness, helpline and hotline activities and the results of the Safer Internet Centres across Europe.

Continue to support the work of the Safer Internet Centres

Follow up on the Connecting Europe Facility, the follow up to the Safer Internet Programme for the period 2014 – 2020

Organise the Safer Internet Forum (17-18 October 2013)

Start preparatory work for Safer Internet Day 2014 (11 February 2014)

For additional analytical, business and investment opportunities information, please contact Global Investment & Business Center, USA at (703) 370-8082. Fax: (703) 370-8083. E-mail: ibpusa3@gmail.com Global Business and Investment Info Databank - www.ibpus.com

Continue to monitor the implementation of "notice and take down" of child abuse images and to strengthen cooperation of Child Sexual Abuse investigators between Member States through the Global Alliance against Child Sexual Abuse online

Continue to support international co-operation.

ACTION 37: FOSTER SELF-REGULATION IN THE USE OF ONLINE SERVICES

Foster multi-stakeholder dialogue and self-regulation of European and global service providers (e.g. social networking platforms, mobile communications providers), especially as regards use of their services by minors.

What is the problem? Children are not safe online

More and more European children go online via mobile phones and game consoles. More than 50% of 13-16 year olds go online from their bedroom and more than half of 9-16 year olds have a social networking profile. At the same time, young people are a vulnerable group as they do not always see the risks of their online actions such as sharing personal information online or talking to people they have never met in real life. In this rapidly changing context, addressing risks and strengthening the online safety of children is a shared responsibility of individuals as much as of private and public bodies, both at home and globally.

Why is EU action required? EU wide action is needed for children's safety online

Many of the providers of products and services that have an impact on the online safety of children, such as social networking sites, mobile phones, online applications and content or games consoles are global or European players.

A general pan-European approach should be adopted since purely national systems risk producing fragmentation.

What has the Commission done so far?

Launch of European strategy for a Better Internet for Children (see action 36)

Brokerage and follow up of CEO Coalition's work to make the Internet a better place for kids

Summary reports of the work carried out and company statements of the Coalition's members were published on Safer Internet Day 2013.

What the Commission will do in 2013:

Continued follow-up of the CEO coalition work through thematic/technical meetings.

Organised high-level meeting chaired by Vice-President Kroes with the CEOs of the Coalition companies (3rd June 2013).

Promote dialogue between youth and industry.

ACTION 38: MEMBER STATES TO ESTABLISH PAN-EUROPEAN COMPUTER EMERGENCY RESPONSE TEAMS

Member States should establish by 2012 a well-functioning network of CERTs at national level covering all of Europe.

What is the problem? Reactions to cyber-attacks are too slow

To respond to online security breaches in real-time conditions, a well-functioning network of Computer Emergency Response Teams ("CERT"s) should be established in Europe.

Why is EU action needed? Reinforce capacities EU-wide to react faster to security threats

The establishment of CERTs will

provide immediate response services to victims of cyber attacks

publish alerts concerning online threats

offer other information to improve computer and network security

The Commission invites Member States to strengthen cooperation between the existing National CERTs and to expand existing cooperation mechanisms like the European Governmental CERTs Group.

What is the European Commission doing?

In 2012

ENISA helped to reinforce cooperation between National / Governmental CERTs in the Member States and on European level.

In 2013

In February 2013, the Commission set out its intention to enhance the cooperation of National / Governmental CERTs as well as the establishment of national competent authorities for network and information security through a legislative proposal on enhanced network and information security across the EU.

ACTION 39: MEMBER STATES TO CARRY OUT CYBER-ATTACK SIMULATIONS

Member States, in cooperation with the Commission should carry out large scale attack simulation and test mitigation strategies as of 2010.

What is the problem? Cyber-attacks threaten internet users

Cyber-attacks are becoming ever more sophisticated. Internet users now face threats from a huge number of viruses, worms and other forms of malware.

Why is EU action needed? Cyber-terrorism is global so EU-wide cooperation is needed

No single country can deal successfully with these threats. International cooperation is essential at the early stages of a cyber-attack. Differences in national approaches and the lack of systematic cross-border cooperation greatly reduce the effectiveness of cyber-attack countermeasures.

Cyber security exercises are still at an early stage in the EU. Member States should therefore develop national contingency plans to deal with cyber-attacks. They should also organise regular exercises for responding to large scale networks security incidents and implementing disaster recovery. These measures should be adopted as steps towards closer pan-European coordination.

What is the European Commission doing?

In 2010:

The 1st pan-European exercise that took place in November 2010 (Cyber Europe 2010) acted as a driver for some Member States to run their own national cyber security exercises.

In 2012:

ENISA worked with Member States on the organisation of the 2nd pan-European exercise in 2012 (Cyber Europe 2012).

ACTION 40: MEMBER STATES TO IMPLEMENT HARMFUL CONTENT ALERT HOTLINES

Member States should fully implement hotlines for reporting illegal online content, organise awareness raising campaigns on online safety for children, and offer teaching online safety and digital literacy in schools, and encourage providers of online services to implement self-regulatory measures regarding online safety for children by 2013.

What is the problem? Children are not safe online

Internet has become one of the main distribution channels for material (images, films, audio files etc.) depicting sexual abuse of children. Internet Watch Foundation confirmed 1.316 child abuse domains in 2009. The content is becoming worse over years: 44% of the images reported to the largest hotline depict serious abuse of a child; 70% of the victims are under the age of 10.

More and more European children go online via mobile phones and game consoles. More than 50% of 13-16 year olds go online from their bedroom and more than half of 9-16 year olds have a social networking profile. At the same time, young people are a vulnerable group as they do not always see the risks of their online actions, such as sharing personal information online or talking to people they have never met in real life.

Why is the EU action required?

To improve online child safety and to ensure that children across the EU enjoy similar levels of protection and service online, an EU-wide coordination is not only needed but necessary

Addressing risks and strengthening the online safety and digital literacy of children is a shared responsibility of individuals as much as of private and public bodies, both at home and globally.

The Commission supports the development of hotlines for reporting illegal online content (see action 36). It also encourages self-regulation by European service providers (see action 37). At the same time, while action in this field should be coordinated at EU level, it has to be implemented at national level. Thus, Member States are expected to provide the necessary financial and political support to Safer Internet Centres in their respective national jurisdictions. They should also develop a strategy on how best to teach online safety in schools.

What has the Commission done so far?

Launch a European strategy for a better internet for children that aims to give children the digital skills and tools they need to fully and safely benefit from being online (see action 36).

Launch a benchmarking exercise of safer internet policies and action across Europe including an analysis of the current resources used for these activities and their breakdown between the Commission and Member States

Online safety in schools:

European Schoolnet (EUN) – co-ordinator of INSAFE network, co-funded by the Safer Internet Programme, launched on Safer Internet Day 2012 the "eSafety label project" to provide Online safety support and accreditation for European schools. This is a multi-stakeholder project coordinated by EUN and involving a number of leading companies (Kaspersky Labs, Liberty Global, Microsoft, Telefonica) and European Education Ministries and educational organisations in Austria, Belgium-Flanders, Estonia Italy, Spain and Portugal). www.esafetylabel.eu.

What will the Commission do?

For additional analytical, business and investment opportunities information, please contact Global Investment & Business Center, USA at (703) 370-8082. Fax: (703) 370-8083. E-mail: ibpusa3@gmail.com Global Business and Investment Info Databank - www.ibpus.com

In 2013:

Continue to support the Safer Internet Centres established in all Member States and that run hotlines, awareness centres and helplines (see action 36).

ACTION 41: MEMBER STATES TO SET UP NATIONAL ALERT PLATFORMS

Member States should set up or adapt national alert platforms to the Europol cybercrime platform, by 2012, starting in 2010.

What is the problem? Cybercrime can not be tackled in Europe without cooperative national alert platforms

To fight cybercrime, Member States should set up a national alert platform. If they have already done so, they should work together with similar platforms in other Member States. All alert platforms in the Member States should adopt appropriate technology to share reported information easily and quickly with each other.

Why is EU action necessary? Cooperation between Member States helps to fight cross-border cybercrime

Member States should develop websites which could serve as a one-stop-shop for the public who can play an active role in reporting illicit online activity. These websites could in addition compile statistics on alerts, thus tracking the development of cybercrime at national level. (See also action 30 and action 31)

What has the European Commission done so far?

For additional analytical, business and investment opportunities information, please contact Global Investment & Business Center, USA at (703) 370-8082. Fax: (703) 370-8083. E-mail: ibpusa3@gmail.com Global Business and Investment Info Databank - www.ibpus.com

In 2011

Encouraged the establishment of national alert platforms in Member States.

In 2012:

Assisted Member States when integrating their alert platforms in the Europol cybercrime platform.

What will the European Commission do now?

In 2013:

Will encourage and work with the European Cybercrime Centre to coordinate with Member States to create structures for sharing information towards combating cybercrime at EU level.

ACTION 123: PROPOSAL FOR DIRECTIVE ON NETWORK AND INFORMATION SECURITY

Presented in February 2013 a legislative proposal on enhanced network and information security across the Union.

What is the problem? Growing number of cyber-attacks on information systems

Network and information systems and services play a vital role in in facilitating the cross-border movement of goods, services and people. Substantial disruption of these systems in one Member State can affect other Member States and the EU as a whole. The resilience and stability of network and information systems is therefore essential to the smooth functioning of the internal market.

The extent and frequency of security incidents, caused by human error or malicious attacks is increasing: the Commission's public consultation found that 57 % of respondents had experienced NIS incidents over the previous year that had a serious impact on their activities. A 2012 Eurobarometer survey found that 38% of EU internet users are concerned about the safety of online payments.

There is currently no effective mechanism at EU level for effective cooperation and collaboration and for secure information sharing on NIS incidents and risks among the Member States.

Why is EU action required? Strengthen security of citizens and businesses

Network and information systems and services play a vital role in in facilitating the cross-border movement of goods, services and people. Substantial disruption of these systems in one Member State can affect other Member States and the EU as a whole. The resilience and stability of network and information systems is therefore essential to the smooth functioning of the internal market.

What will the Commission do?

Proceed with the legislative process towards the adoption of the directive in 2013.

ACTION 124: EU CYBER-SECURITY STRATEGY

The cyber-security strategy – "An Open, Safe and Secure Cyberspace" - represents the EU's comprehensive vision on how best to prevent and respond to cyber disruptions and attacks. This is to further European values of freedom and democracy and ensure the digital economy can safely grow. Specific actions are aimed at enhancing cyber resilience of information systems, reducing cybercrime and strengthening EU international cyber-security policy and cyber defence.

What is the problem?

Cyber-security incidents are increasing in frequency and magnitude, becoming more complex and know no borders. These incidents can cause major damage to safety and the economy. Efforts to prevent, cooperate and be more transparent about cyber incidents must improve.

Why is EU action required? EU helps Member States to cooperate

Previous efforts by the European Commission and individual Member States have been too fragmented to deal with this growing challenge.

What has the Commission done so far?

Presented in February 2013 a proposal, together with the High Representative of the Union for Foreign Affairs and Security Policy, for a 'Cybersecurity Strategy of the European Union'. The proposed Directive lays down measures including: Member State must adopt a NIS strategy and designate a national NIS competent authority with adequate financial and human resources to prevent, handle and respond to NIS risks and incidents;

Creating a cooperation mechanism among Member States and the Commission to share early warnings on risks and incidents through a secure infrastructure, cooperate and organise regular peer reviews;

Operators of critical infrastructures in some sectors (financial services, transport, energy, health), enablers of information society services (notably: app stores e-commerce platforms, Internet payment, cloud computing, search engines, social networks) and public administrations must adopt risk management practices and report major security incidents on their core services.

Together with it, presented in February 2013 a legislative proposal on enhanced network and information security across the Union (action 123 of the Digital Agenda Review package).

Secured ENISA's future – in April 2013 the European Parliament voted to extend ENISA's mandate by seven years.

ACTION 125 EXPAND THE GLOBAL ALLIANCE AGAINST CHILD SEXUAL ABUSE ONLINE

Strengthen cooperation of Child Sexual Abuse investigators between Member States: contribution to the Global Alliance against Child Sexual Abuse online.

What is the problem?

Child sexual abuse online is a crime that is ubiquitous and knows no borders. Child pornography images circulate easily across jurisdictions and perpetuate victimisation of children whose abuse is depicted and disclosed time and again. Child pornography offenders are increasingly operating in international online groups that use sophisticated technology and security protocols to frustrate the efforts of law enforcement to investigate their crimes. Different laws and policies across jurisdictions represent a challenge for law enforcement..

Why is EU action required?

The EU - US Justice and Home Affairs ministerial meeting held in Copenhagen in June 2012 called upon governments around the world to participate in building a Global Alliance against Child Sexual Abuse Online. This initiative seeks to unite decision-makers all around the world to better identify and assist victims and to prosecute the perpetrators.

What has the Commission done so far?

International co-operation

Signature of Joint EU/US Declaration, committing to make the Internet a safer and better place for children by European Commission Vice President for the Digital Agenda Neelie Kroes and the U.S. Secretary of Homeland Security Janet Napolitano

Participation in IGF 2012 in Baku with a workshop on child online protection

Participation of Russia in the INSAFE and INHOPE networks

In December 2012, the Global Alliance against Child Sexual Abuse online was launched . One of the aims is also to establish dedicated law enforcement units for these crimes in all countries, and to make it easier to initiate joint cross-border police investigations. Co-operation with hotline services, where the public can report findings of online child pornography, should be intensified. Countries also commit themselves to making sure that the Interpol international database of child abuse material grows by 10 percent annually.

How will the Global Alliance work?

Authorities, mainly Ministers of Justice and Home Affairs of countries joining the Global Alliance commit to pursue a number of policy targets. These include efforts to identify and protect child victims, investigate cases and prosecute offenders, increase awareness of risks for children online, and reduce the availability of child pornography online. They will aim to reach operational goals and undertake specific action within their jurisdiction for that purpose. Specific actions, their extent and content, will be decided by participant countries, in accordance with their national situation.

To make commitments meaningful, a light monitoring mechanism would be set up. First, Ministers will take stock of existing actions at national level and announce what actions they will be undertaking in the near future. Then, two years later, they will report on the implementation of those actions, and gather again to look back, assess progress and decide what type of additional actions to take.

Secretarial functions to collect the national reports, make an overview on progress and organise regular conferences should be borne by participants on a rotating basis. European Commission services have volunteered to conduct those functions in the first round, and the US is willing to take the second round, followed by other participants.

What are countries in the Global Alliance expected to do?

Ministers from participating countries should commit to pursue a number of policy targets and operational goals (e.g. enhancing investigations) . They would then decide what specific actions to take to achieve them, on the basis of their domestic situation (e.g. set up Joint Investigation Teams, participate in the Virtual Global Task Force) .

Ultimately they are expected to take steps at national level to follow-up on those actions. This implementation part, under the responsibility of each Minister and each country, is the essence of the Global Alliance.

CYBERSECURITY STRATEGY OF THE EUROPEAN UNION: AN OPEN, SAFE AND SECURE CYBERSPACE[3]

1. INTRODUCTION

1.1. CONTEXT

Over the last two decades, the Internet and more broadly cyberspace has had a tremendous impact on all parts of society. Our daily life, fundamental rights, social interactions and economies depend on information and communication technology working seamlessly. An open and free cyberspace has promoted political and social inclusion worldwide; it has broken down barriers between countries, communities and citizens, allowing interaction and sharing of information and ideas across the globe; it has provided a forum for freedom of expression and exercise of fundamental rights, and empowered people in their quest for democratic and more just societies - most strikingly during the Arab Spring.

For cyberspace to remain open and free, the same norms, principles and values that the EU upholds offline, should also apply online. Fundamental rights, democracy and the rule of law need to be protected in cyberspace. Our freedom and prosperity increasingly depend on a robust and innovative Internet, which will continue to flourish if private sector innovation and civil society drive its growth. But freedom online requires safety and security too. Cyberspace should be protected from incidents, malicious activities and misuse; and governments have a significant role in ensuring a free and safe cyberspace. Governments have several tasks: to safeguard access and openness, to respect and protect fundamental rights online and to maintain the reliability and interoperability of the Internet. However, the private sector owns and operates significant parts of cyberspace, and so any initiative aiming to be successful in this area has to recognise its leading role.

Information and communications technology has become the backbone of our economic growth and is a critical resource which all economic sectors rely on. It now underpins the complex systems which keep our economies running in key sectors such as finance, health, energy and transport; while many business models are built on the uninterrupted availability of the Internet and the smooth functioning of information systems.

By completing the Digital Single Market, Europe could boost its GDP by almost €500 billion a year[1]; an average of €1000 per person. For new connected technologies to take off, including e-payments, cloud computing or machine-to-machine communication[2], citizens will need trust and confidence. Unfortunately, a 2012 Eurobarometer survey[3] showed that almost a third of Europeans are not confident in their ability to use the internet for banking or purchases. An overwhelming majority also said they avoid disclosing personal information

1

http://www.epc.eu/dsm/2/Study_by_Copenhagen.pdf

2

[3] JOINT COMMUNICATION TO THE EUROPEAN PARLIAMENT, THE COUNCIL, THE EUROPEAN ECONOMIC AND SOCIAL COMMITTEE AND THE COMMITTEE OF THE REGIONS

For additional analytical, business and investment opportunities information, please contact Global Investment & Business Center, USA at (703) 370-8082. Fax: (703) 370-8083. E-mail: ibpusa3@gmail.com
Global Business and Investment Info Databank - www.ibpus.com

For example, plants embedded with sensors to communicate to the sprinkler system when it is time for them to be watered.

3

2012 Special Eurobarometer 390 on Cybersecurity

EN EN

online because of security concerns. Across the EU, more than one in ten Internet users has already become victim of online fraud.

Recent years have seen that while the digital world brings enormous benefits, it is also vulnerable. Cybersecurity[4] incidents, be it intentional or accidental, are increasing at an alarming pace and could disrupt the supply of essential services we take for granted such as water, healthcare, electricity or mobile services. Threats can have different origins — including criminal, politically motivated, terrorist or state-sponsored attacks as well as natural disasters and unintentional mistakes.

The EU economy is already affected by cybercrime[5] activities against the private sector and individuals. Cybercriminals are using ever more sophisticated methods for intruding into information systems, stealing critical data or holding companies to ransom. The increase of economic espionage and state-sponsored activities in cyberspace poses a new category of threats for EU governments and companies.

In countries outside the EU, governments may also misuse cyberspace for surveillance and control over their own citizens. The EU can counter this situation by promoting freedom online and ensuring respect of fundamental rights online.

All these factors explain why governments across the world have started to develop cyber-security strategies and to consider cyberspace as an increasingly important international issue. The time has come for the EU to step up its actions in this area. This proposal for a Cybersecurity strategy of the European Union, put forward by the Commission and the High Representative of the Union for Foreign Affairs and Security Policy (High Representative) , outlines the EU's vision in this domain, clarifies roles and responsibilities and sets out the actions required based on strong and effective protection and promotion of citizens' rights to make the EU's online environment the safest in the world.

1.2. PRINCIPLES FOR CYBERSECURITY

The borderless and multi-layered Internet has become one of the most powerful instruments for global progress without governmental oversight or regulation. While the private sector should continue to play a leading role in the construction and day-to-day management of the Internet, the need for requirements for transparency, accountability and security is becoming more and more prominent. This strategy clarifies the principles that should guide cybersecurity policy in the EU and internationally.

The EU's core values apply as much in the digital as in the physical world

The same laws and norms that apply in other areas of our day-to-day lives apply also in the cyber domain.

Cyber-security commonly refers to the safeguards and actions that can be used to protect the cyber domain, both in the civilian and military fields, from those threats that are associated with or that may harm its interdependent networks and information infrastructure. Cyber-security strives to preserve the availability and integrity of the networks and infrastructure and the confidentiality of the information contained therein.

Cybercrime commonly refers to a broad range of different criminal activities where computers and information systems are involved either as a primary tool or as a primary target. Cybercrime comprises traditional offences (e.g. fraud, forgery, and identity theft) , content-related offences (e.g. on-line distribution of child pornography or incitement to racial hatred) and offences unique to computers and information systems (e.g. attacks against information systems, denial of service and malware) .

Protecting fundamental rights, freedom of expression, personal data and privacy

Cybersecurity can only be sound and effective if it is based on fundamental rights and freedoms as enshrined in the Charter of Fundamental Rights of the European Union and EU core values. Reciprocally, individuals' rights cannot be secured without safe networks and systems. Any information sharing for the purposes of cyber security, when personal data is at stake, should be compliant with EU data protection law and take full account of the individuals' rights in this field.

Access for all

Limited or no access to the Internet and digital illiteracy constitute a disadvantage to citizens, given how much the digital world pervades activity within society. Everyone should be able to access the Internet and to an unhindered flow of information. The Internet's integrity and security must be guaranteed to allow safe access for all.

Democratic and efficient multi-stakeholder governance

The digital world is not controlled by a single entity. There are currently several stakeholders, of which many are commercial and non-governmental entities, involved in the day-to-day management of Internet resources, protocols and standards and in the future development of the Internet. The EU reaffirms the importance of all stakeholders in the current Internet governance model and supports this multi-stakeholder governance approach[6].

A shared responsibility to ensure security

The growing dependency on information and communications technologies in all domains of human life has led to vulnerabilities which need to be properly defined, thoroughly analysed, remedied or reduced. All relevant actors, whether public authorities, the private sector or individual citizens, need to recognise this shared responsibility, take action to protect themselves and if necessary ensure a coordinated response to strengthen cybersecurity.

2. STRATEGIC PRIORITIES AND ACTIONS

The EU should safeguard an online environment providing the highest possible freedom and security for the benefit of everyone. While acknowledging that it is predominantly the task of Member States to deal with security challenges in cyberspace, this strategy proposes specific actions that can enhance the EU's overall performance. These actions are both short and long term, they include a variety of policy tools[7] and involve different types of actors, be it the EU institutions, Member States or industry.

The EU vision presented in this strategy is articulated in five strategic priorities, which address the challenges highlighted above:

Achieving cyber resilience

Drastically reducing cybercrime

6

See also COM(2009) 277, Communication from the Commission to the European Parliament and the Council on "Internet Governance: the next steps"

7

The actions related to information sharing, when personal data is at stake, should be compliant with EU data protection law.

EN EN

Developing cyberdefence policy and capabilities related to the Common Security and Defence Policy (CSDP)

Develop the industrial and technological resources for cybersecurity

Establish a coherent international cyberspace policy for the European Union and promote core EU values

2.1. ACHIEVING CYBER RESILIENCE

To promote cyber resilience in the EU, both public authorities and the private sector must develop capabilities and cooperate effectively. Building on the positive results achieved via the activities carried out to date[8] further EU action can help in particular to counter cyber risks and threats having a cross-border dimension, and contribute to a coordinated response in emergency situations. This will strongly support the good functioning of the internal market and boost the internal security of the EU.

Europe will remain vulnerable without a substantial effort to enhance public and private capacities, resources and processes to prevent, detect and handle cyber security incidents. This is why the Commission has developed a policy on Network and Information Security (NIS) [9]. The European Network and Information Security Agency ENISA was established in 2004[10] and a new Regulation to strengthen ENISA and modernise its mandate is being negotiated by Council and Parliament[11]. In addition, the Framework Directive for electronic communications[12] requires providers of electronic communications to appropriately manage the risks to their networks and to report significant security breaches. Also, the EU data protection legislation[13] requires data controllers to ensure data protection requirements and safeguards, including measures related to security, and in the field of publicly available e-communication services, data controllers have to notify incidents involving a breach of personal data to the competent national authorities.

Despite progress based on voluntary commitments, there are still gaps across the EU, notably in terms of national capabilities, coordination in cases of incidents spanning across borders, and in

For additional analytical, business and investment opportunities information, please contact Global Investment & Business Center, USA at (703) 370-8082. Fax: (703) 370-8083. E-mail: ibpusa3@gmail.com Global Business and Investment Info Databank - www.ibpus.com

terms of private sector involvement and preparedness:. This strategy is accompanied by a proposal for legislation to notably:

• establish common minimum requirements for NIS at national level which would oblige Member States to: designate national competent authorities for NIS; set up a well-functioning CERT; and adopt a national NIS strategy and a national NIS cooperation plan. Capacity building and coordination also concern the EU institutions: a Computer Emergency Response Team responsible for the security of the IT systems of the EU institutions, agencies and bodies ("CERT-EU") was permanently established in 2012.

[8] See references in this Communication as well as in the Commission Staff Working Document Impact Assessment accompanying the Commission proposal for a Directive on network and information security, in particular sections 4.1.4, 5.2, Annex 2, Annex 6, Annex 8,

9

In 2001, the Commission adopted a Communication on "Network and Information Security: Proposal for A European Policy Approach" (COM(2001) 298) ; in 2006, it adopted a Strategy for a Secure Information Society (COM(2006) 251) . Since 2009, the Commission has also adopted an Action Plan and a Communication on Critical Information Infrastructure Protection (CIIP) (COM(2009) 149, endorsed by Council Resolution 2009/C 321/01; and COM(2011) 163, endorsed by Council Conclusions 10299/11) .

10

Regulation (EC) No 460/2004

11

COM(2010) 521. The actions proposed in this Strategy do not entail amending the existing or future mandate of ENISA.

12

Article 13a&b of Directive 2002/21/EC

13

Article 17 of Directive 95/46/EC; Article 4 of Directive 2002/58/EC

EN EN

set up coordinated prevention, detection, mitigation and response mechanisms, enabling information sharing and mutual assistance amongst the national NIS competent authorities. National NIS competent authorities will be asked to ensure appropriate EU-wide cooperation, notably on the basis of a Union NIS cooperation plan, designed to respond to cyber incidents with cross-border dimension. This cooperation will also build upon the progress made in the context of the "European Forum for Member States (EFMS) "[14], which has held productive discussions and exchanges on NIS public policy and can be integrated in the cooperation mechanism once in place.

For additional analytical, business and investment opportunities information, please contact Global Investment & Business Center, USA at (703) 370-8082. Fax: (703) 370-8083. E-mail: ibpusa3@gmail.com Global Business and Investment Info Databank - www.ibpus.com

improve preparedness and engagement of the private sector. Since the large majority of network and information systems are privately owned and operated, improving engagement with the private sector to foster cybersecurity is crucial. The private sector should develop, at technical level, its own cyber resilience capacities and share best practices across sectors. The tools developed by industry to respond to incidents, identify causes and conduct forensic investigations should also benefit the public sector.

However, private actors still lack effective incentives to provide reliable data on the existence or impact of NIS incidents, to embrace a risk management culture or to invest in security solutions. The proposed legislation therefore aims at making sure that players in a number of key areas (namely energy, transport, banking, stock exchanges, and enablers of key Internet services, as well as public administrations) assess the cybersecurity risks they face, ensure networks and information systems are reliable and resilient via appropriate risk management, and share the identified information with the national NIS competent authorities The take up of a cybersecurity culture could enhance business opportunities and competitiveness in the private sector, which could make cybersecurity a selling point.

Those entities would have to report, to the national NIS competent authorities, incidents with a significant impact on the continuity of core services and supply of goods relying on network and information systems.

National NIS competent authorities should collaborate and exchange information with other regulatory bodies, and in particular personal data protection authorities. NIS competent authorities should in turn report incidents of a suspected serious criminal nature to law enforcement authorities. The national competent authorities should also regularly publish on a dedicated website unclassified information about on-going early warnings on incidents and risks and on coordinated responses. Legal obligations should neither substitute, nor prevent, developing informal and voluntary cooperation, including between public and private sectors, to boost security levels and exchange information and best practices. In particular, the European Public-Private Partnership for Resilience (EP3R[15]) is a sound and valid platform at EU level and should be further developed.

14

The European Forum for Member States was launched via COM(2009) 149 as a platform to foster discussions among Member States public authorities regarding good policy practises on security and resilience of Critical Information Infrastructure

15

The European Public-Private Partnership for Resilience was launched via COM(2009) 149. This platform initiated work and fostered the cooperation between the public and the private sector on the identification of key assets, resources, functions and baseline requirements for resilience as well as cooperation needs and mechanisms to respond to large-scale disruptions affecting electronic communications.

EN EN

The Connecting Europe Facility (CEF) [16] would provide financial support for key infrastructure, linking up Member States' NIS capabilities and so making it easier to cooperate across the EU.

Finally, cyber incident exercises at EU level are essential to simulate cooperation among the Member States and the private sector. The first exercise involving the Member States was carried out in 2010 ("Cyber Europe 2010") and a second exercise, involving also the private sector, took place in October 2012 ("Cyber Europe 2012") . An EU-US table top exercise was carried out in November 2011 ("Cyber Atlantic 2011") . Further exercises are planned for the coming years, including with international partners.

16 1718 https://ec.europa.eu/digital-agenda/en/connecting-europe-facility. CEF Budget line 09.03.02 – Telecommunications networks (to promote the interconnection and interoperability of national public services on-line as well as access to such networks) . CIP-ICT PSP-2012-6, 325188. It has an overall budget of 15 Million Euro, with EU funding amounting to 7.7 Million Euro. http://www.trustindigitallife.eu/

particular through public-private partnerships like EP3R and Trust in Digital Life

Raising awareness

Ensuring cybersecurity is a common responsibility. End users play a crucial role in ensuring the security of networks and information systems: they need to be made aware of the risks they face online and be empowered to take simple steps to guard against them.

Several initiatives have been developed in recent years and should be continued. In particular, ENISA has been involved in raising awareness through publishing reports, organising expert workshops and developing public-private partnerships. Europol, Eurojust and national data protection authorities are also active in raising awareness. In October 2012, ENISA, with some Member States, piloted the "European Cybersecurity Month". Raising awareness is one of the areas the EU-US Working Group on Cybersecurity and Cybercrime[19] is taking forward, and is also essential in the context of the Safer Internet Programme[20] (focused on the safety of children online) .

19

For additional analytical, business and investment opportunities information,
please contact Global Investment & Business Center, USA
at (703) 370-8082. Fax: (703) 370-8083. E-mail: ibpusa3@gmail.com
Global Business and Investment Info Databank - www.ibpus.com

This Working Group, established at the EU-US Summit in November 2010 (MEMO/10/597) is tasked with developing collaborative approaches on a wide range of cybersecurity and cybercrime issues.

20

The Safer Internet Programme funds a network of NGOs active in the field of child welfare online, a network of law enforcement bodies who exchange information and best practices related to criminal exploitation of the Internet in dissemination of child sexual abuse material and a network of researchers who gather information about uses, risks and consequences of online technologies for children's lives.

21

Also with the involvement of relevant national authorities, including NIS competent authorities and data protection authorities.

EN EN

the interface with customers. In particular, industry should reflect on ways to make CEOs and Boards more accountable for ensuring cybersecurity.

2.2. DRASTICALLY REDUCING CYBERCRIME

The more we live in a digital world, the more opportunities for cyber criminals to exploit. Cybercrime is one of the fastest growing forms of crime, with more than one million people worldwide becoming victims each day. Cybercriminals and cybercrime networks are becoming increasingly sophisticated and we need to have the right operational tools and capabilities to tackle them. Cybercrimes are high-profit and low-risk, and criminals often exploit the anonymity of website domains. Cybercrime knows no borders - the global reach of the Internet means that law enforcement must adopt a coordinated and collaborative cross-border approach to respond to this growing threat.

Strong and effective legislation

The EU and the Member States need strong and effective legislation to tackle cybercrime. The Council of Europe Convention on Cybercrime, also known as the Budapest Convention, is a binding international treaty that provides an effective framework for the adoption of national legislation.

The EU has already adopted legislation on cybercrime including a Directive on combating the sexual exploitation of children online and child pornography[22]. The EU is also about to agree on a Directive on attacks against information systems, especially through the use of botnets.

The Commission will:

Ensure swift transposition and implementation of the cybercrime related directives.

Urge those Member States that have not yet ratified the Council of Europe's Budapest Convention on Cybercrime to ratify and implement its provisions as early as possible.

For additional analytical, business and investment opportunities information, please contact Global Investment & Business Center, USA at (703) 370-8082. Fax: (703) 370-8083. E-mail: ibpusa3@gmail.com Global Business and Investment Info Databank - www.ibpus.com

Enhanced operational capability to combat cybercrime

The evolution of cybercrime techniques has accelerated rapidly: law enforcement agencies cannot combat cybercrime with outdated operational tools. Currently, not all EU Member States have the operational capability they need to effectively respond to cybercrime. All Member States need effective national cybercrime units.

Directive 2011/93/EU replacing Council Framework decision 2004/68/JHA

For 2013, under the Prevention and Fight against Crime Programme (ISEC) . After 2013, under the Internal Security Fund (new Instrument under MFF) .

research/academia, law enforcement practitioners and the private sector, similar to the on-going work carried out by the Commission-funded Cybercrime Centres of Excellence already set up in some Member States.

Together with the Member States, coordinate efforts to identify best practices and best available techniques including with the support of JRC to fight cybercrime

(e.g. with respect to the development and use of forensic tools or to threat analysis)

Work closely with the recently launched European Cybercrime Centre (EC3) , within Europol and with Eurojust to align such policy approaches with best practices on the operational side.

Improved coordination at EU level

The EU can complement the work of Member States by facilitating a coordinated and collaborative approach, bringing together law enforcement and judicial authorities and public and private stakeholders from the EU and beyond.

For additional analytical, business and investment opportunities information, please contact Global Investment & Business Center, USA at (703) 370-8082. Fax: (703) 370-8083. E-mail: ibpusa3@gmail.com Global Business and Investment Info Databank - www.ibpus.com

24 2526 On 28 March 2012, the European Commission adopted a Communication "Tackling Crime in a Digital Age: Establishing a European Cybercrime Centre" COM(2012) 196 final Council Conclusions on a Global Alliance against Child Sexual Abuse Online (EU-US Joint Statement) of 7th and 8th June 2012 and Declaration on the launch of the Global Alliance against Child Sexual Abuse Online (http://europa.eu/rapid/press-release_MEMO-12-944_en.htm)

areas of child sexual abuse, payment fraud, botnets and intrusion.

• On a regular basis produce strategic and operational reports on trends and emerging threats to identify priorities and target investigative action by cybercrime teams in the Member States.

THE COMMISSION ASKS THE EUROPEAN POLICE COLLEGE (CEPOL) IN COOPERATION WITH EUROPOL TO:

• Coordinate the design and planning of training courses to equip law enforcement with the knowledge and expertise to effectively tackle cybercrime.

The Commission asks Eurojust to:

- Identify the main obstacles to judicial cooperation on cybercrime investigations and to coordination between Member States and with third countries and support the investigation and prosecution of cybercrime both at the operational and strategic level as well as training activities in the field.

The Commission asks Eurojust and Europol (EC3) to:

- Cooperate closely, inter alia through the exchange of information, in order to increase their effectiveness in combating cybercrime, in accordance with their respective mandates and competence.

2.3. DEVELOPING CYBERDEFENCE POLICY AND CAPABILITIES RELATED TO THE FRAMEWORK OF THE COMMON SECURITY AND DEFENCE POLICY (CSDP)

Cybersecurity efforts in the EU also involve the cyber defence dimension. To increase the resilience of the communication and information systems supporting Member States' defence and national security interests, cyberdefence capability development should concentrate on detection, response and recovery from sophisticated cyber threats

Given that threats are multifaceted, synergies between civilian and military approaches in protecting critical cyber assets should be enhanced. These efforts should be supported by research and development, and closer cooperation between governments, private sector and academia in the EU. To avoid duplications, the EU will explore possibilities on how the EU and NATO can complement their efforts to heighten the resilience of critical governmental, defence and other information infrastructures on which the members of both organisations depend.

2.4. DEVELOP INDUSTRIAL AND TECHNOLOGICAL RESOURCES FOR CYBERSECURITY

Europe has excellent research and development capacities, but many of the global leaders providing innovative ICT products and services are located outside the EU. There is a risk that Europe not only becomes excessively dependent on ICT produced elsewhere, but also on security solutions developed outside its frontiers. It is key to ensure that hardware and software components produced in the EU and in third countries that are used in critical services and infrastructure and increasingly in mobile devices are trustworthy, secure and guarantee the protection of personal data.

Promoting a Single Market for cybersecurity products

A high level of security can only be ensured if all in the value chain (e.g. equipment manufacturers, software developers, information society services providers) make security a priority. It seems[27] however that many players still regard security as little more than an additional burden and there is limited demand for security solutions. There need to be appropriate cybersecurity performance requirements implemented across the whole value chain for ICT products used in Europe. The private sector needs incentives to ensure a high level of cybersecurity; for example, labels indicating adequate cybersecurity performance will enable companies with a good cybersecurity performance and track record to make it a selling point and get a competitive edge. Also, the obligations set out in the proposed NIS Directive would significantly contribute to step up business competitiveness in the sectors covered.

A Europe-wide market demand for highly secure products should also be stimulated. First, this strategy aims to increase cooperation and transparency about security in ICT products. It calls for the establishment of a platform, bringing together relevant European public and private stakeholders, to identify good cybersecurity practices across the value chain and create the favourable market conditions for the development and adoption of secure ICT solutions. A prime focus should be to create incentives to carry out appropriate risk management and adopt security standards and solutions, as well as possibly establish voluntary EU-wide certification schemes building on existing schemes in the EU and internationally. The Commission will promote the adoption of coherent approaches among the Member States to avoid disparities causing locational disadvantages for businesses.

Second, the Commission will support the development of security standards and assist with EU-wide voluntary certification schemes in the area of cloud computing, while taking in due

27

See the Commission Staff Working Document Impact Assessment accompanying the Commission proposal for a Directive on network and information security, Section 4.1.5.2

account the need to ensure data protection. Work should focus on the security of the supply chain, in particular in critical economic sectors (Industrial Control Systems, energy and transport infrastructure) . Such work should build on the on-going standardisation work of the European Standardisation Organisations (CEN, CENELEC and ETSI) [28], of the Cybersecurity Coordination Group (CSCG) as well as on the expertise of ENISA, the Commission and other relevant players.

The Commission will:

Launch in 2013 a public-private platform on NIS solutions to develop incentives for the adoption of secure ICT solutions and the take-up of good cybersecurity performance to be applied to ICT products used in Europe.

Propose in 2014 recommendations to ensure cybersecurity across the ICT value chain, drawing on the work of this platform

Examine how major providers of ICT hardware and software could inform national competent authorities on detected vulnerabilities that could have significant security-implications.

The Commission asks ENISA to:

• Develop, in cooperation with relevant national competent authorities, relevant stakeholders, International and European standardisation bodies and the European Commission Joint Research Centre, technical guidelines and recommendations for the adoption of NIS standards and good practices in the public and private sectors.

The Commission invites public and private stakeholders to:

Stimulate the development and adoption of industry-led security standards, technical norms and security-by-design and privacy-by-design principles by ICT product manufacturers and service providers, including cloud providers; new generations of software and hardware should be equipped with stronger, embedded and user-friendly security features.

Develop industry-led standards for companies' performance on cybersecurity and improve the information available to the public by developing security labels or kite marks helping the consumer navigate the market.

Fostering R&D investments and innovation

R&D can support a strong industrial policy, promote a trustworthy European ICT industry, boost the internal market and reduce European dependence on foreign technologies. R&D should fill the technology gaps in ICT security, prepare for the next generation of security challenges, take into account the constant evolution of user needs and reap the benefits of dual use technologies. It should also continue supporting the development of cryptography. This has to be complemented by efforts to translate R&D results into commercial solutions by providing the necessary incentives and putting in place the appropriate policy conditions.

28

For additional analytical, business and investment opportunities information,
please contact Global Investment & Business Center, USA
at (703) 370-8082. Fax: (703) 370-8083. E-mail: ibpusa3@gmail.com
Global Business and Investment Info Databank - www.ibpus.com

Particularly under the Smart Grids Standard M/490 for the first set of standards for a smart grid and reference architecture.

The EU should make the best of the Horizon 2020[29] Framework Programme for Research and Innovation, to be launched in 2014. The Commission's proposal contains specific objectives for trustworthy ICT as well as for combating cyber-crime, which are in line with this strategy. Horizon 2020 will support security research related to emerging ICT technologies; provide solutions for end-to-end secure ICT systems, services and applications; provide the incentives for the implementation and adoption of existing solutions; and address interoperability among network and information systems. Specific attention will be drawn at EU level to optimising and better coordinating various funding programmes (Horizon 2020, Internal Security Fund, EDA research including European Framework Cooperation) .

The Commission will:

Use Horizon 2020 to address a range of areas in ICT privacy and security, from R&D to innovation and deployment. Horizon 2020 will also develop tools and instruments to fight criminal and terrorist activities targeting the cyber environment.

Establish mechanisms for better coordination of the research agendas of the European Union institutions and the Member States, and incentivise the Member States to invest more in R&D.

The Commission invites the Member States to:

Develop, by the end of 2013, good practices to use the purchasing power of public administrations (such as via public procurement) to stimulate the development and deployment of security features in ICT products and services.

Promote early involvement of industry and academia in developing and coordinating solutions. This should be done by making the most of Europe's Industrial Base and associated R&D technological innovations, and be coordinated between the research agendas of civilian and military organisations;

The Commission asks Europol and ENISA to:

• Identify emerging trends and needs in view of evolving cybercrime and cybersecurity patterns so as to develop adequate digital forensic tools and technologies.

The Commission invites public and private stakeholders to:

• Develop, in cooperation with the insurance sector, harmonised metrics for calculating risk premiums, that would enable companies that have made investments in security to benefit from lower risk premiums.

2.5. Establish a coherent international cyberspace policy for the European Union and promote EU core values

Preserving open, free and secure cyberspace is a global challenge, which the EU should address together with the relevant international partners and organisations, the private sector and civil society.

Horizon2020 is the financial instrument implementing the Innovation Union, a Europe 2020 flagship initiative aimed at securing Europe's global competitiveness. Running from 2014 to 2020, the EU's new Framework Programme for research and innovation will be part of the drive to create new growth and jobs in Europe.

In its international cyberspace policy, the EU will seek to promote openness and freedom of the Internet, encourage efforts to develop norms of behaviour and apply existing international laws in cyberspace. The EU will also work towards closing the digital divide, and will actively participate in international efforts to build cybersecurity capacity. The EU international engagement in cyber issues will be guided by the EU's core values of human dignity, freedom, democracy, equality, the rule of law and the respect for fundamental rights.

Mainstreaming cyberspace issues into EU external relations and Common Foreign and Security Policy

The Commission, the High Representative and the Member States should articulate a coherent EU international cyberspace policy, which will be aimed at increased engagement and stronger relations with key international partners and organisations, as well as with civil society and private sector. EU consultations with international partners on cyber issues should be designed, coordinated and implemented to add value to existing bilateral dialogues between the EU's Member States and third countries. The EU will place a renewed emphasis on dialogue with third countries, with a special focus on like-minded partners that share EU values. It will promote achieving a high level of data protection, including for transfer to a third country of personal data. To address global challenges in cyberspace, the EU will seek closer cooperation with organisations that are active in this field such as the Council of Europe, OECD, UN, OSCE, NATO, AU, ASEAN and OAS. At bilateral level, cooperation with the United States is particularly important and will be further developed, notably in the context of the EU-US Working Group on Cyber-Security and Cyber-Crime.

One of the major elements of the EU international cyber policy will be to promote cyberspace as an area of freedom and fundamental rights. Expanding access to the Internet should advance democratic reform and its promotion worldwide. Increased global connectivity should not be accompanied by censorship or mass surveillance. The EU should promote corporate social responsibility[30], and launch international initiatives to improve global coordination in this field.

The responsibility for a more secure cyberspace lies with all players of the global information society, from citizens to governments. The EU supports the efforts to define norms of behaviour in cyberspace that all stakeholders should adhere to. Just as the EU expects citizens to respect civic duties, social responsibilities and laws online, so should states abide by norms and existing laws. On matters of international security, the EU encourages the development of confidence building measures in cybersecurity, to increase transparency and reduce the risk of misperceptions in state behaviour.

The EU does not call for the creation of new international legal instruments for cyber issues.

The legal obligations enshrined in the International Covenant on Civil and Political Rights, the European Convention on Human Rights and the EU Charter of Fundamental Rights should be also respected online. The EU will focus on how to ensure that these measures are enforced also in cyberspace.

To address cybercrime, the Budapest Convention is an instrument open for adoption by third countries. It provides a model for drafting national cybercrime legislation and a basis for international co-operation in this field.

For additional analytical, business and investment opportunities information, please contact Global Investment & Business Center, USA at (703) 370-8082. Fax: (703) 370-8083. E-mail: ibpusa3@gmail.com Global Business and Investment Info Databank - www.ibpus.com

If armed conflicts extend to cyberspace, International Humanitarian Law and, as appropriate, Human Rights law will apply to the case at hand. Developing capacity building on cybersecurity and resilient information infrastructures in third countries

The smooth functioning of the underlying infrastructures that provide and facilitate communication services will benefit from increased international cooperation. This includes exchanging best practices, sharing information, early warning joint incident management exercises, and so on. The EU will contribute towards this goal by intensifying the on-going international efforts to strengthen Critical Information Infrastructure Protection (CIIP) cooperation networks involving governments and the private sector.

Not all parts of the world benefit from the positive effects of the Internet, due to a lack of open, secure, interoperable and reliable access. The European Union will therefore continue to support countries' efforts in their quest to develop the access and use of the Internet for their people, to ensure its integrity and security and to effectively fight cybercrime.

In cooperation with the Member States, the Commission and the High Representative will:

Work towards a coherent EU International cyberspace policy to increase engagement with key international partners and organisations, to mainstream cyber issues into CFSP, and to improve coordination of global cyber issues;

Support the development of norms of behaviour and confidence building measures in cybersecurity. Facilitate dialogues on how to apply existing international law in cyberspace and promote the Budapest Convention to address cybercrime;

Support the promotion and protection of fundamental rights, including access to information and freedom of expression, focusing on: a) developing new public guidelines on freedom of expression online and offline; b) monitoring the export of products or services that might be used for censorship or mass surveillance online; c) developing measures and tools to expand Internet access, openness and resilience to address censorship or mass surveillance by communication technology; d) empowering stakeholders to use communication technology to promote fundamental rights;

Engage with international partners and organisations, the private sector and civil society to support global capacity-building in third countries to improve access to information and to an open Internet, to prevent and counter cyber threats, including accidental events, cybercrime and cyber terrorism, and to develop donor coordination for steering capacity-building efforts;

Utilise different EU aid instruments for cybersecurity capacity building, including assisting the training of law enforcement, judicial and technical personnel to address cyber threats; as well as supporting the creation of relevant national policies, strategies and institutions in third countries;

Increase policy coordination and information sharing through the international Critical Information Infrastructure Protection networks such as the Meridian network, cooperation among NIS competent authorities and others.

3. ROLES AND RESPONSIBILITIES

Cyber incidents do not stop at borders in the interconnected digital economy and society. All actors, from NIS competent authorities, CERTs and law enforcement to industry, must take responsibility both nationally and at EU-level and work together to strengthen cybersecurity. As different legal frameworks and jurisdictions may be involved, a key challenge for the EU is to clarify the roles and responsibilities of the many actors involved.

Given the complexity of the issue and the diverse range of actors involved, centralised, European supervision is not the answer. National governments are best placed to organise the prevention and response to cyber incidents and attacks and to establish contacts and networks with the private sector and the general public across their established policy streams and legal frameworks. At the same time, due to the potential or actual borderless nature of the risks, an effective national response would often require EU-level involvement. To address cybersecurity in a comprehensive fashion, activities should span across three key pillars— NIS, law enforcement, and defence—which also operate within different legal frameworks:

Network and Information Law enforcement Defence

3.1. COORDINATION BETWEEN NIS COMPETENT AUTHORITIES/CERTS, LAW ENFORCEMENT AND DEFENCE

National level

Member States should have, either already today or as a result of this strategy, structures to deal with cyber resilience, cybercrime and defence; and they should reach the required level of capability to deal with cyber incidents. However, given that a number of entities may have operational responsibilities over different dimensions of cybersecurity, and given the importance of involving the private sector, coordination at national level should be optimised across ministries. Member States should set out in their national cybersecurity strategies the roles and responsibilities of their various national entities.

Information sharing between national entities and with the private sector should be encouraged, to enable the Member States and the private sector to maintain an overall view of different threats and get a better understanding of new trends and techniques used both to commit cyber-attacks and react to them more swiftly. By establishing national NIS cooperation plans to be activated in the case of cyber incidents, the Member States should be able to clearly allocate roles and responsibilities and optimise response actions.

EU level

Just as at national level, there are at EU level a number of actors dealing with cybersecurity. In particular, the ENISA, Europol/EC3 and the EDA are three agencies active from the perspective of NIS, law enforcement and defence respectively. These agencies have Management Boards where the Member States are represented, and offer platforms for coordination at EU level.

Coordination and collaboration will be encouraged among ENISA, Europol/EC3 and EDA in a number of areas where they are jointly involved, notably in terms of trends analysis, risk assessment, training and sharing of best practices. They should collaborate while preserving their specificities. These agencies together with CERT-EU, the Commission and the Member States should support the development of a trusted community of technical and policy experts in this field.

Informal channels for coordination and collaboration will be complemented by more structural links. EU military staff and the EDA cyber defence project team can be used as the vector for coordination in defence. The Programme Board of Europol/EC3 will bring together among others the EUROJUST, CEPOL, the Member States[31], ENISA and the Commission, and offer the chance to share their distinct know-how and to make sure EC3's actions are carried out in partnership, recognising the added expertise and respecting the mandates of all stakeholders. The new mandate of ENISA should make it possible to increase its links with Europol and to reinforce links with industry stakeholders. Most importantly, the Commission's legislative proposal on NIS) would establish a cooperation framework via a network of national NIS competent authorities and address information sharing between NIS and law enforcement authorities.

International

The Commission and the High Representative ensure, together with the Member States, coordinated international action in the field of cybersecurity. In so doing, the Commission and the High Representative will uphold EU core values and promote a peaceful, open and transparent use of cyber technologies. The Commission, the High Representative and the Member States engage in policy dialogue with international partners and with international organisations such as Council of Europe, OECD, OSCE, NATO and UN.

3.2. EU SUPPORT IN CASE OF A MAJOR CYBER INCIDENT OR ATTACK

Major cyber incidents or attacks are likely to have an impact on EU governments, business and individuals. As a result of this strategy, and in particular the proposed directive on NIS, the prevention, detection and response to cyber incidents should improve and Member States and the Commission should keep each other more closely informed about major cyber incidents or attacks. However, the response mechanisms will differ depending on the nature, magnitude and cross-border implications of the incident.

If the incident has a serious impact on the business continuity, the NIS directive proposes that national or Union NIS cooperation plans be triggered, depending on the cross-border nature of the incident. The network of NIS competent authorities would be used in that context to share via representation within the EU Cybercrime Task Force, which is made up of the heads of the EU cybercrime Units of the Member States information and support. This would enable preservation and/or restoration of affected networks and services.

If the incident seems to relate to a crime, Europol/EC3 should be informed so that they - together with the law enforcement authorities from the affected countries – can launch an investigation, preserve the evidence, identify the perpetrators and ultimately make sure they are prosecuted.

If the incident seems to relate to cyber espionage or a state-sponsored attack, or has national security implications, national security and defence authorities will alert their relevant counterparts, so that they know they are under attack and can defend themselves. Early warning mechanisms will then be activated and, if required, so will crisis management or other procedures. A particularly serious cyber incident or attack could constitute sufficient ground for a Member State to invoke the EU Solidarity Clause (Article 222 of the Treaty on the Functioning of the European Union) .

If the incident seems having compromised personal data, the national Data Protection Authorities or the national regulatory authority pursuant to Directive 2002/58/EC should be involved.

Finally, the handling of cyber incidents and attacks will benefit from contact networks and support from international partners. This may include technical mitigation, criminal investigation, or activation of crisis management response mechanisms.

4. CONCLUSION AND FOLLOW-UP

This proposed cybersecurity strategy of the European Union, put forward by the Commission and the High Representative of the Union for Foreign Affairs and Security Policy, outlines the EU's vision and the actions required, based on strongly protecting and promoting citizens' rights, to make the EU's online environment the safest in the world.[32]

This vision can only be realised through a true partnership, between many actors, to take responsibility and meet the challenges ahead.

The Commission and the High Representative therefore invite the Council and the European Parliament to endorse the strategy and to help deliver the outlined actions. Strong support and commitment is also needed from the private sector and civil society, who are key actors to enhance our level of security and safeguard citizens' rights.

The financing of the Strategy will occur within the foreseen amounts for each of the relevant policy areas (CEF, Horizon 2020, Internal Security Fund, CFSP and External Cooperation, notably the Instrument for Stability) as set out in the Commission's proposal for the Multi-Annual Financial Framework 2014-2020 (subject to the approval of the Budget Authority and the final amounts of the adopted MFF for 2014-2020) . With regard to the need to ensure overall compatibility with the number of posts available to decentralised agencies and the sub-ceiling for decentralised agencies in each expenditure heading in the next MFF, the agencies (CEPOL, EDA ENISA, EUROJUST and EUROPOL/EC3) which are requested by this Communication to take on new tasks will be encouraged to do so in so far as the actual capacity of the agency to absorb growing resources has been established and all possibilities for redeployment have been identified.

The time to act is now. The Commission and the High Representative are determined to work together with all actors to deliver the security needed for Europe. To ensure that the strategy is being implemented promptly and assessed in the face of possible developments, they will gather together all relevant parties in a high-level conference and assess progress in 12 months.

PROPOSAL FOR A COUNCIL FRAMEWORK DECISION ON ATTACKS AGAINST INFORMATION SYSTEMS[4]

Proposal for a COUNCIL FRAMEWORK DECISION on attacks against information systems
(presented by the Commission)
EXPLANATORY MEMORANDUM

1. INTRODUCTION

Electronic communication networks and information systems are now an essential part of the daily lives of EU citizens and are fundamental to the success of the EU economy. Networks and information systems are converging and becoming increasingly interconnected. Despite the many and obvious benefits of this development, it has also brought with it the worrying threat of intentional attacks against information systems. These attacks can take a wide variety of forms including illegal access, spread of malicious code and denial of service attacks. It is possible to launch an attack from anywhere in the world, to anywhere in the world, at any time. New, unexpected forms of attacks could occur in the future.

Attacks against information systems constitute a threat to the achievement of a safer Information Society and an Area of Freedom, Security and Justice, and therefore require a response at the level of the European Union. Part of the Commission's contribution to this response is this proposal for a Framework Decision on approximation of criminal law in the area of attacks against information systems.

1.1. TYPES OF ATTACKS AGAINST INFORMATION SYSTEMS

The phrase "information system" is deliberately used here in its broadest sense in recognition of the convergence between electronic communication networks and the various systems they connect. For the purpose of this proposal, information systems therefore include "stand-alone" personal computers, personal digital organisers, mobile telephones, intranets, extranets and, of course, the networks, servers and other infrastructure of the Internet.

In its Communication "Network and Information security - A European Policy Approach" , the Commission has proposed the following description of threats against computer systems:

Communication from the Commission to the Council, the European Parliament, the European Economic and Social Committee and the Committee of the Regions "Network and Information Security: Proposal for a European Policy Approach" of 6.6.2001. COM (2001) 298 final.

(a) Unauthorised access to information systems. This includes the notion of "hacking". Hacking is gaining unauthorised access to a computer or network of computers. It can be undertaken in a variety of ways from simply exploiting inside information to brute force attacks and password interception. It is often - though not always - with malicious intent to either copy, modify or destroy data. Intentional corruption of web-sites or access to services protected by conditional access without payment can be one of the aims of unauthorised access.

(b) Disruption of information systems. Different ways exist to disrupt information systems through malicious attacks. One of the best known ways to deny or degrade the services offered by the Internet is a "denial of service" attack (DoS) . In a way this attack is similar to fax machines being flooded with long and repeated messages. Denial of service attacks attempt to overload web servers or Internet Service Providers (ISPs) with automatically generated messages. Other types

[4] **COM/2002/0173 final - CNS 2002/0086 */** *Official Journal 203 E , 27/08/2002 P. 0109 - 0113*

For additional analytical, business and investment opportunities information, please contact Global Investment & Business Center, USA at (703) 370-8082. Fax: (703) 370-8083. E-mail: ibpusa3@gmail.com Global Business and Investment Info Databank - www.ibpus.com

of attacks can include disrupting servers operating the domain name system (DNS) and attacks directed at "routers". Attacks aimed at disrupting systems have been damaging for certain high profile web-sites like portals. Some studies have calculated that a recent attack caused damage worth several hundred million Euros, in addition to the intangible damage to reputation. Increasingly, companies rely on the availability of their web-sites for their business and those companies which depend on it for "just in time" supply are particularly vulnerable.

(c) Execution of malicious software that modifies or destroys data. The most well known type of malicious software is the virus. Infamous examples include the "I Love You", "Melissa" and "Kournikova" viruses. About 11 % of European users have caught a virus on their home personal computer (PC) . There are other types of malicious software. Some damage the PC itself, whereas others use the PC to attack other networked components. Some programs (often called 'logic bombs') can lie dormant until triggered by some event such as a specific date, at which point they can cause major damage by altering or deleting data. Other programs appear to be benign, but when opened release a malicious attack (often called 'Trojan Horses') . Another variant is a program (often called a worm) that does not infect other programs as a virus, but instead creates copies of itself, which in turn create even more copies and eventually swamp the system.

(d) Interception of communications. Malicious interception of communications compromises the confidentiality and integrity requirements of users. It is often called "sniffing".

(e) Malicious misrepresentation. Information systems offer new opportunities for misrepresentation and fraud. The taking of someone else's identity on the Internet, and using this for malicious purposes, is often called "spoofing".

1.2. THE NATURE OF THE THREAT

There is a clear need to gather reliable information on the scale and nature of attacks against information systems.

Some of the most serious incidents of attacks against information systems are directed against electronic communications network operators and service providers or against electronic commerce companies. More traditional areas can also be severely affected given the ever-increasing amount of inter-connectivity in the modern communications environment: manufacturing industries; service industries; hospitals; other public sector organisations and governments themselves. But victims of attacks are not only organisations; there can be very direct, serious and damaging effects on individuals as well. The economic burden imposed by certain of these attacks on public bodies, companies and individuals alike is considerable and threatens to make information systems more costly and less affordable to users.

The type of attacks described above are often carried out by individuals acting on their own, sometimes by minors who perhaps do not fully appreciate the seriousness of their actions. However, the level of sophistication and ambition of the attack could grow. There is growing and worrying concern of organised criminals using communication networks to launch attacks against information systems for their own purposes. Organised hacking groups specialised in hacking and defacement of web-sites are more and more active at world-wide level. Examples include the Brazilian Silver Lords and the Pakistan Gforce, which try to extort money from their victims by offering them specialised assistance after hacking into their information systems. The arrest of large groups of hackers suggest that hacking could increasingly be an organised crime phenomenon. There have recently been sophisticated, organised attacks against intellectual property as well as attempts to steal substantial funds from banking services .

For additional analytical, business and investment opportunities information,
please contact Global Investment & Business Center, USA
at (703) 370-8082. Fax: (703) 370-8083. E-mail: ibpusa3@gmail.com
Global Business and Investment Info Databank - www.ibpus.com

According to a survey published by the Communications Management Association (CMA) , there have been hacking attacks against a third of UK's big companies and public sector organisations, including government offices, causing damage ranging from infiltrating corporate bank accounts to information theft. See the survey at http:/www.cma.org.

Security breaches at e-commerce merchant databases where access is gained to customers' information, including credit card numbers, are also a cause for concern. These attacks result in increased opportunities for payment fraud and in any case force the banking industry to cancel and re-issue thousands of cards. A further consequence is the intangible damage to the merchant's reputation and to consumer confidence in e-commerce. Preventive measures, such as minimum security requirements for online merchants accepting payment cards, are being discussed under the Action Plan to prevent fraud and counterfeiting of non-cash payments .

Communication from the Commission "Preventing fraud and counterfeiting of non-cash means of payment", COM (2001) 11 final. Adopted by the Commission on 9.2.2001.

This proposal also forms part of the Commission's contribution to the response to the threat of a terrorist attack against vital information systems within the European Union. It supplements the Commission's proposals to replace extradition within the European Union with a European Arrest Warrant and to approximate laws on terrorism , on which political agreement was reached at the Laeken European Council on 14/15 December 2001. . Taken together, these instruments will ensure that Member States of the European Union have effective criminal laws in place to tackle cyber-terrorism, and will enhance international co-operation against terrorism.

Proposal for a Council Framework Decision on the European arrest warrant and the surrender procedures between the Member States. COM(2001) 522 final. Adopted by the Commission on 19.9.2001.

Proposal for a Council Framework Decision on combating terrorism. COM(2001) 521 final. Adopted by the Commission on 19.9.2001

This proposal does not relate only to acts directed at Member States. It also applies to conduct on the territory of the European Union which is directed against information systems on the territory of third countries. This reflects the Commission's commitment to tackle attacks against information systems at a global as well as European Union level.

In fact, there have already been several recent occasions where tensions in international relations have led to a spate of attacks against information systems, often involving attacks against web-sites. More serious attacks could not only lead to serious financial damage but, in some cases, could even lead to loss of life (e.g. hospital systems, air traffic control systems etc) . The importance attached to it by Member States is demonstrated in the priority attached to various Critical Infrastructure Protection initiatives. For example, the EU Information Society Technologies (IST) Programme has established, in collaboration with the US Department of State, a Joint EU/US Task Force on Critical Infrastructure Protection.

The IST Programme is managed by the European Commission. It is part of the 5th Framework Programme, which runs from 1998 to 2002. More information is available at http://www.cordis.lu/ist.

Under the auspices of the Joint Consultative Group of the EC/US Science and Technology Co-operation Agreement.

1.3. THE NEED FOR ACCURATE INFORMATION AND STATISTICS

There are few reliable statistics available on the full scale of the computer-related crime phenomenon. The number of intrusions detected and reported up to now probably under-represent the scope of the problem. According to a US survey , in 1999 only 32% of respondents who have suffered a computer intrusion in the previous year reported it to law enforcement. And this was an improvement on previous years when only 17% had reported. Numerous reasons have been given for non-reporting. Because of limited awareness and experience of system administrators and users, many intrusions are not detected. In addition, many companies are not willing to report cases of computer abuse, to avoid bad publicity and exposure to future attacks. Many police forces do not yet keep statistics on the use of computers and communication systems involved in these and other crimes . Law enforcement authorities lack adequate training to detect, identify and investigate computer related offences. However, the European Union has started to address this issue by collecting some figures on attacks against information systems. In one Member State, it was estimated that there were between 30 000 and 40 000 attacks in 1999 on information systems, whereas no more than 105 official complaints were recorded in this field. Indeed, in 1999, seven Member States recorded a total of only 1844 official reports of crimes against information systems and computer data. Nevertheless, this is twice the figure reported in 1998, when only 972 cases were officially recorded in the seven Member States .

The Computer Security Institute (CSI) and the Federal Bureau of Investigation (FBI) produce an annual "Computer Crime and Security Survey" published early in each year. CSI's website and further details about the survey may be found at www. gocsi.com

The Italian Ministry of Interior recently published statistics on its operational activities against computer-related crime in 1999 and 2000 (see at http://www.mininterno.it/dip_ps/dcpsffp/index.htm) . Official reports of hacking cases in 2000 are 98, four times the figure reported in 1999, when only 21 cases were officially recorded.

Council doc. 8123/01 ENFOPOL 38. Available from the Council website http://db.consilium.eu.int/jai

In addition, a recent survey reported that 13 per cent of companies that had been victim to economic crime stated one of the crimes was cybercrime. The survey also reported increasing concern about cybercrime, with 43 per cent of respondents believing cybercrime would be a future risk. Another study concluded that hackers and viruses now pose the main cybercrime threat to organisations, with the main perpetrators being hackers (45 per cent) , former employees (13 per cent) , organised crime (13 per cent) and current employees (11 per cent) . Such figures can be expected to continue to grow as the use of information systems and interconnectivity increases, and the willingness to report attacks improves. But it is clear that urgent measures are needed to produce a statistical tool for use by all Member States so that computer-related crime within the European Union can be measured both quantitatively and qualitatively. The starting point for such an analysis is a common definition at the level of the European Union of the offences involved in attacks against information systems.

European Economic Crime Survey 2001, PricewaterhouseCoopers 2001 (http://www.pwcglobal.com)

The Cybercrime Survey 2001, Confederation of British Industry (see http://www.cbi.org.uk)

1.4. EUROPEAN UNION POLICY BACKGROUND

For additional analytical, business and investment opportunities information, please contact Global Investment & Business Center, USA at (703) 370-8082. Fax: (703) 370-8083. E-mail: ibpusa3@gmail.com Global Business and Investment Info Databank - www.ibpus.com

Against this background, at the Lisbon European Council of March 2000, the European Council stressed the importance of the transition to a competitive, dynamic and knowledge-based economy, and invited the Council and the Commission to draw up an eEurope Action plan to make the most of this opportunity. This Action Plan, prepared by the Commission and the Council, adopted by the Feira Summit of the European Council in June 2000, includes actions to enhance network security and the establishment of a co-ordinated and coherent approach to cybercrime by the end of 2002.

Presidency Conclusions of the Lisbon European Council of 23 and 24 March 2000, available at

As part of the Commission's contribution to this mandate on cybercrime, the Commission published a Communication entitled "Creating a Safer Information Society by Improving the Security of Information Infrastructures and Combating Computer-related Crime" This proposed a balanced approach to tackling the problems of cybercrime, by taking full account of the views of all the interested parties including law enforcement agencies, service providers, network operators, other industry groups, consumer groups, data protection authorities and privacy groups. The Communication proposed a number of legislative and non-legislative initiatives.

An important example of an ongoing action is within the IDA Programme, where Member States and the Commission are already working on a common security policy and implementing a secure network for exchange of administrative information.

One of the key issues addressed by the Communication was the need for effective action to deal with threats to the authenticity, integrity, confidentiality and availability of information systems and networks. Much has already been achieved in the field of Community law. There are already several legal measures in place at Community level with specific implications for network and information security.

This Framework Decision supplements what has already been achieved in the field of Community law to protect information systems, such as under Directives 95/46/EC, Directive 97/66/EC and Directive 98/84/EC on the legal protection of services based on, or consisting of, conditional access. In particular, the European telecommunication and data protection framework (Directives 95/46/EC and 97/66/EC) contains provisions to ensure that providers of publicly available telecommunications services must take appropriate technical and organisational measures to safeguard the security and confidentiality of their services, and that these measures must ensure a level of security appropriate to the risk presented.

One of the most important and effective ways to address these problems is through prevention and education. The Communication underlined the importance of the availability, development, deployment and effective use of preventive technologies. It highlighted that there was a need to raise public awareness on the risks posed by computer-related crime, promote best practices for IT security, develop effective tools and procedures to combat computer-related crime as well as encourage further development of early warning and crisis management mechanisms. The EU Information Society Technologies (IST) Programme provides a framework to develop capability and technologies to understand and tackle emerging challenges related to computer crime.

The IST Programme is managed by the European Commission. It is part of the 5th Framework Programme, which runs from 1998 to 2002. More information is available at http://www.cordis.lu/ist.

More recently, the Stockholm European Council on 23-24 March recognised the need for further action in the area of network and information security and concluded "the Council together with the Commission will develop a comprehensive strategy on security of electronic networks including practical implementing action. This should be presented in time for the Göteborg

For additional analytical, business and investment opportunities information, please contact Global Investment & Business Center, USA at (703) 370-8082. Fax: (703) 370-8083. E-mail: ibpusa3@gmail.com
Global Business and Investment Info Databank - www.ibpus.com

European Council." The Commission responded to this call with its Communication on "Network and Information Security: A European Policy approach" [17] . This analysed the current problems in network security, and provided a strategic outline for action in this area. It was followed by a Council Resolution of 6 December 2001 on a common approach and specific actions in the area of network and information security. These initiatives are not in themselves sufficient to provide all the necessary responses to serious attacks against information systems. Both Commission Communications also recognised that there was an urgent need for approximation of substantive criminal law within the European Union in the area of attacks against information systems. This reflected the conclusions of the Tampere Summit of the European Council in October 1999 [18] which include high-tech crime in a limited list of areas where efforts should be made to agree on common definitions, incriminations and sanctions, and was included in Recommendation 7 of the European Union strategy for the new Millennium on the prevention and control of organised crime adopted by the JHA Council in March 2000. [19] This proposal for a Framework Decision is also part of the Commission Work Programme for the Year 2001 [20] and the Scoreboard for the establishment of an area of Freedom, Security and Justice, produced by the Commission on 30 October 2001 [21].

1.5. The need for approximation of criminal law

Member States' laws in this area contain some significant gaps and differences which could hamper the fight against organised crime and terrorism, as well as serious attacks against information systems by individuals. Approximation of substantive law in the area of high tech crime will ensure that national legislation is sufficiently comprehensive so that all forms of serious attacks against information systems can be investigated using the techniques and methods available under the criminal law. Perpetrators of these offences need to be identified, brought to justice, and the courts need to have appropriate and proportionate penalties at their disposal. This will send a strong deterrent message to those contemplating attacks against information systems.

In addition, these gaps and differences could act as a barrier to effective police and judicial co-operation in the area of attacks against information systems. Attacks against information systems could often be trans-national in nature, and would require international police and judicial co-operation. Approximation of laws will therefore improve this co-operation by ensuring that the dual criminality requirement is fulfilled (in which an activity must be an offence in both countries before mutual legal assistance can usually be provided to assist a criminal investigation) . This will benefit EU Member States in co-operation between themselves, as well as improving co-operation between EU Member States and third countries (provided that an appropriate mutual legal assistance agreement exists) .

There is also a need to supplement existing instruments at European Union level. The Framework Decision on the European Arrest Warrant [22], the Annex to the Europol Convention [23] and the Council Decision setting up Eurojust [24] contain references to computer-related crime which need to be defined more precisely. For the purposes of such instruments, computer-related crime should be understood as including attacks against information systems as defined in this Framework Decision, which will provide a much greater level of approximation of the constituent elements of such offences. This Framework Decision also complements the Framework Decision on combating terrorism [25] which covers terrorist actions causing extensive destruction of an infrastructure facility, including an information system, likely to endanger human life or result in major economic loss.

1.6. Scope and purpose of the proposed Framework Decision

The objectives of this Council Framework Decision are therefore to approximate criminal law in the area of attacks against information systems and to ensure the greatest possible police and judicial co-operation in the area of criminal offences related to attacks against information

For additional analytical, business and investment opportunities information, please contact Global Investment & Business Center, USA at (703) 370-8082. Fax: (703) 370-8083. E-mail: ibpusa3@gmail.com Global Business and Investment Info Databank - www.ibpus.com

systems. Moreover, this proposal contributes to the efforts of the European Union in the fight against organised crime and terrorism. It is not intended to require Member States to criminalise minor or trivial conduct.

It is clear from Article 47 of the Treaty on European Union that this Framework Decision is without prejudice to Community law. In particular, it does not affect privacy or data protection rights and obligations provided for under Community law such as in Directives 95/46 and 97/66. It is not intended to require Member States to criminalise breaches of rules on access to / disclosure of personal data, secrecy of communications, security of processing of personal data, electronic signatures [26] or intellectual property violations and it does not prejudice the Directive 98/84/EC on the legal protection of services based on, or consisting of, conditional access [27]. These are important issues, but they are already covered by existing Community legislation. Any approximation of criminal law in these areas to meet Community law objectives, such as the protection of personal data, the remuneration of service providers using conditional access or intellectual property, therefore needs to be considered using the framework of Community law rather than Title VI of the TEU. For these reasons, this Framework Decision limits itself to addressing the conduct described in points (a) -(c) in section 1.1.

Legislative action at the level of the European Union also needs to take into account developments in other international fora. In the context of approximation of substantive criminal law on attacks against information systems, the Council of Europe (C.o.E.) is currently the most far-advanced. The Council of Europe started preparing an international Convention on cyber-crime in February 1997, and the Convention was formally adopted and opened for signature in November 2001. [28] The Convention seeks to approximate a range of criminal offences including offences against the confidentiality, integrity and availability of computer systems and data. This Framework Decision is intended to be consistent with the approach adopted in the Council of Europe Convention for these offences.

[28] The text is available on the web, in two languages, in French : http://conventions.coe.int/treaty/fr/projets/cybercrime.htm.

In G8 discussions on high tech crime, two major categories of threats have been identified. First, threats to computer infrastructures, which concern operations to disrupt, deny, degrade or destroy information resident in computers and computer networks, or the computer and networks themselves. Secondly, computer-assisted threats, which concern malicious activities, such as fraud, money laundering, child pornography, infringement to intellectual property rights and drug trafficking, which are facilitated by the use of a computer. This proposal deals with the first category of threats.

Approximation at the level of the EU should take into account developments in international fora and should be consistent with current Community policies. This proposal also seeks to provide greater approximation within the EU than has been possible in other international fora.

2. LEGAL BASIS

The objective of the establishment of an area of freedom, security and justice must be achieved by preventing and combating crime, organised or otherwise, including terrorism, through closer co-operation between law enforcement and judicial authorities in the Member States and approximation of rules in criminal matters of the Member States. This proposal for a Framework Decision is therefore aimed at approximating laws and regulations of the Member States in the area of police and judicial co-operation in criminal matters. It concerns "minimum rules relating to the constituent elements of criminal acts", in particular, to a substantial degree, in the fields of organised crime and terrorism. It also involves "ensuring compatibility in rules applicable in the

Member States" in order to facilitate and accelerate co-operation between judicial authorities. The legal basis indicated in the preamble of the proposal is therefore Articles 29, 30(a) , 31 and 34(2) (b) of the Treaty on European Union. The proposal will not entail financial implications for the budget of the European Communities.

3. THE FRAMEWORK DECISION: ARTICLES

Article 1 - Scope and purpose of the Framework Decision

This Article explicitly states that the objectives of this Framework Decision are to approximate criminal law in the area of serious attacks against information systems, in particular to contribute to the fight against organised crime and terrorism, and by doing so to ensure the greatest possible judicial co-operation in the area of criminal offences related to attacks against information systems. In accordance with Article 47 of the Treaty on European Union, this Framework Decision is also without prejudice to Community law. In particular this includes privacy or data protection rights and obligations provided for under the Directives 95/46 and 97/66. It is not intended to require Member States to criminalise breaches of rules on access to / disclosure of personal data, secrecy of communications, security of processing of personal data, electronic signatures [29] or intellectual property violations and it does not prejudice the Directive 98/84/EC on the legal protection of services based on, or consisting of, conditional access [30].

This Framework Decision is not intended to require Member States to criminalise minor or trivial conduct. Articles 3 and 4 define the criteria which need to be met in order for the action to be criminalised These criteria are consistent with the derogation and reservation possibilities in the draft Council of Europe Cybercrime Convention.

All the criminal offences covered in the framework decision need to be committed with intent. The term "intentional" is used explicitly in Articles 3, 4 and 5. This should be interpreted in accordance with the normal criminal law principles in Member States governing intent. Thus, this Framework Decision does not require criminalisation of actions where there is gross negligence or other recklessness, but no intent as such. An intent to unlawfully access or interfere with information systems in general should also be sufficient, rather than it being necessary to prove that the intent was directed at a specific information system.

Article 2 - Definitions

The proposed Council Framework Decision contains the following definitions:

(a) "Electronic communications network". This definition is the same as that adopted by the Council and European Parliament on 14 February 2002 in the Directive on a common regulatory framework for electronic communications networks and services

(b) "Computer". This definition is based on Article 1 of the draft Council of Europe Convention on Cybercrime. The definition also includes for example "stand-alone" personal computers, personal digital organisers, digital set-top boxes, personal video recorders and mobile telephones (provided they have some data processing functions, e.g. WAP and third generation) , which would not be covered solely by the definition of electronic communication networks.

(c) "Computer data". This definition is built upon the ISO [32] definition of data. It is not intended to include physical items such as books. However, it does include a book stored in the form of computer data (e.g. saved in electronic form as a word processing file) or turned into computer data by means of scanning. For this reason, the definition makes clear that computer data needs

For additional analytical, business and investment opportunities information, please contact Global Investment & Business Center, USA at (703) 370-8082. Fax: (703) 370-8083. E-mail: ibpusa3@gmail.com Global Business and Investment Info Databank - www.ibpus.com

to have been "created or put into a form" suitable for processing in an information system or suitable for causing a function of an information system.

(d) "Information System". The definition of information systems is originally drawn from that adopted by the OECD in 1992 in its Guidelines for the Security of Information Systems and the previous definitions by referring to electronic communications networks, computers and computer data. The term has also been used in previous community law instruments, such as the Council Decision of 31 March 1992 "in the field of security of information systems" and the Council Recommendation of 7 April 1995 "on common information technology security evaluation criteria". It is intended to be technology neutral, and to reflect accurately the concept of interconnected networks and systems containing data. It covers both the hardware and the software of the system, though not the content of the information itself. It also covers stand-alone systems. In the Commission's view, it is desirable to extend the protection afforded by the criminal law to stand-alone computers as well and not to limit it only to systems that are inter-connected.

(e) "Legal person". This is a standard definition from previous Council Framework Decisions.

(f) "Authorised person". This means any person who has the right, by contract or by law, or the lawful permission, to use, manage, control, test, conduct legitimate scientific research or otherwise operate an information system and who is acting in accordance with that right or permission. This includes persons acting in accordance with the lawful consent of someone given such an explicit authorisation. It is particularly important that the following categories of persons and legitimate activities (within the limits of the person's rights, permissions and responsibilities, and in accordance with Community laws on data protection and secrecy of communications) should not be criminalised when this Framework Decision is transposed into domestic law:

- actions of ordinary users, whether private or business users, including their use of encryption to protect their own communications and data;

- reverse engineering, within the limits provided by Directive 91/250 of 14 May 1991 "on the legal protection of computer programs" [33]

- actions of managers, controllers and operators of networks and systems;

- actions of authorised persons testing a system, whether within the company or person appointed externally and given permission to test the security of a system;

- legitimate scientific research.

(g) "Without right". This is a broad notion, and leaves some flexibility to Member States to decide the precise scope of the offence. Nevertheless, to assist in the implementation of the Council Framework Decision in domestic laws, the Commission believes that it is necessary to indicate that certain activities should not fall within the scope of the offence. It is not possible, and probably not desirable, to draw up a comprehensive, exclusive list of exemptions at the level of the European Union. But the phrase "without right" builds on the previous definitions so as to exclude conduct by authorised persons. It also excludes any other conduct recognised as lawful under domestic law, including standard legal defences and other types of authority recognised in domestic law.

ARTICLE 3 - ATTACK THROUGH ILLEGAL ACCESS TO INFORMATION SYSTEMS

This offence is intended to cover the offence of illegal access to information systems. This includes the notion of "hacking" an information system. Member States are free to exclude minor or trivial cases from the scope of the offence when transposing the Framework Decision into domestic law.

The offence is required to be established in Member States' laws only to the extent that the offence is committed:

(i) against any part of an information system which is subject to specific protection measures; or

(ii) with the intent to cause damage to a natural or legal person; or

(iii) with the intent to result in an economic benefit.

The Commission does not wish to undermine in any way the importance it attached to the use of effective technical measures to protect information systems. Nevertheless, it is an unfortunate fact that a high proportion of users leave themselves exposed to attacks by not having adequate (or even any) technical protection. To deter attacks against these users, it is necessary that criminal law covers unauthorised access to their systems even though there may not be adequate technical protection for their systems. For this reason, and provided that there is either an intent to cause damage or an intent to result in an economic benefit, there is no requirement that security measures must have been overcome for the offence to have been committed.

ARTICLE 4 - ILLEGAL INTERFERENCE WITH INFORMATION SYSTEMS

This offence covers the intentional conduct, without right, of one of the following actions:

(a) the serious hindering or interruption, without right, of the functioning of an information system by inputting, transmitting, damaging, deleting, deteriorating, altering or suppressing computer data computer data. The elements of inputting or transmitting computer data specifically address the problem of so-called "denial of service attacks" where there is a deliberate attempt to overwhelm an information system. The offence also covers the "interruption" of the functioning of an information system, which could be inferred from the phrase "hindering" but is included here explicitly for the sake of clarity. The other elements in the offence (damaging, deleting, deteriorating, altering or suppressing computer data) specifically address the problem of viruses, and other types of attacks, which are directed at hindering or interrupting the functions of the information system itself.

(b) the deletion, deterioration, alteration, suppression or rendering inaccessible of computer data on an information system where it is committed with the intention to cause damage to a natural or legal person. This covers virus attacks aimed at the content (or computer data) on the information system, as well as corruption of web-sites.

Subparagraph (a) uses the word "serious hindering or interruption" as a constituent element of the offence in order to describe the effects of such an attack. The meaning of the word "serious hindering" is not defined, as hindering could take different forms and its level could vary depending upon the type of the attack and the technical capacities of the information system being attacked. Each Member State shall determine for itself what criteria must be fulfilled in order for an information system to be considered as "seriously hindered". However, minor nuisances or disruptions in the functioning of the services should not be considered as fulfilling the threshold of seriousness.

As above, Member States are free to exclude minor or trivial cases from the scope of the offence when transposing the Framework Decision into domestic law.

For additional analytical, business and investment opportunities information, please contact Global Investment & Business Center, USA at (703) 370-8082. Fax: (703) 370-8083. E-mail: ibpusa3@gmail.com Global Business and Investment Info Databank - www.ibpus.com

Article 5 - Instigation, aiding, abetting and attempt

Article 5(1) puts an obligation on Member States to ensure that the intentional instigation of, aiding or abetting offences against information systems as described in Articles 3 and 4 are punishable.

Article 5(2) specifically concerns attempt. It puts an obligation on Member States to ensure that attempt to commit any of the offences against information systems described in Articles 3 and 4 is punishable.

Article 6 - Penalties

Paragraph 1 requires Member States to take the necessary measures to ensure that the offences defined in Articles 3-5 are punishable by effective, proportionate and dissuasive penalties [34]. By virtue of this paragraph, Member States are required to lay down penalties commensurate with the gravity of the offence, which includes custodial sentences with a maximum term of imprisonment of no less than one year in serious cases. Serious cases shall be understood as excluding cases where the conduct resulted in no damage or economic benefit.

[34] The phrase is taken from the Judgment given by the Court of Justice on 21 September 1989 in Case 68/88 [1989] ECR 2965.

The maximum penalty of at least one year imprisonment in serious cases brings these offences within the scope of the European Arrest Warrant as well as other instruments such as the Council Framework Decision of 26 June 2001 [35] on money laundering, the identification, tracing, freezing, seizing and confiscation of the instrumentalities and the proceeds from crime.

[35] OJ L 182, 5.7.2001, p.1

In keeping with the nature of all framework decisions, which are binding on the Member States as regards the result to be achieved, but leave the choice of form and means to their discretion, the Member States retain some degree of flexibility to adapt their legislation to these rules and to determine the severity of the penalties that apply, within the limits imposed by the Framework Decision, particularly the aggravating circumstances in Article 7. The Commission would stress that it is for the Member States to decide the criteria for determining the gravity of an offence, on the basis of their respective legal systems.

Punishment need not always take the form of imprisonment. Paragraph 2 provides the possibility for Member States to impose fines in addition to or as an alternative to custodial sentences, in line with their respective traditions and legal systems.

Article 7 - Aggravating circumstances

This Article provides for Member States to increase the penalties defined in Article 6 under certain circumstances. The Commission would stress that the list of aggravating circumstances provided in this Article is without prejudice to any other circumstances regarded as aggravating in Member States' legislation. This list takes into account the aggravating circumstances described in the national provisions in Member States and as laid down in previous Commission proposals for Framework Decisions.

If one of the following conditions listed in paragraph 1 is fulfilled then the maximum term of imprisonment may not be less than four years:

For additional analytical, business and investment opportunities information, please contact Global Investment & Business Center, USA at (703) 370-8082. Fax: (703) 370-8083. E-mail: ibpusa3@gmail.com Global Business and Investment Info Databank - www.ibpus.com

(a) the offence has been committed within the framework of a criminal organisation as defined by Joint Action 98/733 JHA, apart from the penalty level referred to therein;

(b) the offence caused, or resulted in, substantial direct or indirect economic loss, physical harm to a natural person or substantial damage to part of the critical infrastructure of the Member State; or

(c) the offence resulted in substantial proceeds.

Member States are also required to ensure that the offences referred to in Articles 3, 4 and 5 are punishable by custodial sentences greater than those foreseen under Article 6, when the offender has been convicted of such an offence by a final judgement in a Member State.

Article 8 - Particular circumstances

This article provides for circumstances in which a Member State may decide to reduce the penalties referred to in Articles 6 and 7 where, in the opinion of the competent judicial authority, the offender caused only minor damage.

Article 9 - Liability of legal persons

In line with the approach taken in a number of legal instruments adopted at EU level to combat different types of criminality, it is necessary also to cover the situation in which legal persons are involved in attacks against information systems. Article 9 therefore contains provisions for holding a legal person liable for the offences envisaged by Articles 3, 4 and 5, committed for their benefit by any person with certain leading positions, acting either individually or as a part of the organ of the legal person. The term liability should be construed so as to include either criminal or civil liability.

In addition, according to standard practice, paragraph 2 provides that a legal person can also be held liable when the lack of supervision or control by a person in a position to exercise control, has rendered possible the commission of the offences for its benefit. Paragraph 3 indicates that legal proceedings against a legal person do not preclude parallel legal proceedings against a natural person.

Article 10 - Sanctions on legal persons

Article 10 sets out a requirement for sanctions for legal persons held liable for the offences referred to in Articles 3, 4 and 5. It requires effective, proportionate and dissuasive sanctions, where the minimum obligation is to impose criminal or non-criminal fines. Other sanctions that could typically apply to legal persons are also indicated.

Article 11 - Jurisdiction

The international nature of offences involving attacks against information systems means that an effective legal response requires procedural provisions on jurisdiction and extradition which should be clear and far-reaching at the European Union level, to ensure that offenders cannot escape prosecution.

Paragraph 1 sets out a series of criteria for conferring jurisdiction on national judicial authorities to prosecute and investigate cases involving the offences referred to in this framework decision. A Member State will establish its jurisdiction in three situations:

(a) where the offence is committed in whole or in part on its territory, irrespective of the status of the legal person or the nationality of the natural person involved (territoriality principle) ;

(b) where the offender is a national of that Member State (active personality principle) and the act affects individuals or groups of that State. Member States that make no provision for extradition are responsible for prosecuting their own nationals who have committed offences abroad;

(c) where the offence is committed for the benefit of a legal person established in the territory of that Member State.

Paragraph 2 is intended to ensure that when establishing its jurisdiction over the offences based on the territoriality principle in paragraph 1(a) , each Member State ensures that its jurisdiction includes cases where:

(a) the offender commits the offence when physically present on its territory, whether or not the offence is against an information system on its territory. For example, a person obtaining illegal access to (hacking) an information system in a third country from the territory of the Member State; or

(b) the offence is against an information system on its territory, whether or not the offender commits the offence when physically present on its territory. For example, a person obtaining illegal access to (hacking) an information system on the territory of the Member State from the territory of a third country.

Given that not all Member States' legal traditions recognise extraterritorial jurisdiction for all types of criminal offence, paragraph 3 allows them not to apply the rules on jurisdiction set out in paragraph 1 as regards the situations covered by paragraph 1(b) and (c) .

Paragraph 4 requires each Member State to take the necessary measures also to establish its jurisdiction over the offences referred to in Articles 3 to 5 in cases where it refuses to hand over or extradite a person suspected or convicted of such an offence to another Member State or to a third country.

Paragraph 5 covers multi-jurisdictional cases, and aims to ensure full co-operation between the Member States in order to centralise, if possible, proceedings in a single Member State. To this end, it is recalled that Member States may have recourse to any body or mechanism established within the European Union in order to facilitate co-operation between their judicial authorities and the co-ordination of their action. This would include Eurojust and the European Judicial Network.

Paragraph 6 states that the Member States shall inform the General Secretariat of the Council and the Commission where they decide to apply paragraph 3.

Article 12 - Exchange of Information

The purpose of Article 12 is to facilitate the exchange of information by ensuring that there are operational points of contact. This is important for effective police co-operation. In particular, the need for all Member States to join the G8 network of points of contact was recognised by the Justice and Home Affairs Council on 19 March 1998 and more recently when it adopted a Council Recommendation on contact points maintaining a 24-hour service for combating high-tech crime [36].

[36] OJ C 187, 3.7.2001, p. 5

For additional analytical, business and investment opportunities information, please contact Global Investment & Business Center, USA at (703) 370-8082. Fax: (703) 370-8083. E-mail: ibpusa3@gmail.com Global Business and Investment Info Databank - www.ibpus.com

Article 13 - Implementation

Article 13 concerns the implementation and follow-up of this Framework Decision. Member States are required to take the necessary measures to comply with this Framework Decision not later than 31 December 2003.

Member States shall transmit by that date to the General Secretariat of the Council and to the Commission the provisions transposing the obligations imposed on them under this Framework Decision into national law. The Council shall assess within one year, on the basis of that information and a Commission's written report, the extent to which Member States have complied with the obligations imposed by the Framework Decision.

Article 14 - Entry into force

Article 14 states that the Framework Decision will enter into force on the twentieth day following that of its publication in the Official Journal of the European Communities.

2002/0086 (CNS)

Proposal for a COUNCIL FRAMEWORK DECISION on attacks against information systems

THE COUNCIL OF THE EUROPEAN UNION,

Having regard to the Treaty on European Union, and in particular Articles 29, 30(1) (a) , 31 and 34(2) (b) thereof,

Having regard to the proposal of the Commission [37],

[37] OJ C . . p .

Having regard to the opinion of the European Parliament [38],

[38] OJ C . . p

Whereas:

(1) There is evidence of attacks against information systems, in particular as a result of the threat from organised crime, and increasing concern at the potential of terrorist attacks against information systems which form part of the critical infrastructure of the Member States. This constitutes a threat to the achievement of a safer Information Society and an Area of Freedom, Security and Justice, and therefore requires a response at the level of the European Union.

(2) An effective response to those threats requires a comprehensive approach to network and information security, as underlined in the eEurope Action Plan, in the Communication by the Commission "Network and Information Security: Proposal for a European Policy Approach" [39] and in the Council Resolution of 6 December 2001 on a common approach and specific actions in the area of network and information security.

[39] COM (2001) 298

For additional analytical, business and investment opportunities information, please contact Global Investment & Business Center, USA at (703) 370-8082. Fax: (703) 370-8083. E-mail: ibpusa3@gmail.com Global Business and Investment Info Databank - www.ibpus.com

(3) The need to further increase awareness of the problems related to information security and provide practical assistance has also been stressed in the European Parliament Resolution of 5th September 2001 [40].

[40] [2001/2098(INI)]

(4) Significant gaps and differences in Member States' laws in this area hamper the fight against organised crime and terrorism, and act as a barrier to effective police and judicial co-operation in the area of attacks against information systems. The trans-national and borderless character of modern electronic communication networks means that attacks against information systems are often international in nature, thus underlining the urgent need for further action to approximate criminal laws in this area.

(5) The Action Plan of the Council and the Commission on how to best implement the provisions of the Treaty of Amsterdam on an area of freedom, security and justice [41], the Tampere European Council on 15-16 October 1999, the Santa Maria da Feira European Council on 19-20 June 2000, the Commission in the Scoreboard [42] and the European Parliament in its Resolution of 19 May 2000 [43] indicate or call for legislative action against high technology crime, including common definitions, incriminations and sanctions.

[41] OJ C 19, 23.1.1999

[42] COM (2001) 278 final

[43] A5-0127/2000

(6) It is necessary to complement the work performed by international organisations, in particular the Council of Europe's work on approximating criminal law and the G8's work on transnational co-operation in the area of high tech crime, by providing a common approach in the European Union in this area. This call was further elaborated by the Communication from the Commission to the Council, the European Parliament, the Economic and Social Committee and the Committee of the Regions on "Creating a Safer Information Society by Improving the Security of Information Infrastructures and Combating Computer-related Crime" [44].

[44] COM (2000) 890

(7) Criminal law in the area of attacks against information systems should be approximated in order to ensure the greatest possible police and judicial co-operation in the area of criminal offences related to attacks against information systems, and to contribute to the fight against organised crime and terrorism.

(8) The Framework Decision on the European Arrest Warrant [45], the Annex to the Europol Convention and the Council Decision setting up Eurojust contain references to computer-related crime which needs to be defined more precisely. For the purposes of such instruments, computer-related crime should be understood as including attacks against information systems as defined in this Framework Decision which provides a much greater level of approximation of the constituent elements of such offences. This Framework Decision also complements the Framework Decision on combating terrorism [46] which covers terrorist actions causing extensive destruction of an infrastructure facility, including an information system, likely to endanger human life or result in major economic loss.

[45] OJ C . . p

[46] OJ C . . p

For additional analytical, business and investment opportunities information, please contact Global Investment & Business Center, USA at (703) 370-8082. Fax: (703) 370-8083. E-mail: ibpusa3@gmail.com Global Business and Investment Info Databank - www.ibpus.com

(9) All Member States have ratified the Council of Europe Convention of 28 January 1981 for the protection of individuals with regard to automatic processing of personal data. The personal data processed in the context of the implementation of this Framework Decision will be protected in accordance with the principles of the said Convention.

(10) Common definitions in this area, particularly of information systems and computer data, are important to ensure a consistent approach in Member States in the application of this Framework Decision.

(11) There is a need to achieve a common approach to the constituent elements of criminal offences by providing for a common offence of illegal access to an information system, and illegal interference with an information system.

(12) There is a need to avoid over-criminalisation, particularly of trivial or minor conduct, as well as the need to avoid criminalising right-holders and authorised persons such as legitimate private or business users, managers, controllers and operators of networks and systems, legitimate scientific researchers, and authorised persons testing a system, whether a person within the company or a person appointed externally and given permission to test the security of a system.

(13) There is a need for Member States to provide penalties for attacks against information systems which are effective, proportionate and dissuasive, including custodial sentences in serious cases;

(14) It is necessary to provide for more severe penalties when certain circumstances accompanying an attack against an information system make it an even greater threat to society. In such cases, sanctions on perpetrators should be sufficient to allow for attacks against information systems to be included within the scope of instruments already adopted for the purpose of combating organised crime such as the 98/733/JHA Joint Action of 21 December 1998 adopted by the Council on the basis of Article K.3 of the Treaty on European Union on making it a criminal offence to participate in a criminal organisation in the Member States of the European Union [47].

[47] OJ L 351, 29.12.1998, p. 1

(15) Measures should be taken to enable legal persons to be held liable for the criminal offences referred to by this act which are committed for their benefit, and to ensure that each Member State has jurisdiction over offences committed against information systems in situations where the offender is physically present on its territory or where the information system is on its territory.

(16) Measures should also be foreseen for the purposes of co-operation between Member States with a view to ensuring effective action against attacks against information systems. Operational contact points should be established for the exchange of information.

(17) Since the objectives of ensuring that attacks against information systems be sanctioned in all Member States by effective, proportionate and dissuasive criminal penalties and improving and encouraging judicial co-operation by removing potential obstacles, cannot be sufficiently achieved by the Member States individually, as rules have to be common and compatible, and can therefore be better achieved at the level of the Union, the Union may adopt measures, in accordance with the principle of subsidiarity as referred to in Article 2 of the EU Treaty and as set out in Article 5 of the EC Treaty. In accordance with the principle of proportionality, as set out in the latter Article, this Framework Decision does not go beyond what is necessary in order to achieve those objectives.

For additional analytical, business and investment opportunities information, please contact Global Investment & Business Center, USA at (703) 370-8082. Fax: (703) 370-8083. E-mail: ibpusa3@gmail.com Global Business and Investment Info Databank - www.ibpus.com

(18) This Framework Decision is without prejudice to the powers of the European Community.

(19) This Framework Decision respects the fundamental rights and observes the principles recognised in particular by the Charter of Fundamental Rights of the European Union, and notably Chapters II and VI thereof.

HAS ADOPTED THIS FRAMEWORK DECISION:

ARTICLE 1 SCOPE AND OBJECTIVE OF THE FRAMEWORK DECISION

The objective of this Framework Decision is to improve co-operation between judicial and other competent authorities, including the police and other specialised law enforcement services of the Member States, through approximating rules on criminal law in the Member States in the area of attacks against information systems.

ARTICLE 2 DEFINITIONS

For the purposes of this Framework Decision, the following definitions shall apply:

(a) "Electronic communications network" means transmission systems and, where applicable, switching or routing equipment and other resources which permit the conveyance of signals by wire, by radio, by optical or by other electromagnetic means, including satellite networks, fixed (circuit- and packet-switched, including Internet) and mobile terrestrial networks, electricity cable systems, to the extent that they are used for the purpose of transmitting signals, networks used for radio and television broadcasting, and cable TV networks, irrespective of the type of information conveyed

(b) "Computer" means any device or group of inter-connected or related devices, one or more of which, pursuant to a program, performs automatic processing of computer data.

(c) "Computer data" means any representation of facts, information or concepts which has been created or put into a form suitable for processing in an information system, including a program suitable for causing an information system to perform a function.

(d) "Information System" means computers and electronic communication networks, as well as computer data stored, processed, retrieved or transmitted by them for the purposes of their operation, use, protection and maintenance.

(e) "Legal person" means any entity having such status under the applicable law, except for States or other public bodies in the exercise of State authority and for public international organisations.

(f) "Authorised person" means any natural or legal person who has the right, by contract or by law, or the lawful permission, to use, manage, control, test, conduct legitimate scientific research or otherwise operate an information system and who is acting in accordance with that right or permission.

(g) "Without right" means that conduct by authorised persons or other conduct recognised as lawful under domestic law is excluded.

ARTICLE 3 ILLEGAL ACCESS TO INFORMATION SYSTEMS

For additional analytical, business and investment opportunities information, please contact Global Investment & Business Center, USA at (703) 370-8082. Fax: (703) 370-8083. E-mail: ibpusa3@gmail.com Global Business and Investment Info Databank - www.ibpus.com

Member States shall ensure that the intentional access, without right, to the whole or any part of an information system is punishable as a criminal offence where it is committed:

(i) against any part of an information system which is subject to specific protection measures; or

(ii) with the intent to cause damage to a natural or legal person; or

(iii) with the intent to result in an economic benefit.

ARTICLE 4 ILLEGAL INTERFERENCE WITH INFORMATION SYSTEMS

Member States shall ensure that the following intentional conduct, without right, is punishable as a criminal offence:

(a) the serious hindering or interruption of the functioning of an information system by inputting, transmitting, damaging, deleting, deteriorating, altering, suppressing or rendering inaccessible computer data;

(b) the deletion, deterioration, alteration, suppression or rendering inaccessible of computer data on an information system where it is committed with the intention to cause damage to a natural or legal person.

ARTICLE 5 INSTIGATION, AIDING, ABETTING AND ATTEMPT

1. Member States shall ensure that the intentional instigation of, aiding or abetting an offence referred to in Articles 3 and 4 is punishable.

2. Member State shall ensure that attempt to commit the offences referred to in Articles 3 and 4 is punishable.

ARTICLE 6 PENALTIES

1. Member States shall ensure that offences referred to in Articles 3, 4 and 5 are punishable by effective, proportionate and dissuasive penalties including a custodial sentence with a maximum term of imprisonment of no less than one year in serious cases. Serious cases shall be understood as excluding cases where the conduct resulted in no damage or economic benefit

2. Member States shall provide for the possibility of imposing fines in addition to or as an alternative to custodial sentences.

ARTICLE 7 AGGRAVATING CIRCUMSTANCES

1. Member States shall ensure that the offences referred to in Articles 3, 4 and 5 are punishable by a custodial sentence with a maximum term of imprisonment of no less than four years when they are committed under the following circumstances:

(a) the offence has been committed within the framework of a criminal organisation as defined in Joint Action 98/733/ JHA of 21 December 1998 on making it a criminal offence to participate in a

For additional analytical, business and investment opportunities information, please contact Global Investment & Business Center, USA at (703) 370-8082. Fax: (703) 370-8083. E-mail: ibpusa3@gmail.com Global Business and Investment Info Databank - www.ibpus.com

criminal organisation in the Member States of the European Union, apart from the penalty level referred to therein;

(b) the offence caused, or resulted in, substantial direct or indirect economic loss, physical harm to a natural person or substantial damage to part of the critical infrastructure of the Member State;

(c) the offence resulted in substantial proceeds; or

2. Member States shall ensure that the offences referred to in Articles 3 and 4 are punishable by custodial sentences greater than those foreseen under Article 6, when the offender has been convicted of such an offence by a final judgement in a Member State.

ARTICLE 8 PARTICULAR CIRCUMSTANCES

Notwithstanding Articles 6 and 7, Member States shall ensure the penalties referred to in Articles 6 and 7 can be reduced, where, in the opinion of the competent judicial authority, the offender caused only minor damage.

ARTICLE 9 LIABILITY OF LEGAL PERSONS

1. Member States shall ensure that legal persons can be held liable for conducts referred to in Articles 3, 4 and 5, committed for their benefit by any person, acting either individually or as part of an organ of the legal person, who has a leading position within the legal person, based on:

(a) a power of representation of the legal person, or

(b) an authority to take decisions on behalf of the legal person, or

(c) an authority to exercise control within the legal person.

2. Apart from the cases provided for in paragraph 1, Member States shall ensure that a legal person can be held liable where the lack of supervision or control by a person referred to in paragraph 1 has made possible the commission of the offences referred to in Articles 3, 4 and 5 for the benefit of that legal person by a person under its authority.

3. Liability of a legal person under paragraphs 1 and 2 shall not exclude criminal proceedings against natural persons who commit offences or engage in the conduct referred to in Articles 3, 4 and 5.

ARTICLE 10 SANCTIONS FOR LEGAL PERSONS

1. Member States shall ensure that a legal person held liable pursuant to Article 9(1) is punishable by effective, proportionate and dissuasive sanctions, which shall include criminal or non-criminal fines and may include other sanctions, such as:

a) exclusion from entitlement to public benefits or aid;

b) temporary or permanent disqualification from the practice of commercial activities;

c) placing under judicial supervision; or

d) a judicial winding-up order.

For additional analytical, business and investment opportunities information, please contact Global Investment & Business Center, USA at (703) 370-8082. Fax: (703) 370-8083. E-mail: ibpusa3@gmail.com Global Business and Investment Info Databank - www.ibpus.com

2. Member States shall ensure that a legal person held liable pursuant to Article 9(2) is punishable by effective, proportionate and dissuasive sanctions or measures.

ARTICLE 11 JURISDICTION

1. Each Member State shall establish its jurisdiction with regard to the offences referred to in Articles 3, 4 and 5 where the offence has been committed:

(a) in whole or in part within its territory; or

(b) by one of its nationals and the act affects individuals or groups of that State; or

(c) for the benefit of a legal person that has its head office in the territory of that Member State.

2. When establishing jurisdiction in accordance with paragraph (1) (a) , each Member State shall ensure that it includes cases where:

(a) the offender commits the offence when physically present on its territory, whether or not the offence is against an information system on its territory; or

(b) the offence is against an information system on its territory, whether or not the offender commits the offence when physically present on its territory.

3. A Member State may decide not to apply, or to apply only in specific cases or circumstances, the jurisdiction rule set out in paragraphs 1(b) and 1(c) .

4. Each Member State shall take the necessary measures also to establish its jurisdiction over the offences referred to in Articles 3 to 5 in cases where it refuses to hand over or extradite a person suspected or convicted of such an offence to another Member State or to a third country.

5. Where an offence falls within the jurisdiction of more than one Member State and when any of the States concerned can validly prosecute on the basis of the same facts, the Member States concerned shall co-operate in order to decide which of them will prosecute the offenders with the aim, if possible, of centralising proceedings in a single Member State. To this end, the Member States may have recourse to any body or mechanism established within the European Union in order to facilitate co-operation between their judicial authorities and the co-ordination of their action.

6. Member States shall inform the General Secretariat of the Council and the Commission accordingly where they decide to apply paragraph 3, where appropriate with an indication of the specific cases or circumstances in which the decision applies.

ARTICLE 12 EXCHANGE OF INFORMATION

1. For the purpose of exchange of information relating to the offences referred to in Articles 3, 4 and 5, and in accordance with data protection rules, Member States shall ensure that they establish operational points of contact available twenty four hours a day and seven days a week.

2. Each Member State shall inform the General Secretariat of the Council and the Commission of its appointed point of contact for the purpose of exchanging information on offences relating to

For additional analytical, business and investment opportunities information, please contact Global Investment & Business Center, USA at (703) 370-8082. Fax: (703) 370-8083. E-mail: ibpusa3@gmail.com Global Business and Investment Info Databank - www.ibpus.com

attacks against information systems. The General Secretariat shall notify that information to the other Member States.

Article 13 Implementation

1. Member States shall bring into force the measures necessary to comply with this Framework Decision by 31 December 2003.

2. They shall communicate to the General Secretariat of the Council and to the Commission the text of any provisions they adopt and information on any other measures taken to comply with this Framework Decision.

3. On that basis, the Commission shall, by 31December 2004, submit a report to the European Parliament and to the Council on the operation of this Framework Decision, accompanied where necessary by legislative proposals.

4. The Council shall assess the extent to which Member States have complied with this Framework Decision.

Article 14 Entry into force

This Framework Decision shall enter into force on the twentieth day following that of its publication in the Official Journal of the European Communities.

Done at Brussels,
For the Council
The President

For additional analytical, business and investment opportunities information, please contact Global Investment & Business Center, USA at (703) 370-8082. Fax: (703) 370-8083. E-mail: ibpusa3@gmail.com Global Business and Investment Info Databank - www.ibpus.com

BASIC INTERNATIONAL AND EU OFFICIAL MATERIALS

CODE OF EU ONLINE RIGHTS

RIGHTS & PRINCIPLES APPLICABLE WHEN YOU ACCESS AND USE ONLINE SERVICES

Access to an internet connection

EU citizens must have the possibility to access a minimum set of electronic communications services of good quality at an affordable price. This is also known as the 'universal service' principle.

Use of services of your choice

Everyone in the EU shall be able to access and distribute any information, and to run any application and service of their choice through electronic communication networks. This is also known as the principle of 'open and neutral character of the internet'.

Non-discrimination

When EU consumers try to access services online, service providers shall not apply less favourable conditions on grounds of their Member State of residence unless the differences are justified by objective criteria.

Protection of personal data

In the EU, personal data protection is a fundamental right enshrined in the Lisbon Treaty and the Charter of Fundamental Rights of the European Union. Every EU citizen has the right to adequate protection of his personal data. These general data protection rights also apply online, where individuals have in addition the following rights:
To be fully informed and give their agreement if a website stores and retrieves information from their terminal equipment or wants to track them when they surf the internet;
Confidentiality of their online communications, such as emails;
To be notified if their personal data held by their Internet Service Provider has been compromised, e.g. lost or stolen, and their privacy is likely to be adversely affected;
Not to be sent unsolicited commercial communications, known as 'spam', unless they have given their agreement.

CHAPTER 1: ACCESS TO ELECTRONIC COMMUNICATIONS NETWORKS AND SERVICES1

(1) Everyone in the EU must have the possibility to access a minimum set of electronic communications services of good quality at an affordable price. This is also known as the 'universal service' principle.

As regards rights of access to internet, all reasonable requests for connection at a fixed location to a public communications network must be met by at least one operator.

Such connection must be capable of supporting voice, fax and data communications at data rates that are sufficient to permit functional internet access and the provision of voice telephony services.

For additional analytical, business and investment opportunities information, please contact Global Investment & Business Center, USA at (703) 370-8082. Fax: (703) 370-8083. E-mail: ibpusa3@gmail.com Global Business and Investment Info Databank - www.ibpus.com

This also applies to disabled end-users who must have equivalent access and choice to that enjoyed by the majority of consumers.2

CHAPTER 2: ACCESS TO SERVICES AND APPLICATIONS OF YOUR CHOICE3

(1) Everyone in the EU shall be able to access and distribute any information and to run any application and service of their choice through electronic communication networks.

The fundamental rights and freedoms of natural persons as guaranteed by the Charter of Fundamental Rights of the European Union, the European Convention for the Protection of Human Rights and Fundamental Freedoms, and the general principles of EU Law shall be respected in this context.

For this reason, any measure related to consumers' access to or use of services and applications liable to restrict those fundamental rights or freedoms could only be imposed by a Member State if appropriate, proportionate and necessary within a democratic society.4

(2) Regulatory authorities in the electronic communications area must promote the ability of everyone in the EU to access and distribute any information and to run any application and service of their choice. This is also known as the principle of 'open and neutral character of the internet'.5

These regulatory authorities have the power to set minimum quality of service requirements in case of problems to safeguard the openness of the internet. In order to prevent the degradation of service and the hindering or slowing down of traffic over networks, Member States shall ensure that national regulatory authorities are able to set minimum quality of service requirements on an undertaking or undertakings providing public communications networks.6

(3) Every disabled consumer must benefit from the choice of e-communication providers and services available to the majority of consumers.7

For consumers with a visual or hearing disability providers of audiovisual media services are encouraged to ensure that their programmes, e.g. films, sports events, situation comedies, documentaries, children's programmes or original dramas, as well as commercial communications are gradually made accessible to them.8

This obligation applies irrespective of the type of service and of the delivery platform, as long as the latter relies on electronic communications networks, therefore covering also audiovisual media services purchased online.

(4) Minors are protected in relation to audiovisual media programmes and commercial communications which might seriously impair their physical, mental and moral development. Such content can only be made available online in the EU on explicit request, and only in a manner that ensures that minors will not normally hear or see such services.9

(5) Incitement to hatred based on race, sex, religion or nationality is forbidden in audiovisual media services. Governments must ensure that neither audiovisual media programmes nor audiovisual commercial communications that are delivered online contain any such incitement.10

For additional analytical, business and investment opportunities information, please contact Global Investment & Business Center, USA at (703) 370-8082. Fax: (703) 370-8083. E-mail: ibpusa3@gmail.com Global Business and Investment Info Databank - www.ibpus.com

CHAPTER 3: NON-DISCRIMINATION WHEN ACCESSING SERVICES PROVIDED ONLINE11

(1) Consumers who wish to acquire online services12 in another Member State shall be granted access by traders to public information on the conditions of access.

(2) Consumers shall not be refused access to services online on grounds of their Member State of residence unless the refusal is justified by objective criteria in accordance to the Commission Staff Working Document with a view to establishing guidance on the application of Article 20(2) of Directive 2006/123/EC on services in the internal market ('the Services Directive') .13 Where possible, traders shall inform consumers of this justification for non-delivery of a service into certain territories in the information that they make available to the public at large. When this is not possible, they shall provide such information upon the consumer's request.

(3) When consumers try to access services online, service providers shall not apply less favourable conditions of access to the service to consumers on grounds of their Member State of residence unless the differences are justified by objective criteria.14 Upon the consumer's request, traders shall use their best endeavours to inform consumers of the justification for differences in treatment.

CHAPTER 4: PRIVACY, PROTECTION OF PERSONAL DATA AND SECURITY15

(1) Personal data protection is a fundamental right, and is also enshrined in the Lisbon Treaty. The Charter of Fundamental Rights of the European Union provides that "Everyone has the right to the protection of personal data concerning him or her. Such data must be processed fairly for specified purposes and on the basis of the consent of the person concerned or some other legitimate basis laid down by law. Everyone has the right of access to data which has been collected concerning him or her, and the right to have it rectified".16

Every individual has the right to adequate protection of his personal data17 . Processing of personal data must be necessary, fair, lawful and proportionate. The data that individuals provide directly or indirectly must not be used for purposes other than originally intended. Nor can such data be passed on indiscriminately to entities that the individual has not chosen to be involved with. These rights apply to everyone, irrespective of nationality or place of residence. Personal data revealing racial or ethnic origin, political opinions, religious or philosophical beliefs, trade-union membership, and the processing of data concerning health or sex life is only permitted with explicit consent of the individual, where allowed by national legislation.18

(2) Individuals have the right to receive information from people and companies holding some of their personal data in their files, such as websites, data bases, service providers etc. ("data controllers") , and they have the right to correct or erase this data if it is incomplete or inaccurate:

Data controllers are required to inform consumers when they collect personal data about them;

Individuals have the right to know the name of the controller, the intended use of the data processing, and to whom the data may be transferred;

Individuals are entitled to ask the data controller whether he is processing personal data about them;

Individuals have the right to receive a copy of the data that relates to them in intelligible form;

For additional analytical, business and investment opportunities information, please contact Global Investment & Business Center, USA at (703) 370-8082. Fax: (703) 370-8083. E-mail: ibpusa3@gmail.com Global Business and Investment Info Databank - www.ibpus.com

Individuals have the right to ask for the deletion, blocking or erasing of the data if it is incomplete, inaccurate or obtained unlawfully. Individuals have the right to object to the processing of personal data.

(3) Individuals have the right not to be subject to a decision which produces legal effects concerning them or that significantly affects them and which is based solely on automated processing of data intended to evaluate certain personal aspects relating to them, such as their performance at work, credit worthiness, reliability, conduct, etc.19

(4) These rights also apply online, where individuals have in addition the following rights:20

To be fully informed and give their agreement if a website stores and retrieves information from their terminal equipment or wants to track them when they surf the internet;

Confidentiality of their online communications, such as emails;

To be notified if their personal data held by their Internet Service Provider has been compromised, e.g. lost or stolen, and their privacy is likely to be adversely affected;

Not to be sent unsolicited commercial communications, known as 'spam', unless they have given their agreement.

RIGHTS & PRINCIPLES APPLICABLE WHEN YOU BUY GOODS OR SERVICES ONLINE

Every consumer in the EU has the right to receive clear, correct and comprehensible key information from a trader about the product or service before making an online purchase. This information must include aspects such as the characteristics of the product, the price inclusive of taxes, delivery costs and the existence of a right of withdrawal or cancellation.

Contractual information

Every online consumer concluding a contract in the EU has the right to have easy, direct and permanent access to -at least- the following:

Name and address of the provider

Electronic mail address or website

VAT details where applicable

Any other detail allowing rapid and effective contact with the provider.

Subscribers of electronic communications services have the right to receive information from the provider, e.g. on applicable prices, tariffs and charges.

Right to fair contract conditions

Any consumer in the EU, also in the digital environment, is protected from unfair standard contract terms by traders that create an unreasonable imbalance to the detriment of the consumer. Unfair terms are in particular:

when a consumer did not have any real opportunity to become acquainted with the contract before its conclusion, but which bind the consumer;

when the contract exclude or hinder the consumer's right to take legal action;

when the contract is automatically extended to a fixed duration with an unreasonably short deadline;

when the price increases considerably without giving the consumer the right to cancel the contract.

Protection against unfair practices

Any consumer in the EU, including the digital consumer, has the right either to complain to the national enforcement authorities or to take legal action against a trader in the EU that uses unfair commercial practices.

Examples of unfair commercial practices are:

a trader is not allowed to make an invitation to purchase products at a specified price if he then refuses either to take orders for them or to deliver them within a reasonable time, with the intention of promoting a different product ('bait and switch') ;

a trader is not allowed to describe a product as "gratis", "free", "without charge" or similar if the consumer has to pay anything other than the unavoidable cost of responding to the commercial practice and collecting or paying for the delivery of the item;

a consumer cannot be asked to pay for or to return unsolicited products supplied by a trader ('inertia selling') .

Delivery of goods and services without defects and in due time

Any consumer in the EU must receive goods or services ordered online from a trader within 30 days, unless something else has been agreed with the seller.

If the good or service was not delivered within this time-frame, the consumer has a right to be reimbursed.

Consumers can request repair or replacement free of charge if goods they receive are faulty or do not correspond to what they have ordered. The trader has to repair or replace the good within a reasonable time and with limited inconvenience to the consumer.

Right of withdrawal from a contract

Consumers in the EU have at least seven days to change their mind about goods or services they have ordered online from a trader.

For goods, the withdrawal period starts from the date of delivery, for services in general from the date the on-line order was placed.

Consumers can then withdraw from the contract without penalty and without giving any reason. Reimbursement of sums paid must be carried out as soon as possible and in any case within 30 days.

The only charge that can be made to the consumer in this case is the direct cost of returning the goods.

CHAPTER 5: INFORMATION PRIOR TO THE CONCLUSION OF A CONTRACT ONLINE 21

(1) Every consumer in the EU has the right to receive clear, correct and comprehensible key information from a trader about the product or service before making an online purchase.

This information must include the main characteristics of the product, price inclusive of taxes, delivery costs, the arrangements for payment, delivery or performance, identity and geographical address of the trader, the existence of a right of withdrawal or cancellation (for products which involve such right) , the period for which the offer or the price remains valid, and, if applicable, the minimum duration of the contract.22 Unless contracts are concluded exclusively by exchange of electronic mail or by equivalent individual communications, this information must also contain the different technical steps to follow to conclude the contract; whether or not the contract will be filed and accessible; the technical means for identifying and correcting input errors, and the languages offered for the conclusion of the contract.23

When the consumer places his order online, he has the right to receive an acknowledgment of the receipt of the order without undue delay and by electronic means.24

(2) The right to receive key information in good time before being bound by any distance contract or offer is also applicable to financial services including banking, credit, insurance, personal pension, investment of payment in nature. The information should be presented in a clear and comprehensive manner and should include details on the supplier and the main characteristics of the financial service, such as price including all taxes, arrangements for payment or performance. Suppliers should also inform consumers about their contractual rights, such as to withdraw from the contract or to terminate the contract earlier, and about possible action in case of a problem.

For practical reasons, in the case of financial services, consumers may receive a limited amount of information when they speak over the phone with the supplier of financial services and when, at their request, the contract is concluded online. The full information would in that case be given immediately after concluding the contract.25

CHAPTER 6: TIMELY, CLEAR AND COMPLETE CONTRACTUAL INFORMATION26

(1) Every online consumer concluding a contract in the EU has the right to have easy, direct and permanent access to at least the name and geographic address of the provider, the electronic mail address or website, the trade register in which the provider is entered and his registration number, the professional title and professional body with which the provider is registered, the VAT details where applicable and any other detail allowing rapid and effective contact with the provider.27 The online consumer must also have access to codes of conduct to which the provider subscribes and to contract terms and general conditions in a way that allows him to store and reproduce (print) them. This right does not apply where contracts are concluded exclusively by exchange of electronic mail or by equivalent individual communications.28

(2) Every consumer has the right to receive, after having ordered the goods or services, confirmation of the key elements of the contract in writing or on a durable medium, such as e-mail. This information must be given at the latest at the time of delivery of goods or, for services, in good time during their performance. However, the trader does not need to repeat information already given before.

The confirmation must always include information under what conditions and how the consumer can withdraw from the contract, an address where the consumer can direct complaints, information on after-sales services and guarantees which exist and, for contracts of more than a year or of indefinite duration, the conditions for cancelling the contract.29

(3) After concluding a contract on financial services online consumers have the right to receive, in good time before being bound by the distance contract, detailed information on the terms of the contract, e.g. the characteristics of the service, the price and arrangements for payment and performance. Suppliers should also inform consumers about their contractual rights, how to withdraw from the contract or to terminate the contract earlier, any information on existing after-sales services and guarantees and possible actions in case of a problem.30

(4) Subscribers of electronic communications services, including those used for the delivery of information society services, have the right to receive information from the provider e.g. on applicable prices, tariffs and charges, including tariff options and packages, standard terms and conditions for access to and use of the services provided and quality of the service. Moreover disabled subscribers shall be regularly informed of the products and services designed for them.31

(5) Before making an online payment transaction every consumer has the right to receive all relevant payment details, in particular, terms and conditions of the service, including information on the payment service provider responsible for the transaction; information about the characteristics of the payment service and the processing time; information about charges applicable for the transaction and on the refund rights; information about any additional charges or discounts applied by the merchant.

After each payment transaction the consumer shall receive the confirmation, which will contain at least the amount of the purchase, the date of the transaction, and a breakdown of any charges applied.32

CHAPTER 7: FAIR CONTRACT TERMS & CONDITIONS33

(1) Any consumer in the EU, also in the digital environment, is protected from unfair standard contract terms by traders that create an unreasonable imbalance to the detriment of the consumer. If a contract contains such terms, the consumer is not bound by them, although the contract itself usually remains valid. Unfair terms are in particular:34

- Contract terms that a consumer did not have any real opportunity to become acquainted with before the conclusion of the contract, but which bind the consumer;

- Contract terms that exclude or hinder the consumer's right to take legal action or exercise any other legal remedy (e.g. by requiring them to take disputes exclusively to arbitration) ;

- Contract terms automatically extending a contract of fixed duration when the deadline fixed for the consumer to express his desire not to extend it is unreasonably short;

- Contract terms that allow considerable price increases without giving the consumer the right to cancel the contract.

(2) The consumer has the right to contractual terms written in plain and understandable language and this applies as well online. Where there is doubt about the meaning of a term, the interpretation most favourable to the consumer shall prevail.35

(3) Subscribers of electronic communications services have the right to minimum standard contract terms and conditions with companies providing internet access. Subscribers also have the right to be informed well in advance if the service provider wants to amend the contract and to withdraw from the contract without penalty if they do not accept the new conditions; they also have the option to subscribe to a 12-month maximum contract period for online connection, and not to be obliged to subscribe to contracts for an initial period of more than 24 months.36

(4) When paying online for goods and services, the same charges for a transaction in euro apply whether the merchant is located in the country of the consumer or in another EU Member State. This includes payments in euro by credit (bank) transfers, by direct debit and by credit card.37

CHAPTER 8: PROTECTION AGAINST UNFAIR PRACTICES38

(1) Any consumer, including the digital consumer, has the right either to complain to the national enforcement authorities39 or to take legal action against a trader in the EU that uses unfair commercial practices.

For example, after making an online purchase, consumers cannot be made subject to onerous or disproportionate non-contractual obstacles (such as filling in a large amount of forms or being asked to call a specific phone number when no one is answering the call) in order to prevent them from terminating the contract or switching to another product or trader.40

(2) Consumers must not be misled or exposed to aggressive marketing and this applies also in the digital environment. Any claim made by traders in the EU has to be truthful, clear, accurate and substantiated, enabling consumers to make informed and meaningful choices.41 Comparative advertising must compare goods or services meeting the same needs or intended for the same purpose and it must objectively compare material, relevant, verifiable and representative features.42

Examples of unfair commercial practices:

- a trader is not allowed to make an invitation to purchase products at a specified price if he then refuses either to take orders for them or to deliver them within a reasonable time, with the intention of promoting a different product ('bait and switch') ;

- a trader is not allowed to describe a product as "gratis", "free", "without charge" or similar if the consumer has to pay anything other than the unavoidable cost of responding to the commercial practice and collecting or paying for the delivery of the item;43

- a consumer cannot be asked to pay for or to return unsolicited products supplied by a trader ('inertia selling') .

(3) When buying products online, including financial services, consumers are protected from abusive marketing practices seeking to require them to buy something they have not solicited. They are also protected against other practices, such as unsolicited phone calls and e-mails.44

CHAPTER 9: DELIVERY OF GOODS AND SERVICES WITHOUT DEFECTS AND IN DUE TIME45

(1) Any consumer in the EU must receive goods or services ordered online from a trader within 30 days, unless something else has been agreed with the seller. If the good or service was not delivered within this time-frame, the consumer has a right to be reimbursed.46

(2) Consumers can request repair or replacement free of charge if goods they receive are faulty or do not correspond to what they have ordered. The trader has to repair or replace the good within a reasonable time and with limited inconvenience to the consumer.

If the trader fails to repair or replace the good within a reasonable time, consumers may instead ask for a refund or a price reduction. The legal guarantee has a duration of at least two years from delivery of the goods, but after six months the consumer has to prove that the defect already existed at the time of delivery. Within six months of delivery it is assumed that the defect existed at the time of delivery unless the seller can prove that this is not the case.47

If the manufacturer or seller grants commercial guarantees or warranties promising free repair and replacement within a certain period, an online consumer can also turn to the one offering such a guarantee.

(3) In the EU, consumers have the right to have their online payment transactions treated within strict limits by the payment service providers. As a rule the amount of the transaction shall be credited to the payee's account no later than on a next business day. Exceptions apply to direct debit payments (they are executed on the agreed day) and payments initiated in paper form (one additional day for processing) .48

(4) In case of an unauthorised payment transaction (e.g. mistakes of the merchant, bank or fraud attempts not related to the payer) the payer has the right to obtain an immediate refund of the total amount of the transaction by the payment service provider.49

CHAPTER 10: WITHDRAWAL FROM A CONTRACT50

(1) Consumers in the EU have at least seven days to change their mind about goods or services they have ordered online from a trader. For goods, the withdrawal period starts from the date of delivery, for services in general from the date the on-line order was placed. Consumers can then withdraw from the contract without penalty and without giving any reason. Reimbursement of sums paid must be carried out as soon as possible and in any case within 30 days. The only charge that can be made to the consumer in this case is the direct cost of returning the goods.51

This right does not apply, however, if the provision of a service has begun, with the consumer's agreement, before the end of the seven working day period for the exercise of the right of withdrawal; for accommodation, transport, catering or leisure services, unless the date or period of this service is open and not specified; or goods or services the price of which is dependent on fluctuations in the financial markets which cannot be controlled by the supplier; for personalised or 'tailor-made' goods; for the supply of goods which are liable to deteriorate or expire rapidly; for the supply of audio or video recordings or computer software which were unsealed by the consumer; for the supply of newspapers, periodicals and magazines; for gaming and lottery services.

In the case of buying financial services online consumers can withdraw from the contract within 14 days without any penalty and without giving any reason.52

This right does not apply, however, to financial services whose price depends on fluctuations in the financial market outside the supplier control; travel and baggage insurance policies or similar short-term insurance policies of less than one month's duration; contracts whose performance has been fully completed by both parties at the consumer's express request before the consumer exercises his right of withdrawal.

THE CONVENTION ON CYBERCRIME

PREAMBLE

The member States of the Council of Europe and the other States signatory hereto,

Considering that the aim of the Council of Europe is to achieve a greater unity between its members;

Recognising the value of fostering co-operation with the other States parties to this Convention;

Convinced of the need to pursue, as a matter of priority, a common criminal policy aimed at the protection of society against cybercrime, *inter alia,* by adopting appropriate legislation and fostering international co-operation;

Conscious of the profound changes brought about by the digitalisation, convergence and continuing globalisation of computer networks;

Concerned by the risk that computer networks and electronic information may also be used for committing criminal offences and that evidence relating to such offences may be stored and transferred by these networks;

Recognising the need for co-operation between States and private industry in combating cybercrime and the need to protect legitimate interests in the use and development of information technologies;

Believing that an effective fight against cybercrime requires increased, rapid and well-functioning international co-operation in criminal matters;

Convinced that the present Convention is necessary to deter action directed against the confidentiality, integrity and availability of computer systems, networks and computer data as well as the misuse of such systems, networks and data by providing for the criminalisation of such conduct, as described in this Convention, and the adoption of powers sufficient for effectively combating such criminal offences, by facilitating their detection, investigation and prosecution at both the domestic and international levels and by providing arrangements for fast and reliable international co-operation;

Mindful of the need to ensure a proper balance between the interests of law enforcement and respect for fundamental human rights as enshrined in the 1950 Council of Europe Convention for the Protection of Human Rights and Fundamental Freedoms, the 1966 United Nations International Covenant on Civil and Political Rights and other applicable international human rights treaties, which reaffirm the right of everyone to hold opinions without interference, as well as the right to freedom of expression, including the freedom to seek, receive, and impart information and ideas of all kinds, regardless of frontiers, and the rights concerning the respect for privacy;

For additional analytical, business and investment opportunities information, please contact Global Investment & Business Center, USA at (703) 370-8082. Fax: (703) 370-8083. E-mail: ibpusa3@gmail.com Global Business and Investment Info Databank - www.ibpus.com

Mindful also of the right to the protection of personal data, as conferred, for example, by the 1981 Council of Europe Convention for the Protection of Individuals with regard to Automatic Processing of Personal Data;

Considering the 1989 United Nations Convention on the Rights of the Child and the 1999 International Labour Organization Worst Forms of Child Labour Convention;

Taking into account the existing Council of Europe conventions on co-operation in the penal field, as well as similar treaties which exist between Council of Europe member States and other States, and stressing that the present Convention is intended to supplement those conventions in order to make criminal investigations and proceedings concerning criminal offences related to computer systems and data more effective and to enable the collection of evidence in electronic form of a criminal offence;

Welcoming recent developments which further advance international understanding and co-operation in combating cybercrime, including action taken by the United Nations, the OECD, the European Union and the G8;

Recalling Committee of Ministers Recommendations No. R (85) 10 concerning the practical application of the European Convention on Mutual Assistance in Criminal Matters in respect of letters rogatory for the interception of telecommunications, No. R (88) 2 on piracy in the field of copyright and neighbouring rights, No. R (87) 15 regulating the use of personal data in the police sector, No. R (95) 4 on the protection of personal data in the area of telecommunication services, with particular reference to telephone services, as well as No. R (89) 9 on computer-related crime providing guidelines for national legislatures concerning the definition of certain computer crimes and No. R (95) 13 concerning problems of criminal procedural law connected with information technology;

Having regard to Resolution No. 1 adopted by the European Ministers of Justice at their 21st Conference (Prague, 10 and 11 June 1997) , which recommended that the Committee of Ministers support the work on cybercrime carried out by the European Committee on Crime Problems (CDPC) in order to bring domestic criminal law provisions closer to each other and enable the use of effective means of investigation into such offences, as well as to Resolution No. 3 adopted at the 23rd Conference of the European Ministers of Justice (London, 8 and 9 June 2000) , which encouraged the negotiating parties to pursue their efforts with a view to finding appropriate solutions to enable the largest possible number of States to become parties to the Convention and acknowledged the need for a swift and efficient system of international co-operation, which duly takes into account the specific requirements of the fight against cybercrime;

Having also regard to the Action Plan adopted by the Heads of State and Government of the Council of Europe on the occasion of their Second Summit (Strasbourg, 10 and 11 October 1997) , to seek common responses to the development of the new information technologies based on the standards and values of the Council of Europe;

Have agreed as follows:

CHAPTER I – USE OF TERMS

Article 1 – Definitions

For the purposes of this Convention:

For additional analytical, business and investment opportunities information, please contact Global Investment & Business Center, USA at (703) 370-8082. Fax: (703) 370-8083. E-mail: ibpusa3@gmail.com Global Business and Investment Info Databank - www.ibpus.com

a "computer system" means any device or a group of interconnected or related devices, one or more of which, pursuant to a program, performs automatic processing of data;

b "computer data" means any representation of facts, information or concepts in a form suitable for processing in a computer system, including a program suitable to cause a computer system to perform a function;

c "service provider" means:

i any public or private entity that provides to users of its service the ability to communicate by means of a computer system, and

ii any other entity that processes or stores computer data on behalf of such communication service or users of such service.

d "traffic data" means any computer data relating to a communication by means of a computer system, generated by a computer system that formed a part in the chain of communication, indicating the communication's origin, destination, route, time, date, size, duration, or type of underlying service.

CHAPTER II – MEASURES TO BE TAKEN AT THE NATIONAL LEVEL

Section 1 – Substantive criminal law

Title 1 – Offences against the confidentiality, integrity and availability of computer data and systems

Article 2 – Illegal access

Each Party shall adopt such legislative and other measures as may be necessary to establish as criminal offences under its domestic law, when committed intentionally, the access to the whole or any part of a computer system without right. A Party may require that the offence be committed by infringing security measures, with the intent of obtaining computer data or other dishonest intent, or in relation to a computer system that is connected to another computer system.

Article 3 – Illegal interception

Each Party shall adopt such legislative and other measures as may be necessary to establish as criminal offences under its domestic law, when committed intentionally, the interception without right, made by technical means, of non-public transmissions of computer data to, from or within a computer system, including electromagnetic emissions from a computer system carrying such computer data. A Party may require that the offence be committed with dishonest intent, or in relation to a computer system that is connected to another computer system.

Article 4 – Data interference

1 Each Party shall adopt such legislative and other measures as may be necessary to establish as criminal offences under its domestic law, when committed intentionally, the damaging, deletion, deterioration, alteration or suppression of computer data without right.

For additional analytical, business and investment opportunities information, please contact Global Investment & Business Center, USA at (703) 370-8082. Fax: (703) 370-8083. E-mail: ibpusa3@gmail.com Global Business and Investment Info Databank - www.ibpus.com

2 A Party may reserve the right to require that the conduct described in paragraph 1 result in serious harm.

Article 5 – System interference

Each Party shall adopt such legislative and other measures as may be necessary to establish as criminal offences under its domestic law, when committed intentionally, the serious hindering without right of the functioning of a computer system by inputting, transmitting, damaging, deleting, deteriorating, altering or suppressing computer data.

Article 6 – Misuse of devices

1 Each Party shall adopt such legislative and other measures as may be necessary to establish as criminal offences under its domestic law, when committed intentionally and without right:

a the production, sale, procurement for use, import, distribution or otherwise making available of:

i a device, including a computer program, designed or adapted primarily for the purpose of committing any of the offences established in accordance with Articles 2 through 5;

ii a computer password, access code, or similar data by which the whole or any part of a computer system is capable of being accessed,

with intent that it be used for the purpose of committing any of the offences established in Articles 2 through 5; and

b the possession of an item referred to in paragraphs a.i or ii above, with intent that it be used for the purpose of committing any of the offences established in Articles 2 through 5. A Party may require by law that a number of such items be possessed before criminal liability attaches.

2 This article shall not be interpreted as imposing criminal liability where the production, sale, procurement for use, import, distribution or otherwise making available or possession referred to in paragraph 1 of this article is not for the purpose of committing an offence established in accordance with Articles 2 through 5 of this Convention, such as for the authorised testing or protection of a computer system.

3 Each Party may reserve the right not to apply paragraph 1 of this article, provided that the reservation does not concern the sale, distribution or otherwise making available of the items referred to in paragraph 1 a.ii of this article.

Title 2 – Computer-related offences

Article 7 – Computer-related forgery

Each Party shall adopt such legislative and other measures as may be necessary to establish as criminal offences under its domestic law, when committed intentionally and without right, the input, alteration, deletion, or suppression of computer data, resulting in inauthentic data with the intent that it be considered or acted upon for legal purposes as if it were authentic, regardless whether or not the data is directly readable and intelligible. A Party may require an intent to defraud, or similar dishonest intent, before criminal liability attaches.

For additional analytical, business and investment opportunities information, please contact Global Investment & Business Center, USA at (703) 370-8082. Fax: (703) 370-8083. E-mail: ibpusa3@gmail.com Global Business and Investment Info Databank - www.ibpus.com

Article 8 – Computer-related fraud

Each Party shall adopt such legislative and other measures as may be necessary to establish as criminal offences under its domestic law, when committed intentionally and without right, the causing of a loss of property to another person by:

a any input, alteration, deletion or suppression of computer data,

b any interference with the functioning of a computer system,

with fraudulent or dishonest intent of procuring, without right, an economic benefit for oneself or for another person.

Title 3 – Content-related offences

Article 9 – Offences related to child pornography

1 Each Party shall adopt such legislative and other measures as may be necessary to establish as criminal offences under its domestic law, when committed intentionally and without right, the following conduct:

a producing child pornography for the purpose of its distribution through a computer system;

b offering or making available child pornography through a computer system;

c distributing or transmitting child pornography through a computer system;

d procuring child pornography through a computer system for oneself or for another person;

e possessing child pornography in a computer system or on a computer-data storage medium.

2 For the purpose of paragraph 1 above, the term "child pornography" shall include pornographic material that visually depicts:

a a minor engaged in sexually explicit conduct;

b a person appearing to be a minor engaged in sexually explicit conduct;

c realistic images representing a minor engaged in sexually explicit conduct.

3 For the purpose of paragraph 2 above, the term "minor" shall include all persons under 18 years of age. A Party may, however, require a lower age-limit, which shall be not less than 16 years.

4 Each Party may reserve the right not to apply, in whole or in part, paragraphs 1, sub-paragraphs d. and e, and 2, sub-paragraphs b. and c.

Title 4 – Offences related to infringements of copyright and related rights

For additional analytical, business and investment opportunities information, please contact Global Investment & Business Center, USA at (703) 370-8082. Fax: (703) 370-8083. E-mail: ibpusa3@gmail.com Global Business and Investment Info Databank - www.ibpus.com

Article 10 – Offences related to infringements of copyright and related rights

1 Each Party shall adopt such legislative and other measures as may be necessary to establish as criminal offences under its domestic law the infringement of copyright, as defined under the law of that Party, pursuant to the obligations it has undertaken under the Paris Act of 24 July 1971 revising the Bern Convention for the Protection of Literary and Artistic Works, the Agreement on Trade-Related Aspects of Intellectual Property Rights and the WIPO Copyright Treaty, with the exception of any moral rights conferred by such conventions, where such acts are committed wilfully, on a commercial scale and by means of a computer system.

2 Each Party shall adopt such legislative and other measures as may be necessary to establish as criminal offences under its domestic law the infringement of related rights, as defined under the law of that Party, pursuant to the obligations it has undertaken under the International Convention for the Protection of Performers, Producers of Phonograms and Broadcasting Organisations (Rome Convention) , the Agreement on Trade-Related Aspects of Intellectual Property Rights and the WIPO Performances and Phonograms Treaty, with the exception of any moral rights conferred by such conventions, where such acts are committed wilfully, on a commercial scale and by means of a computer system.

3 A Party may reserve the right not to impose criminal liability under paragraphs 1 and 2 of this article in limited circumstances, provided that other effective remedies are available and that such reservation does not derogate from the Party's international obligations set forth in the international instruments referred to in paragraphs 1 and 2 of this article.

Title 5 – Ancillary liability and sanctions

Article 11 – Attempt and aiding or abetting

1 Each Party shall adopt such legislative and other measures as may be necessary to establish as criminal offences under its domestic law, when committed intentionally, aiding or abetting the commission of any of the offences established in accordance with Articles 2 through 10 of the present Convention with intent that such offence be committed.

2 Each Party shall adopt such legislative and other measures as may be necessary to establish as criminal offences under its domestic law, when committed intentionally, an attempt to commit any of the offences established in accordance with Articles 3 through 5, 7, 8, and 9.1.a and c. of this Convention.

3 Each Party may reserve the right not to apply, in whole or in part, paragraph 2 of this article.

Article 12 – Corporate liability

1 Each Party shall adopt such legislative and other measures as may be necessary to ensure that legal persons can be held liable for a criminal offence established in accordance with this Convention, committed for their benefit by any natural person, acting either individually or as part of an organ of the legal person, who has a leading position within it, based on:

a a power of representation of the legal person;

b an authority to take decisions on behalf of the legal person;

c an authority to exercise control within the legal person.

For additional analytical, business and investment opportunities information, please contact Global Investment & Business Center, USA at (703) 370-8082. Fax: (703) 370-8083. E-mail: ibpusa3@gmail.com Global Business and Investment Info Databank - www.ibpus.com

2 In addition to the cases already provided for in paragraph 1 of this article, each Party shall take the measures necessary to ensure that a legal person can be held liable where the lack of supervision or control by a natural person referred to in paragraph 1 has made possible the commission of a criminal offence established in accordance with this Convention for the benefit of that legal person by a natural person acting under its authority.

3 Subject to the legal principles of the Party, the liability of a legal person may be criminal, civil or administrative.

4 Such liability shall be without prejudice to the criminal liability of the natural persons who have committed the offence.

Article 13 – Sanctions and measures

1 Each Party shall adopt such legislative and other measures as may be necessary to ensure that the criminal offences established in accordance with Articles 2 through 11 are punishable by effective, proportionate and dissuasive sanctions, which include deprivation of liberty.

2 Each Party shall ensure that legal persons held liable in accordance with Article 12 shall be subject to effective, proportionate and dissuasive criminal or non-criminal sanctions or measures, including monetary sanctions.

Section 2 – Procedural law

Title 1 – Common provisions

Article 14 – Scope of procedural provisions

1 Each Party shall adopt such legislative and other measures as may be necessary to establish the powers and procedures provided for in this section for the purpose of specific criminal investigations or proceedings.

2 Except as specifically provided otherwise in Article 21, each Party shall apply the powers and procedures referred to in paragraph 1 of this article to:

a the criminal offences established in accordance with Articles 2 through 11 of this Convention;

b other criminal offences committed by means of a computer system; and

c the collection of evidence in electronic form of a criminal offence.

3 a. Each Party may reserve the right to apply the measures referred to in Article 20 only to offences or categories of offences specified in the reservation, provided that the range of such offences or categories of offences is not more restricted than the range of offences to which it applies the measures referred to in Article 21. Each Party shall consider restricting such a reservation to enable the broadest application of the measure referred to in Article 20.

b Where a Party, due to limitations in its legislation in force at the time of the adoption of the present Convention, is not able to apply the measures referred to in Articles 20 and 21 to communications being transmitted within a computer system of a service provider, which system:

i is being operated for the benefit of a closed group of users, and

ii does not employ public communications networks and is not connected with another computer system, whether public or private,

that Party may reserve the right not to apply these measures to such communications. Each Party shall consider restricting such a reservation to enable the broadest application of the measures referred to in Articles 20 and 21.

Article 15 – Conditions and safeguards

1 Each Party shall ensure that the establishment, implementation and application of the powers and procedures provided for in this Section are subject to conditions and safeguards provided for under its domestic law, which shall provide for the adequate protection of human rights and liberties, including rights arising pursuant to obligations it has undertaken under the 1950 Council of Europe Convention for the Protection of Human Rights and Fundamental Freedoms, the 1966 United Nations International Covenant on Civil and Political Rights, and other applicable international human rights instruments, and which shall incorporate the principle of proportionality.

2 Such conditions and safeguards shall, as appropriate in view of the nature of the procedure or power concerned, *inter alia,* include judicial or other independent supervision, grounds justifying application, and limitation of the scope and the duration of such power or procedure.

3 To the extent that it is consistent with the public interest, in particular the sound administration of justice, each Party shall consider the impact of the powers and procedures in this section upon the rights, responsibilities and legitimate interests of third parties.

Title 2 – Expedited preservation of stored computer data

Article 16 – Expedited preservation of stored computer data

1 Each Party shall adopt such legislative and other measures as may be necessary to enable its competent authorities to order or similarly obtain the expeditious preservation of specified computer data, including traffic data, that has been stored by means of a computer system, in particular where there are grounds to believe that the computer data is particularly vulnerable to loss or modification.

2 Where a Party gives effect to paragraph 1 above by means of an order to a person to preserve specified stored computer data in the person's possession or control, the Party shall adopt such legislative and other measures as may be necessary to oblige that person to preserve and maintain the integrity of that computer data for a period of time as long as necessary, up to a maximum of ninety days, to enable the competent authorities to seek its disclosure. A Party may provide for such an order to be subsequently renewed.

3 Each Party shall adopt such legislative and other measures as may be necessary to oblige the custodian or other person who is to preserve the computer data to keep confidential the undertaking of such procedures for the period of time provided for by its domestic law.

4 The powers and procedures referred to in this article shall be subject to Articles 14 and 15.

Article 17 – Expedited preservation and partial disclosure of traffic data

For additional analytical, business and investment opportunities information, please contact Global Investment & Business Center, USA at (703) 370-8082. Fax: (703) 370-8083. E-mail: ibpusa3@gmail.com Global Business and Investment Info Databank - www.ibpus.com

1 Each Party shall adopt, in respect of traffic data that is to be preserved under Article 16, such legislative and other measures as may be necessary to:

a ensure that such expeditious preservation of traffic data is available regardless of whether one or more service providers were involved in the transmission of that communication; and

b ensure the expeditious disclosure to the Party's competent authority, or a person designated by that authority, of a sufficient amount of traffic data to enable the Party to identify the service providers and the path through which the communication was transmitted.

2 The powers and procedures referred to in this article shall be subject to Articles 14 and 15.

Title 3 – Production order

Article 18 – Production order

1 Each Party shall adopt such legislative and other measures as may be necessary to empower its competent authorities to order:

a a person in its territory to submit specified computer data in that person's possession or control, which is stored in a computer system or a computer-data storage medium; and

b a service provider offering its services in the territory of the Party to submit subscriber information relating to such services in that service provider's possession or control.

2 The powers and procedures referred to in this article shall be subject to Articles 14 and 15.

3 For the purpose of this article, the term "subscriber information" means any information contained in the form of computer data or any other form that is held by a service provider, relating to subscribers of its services other than traffic or content data and by which can be established:

a the type of communication service used, the technical provisions taken thereto and the period of service;

b the subscriber's identity, postal or geographic address, telephone and other access number, billing and payment information, available on the basis of the service agreement or arrangement;

c any other information on the site of the installation of communication equipment, available on the basis of the service agreement or arrangement.

Title 4 – Search and seizure of stored computer data

Article 19 – Search and seizure of stored computer data

1 Each Party shall adopt such legislative and other measures as may be necessary to empower its competent authorities to search or similarly access:

a a computer system or part of it and computer data stored therein; and

b a computer-data storage medium in which computer data may be stored

For additional analytical, business and investment opportunities information, please contact Global Investment & Business Center, USA at (703) 370-8082. Fax: (703) 370-8083. E-mail: ibpusa3@gmail.com Global Business and Investment Info Databank - www.ibpus.com

in its territory.

2 Each Party shall adopt such legislative and other measures as may be necessary to ensure that where its authorities search or similarly access a specific computer system or part of it, pursuant to paragraph 1.a, and have grounds to believe that the data sought is stored in another computer system or part of it in its territory, and such data is lawfully accessible from or available to the initial system, the authorities shall be able to expeditiously extend the search or similar accessing to the other system.

3 Each Party shall adopt such legislative and other measures as may be necessary to empower its competent authorities to seize or similarly secure computer data accessed according to paragraphs 1 or 2. These measures shall include the power to:

a seize or similarly secure a computer system or part of it or a computer-data storage medium;

b make and retain a copy of those computer data;

c maintain the integrity of the relevant stored computer data;

d render inaccessible or remove those computer data in the accessed computer system.

4 Each Party shall adopt such legislative and other measures as may be necessary to empower its competent authorities to order any person who has knowledge about the functioning of the computer system or measures applied to protect the computer data therein to provide, as is reasonable, the necessary information, to enable the undertaking of the measures referred to in paragraphs 1 and 2.

5 The powers and procedures referred to in this article shall be subject to Articles 14 and 15.

Title 5 – Real-time collection of computer data

Article 20 – Real-time collection of traffic data

1 Each Party shall adopt such legislative and other measures as may be necessary to empower its competent authorities to:

a collect or record through the application of technical means on the territory of that Party, and

b compel a service provider, within its existing technical capability:

i to collect or record through the application of technical means on the territory of that Party; or

ii to co-operate and assist the competent authorities in the collection or recording of,

traffic data, in real-time, associated with specified communications in its territory transmitted by means of a computer system.

2 Where a Party, due to the established principles of its domestic legal system, cannot adopt the measures referred to in paragraph 1.a, it may instead adopt legislative and other measures as may be necessary to ensure the real-time collection or recording of traffic data associated with

specified communications transmitted in its territory, through the application of technical means on that territory.

3 Each Party shall adopt such legislative and other measures as may be necessary to oblige a service provider to keep confidential the fact of the execution of any power provided for in this article and any information relating to it.

4 The powers and procedures referred to in this article shall be subject to Articles 14 and 15.

Article 21 – Interception of content data

1 Each Party shall adopt such legislative and other measures as may be necessary, in relation to a range of serious offences to be determined by domestic law, to empower its competent authorities to:

a collect or record through the application of technical means on the territory of that Party, and

b compel a service provider, within its existing technical capability:

i to collect or record through the application of technical means on the territory of that Party, or

ii to co-operate and assist the competent authorities in the collection or recording of,

content data, in real-time, of specified communications in its territory transmitted by means of a computer system.

2 Where a Party, due to the established principles of its domestic legal system, cannot adopt the measures referred to in paragraph 1.a, it may instead adopt legislative and other measures as may be necessary to ensure the real-time collection or recording of content data on specified communications in its territory through the application of technical means on that territory.

3 Each Party shall adopt such legislative and other measures as may be necessary to oblige a service provider to keep confidential the fact of the execution of any power provided for in this article and any information relating to it.

4 The powers and procedures referred to in this article shall be subject to Articles 14 and 15.

Section 3 – Jurisdiction

Article 22 – Jurisdiction

1 Each Party shall adopt such legislative and other measures as may be necessary to establish jurisdiction over any offence established in accordance with Articles 2 through 11 of this Convention, when the offence is committed:

a in its territory; or

b on board a ship flying the flag of that Party; or

c on board an aircraft registered under the laws of that Party; or

For additional analytical, business and investment opportunities information, please contact Global Investment & Business Center, USA at (703) 370-8082. Fax: (703) 370-8083. E-mail: ibpusa3@gmail.com Global Business and Investment Info Databank - www.ibpus.com

d by one of its nationals, if the offence is punishable under criminal law where it was committed or if the offence is committed outside the territorial jurisdiction of any State.

2 Each Party may reserve the right not to apply or to apply only in specific cases or conditions the jurisdiction rules laid down in paragraphs 1.b through 1.d of this article or any part thereof.

3 Each Party shall adopt such measures as may be necessary to establish jurisdiction over the offences referred to in Article 24, paragraph 1, of this Convention, in cases where an alleged offender is present in its territory and it does not extradite him or her to another Party, solely on the basis of his or her nationality, after a request for extradition.

4 This Convention does not exclude any criminal jurisdiction exercised by a Party in accordance with its domestic law.

5 When more than one Party claims jurisdiction over an alleged offence established in accordance with this Convention, the Parties involved shall, where appropriate, consult with a view to determining the most appropriate jurisdiction for prosecution.

CHAPTER III – INTERNATIONAL CO-OPERATION

Section 1 – General principles

Title 1 – General principles relating to international co-operation

Article 23 – General principles relating to international co-operation

The Parties shall co-operate with each other, in accordance with the provisions of this chapter, and through the application of relevant international instruments on international co-operation in criminal matters, arrangements agreed on the basis of uniform or reciprocal legislation, and domestic laws, to the widest extent possible for the purposes of investigations or proceedings concerning criminal offences related to computer systems and data, or for the collection of evidence in electronic form of a criminal offence.

Title 2 – Principles relating to extradition

Article 24 – Extradition

1 a. This article applies to extradition between Parties for the criminal offences established in accordance with Articles 2 through 11 of this Convention, provided that they are punishable under the laws of both Parties concerned by deprivation of liberty for a maximum period of at least one year, or by a more severe penalty.

b. Where a different minimum penalty is to be applied under an arrangement agreed on the basis of uniform or reciprocal legislation or an extradition treaty, including the European Convention on Extradition (ETS No. 24) , applicable between two or more parties, the minimum penalty provided for under such arrangement or treaty shall apply.

2 The criminal offences described in paragraph 1 of this article shall be deemed to be included as extraditable offences in any extradition treaty existing between or among the Parties. The Parties undertake to include such offences as extraditable offences in any extradition treaty to be concluded between or among them.

For additional analytical, business and investment opportunities information, please contact Global Investment & Business Center, USA at (703) 370-8082. Fax: (703) 370-8083. E-mail: ibpusa3@gmail.com Global Business and Investment Info Databank - www.ibpus.com

3 If a Party that makes extradition conditional on the existence of a treaty receives a request for extradition from another Party with which it does not have an extradition treaty, it may consider this Convention as the legal basis for extradition with respect to any criminal offence referred to in paragraph 1 of this article.

4 Parties that do not make extradition conditional on the existence of a treaty shall recognise the criminal offences referred to in paragraph 1 of this article as extraditable offences between themselves.

5 Extradition shall be subject to the conditions provided for by the law of the requested Party or by applicable extradition treaties, including the grounds on which the requested Party may refuse extradition.

6 If extradition for a criminal offence referred to in paragraph 1 of this article is refused solely on the basis of the nationality of the person sought, or because the requested Party deems that it has jurisdiction over the offence, the requested Party shall submit the case at the request of the requesting Party to its competent authorities for the purpose of prosecution and shall report the final outcome to the requesting Party in due course. Those authorities shall take their decision and conduct their investigations and proceedings in the same manner as for any other offence of a comparable nature under the law of that Party.

7 a. Each Party shall, at the time of signature or when depositing its instrument of ratification, acceptance, approval or accession, communicate to the Secretary General of the Council of Europe the name and address of each authority responsible for making or receiving requests for extradition or provisional arrest in the absence of a treaty.

b. The Secretary General of the Council of Europe shall set up and keep updated a register of authorities so designated by the Parties. Each Party shall ensure that the details held on the register are correct at all times.

Title 3 – General principles relating to mutual assistance

Article 25 – General principles relating to mutual assistance

1 The Parties shall afford one another mutual assistance to the widest extent possible for the purpose of investigations or proceedings concerning criminal offences related to computer systems and data, or for the collection of evidence in electronic form of a criminal offence.

2 Each Party shall also adopt such legislative and other measures as may be necessary to carry out the obligations set forth in Articles 27 through 35.

3 Each Party may, in urgent circumstances, make requests for mutual assistance or communications related thereto by expedited means of communication, including fax or e-mail, to the extent that such means provide appropriate levels of security and authentication (including the use of encryption, where necessary) , with formal confirmation to follow, where required by the requested Party. The requested Party shall accept and respond to the request by any such expedited means of communication.

4 Except as otherwise specifically provided in articles in this chapter, mutual assistance shall be subject to the conditions provided for by the law of the requested Party or by applicable mutual assistance treaties, including the grounds on which the requested Party may refuse co-operation. The requested Party shall not exercise the right to refuse mutual assistance in relation to the

For additional analytical, business and investment opportunities information, please contact Global Investment & Business Center, USA at (703) 370-8082. Fax: (703) 370-8083. E-mail: ibpusa3@gmail.com Global Business and Investment Info Databank - www.ibpus.com

offences referred to in Articles 2 through 11 solely on the ground that the request concerns an offence which it considers a fiscal offence.

5 Where, in accordance with the provisions of this chapter, the requested Party is permitted to make mutual assistance conditional upon the existence of dual criminality, that condition shall be deemed fulfilled, irrespective of whether its laws place the offence within the same category of offence or denominate the offence by the same terminology as the requesting Party, if the conduct underlying the offence for which assistance is sought is a criminal offence under its laws.

Article 26 – Spontaneous information

1 A Party may, within the limits of its domestic law and without prior request, forward to another Party information obtained within the framework of its own investigations when it considers that the disclosure of such information might assist the receiving Party in initiating or carrying out investigations or proceedings concerning criminal offences established in accordance with this Convention or might lead to a request for co-operation by that Party under this chapter.

2 Prior to providing such information, the providing Party may request that it be kept confidential or only used subject to conditions. If the receiving Party cannot comply with such request, it shall notify the providing Party, which shall then determine whether the information should nevertheless be provided. If the receiving Party accepts the information subject to the conditions, it shall be bound by them.

Title 4 – Procedures pertaining to mutual assistance requests in the absence of applicable international agreements

Article 27 – Procedures pertaining to mutual assistance requests in the absence of applicable international agreements

1 Where there is no mutual assistance treaty or arrangement on the basis of uniform or reciprocal legislation in force between the requesting and requested Parties, the provisions of paragraphs 2 through 9 of this article shall apply. The provisions of this article shall not apply where such treaty, arrangement or legislation exists, unless the Parties concerned agree to apply any or all of the remainder of this article in lieu thereof.

2 a. Each Party shall designate a central authority or authorities responsible for sending and answering requests for mutual assistance, the execution of such requests or their transmission to the authorities competent for their execution.

b. The central authorities shall communicate directly with each other;

c. Each Party shall, at the time of signature or when depositing its instrument of ratification, acceptance, approval or accession, communicate to the Secretary General of the Council of Europe the names and addresses of the authorities designated in pursuance of this paragraph;

d. The Secretary General of the Council of Europe shall set up and keep updated a register of central authorities designated by the Parties. Each Party shall ensure that the details held on the register are correct at all times.

3 Mutual assistance requests under this article shall be executed in accordance with the procedures specified by the requesting Party, except where incompatible with the law of the requested Party.

For additional analytical, business and investment opportunities information, please contact Global Investment & Business Center, USA at (703) 370-8082. Fax: (703) 370-8083. E-mail: ibpusa3@gmail.com Global Business and Investment Info Databank - www.ibpus.com

4 The requested Party may, in addition to the grounds for refusal established in Article 25, paragraph 4, refuse assistance if:

a the request concerns an offence which the requested Party considers a political offence or an offence connected with a political offence, or

b it considers that execution of the request is likely to prejudice its sovereignty, security, *ordre public* or other essential interests.

5 The requested Party may postpone action on a request if such action would prejudice criminal investigations or proceedings conducted by its authorities.

6 Before refusing or postponing assistance, the requested Party shall, where appropriate after having consulted with the requesting Party, consider whether the request may be granted partially or subject to such conditions as it deems necessary.

7 The requested Party shall promptly inform the requesting Party of the outcome of the execution of a request for assistance. Reasons shall be given for any refusal or postponement of the request. The requested Party shall also inform the requesting Party of any reasons that render impossible the execution of the request or are likely to delay it significantly.

8 The requesting Party may request that the requested Party keep confidential the fact of any request made under this chapter as well as its subject, except to the extent necessary for its execution. If the requested Party cannot comply with the request for confidentiality, it shall promptly inform the requesting Party, which shall then determine whether the request should nevertheless be executed.

9 a. In the event of urgency, requests for mutual assistance or communications related thereto may be sent directly by judicial authorities of the requesting Party to such authorities of the requested Party. In any such cases, a copy shall be sent at the same time to the central authority of the requested Party through the central authority of the requesting Party.

b. Any request or communication under this paragraph may be made through the International Criminal Police Organisation (Interpol) .

c. Where a request is made pursuant to sub-paragraph a. of this article and the authority is not competent to deal with the request, it shall refer the request to the competent national authority and inform directly the requesting Party that it has done so.

d. Requests or communications made under this paragraph that do not involve coercive action may be directly transmitted by the competent authorities of the requesting Party to the competent authorities of the requested Party.

e. Each Party may, at the time of signature or when depositing its instrument of ratification, acceptance, approval or accession, inform the Secretary General of the Council of Europe that, for reasons of efficiency, requests made under this paragraph are to be addressed to its central authority.

Article 28 – Confidentiality and limitation on use

1 When there is no mutual assistance treaty or arrangement on the basis of uniform or reciprocal legislation in force between the requesting and the requested Parties, the provisions of this article

For additional analytical, business and investment opportunities information, please contact Global Investment & Business Center, USA at (703) 370-8082. Fax: (703) 370-8083. E-mail: ibpusa3@gmail.com Global Business and Investment Info Databank - www.ibpus.com

shall apply. The provisions of this article shall not apply where such treaty, arrangement or legislation exists, unless the Parties concerned agree to apply any or all of the remainder of this article in lieu thereof.

2 The requested Party may make the supply of information or material in response to a request dependent on the condition that it is:

a kept confidential where the request for mutual legal assistance could not be complied with in the absence of such condition, or

b not used for investigations or proceedings other than those stated in the request.

3 If the requesting Party cannot comply with a condition referred to in paragraph 2, it shall promptly inform the other Party, which shall then determine whether the information should nevertheless be provided. When the requesting Party accepts the condition, it shall be bound by it.

4 Any Party that supplies information or material subject to a condition referred to in paragraph 2 may require the other Party to explain, in relation to that condition, the use made of such information or material.

Section 2 – Specific provisions

Title 1 – Mutual assistance regarding provisional measures

Article 29 – Expedited preservation of stored computer data

1 A Party may request another Party to order or otherwise obtain the expeditious preservation of data stored by means of a computer system, located within the territory of that other Party and in respect of which the requesting Party intends to submit a request for mutual assistance for the search or similar access, seizure or similar securing, or disclosure of the data.

2 A request for preservation made under paragraph 1 shall specify:

a the authority seeking the preservation;

b the offence that is the subject of a criminal investigation or proceedings and a brief summary of the related facts;

c the stored computer data to be preserved and its relationship to the offence;

d any available information identifying the custodian of the stored computer data or the location of the computer system;

e the necessity of the preservation; and

f that the Party intends to submit a request for mutual assistance for the search or similar access, seizure or similar securing, or disclosure of the stored computer data.

3 Upon receiving the request from another Party, the requested Party shall take all appropriate measures to preserve expeditiously the specified data in accordance with its domestic law. For

For additional analytical, business and investment opportunities information, please contact Global Investment & Business Center, USA at (703) 370-8082. Fax: (703) 370-8083. E-mail: ibpusa3@gmail.com Global Business and Investment Info Databank - www.ibpus.com

the purposes of responding to a request, dual criminality shall not be required as a condition to providing such preservation.

4 A Party that requires dual criminality as a condition for responding to a request for mutual assistance for the search or similar access, seizure or similar securing, or disclosure of stored data may, in respect of offences other than those established in accordance with Articles 2 through 11 of this Convention, reserve the right to refuse the request for preservation under this article in cases where it has reasons to believe that at the time of disclosure the condition of dual criminality cannot be fulfilled.

5 In addition, a request for preservation may only be refused if:

a the request concerns an offence which the requested Party considers a political offence or an offence connected with a political offence, or

b the requested Party considers that execution of the request is likely to prejudice its sovereignty, security, *ordre public* or other essential interests.

6 Where the requested Party believes that preservation will not ensure the future availability of the data or will threaten the confidentiality of or otherwise prejudice the requesting Party's investigation, it shall promptly so inform the requesting Party, which shall then determine whether the request should nevertheless be executed.

7 Any preservation effected in response to the request referred to in paragraph 1 shall be for a period not less than sixty days, in order to enable the requesting Party to submit a request for the search or similar access, seizure or similar securing, or disclosure of the data. Following the receipt of such a request, the data shall continue to be preserved pending a decision on that request.

Article 30 – Expedited disclosure of preserved traffic data

1 Where, in the course of the execution of a request made pursuant to Article 29 to preserve traffic data concerning a specific communication, the requested Party discovers that a service provider in another State was involved in the transmission of the communication, the requested Party shall expeditiously disclose to the requesting Party a sufficient amount of traffic data to identify that service provider and the path through which the communication was transmitted.

2 Disclosure of traffic data under paragraph 1 may only be withheld if:

a the request concerns an offence which the requested Party considers a political offence or an offence connected with a political offence; or

b the requested Party considers that execution of the request is likely to prejudice its sovereignty, security, *ordre public* or other essential interests.

Title 2 – Mutual assistance regarding investigative powers

Article 31 – Mutual assistance regarding accessing of stored computer data

For additional analytical, business and investment opportunities information, please contact Global Investment & Business Center, USA at (703) 370-8082. Fax: (703) 370-8083. E-mail: ibpusa3@gmail.com Global Business and Investment Info Databank - www.ibpus.com

1 A Party may request another Party to search or similarly access, seize or similarly secure, and disclose data stored by means of a computer system located within the territory of the requested Party, including data that has been preserved pursuant to Article 29.

2 The requested Party shall respond to the request through the application of international instruments, arrangements and laws referred to in Article 23, and in accordance with other relevant provisions of this chapter.

3 The request shall be responded to on an expedited basis where:

a there are grounds to believe that relevant data is particularly vulnerable to loss or modification; or

b the instruments, arrangements and laws referred to in paragraph 2 otherwise provide for expedited co-operation.

Article 32 – Trans-border access to stored computer data with consent or where publicly available

A Party may, without the authorisation of another Party:

a access publicly available (open source) stored computer data, regardless of where the data is located geographically; or

b access or receive, through a computer system in its territory, stored computer data located in another Party, if the Party obtains the lawful and voluntary consent of the person who has the lawful authority to disclose the data to the Party through that computer system.

Article 33 – Mutual assistance regarding the real-time collection of traffic data

1 The Parties shall provide mutual assistance to each other in the real-time collection of traffic data associated with specified communications in their territory transmitted by means of a computer system. Subject to the provisions of paragraph 2, this assistance shall be governed by the conditions and procedures provided for under domestic law.

2 Each Party shall provide such assistance at least with respect to criminal offences for which real-time collection of traffic data would be available in a similar domestic case.

Article 34 – Mutual assistance regarding the interception of content data

The Parties shall provide mutual assistance to each other in the real-time collection or recording of content data of specified communications transmitted by means of a computer system to the extent permitted under their applicable treaties and domestic laws.

Title 3 – 24/7 Network

Article 35 – 24/7 Network

1 Each Party shall designate a point of contact available on a twenty-four hour, seven-day-a-week basis, in order to ensure the provision of immediate assistance for the purpose of investigations or proceedings concerning criminal offences related to computer systems and data,

For additional analytical, business and investment opportunities information, please contact Global Investment & Business Center, USA at (703) 370-8082. Fax: (703) 370-8083. E-mail: ibpusa3@gmail.com Global Business and Investment Info Databank - www.ibpus.com

or for the collection of evidence in electronic form of a criminal offence. Such assistance shall include facilitating, or, if permitted by its domestic law and practice, directly carrying out the following measures:

a the provision of technical advice;

b the preservation of data pursuant to Articles 29 and 30;

c the collection of evidence, the provision of legal information, and locating of suspects.

2 a. A Party's point of contact shall have the capacity to carry out communications with the point of contact of another Party on an expedited basis.

b. If the point of contact designated by a Party is not part of that Party's authority or authorities responsible for international mutual assistance or extradition, the point of contact shall ensure that it is able to co-ordinate with such authority or authorities on an expedited basis.

3 Each Party shall ensure that trained and equipped personnel are available, in order to facilitate the operation of the network.

CHAPTER IV – FINAL PROVISIONS

Article 36 – Signature and entry into force

1 This Convention shall be open for signature by the member States of the Council of Europe and by non-member States which have participated in its elaboration.

2 This Convention is subject to ratification, acceptance or approval. Instruments of ratification, acceptance or approval shall be deposited with the Secretary General of the Council of Europe.

3 This Convention shall enter into force on the first day of the month following the expiration of a period of three months after the date on which five States, including at least three member States of the Council of Europe, have expressed their consent to be bound by the Convention in accordance with the provisions of paragraphs 1 and 2.

4 In respect of any signatory State which subsequently expresses its consent to be bound by it, the Convention shall enter into force on the first day of the month following the expiration of a period of three months after the date of the expression of its consent to be bound by the Convention in accordance with the provisions of paragraphs 1 and 2.

Article 37 – Accession to the Convention

1 After the entry into force of this Convention, the Committee of Ministers of the Council of Europe, after consulting with and obtaining the unanimous consent of the Contracting States to the Convention, may invite any State which is not a member of the Council and which has not participated in its elaboration to accede to this Convention. The decision shall be taken by the majority provided for in Article 20.d. of the Statute of the Council of Europe and by the unanimous vote of the representatives of the Contracting States entitled to sit on the Committee of Ministers.

2 In respect of any State acceding to the Convention under paragraph 1 above, the Convention shall enter into force on the first day of the month following the expiration of a period of three

For additional analytical, business and investment opportunities information, please contact Global Investment & Business Center, USA at (703) 370-8082. Fax: (703) 370-8083. E-mail: ibpusa3@gmail.com Global Business and Investment Info Databank - www.ibpus.com

months after the date of deposit of the instrument of accession with the Secretary General of the Council of Europe.

Article 38 – Territorial application

1 Any State may, at the time of signature or when depositing its instrument of ratification, acceptance, approval or accession, specify the territory or territories to which this Convention shall apply.

2 Any State may, at any later date, by a declaration addressed to the Secretary General of the Council of Europe, extend the application of this Convention to any other territory specified in the declaration. In respect of such territory the Convention shall enter into force on the first day of the month following the expiration of a period of three months after the date of receipt of the declaration by the Secretary General.

3 Any declaration made under the two preceding paragraphs may, in respect of any territory specified in such declaration, be withdrawn by a notification addressed to the Secretary General of the Council of Europe. The withdrawal shall become effective on the first day of the month following the expiration of a period of three months after the date of receipt of such notification by the Secretary General.

Article 39 – Effects of the Convention

1 The purpose of the present Convention is to supplement applicable multilateral or bilateral treaties or arrangements as between the Parties, including the provisions of:

– the European Convention on Extradition, opened for signature in Paris, on 13 December 1957 (ETS No. 24) ;

– the European Convention on Mutual Assistance in Criminal Matters, opened for signature in Strasbourg, on 20 April 1959 (ETS No. 30) ;

– the Additional Protocol to the European Convention on Mutual Assistance in Criminal Matters, opened for signature in Strasbourg, on 17 March 1978 (ETS No. 99) .

2 If two or more Parties have already concluded an agreement or treaty on the matters dealt with in this Convention or have otherwise established their relations on such matters, or should they in future do so, they shall also be entitled to apply that agreement or treaty or to regulate those relations accordingly. However, where Parties establish their relations in respect of the matters dealt with in the present Convention other than as regulated therein, they shall do so in a manner that is not inconsistent with the Convention's objectives and principles.

3 Nothing in this Convention shall affect other rights, restrictions, obligations and responsibilities of a Party.

Article 40 – Declarations

By a written notification addressed to the Secretary General of the Council of Europe, any State may, at the time of signature or when depositing its instrument of ratification, acceptance, approval or accession, declare that it avails itself of the possibility of requiring additional elements as provided for under Articles 2, 3, 6 paragraph 1.b, 7, 9 paragraph 3, and 27, paragraph 9.e.

For additional analytical, business and investment opportunities information, please contact Global Investment & Business Center, USA at (703) 370-8082. Fax: (703) 370-8083. E-mail: ibpusa3@gmail.com Global Business and Investment Info Databank - www.ibpus.com

Article 41 – Federal clause

1 A federal State may reserve the right to assume obligations under Chapter II of this Convention consistent with its fundamental principles governing the relationship between its central government and constituent States or other similar territorial entities provided that it is still able to co-operate under Chapter III.

2 When making a reservation under paragraph 1, a federal State may not apply the terms of such reservation to exclude or substantially diminish its obligations to provide for measures set forth in Chapter II. Overall, it shall provide for a broad and effective law enforcement capability with respect to those measures.

3 With regard to the provisions of this Convention, the application of which comes under the jurisdiction of constituent States or other similar territorial entities, that are not obliged by the constitutional system of the federation to take legislative measures, the federal government shall inform the competent authorities of such States of the said provisions with its favourable opinion, encouraging them to take appropriate action to give them effect.

Article 42 – Reservations

By a written notification addressed to the Secretary General of the Council of Europe, any State may, at the time of signature or when depositing its instrument of ratification, acceptance, approval or accession, declare that it avails itself of the reservation(s) provided for in Article 4, paragraph 2, Article 6, paragraph 3, Article 9, paragraph 4, Article 10, paragraph 3, Article 11, paragraph 3, Article 14, paragraph 3, Article 22, paragraph 2, Article 29, paragraph 4, and Article 41, paragraph 1. No other reservation may be made.

Article 43 – Status and withdrawal of reservations

1 A Party that has made a reservation in accordance with Article 42 may wholly or partially withdraw it by means of a notification addressed to the Secretary General of the Council of Europe. Such withdrawal shall take effect on the date of receipt of such notification by the Secretary General. If the notification states that the withdrawal of a reservation is to take effect on a date specified therein, and such date is later than the date on which the notification is received by the Secretary General, the withdrawal shall take effect on such a later date.

2 A Party that has made a reservation as referred to in Article 42 shall withdraw such reservation, in whole or in part, as soon as circumstances so permit.

3 The Secretary General of the Council of Europe may periodically enquire with Parties that have made one or more reservations as referred to in Article 42 as to the prospects for withdrawing such reservation(s) .

Article 44 – Amendments

1 Amendments to this Convention may be proposed by any Party, and shall be communicated by the Secretary General of the Council of Europe to the member States of the Council of Europe, to the non-member States which have participated in the elaboration of this Convention as well as to any State which has acceded to, or has been invited to accede to, this Convention in accordance with the provisions of Article 37.

For additional analytical, business and investment opportunities information, please contact Global Investment & Business Center, USA at (703) 370-8082. Fax: (703) 370-8083. E-mail: ibpusa3@gmail.com Global Business and Investment Info Databank - www.ibpus.com

2 Any amendment proposed by a Party shall be communicated to the European Committee on Crime Problems (CDPC) , which shall submit to the Committee of Ministers its opinion on that proposed amendment.

3 The Committee of Ministers shall consider the proposed amendment and the opinion submitted by the CDPC and, following consultation with the non-member States Parties to this Convention, may adopt the amendment.

4 The text of any amendment adopted by the Committee of Ministers in accordance with paragraph 3 of this article shall be forwarded to the Parties for acceptance.

5 Any amendment adopted in accordance with paragraph 3 of this article shall come into force on the thirtieth day after all Parties have informed the Secretary General of their acceptance thereof.

Article 45 – Settlement of disputes

1 The European Committee on Crime Problems (CDPC) shall be kept informed regarding the interpretation and application of this Convention.

2 In case of a dispute between Parties as to the interpretation or application of this Convention, they shall seek a settlement of the dispute through negotiation or any other peaceful means of their choice, including submission of the dispute to the CDPC, to an arbitral tribunal whose decisions shall be binding upon the Parties, or to the International Court of Justice, as agreed upon by the Parties concerned.

Article 46 – Consultations of the Parties

1 The Parties shall, as appropriate, consult periodically with a view to facilitating:

a the effective use and implementation of this Convention, including the identification of any problems thereof, as well as the effects of any declaration or reservation made under this Convention;

b the exchange of information on significant legal, policy or technological developments pertaining to cybercrime and the collection of evidence in electronic form;

c consideration of possible supplementation or amendment of the Convention.

2 The European Committee on Crime Problems (CDPC) shall be kept periodically informed regarding the result of consultations referred to in paragraph 1.

3 The CDPC shall, as appropriate, facilitate the consultations referred to in paragraph 1 and take the measures necessary to assist the Parties in their efforts to supplement or amend the Convention. At the latest three years after the present Convention enters into force, the European Committee on Crime Problems (CDPC) shall, in co-operation with the Parties, conduct a review of all of the Convention's provisions and, if necessary, recommend any appropriate amendments.

4 Except where assumed by the Council of Europe, expenses incurred in carrying out the provisions of paragraph 1 shall be borne by the Parties in the manner to be determined by them.

For additional analytical, business and investment opportunities information, please contact Global Investment & Business Center, USA at (703) 370-8082. Fax: (703) 370-8083. E-mail: ibpusa3@gmail.com Global Business and Investment Info Databank - www.ibpus.com

5 The Parties shall be assisted by the Secretariat of the Council of Europe in carrying out their functions pursuant to this article.

Article 47 – Denunciation

1 Any Party may, at any time, denounce this Convention by means of a notification addressed to the Secretary General of the Council of Europe.

2 Such denunciation shall become effective on the first day of the month following the expiration of a period of three months after the date of receipt of the notification by the Secretary General.

Article 48 – Notification

The Secretary General of the Council of Europe shall notify the member States of the Council of Europe, the non-member States which have participated in the elaboration of this Convention as well as any State which has acceded to, or has been invited to accede to, this Convention of:

a any signature;

b the deposit of any instrument of ratification, acceptance, approval or accession;

c any date of entry into force of this Convention in accordance with Articles 36 and 37;

d any declaration made under Article 40 or reservation made in accordance with Article 42;

e any other act, notification or communication relating to this Convention.

In witness whereof the undersigned, being duly authorised thereto, have signed this Convention.

Done at Budapest, this 23rd day of November 2001, in English and in French, both texts being equally authentic, in a single copy which shall be deposited in the archives of the Council of Europe. The Secretary General of the Council of Europe shall transmit certified copies to each member State of the Council of Europe, to the non-member States which have participated in the elaboration of this Convention, and to any State invited to accede to it.

DIRECTIVE ON PRIVACY AND ELECTRONIC COMMUNICATIONS

Directive 2002/58/EC of the European Parliament and of the Council

of 12 July 2002

concerning the processing of personal data and the protection of privacy in the electronic communications sector (Directive on privacy and electronic communications)

THE EUROPEAN PARLIAMENT AND THE COUNCIL OF THE EUROPEAN UNION,

Having regard to the Treaty establishing the European Community, and in particular Article 95 thereof,

Having regard to the proposal from the Commission(1) ,

Having regard to the opinion of the Economic and Social Committee(2) ,

Having consulted the Committee of the Regions,

Acting in accordance with the procedure laid down in Article 251 of the Treaty(3) ,

Whereas:

(1) Directive 95/46/EC of the European Parliament and of the Council of 24 October 1995 on the protection of individuals with regard to the processing of personal data and on the free movement of such data(4) requires Member States to ensure the rights and freedoms of natural persons with regard to the processing of personal data, and in particular their right to privacy, in order to ensure the free flow of personal data in the Community.

(2) This Directive seeks to respect the fundamental rights and observes the principles recognised in particular by the Charter of fundamental rights of the European Union. In particular, this Directive seeks to ensure full respect for the rights set out in Articles 7 and 8 of that Charter.

(3) Confidentiality of communications is guaranteed in accordance with the international instruments relating to human rights, in particular the European Convention for the Protection of Human Rights and Fundamental Freedoms, and the constitutions of the Member States.

(4) Directive 97/66/EC of the European Parliament and of the Council of 15 December 1997 concerning the processing of personal data and the protection of privacy in the telecommunications sector(5) translated the principles set out in Directive 95/46/EC into specific rules for the telecommunications sector. Directive 97/66/EC has to be adapted to developments in the markets and technologies for electronic communications services in order to provide an equal level of protection of personal data and privacy for users of publicly available electronic communications services, regardless of the technologies used. That Directive should therefore be repealed and replaced by this Directive.

(5) New advanced digital technologies are currently being introduced in public communications networks in the Community, which give rise to specific requirements concerning the protection of personal data and privacy of the user. The development of the information society is characterised by the introduction of new electronic communications services. Access to digital mobile networks has become available and affordable for a large public. These digital networks have large capacities and possibilities for processing personal data. The successful cross-border development of these services is partly dependent on the confidence of users that their privacy will not be at risk.

(6) The Internet is overturning traditional market structures by providing a common, global infrastructure for the delivery of a wide range of electronic communications services. Publicly available electronic communications services over the Internet open new possibilities for users but also new risks for their personal data and privacy.

(7) In the case of public communications networks, specific legal, regulatory and technical provisions should be made in order to protect fundamental rights and freedoms of natural persons and legitimate interests of legal persons, in particular with regard to the increasing capacity for automated storage and processing of data relating to subscribers and users.

(8) Legal, regulatory and technical provisions adopted by the Member States concerning the protection of personal data, privacy and the legitimate interest of legal persons, in the electronic communication sector, should be harmonised in order to avoid obstacles to the internal market for electronic communication in accordance with Article 14 of the Treaty. Harmonisation should be

For additional analytical, business and investment opportunities information, please contact Global Investment & Business Center, USA at (703) 370-8082. Fax: (703) 370-8083. E-mail: ibpusa3@gmail.com Global Business and Investment Info Databank - www.ibpus.com

limited to requirements necessary to guarantee that the promotion and development of new electronic communications services and networks between Member States are not hindered.

(9) The Member States, providers and users concerned, together with the competent Community bodies, should cooperate in introducing and developing the relevant technologies where this is necessary to apply the guarantees provided for by this Directive and taking particular account of the objectives of minimising the processing of personal data and of using anonymous or pseudonymous data where possible.

(10) In the electronic communications sector, Directive 95/46/EC applies in particular to all matters concerning protection of fundamental rights and freedoms, which are not specifically covered by the provisions of this Directive, including the obligations on the controller and the rights of individuals. Directive 95/46/EC applies to non-public communications services.

(11) Like Directive 95/46/EC, this Directive does not address issues of protection of fundamental rights and freedoms related to activities which are not governed by Community law. Therefore it does not alter the existing balance between the individual's right to privacy and the possibility for Member States to take the measures referred to in Article 15(1) of this Directive, necessary for the protection of public security, defence, State security (including the economic well-being of the State when the activities relate to State security matters) and the enforcement of criminal law. Consequently, this Directive does not affect the ability of Member States to carry out lawful interception of electronic communications, or take other measures, if necessary for any of these purposes and in accordance with the European Convention for the Protection of Human Rights and Fundamental Freedoms, as interpreted by the rulings of the European Court of Human Rights. Such measures must be appropriate, strictly proportionate to the intended purpose and necessary within a democratic society and should be subject to adequate safeguards in accordance with the European Convention for the Protection of Human Rights and Fundamental Freedoms.

(12) Subscribers to a publicly available electronic communications service may be natural or legal persons. By supplementing Directive 95/46/EC, this Directive is aimed at protecting the fundamental rights of natural persons and particularly their right to privacy, as well as the legitimate interests of legal persons. This Directive does not entail an obligation for Member States to extend the application of Directive 95/46/EC to the protection of the legitimate interests of legal persons, which is ensured within the framework of the applicable Community and national legislation.

(13) The contractual relation between a subscriber and a service provider may entail a periodic or a one-off payment for the service provided or to be provided. Prepaid cards are also considered as a contract.

(14) Location data may refer to the latitude, longitude and altitude of the user's terminal equipment, to the direction of travel, to the level of accuracy of the location information, to the identification of the network cell in which the terminal equipment is located at a certain point in time and to the time the location information was recorded.

(15) A communication may include any naming, numbering or addressing information provided by the sender of a communication or the user of a connection to carry out the communication. Traffic data may include any translation of this information by the network over which the communication is transmitted for the purpose of carrying out the transmission. Traffic data may, inter alia, consist of data referring to the routing, duration, time or volume of a communication, to the protocol used, to the location of the terminal equipment of the sender or recipient, to the network on which the communication originates or terminates, to the beginning, end or duration of

For additional analytical, business and investment opportunities information, please contact Global Investment & Business Center, USA at (703) 370-8082. Fax: (703) 370-8083. E-mail: ibpusa3@gmail.com Global Business and Investment Info Databank - www.ibpus.com

a connection. They may also consist of the format in which the communication is conveyed by the network.

(16) Information that is part of a broadcasting service provided over a public communications network is intended for a potentially unlimited audience and does not constitute a communication in the sense of this Directive. However, in cases where the individual subscriber or user receiving such information can be identified, for example with video-on-demand services, the information conveyed is covered within the meaning of a communication for the purposes of this Directive.

(17) For the purposes of this Directive, consent of a user or subscriber, regardless of whether the latter is a natural or a legal person, should have the same meaning as the data subject's consent as defined and further specified in Directive 95/46/EC. Consent may be given by any appropriate method enabling a freely given specific and informed indication of the user's wishes, including by ticking a box when visiting an Internet website.

(18) Value added services may, for example, consist of advice on least expensive tariff packages, route guidance, traffic information, weather forecasts and tourist information.

(19) The application of certain requirements relating to presentation and restriction of calling and connected line identification and to automatic call forwarding to subscriber lines connected to analogue exchanges should not be made mandatory in specific cases where such application would prove to be technically impossible or would require a disproportionate economic effort. It is important for interested parties to be informed of such cases and the Member States should therefore notify them to the Commission.

(20) Service providers should take appropriate measures to safeguard the security of their services, if necessary in conjunction with the provider of the network, and inform subscribers of any special risks of a breach of the security of the network. Such risks may especially occur for electronic communications services over an open network such as the Internet or analogue mobile telephony. It is particularly important for subscribers and users of such services to be fully informed by their service provider of the existing security risks which lie outside the scope of possible remedies by the service provider. Service providers who offer publicly available electronic communications services over the Internet should inform users and subscribers of measures they can take to protect the security of their communications for instance by using specific types of software or encryption technologies. The requirement to inform subscribers of particular security risks does not discharge a service provider from the obligation to take, at its own costs, appropriate and immediate measures to remedy any new, unforeseen security risks and restore the normal security level of the service. The provision of information about security risks to the subscriber should be free of charge except for any nominal costs which the subscriber may incur while receiving or collecting the information, for instance by downloading an electronic mail message. Security is appraised in the light of Article 17 of Directive 95/46/EC.

(21) Measures should be taken to prevent unauthorised access to communications in order to protect the confidentiality of communications, including both the contents and any data related to such communications, by means of public communications networks and publicly available electronic communications services. National legislation in some Member States only prohibits intentional unauthorised access to communications.

(22) The prohibition of storage of communications and the related traffic data by persons other than the users or without their consent is not intended to prohibit any automatic, intermediate and transient storage of this information in so far as this takes place for the sole purpose of carrying out the transmission in the electronic communications network and provided that the information is not stored for any period longer than is necessary for the transmission and for traffic management purposes, and that during the period of storage the confidentiality remains

guaranteed. Where this is necessary for making more efficient the onward transmission of any publicly accessible information to other recipients of the service upon their request, this Directive should not prevent such information from being further stored, provided that this information would in any case be accessible to the public without restriction and that any data referring to the individual subscribers or users requesting such information are erased.

(23) Confidentiality of communications should also be ensured in the course of lawful business practice. Where necessary and legally authorised, communications can be recorded for the purpose of providing evidence of a commercial transaction. Directive 95/46/EC applies to such processing. Parties to the communications should be informed prior to the recording about the recording, its purpose and the duration of its storage. The recorded communication should be erased as soon as possible and in any case at the latest by the end of the period during which the transaction can be lawfully challenged.

(24) Terminal equipment of users of electronic communications networks and any information stored on such equipment are part of the private sphere of the users requiring protection under the European Convention for the Protection of Human Rights and Fundamental Freedoms. So-called spyware, web bugs, hidden identifiers and other similar devices can enter the user's terminal without their knowledge in order to gain access to information, to store hidden information or to trace the activities of the user and may seriously intrude upon the privacy of these users. The use of such devices should be allowed only for legitimate purposes, with the knowledge of the users concerned.

(25) However, such devices, for instance so-called "cookies", can be a legitimate and useful tool, for example, in analysing the effectiveness of website design and advertising, and in verifying the identity of users engaged in on-line transactions. Where such devices, for instance cookies, are intended for a legitimate purpose, such as to facilitate the provision of information society services, their use should be allowed on condition that users are provided with clear and precise information in accordance with Directive 95/46/EC about the purposes of cookies or similar devices so as to ensure that users are made aware of information being placed on the terminal equipment they are using. Users should have the opportunity to refuse to have a cookie or similar device stored on their terminal equipment. This is particularly important where users other than the original user have access to the terminal equipment and thereby to any data containing privacy-sensitive information stored on such equipment. Information and the right to refuse may be offered once for the use of various devices to be installed on the user's terminal equipment during the same connection and also covering any further use that may be made of those devices during subsequent connections. The methods for giving information, offering a right to refuse or requesting consent should be made as user-friendly as possible. Access to specific website content may still be made conditional on the well-informed acceptance of a cookie or similar device, if it is used for a legitimate purpose.

(26) The data relating to subscribers processed within electronic communications networks to establish connections and to transmit information contain information on the private life of natural persons and concern the right to respect for their correspondence or concern the legitimate interests of legal persons. Such data may only be stored to the extent that is necessary for the provision of the service for the purpose of billing and for interconnection payments, and for a limited time. Any further processing of such data which the provider of the publicly available electronic communications services may want to perform, for the marketing of electronic communications services or for the provision of value added services, may only be allowed if the subscriber has agreed to this on the basis of accurate and full information given by the provider of the publicly available electronic communications services about the types of further processing it intends to perform and about the subscriber's right not to give or to withdraw his/her consent to such processing. Traffic data used for marketing communications services or for the provision of value added services should also be erased or made anonymous after the provision of the

service. Service providers should always keep subscribers informed of the types of data they are processing and the purposes and duration for which this is done.

(27) The exact moment of the completion of the transmission of a communication, after which traffic data should be erased except for billing purposes, may depend on the type of electronic communications service that is provided. For instance for a voice telephony call the transmission will be completed as soon as either of the users terminates the connection. For electronic mail the transmission is completed as soon as the addressee collects the message, typically from the server of his service provider.

(28) The obligation to erase traffic data or to make such data anonymous when it is no longer needed for the purpose of the transmission of a communication does not conflict with such procedures on the Internet as the caching in the domain name system of IP addresses or the caching of IP addresses to physical address bindings or the use of log-in information to control the right of access to networks or services.

(29) The service provider may process traffic data relating to subscribers and users where necessary in individual cases in order to detect technical failure or errors in the transmission of communications. Traffic data necessary for billing purposes may also be processed by the provider in order to detect and stop fraud consisting of unpaid use of the electronic communications service.

(30) Systems for the provision of electronic communications networks and services should be designed to limit the amount of personal data necessary to a strict minimum. Any activities related to the provision of the electronic communications service that go beyond the transmission of a communication and the billing thereof should be based on aggregated, traffic data that cannot be related to subscribers or users. Where such activities cannot be based on aggregated data, they should be considered as value added services for which the consent of the subscriber is required.

(31) Whether the consent to be obtained for the processing of personal data with a view to providing a particular value added service should be that of the user or of the subscriber, will depend on the data to be processed and on the type of service to be provided and on whether it is technically, procedurally and contractually possible to distinguish the individual using an electronic communications service from the legal or natural person having subscribed to it.

(32) Where the provider of an electronic communications service or of a value added service subcontracts the processing of personal data necessary for the provision of these services to another entity, such subcontracting and subsequent data processing should be in full compliance with the requirements regarding controllers and processors of personal data as set out in Directive 95/46/EC. Where the provision of a value added service requires that traffic or location data are forwarded from an electronic communications service provider to a provider of value added services, the subscribers or users to whom the data are related should also be fully informed of this forwarding before giving their consent for the processing of the data.

(33) The introduction of itemised bills has improved the possibilities for the subscriber to check the accuracy of the fees charged by the service provider but, at the same time, it may jeopardise the privacy of the users of publicly available electronic communications services. Therefore, in order to preserve the privacy of the user, Member States should encourage the development of electronic communication service options such as alternative payment facilities which allow anonymous or strictly private access to publicly available electronic communications services, for example calling cards and facilities for payment by credit card. To the same end, Member States may ask the operators to offer their subscribers a different type of detailed bill in which a certain number of digits of the called number have been deleted.

For additional analytical, business and investment opportunities information, please contact Global Investment & Business Center, USA at (703) 370-8082. Fax: (703) 370-8083. E-mail: ibpusa3@gmail.com Global Business and Investment Info Databank - www.ibpus.com

(34) It is necessary, as regards calling line identification, to protect the right of the calling party to withhold the presentation of the identification of the line from which the call is being made and the right of the called party to reject calls from unidentified lines. There is justification for overriding the elimination of calling line identification presentation in specific cases. Certain subscribers, in particular help lines and similar organisations, have an interest in guaranteeing the anonymity of their callers. It is necessary, as regards connected line identification, to protect the right and the legitimate interest of the called party to withhold the presentation of the identification of the line to which the calling party is actually connected, in particular in the case of forwarded calls. The providers of publicly available electronic communications services should inform their subscribers of the existence of calling and connected line identification in the network and of all services which are offered on the basis of calling and connected line identification as well as the privacy options which are available. This will allow the subscribers to make an informed choice about the privacy facilities they may want to use. The privacy options which are offered on a per-line basis do not necessarily have to be available as an automatic network service but may be obtainable through a simple request to the provider of the publicly available electronic communications service.

(35) In digital mobile networks, location data giving the geographic position of the terminal equipment of the mobile user are processed to enable the transmission of communications. Such data are traffic data covered by Article 6 of this Directive. However, in addition, digital mobile networks may have the capacity to process location data which are more precise than is necessary for the transmission of communications and which are used for the provision of value added services such as services providing individualised traffic information and guidance to drivers. The processing of such data for value added services should only be allowed where subscribers have given their consent. Even in cases where subscribers have given their consent, they should have a simple means to temporarily deny the processing of location data, free of charge.

(36) Member States may restrict the users' and subscribers' rights to privacy with regard to calling line identification where this is necessary to trace nuisance calls and with regard to calling line identification and location data where this is necessary to allow emergency services to carry out their tasks as effectively as possible. For these purposes, Member States may adopt specific provisions to entitle providers of electronic communications services to provide access to calling line identification and location data without the prior consent of the users or subscribers concerned.

(37) Safeguards should be provided for subscribers against the nuisance which may be caused by automatic call forwarding by others. Moreover, in such cases, it must be possible for subscribers to stop the forwarded calls being passed on to their terminals by simple request to the provider of the publicly available electronic communications service.

(38) Directories of subscribers to electronic communications services are widely distributed and public. The right to privacy of natural persons and the legitimate interest of legal persons require that subscribers are able to determine whether their personal data are published in a directory and if so, which. Providers of public directories should inform the subscribers to be included in such directories of the purposes of the directory and of any particular usage which may be made of electronic versions of public directories especially through search functions embedded in the software, such as reverse search functions enabling users of the directory to discover the name and address of the subscriber on the basis of a telephone number only.

(39) The obligation to inform subscribers of the purpose(s) of public directories in which their personal data are to be included should be imposed on the party collecting the data for such inclusion. Where the data may be transmitted to one or more third parties, the subscriber should be informed of this possibility and of the recipient or the categories of possible recipients. Any

For additional analytical, business and investment opportunities information, please contact Global Investment & Business Center, USA at (703) 370-8082. Fax: (703) 370-8083. E-mail: ibpusa3@gmail.com Global Business and Investment Info Databank - www.ibpus.com

transmission should be subject to the condition that the data may not be used for other purposes than those for which they were collected. If the party collecting the data from the subscriber or any third party to whom the data have been transmitted wishes to use the data for an additional purpose, the renewed consent of the subscriber is to be obtained either by the initial party collecting the data or by the third party to whom the data have been transmitted.

(40) Safeguards should be provided for subscribers against intrusion of their privacy by unsolicited communications for direct marketing purposes in particular by means of automated calling machines, telefaxes, and e-mails, including SMS messages. These forms of unsolicited commercial communications may on the one hand be relatively easy and cheap to send and on the other may impose a burden and/or cost on the recipient. Moreover, in some cases their volume may also cause difficulties for electronic communications networks and terminal equipment. For such forms of unsolicited communications for direct marketing, it is justified to require that prior explicit consent of the recipients is obtained before such communications are addressed to them. The single market requires a harmonised approach to ensure simple, Community-wide rules for businesses and users.

(41) Within the context of an existing customer relationship, it is reasonable to allow the use of electronic contact details for the offering of similar products or services, but only by the same company that has obtained the electronic contact details in accordance with Directive 95/46/EC. When electronic contact details are obtained, the customer should be informed about their further use for direct marketing in a clear and distinct manner, and be given the opportunity to refuse such usage. This opportunity should continue to be offered with each subsequent direct marketing message, free of charge, except for any costs for the transmission of this refusal.

(42) Other forms of direct marketing that are more costly for the sender and impose no financial costs on subscribers and users, such as person-to-person voice telephony calls, may justify the maintenance of a system giving subscribers or users the possibility to indicate that they do not want to receive such calls. Nevertheless, in order not to decrease existing levels of privacy protection, Member States should be entitled to uphold national systems, only allowing such calls to subscribers and users who have given their prior consent.

(43) To facilitate effective enforcement of Community rules on unsolicited messages for direct marketing, it is necessary to prohibit the use of false identities or false return addresses or numbers while sending unsolicited messages for direct marketing purposes.

(44) Certain electronic mail systems allow subscribers to view the sender and subject line of an electronic mail, and also to delete the message, without having to download the rest of the electronic mail's content or any attachments, thereby reducing costs which could arise from downloading unsolicited electronic mails or attachments. These arrangements may continue to be useful in certain cases as an additional tool to the general obligations established in this Directive.

(45) This Directive is without prejudice to the arrangements which Member States make to protect the legitimate interests of legal persons with regard to unsolicited communications for direct marketing purposes. Where Member States establish an opt-out register for such communications to legal persons, mostly business users, the provisions of Article 7 of Directive 2000/31/EC of the European Parliament and of the Council of 8 June 2000 on certain legal aspects of information society services, in particular electronic commerce, in the internal market (Directive on electronic commerce) (6) are fully applicable.

(46) The functionalities for the provision of electronic communications services may be integrated in the network or in any part of the terminal equipment of the user, including the software. The protection of the personal data and the privacy of the user of publicly available electronic communications services should be independent of the configuration of the various components

For additional analytical, business and investment opportunities information, please contact Global Investment & Business Center, USA at (703) 370-8082. Fax: (703) 370-8083. E-mail: ibpusa3@gmail.com Global Business and Investment Info Databank - www.ibpus.com

necessary to provide the service and of the distribution of the necessary functionalities between these components. Directive 95/46/EC covers any form of processing of personal data regardless of the technology used. The existence of specific rules for electronic communications services alongside general rules for other components necessary for the provision of such services may not facilitate the protection of personal data and privacy in a technologically neutral way. It may therefore be necessary to adopt measures requiring manufacturers of certain types of equipment used for electronic communications services to construct their product in such a way as to incorporate safeguards to ensure that the personal data and privacy of the user and subscriber are protected. The adoption of such measures in accordance with Directive 1999/5/EC of the European Parliament and of the Council of 9 March 1999 on radio equipment and telecommunications terminal equipment and the mutual recognition of their conformity(7) will ensure that the introduction of technical features of electronic communication equipment including software for data protection purposes is harmonised in order to be compatible with the implementation of the internal market.

(47) Where the rights of the users and subscribers are not respected, national legislation should provide for judicial remedies. Penalties should be imposed on any person, whether governed by private or public law, who fails to comply with the national measures taken under this Directive.

(48) It is useful, in the field of application of this Directive, to draw on the experience of the Working Party on the Protection of Individuals with regard to the Processing of Personal Data composed of representatives of the supervisory authorities of the Member States, set up by Article 29 of Directive 95/46/EC.

(49) To facilitate compliance with the provisions of this Directive, certain specific arrangements are needed for processing of data already under way on the date that national implementing legislation pursuant to this Directive enters into force,

HAVE ADOPTED THIS DIRECTIVE:

Article 1

Scope and aim

1. This Directive harmonises the provisions of the Member States required to ensure an equivalent level of protection of fundamental rights and freedoms, and in particular the right to privacy, with respect to the processing of personal data in the electronic communication sector and to ensure the free movement of such data and of electronic communication equipment and services in the Community.

2. The provisions of this Directive particularise and complement Directive 95/46/EC for the purposes mentioned in paragraph 1. Moreover, they provide for protection of the legitimate interests of subscribers who are legal persons.

3. This Directive shall not apply to activities which fall outside the scope of the Treaty establishing the European Community, such as those covered by Titles V and VI of the Treaty on European Union, and in any case to activities concerning public security, defence, State security (including the economic well-being of the State when the activities relate to State security matters) and the activities of the State in areas of criminal law.

ARTICLE 2 DEFINITIONS

Save as otherwise provided, the definitions in Directive 95/46/EC and in Directive 2002/21/EC of the European Parliament and of the Council of 7 March 2002 on a common regulatory framework for electronic communications networks and services (Framework Directive) (8) shall apply.

The following definitions shall also apply:

(a) "user" means any natural person using a publicly available electronic communications service, for private or business purposes, without necessarily having subscribed to this service;

(b) "traffic data" means any data processed for the purpose of the conveyance of a communication on an electronic communications network or for the billing thereof;

(c) "location data" means any data processed in an electronic communications network, indicating the geographic position of the terminal equipment of a user of a publicly available electronic communications service;

(d) "communication" means any information exchanged or conveyed between a finite number of parties by means of a publicly available electronic communications service. This does not include any information conveyed as part of a broadcasting service to the public over an electronic communications network except to the extent that the information can be related to the identifiable subscriber or user receiving the information;

(e) "call" means a connection established by means of a publicly available telephone service allowing two-way communication in real time;

(f) "consent" by a user or subscriber corresponds to the data subject's consent in Directive 95/46/EC;

(g) "value added service" means any service which requires the processing of traffic data or location data other than traffic data beyond what is necessary for the transmission of a communication or the billing thereof;

(h) "electronic mail" means any text, voice, sound or image message sent over a public communications network which can be stored in the network or in the recipient's terminal equipment until it is collected by the recipient.

ARTICLE 3 SERVICES CONCERNED

1. This Directive shall apply to the processing of personal data in connection with the provision of publicly available electronic communications services in public communications networks in the Community.

2. Articles 8, 10 and 11 shall apply to subscriber lines connected to digital exchanges and, where technically possible and if it does not require a disproportionate economic effort, to subscriber lines connected to analogue exchanges.

3. Cases where it would be technically impossible or require a disproportionate economic effort to fulfil the requirements of Articles 8, 10 and 11 shall be notified to the Commission by the Member States.

ARTICLE 4 SECURITY

1. The provider of a publicly available electronic communications service must take appropriate technical and organisational measures to safeguard security of its services, if necessary in conjunction with the provider of the public communications network with respect to network

For additional analytical, business and investment opportunities information, please contact Global Investment & Business Center, USA at (703) 370-8082. Fax: (703) 370-8083. E-mail: ibpusa3@gmail.com Global Business and Investment Info Databank - www.ibpus.com

security. Having regard to the state of the art and the cost of their implementation, these measures shall ensure a level of security appropriate to the risk presented.

2. In case of a particular risk of a breach of the security of the network, the provider of a publicly available electronic communications service must inform the subscribers concerning such risk and, where the risk lies outside the scope of the measures to be taken by the service provider, of any possible remedies, including an indication of the likely costs involved.

ARTICLE 5 CONFIDENTIALITY OF THE COMMUNICATIONS

1. Member States shall ensure the confidentiality of communications and the related traffic data by means of a public communications network and publicly available electronic communications services, through national legislation. In particular, they shall prohibit listening, tapping, storage or other kinds of interception or surveillance of communications and the related traffic data by persons other than users, without the consent of the users concerned, except when legally authorised to do so in accordance with Article 15(1) . This paragraph shall not prevent technical storage which is necessary for the conveyance of a communication without prejudice to the principle of confidentiality.

2. Paragraph 1 shall not affect any legally authorised recording of communications and the related traffic data when carried out in the course of lawful business practice for the purpose of providing evidence of a commercial transaction or of any other business communication.

3. Member States shall ensure that the use of electronic communications networks to store information or to gain access to information stored in the terminal equipment of a subscriber or user is only allowed on condition that the subscriber or user concerned is provided with clear and comprehensive information in accordance with Directive 95/46/EC, inter alia about the purposes of the processing, and is offered the right to refuse such processing by the data controller. This shall not prevent any technical storage or access for the sole purpose of carrying out or facilitating the transmission of a communication over an electronic communications network, or as strictly necessary in order to provide an information society service explicitly requested by the subscriber or user.

ARTICLE 6 TRAFFIC DATA

1. Traffic data relating to subscribers and users processed and stored by the provider of a public communications network or publicly available electronic communications service must be erased or made anonymous when it is no longer needed for the purpose of the transmission of a communication without prejudice to paragraphs 2, 3 and 5 of this Article and Article 15(1) .

2. Traffic data necessary for the purposes of subscriber billing and interconnection payments may be processed. Such processing is permissible only up to the end of the period during which the bill may lawfully be challenged or payment pursued.

3. For the purpose of marketing electronic communications services or for the provision of value added services, the provider of a publicly available electronic communications service may process the data referred to in paragraph 1 to the extent and for the duration necessary for such services or marketing, if the subscriber or user to whom the data relate has given his/her consent. Users or subscribers shall be given the possibility to withdraw their consent for the processing of traffic data at any time.

4. The service provider must inform the subscriber or user of the types of traffic data which are processed and of the duration of such processing for the purposes mentioned in paragraph 2 and, prior to obtaining consent, for the purposes mentioned in paragraph 3.

5. Processing of traffic data, in accordance with paragraphs 1, 2, 3 and 4, must be restricted to persons acting under the authority of providers of the public communications networks and publicly available electronic communications services handling billing or traffic management, customer enquiries, fraud detection, marketing electronic communications services or providing a value added service, and must be restricted to what is necessary for the purposes of such activities.

6. Paragraphs 1, 2, 3 and 5 shall apply without prejudice to the possibility for competent bodies to be informed of traffic data in conformity with applicable legislation with a view to settling disputes, in particular interconnection or billing disputes.

ARTICLE 7 ITEMISED BILLING

1. Subscribers shall have the right to receive non-itemised bills.

2. Member States shall apply national provisions in order to reconcile the rights of subscribers receiving itemised bills with the right to privacy of calling users and called subscribers, for example by ensuring that sufficient alternative privacy enhancing methods of communications or payments are available to such users and subscribers.

ARTICLE 8 PRESENTATION AND RESTRICTION OF CALLING AND CONNECTED LINE IDENTIFICATION

1. Where presentation of calling line identification is offered, the service provider must offer the calling user the possibility, using a simple means and free of charge, of preventing the presentation of the calling line identification on a per-call basis. The calling subscriber must have this possibility on a per-line basis.

2. Where presentation of calling line identification is offered, the service provider must offer the called subscriber the possibility, using a simple means and free of charge for reasonable use of this function, of preventing the presentation of the calling line identification of incoming calls.

3. Where presentation of calling line identification is offered and where the calling line identification is presented prior to the call being established, the service provider must offer the called subscriber the possibility, using a simple means, of rejecting incoming calls where the presentation of the calling line identification has been prevented by the calling user or subscriber.

4. Where presentation of connected line identification is offered, the service provider must offer the called subscriber the possibility, using a simple means and free of charge, of preventing the presentation of the connected line identification to the calling user.

5. Paragraph 1 shall also apply with regard to calls to third countries originating in the Community. Paragraphs 2, 3 and 4 shall also apply to incoming calls originating in third countries.

6. Member States shall ensure that where presentation of calling and/or connected line identification is offered, the providers of publicly available electronic communications services inform the public thereof and of the possibilities set out in paragraphs 1, 2, 3 and 4.

ARTICLE 9 LOCATION DATA OTHER THAN TRAFFIC DATA

1. Where location data other than traffic data, relating to users or subscribers of public communications networks or publicly available electronic communications services, can be processed, such data may only be processed when they are made anonymous, or with the consent of the users or subscribers to the extent and for the duration necessary for the provision of a value added service. The service provider must inform the users or subscribers, prior to obtaining their consent, of the type of location data other than traffic data which will be processed,

For additional analytical, business and investment opportunities information, please contact Global Investment & Business Center, USA at (703) 370-8082. Fax: (703) 370-8083. E-mail: ibpusa3@gmail.com Global Business and Investment Info Databank - www.ibpus.com

of the purposes and duration of the processing and whether the data will be transmitted to a third party for the purpose of providing the value added service. Users or subscribers shall be given the possibility to withdraw their consent for the processing of location data other than traffic data at any time.

2. Where consent of the users or subscribers has been obtained for the processing of location data other than traffic data, the user or subscriber must continue to have the possibility, using a simple means and free of charge, of temporarily refusing the processing of such data for each connection to the network or for each transmission of a communication.

3. Processing of location data other than traffic data in accordance with paragraphs 1 and 2 must be restricted to persons acting under the authority of the provider of the public communications network or publicly available communications service or of the third party providing the value added service, and must be restricted to what is necessary for the purposes of providing the value added service.

ARTICLE 10 EXCEPTIONS

Member States shall ensure that there are transparent procedures governing the way in which a provider of a public communications network and/or a publicly available electronic communications service may override:

(a) the elimination of the presentation of calling line identification, on a temporary basis, upon application of a subscriber requesting the tracing of malicious or nuisance calls. In this case, in accordance with national law, the data containing the identification of the calling subscriber will be stored and be made available by the provider of a public communications network and/or publicly available electronic communications service;

(b) the elimination of the presentation of calling line identification and the temporary denial or absence of consent of a subscriber or user for the processing of location data, on a per-line basis for organisations dealing with emergency calls and recognised as such by a Member State, including law enforcement agencies, ambulance services and fire brigades, for the purpose of responding to such calls.

ARTICLE 11 AUTOMATIC CALL FORWARDING

Member States shall ensure that any subscriber has the possibility, using a simple means and free of charge, of stopping automatic call forwarding by a third party to the subscriber's terminal.

ARTICLE 12 DIRECTORIES OF SUBSCRIBERS

1. Member States shall ensure that subscribers are informed, free of charge and before they are included in the directory, about the purpose(s) of a printed or electronic directory of subscribers available to the public or obtainable through directory enquiry services, in which their personal data can be included and of any further usage possibilities based on search functions embedded in electronic versions of the directory.

2. Member States shall ensure that subscribers are given the opportunity to determine whether their personal data are included in a public directory, and if so, which, to the extent that such data are relevant for the purpose of the directory as determined by the provider of the directory, and to verify, correct or withdraw such data. Not being included in a public subscriber directory, verifying, correcting or withdrawing personal data from it shall be free of charge.

3. Member States may require that for any purpose of a public directory other than the search of contact details of persons on the basis of their name and, where necessary, a minimum of other identifiers, additional consent be asked of the subscribers.

For additional analytical, business and investment opportunities information, please contact Global Investment & Business Center, USA at (703) 370-8082. Fax: (703) 370-8083. E-mail: ibpusa3@gmail.com Global Business and Investment Info Databank - www.ibpus.com

4. Paragraphs 1 and 2 shall apply to subscribers who are natural persons. Member States shall also ensure, in the framework of Community law and applicable national legislation, that the legitimate interests of subscribers other than natural persons with regard to their entry in public directories are sufficiently protected.

ARTICLE 13 UNSOLICITED COMMUNICATIONS

1. The use of automated calling systems without human intervention (automatic calling machines) , facsimile machines (fax) or electronic mail for the purposes of direct marketing may only be allowed in respect of subscribers who have given their prior consent.

2. Notwithstanding paragraph 1, where a natural or legal person obtains from its customers their electronic contact details for electronic mail, in the context of the sale of a product or a service, in accordance with Directive 95/46/EC, the same natural or legal person may use these electronic contact details for direct marketing of its own similar products or services provided that customers clearly and distinctly are given the opportunity to object, free of charge and in an easy manner, to such use of electronic contact details when they are collected and on the occasion of each message in case the customer has not initially refused such use.

3. Member States shall take appropriate measures to ensure that, free of charge, unsolicited communications for purposes of direct marketing, in cases other than those referred to in paragraphs 1 and 2, are not allowed either without the consent of the subscribers concerned or in respect of subscribers who do not wish to receive these communications, the choice between these options to be determined by national legislation.

4. In any event, the practice of sending electronic mail for purposes of direct marketing disguising or concealing the identity of the sender on whose behalf the communication is made, or without a valid address to which the recipient may send a request that such communications cease, shall be prohibited.

5. Paragraphs 1 and 3 shall apply to subscribers who are natural persons. Member States shall also ensure, in the framework of Community law and applicable national legislation, that the legitimate interests of subscribers other than natural persons with regard to unsolicited communications are sufficiently protected.

ARTICLE 14 TECHNICAL FEATURES AND STANDARDISATION

1. In implementing the provisions of this Directive, Member States shall ensure, subject to paragraphs 2 and 3, that no mandatory requirements for specific technical features are imposed on terminal or other electronic communication equipment which could impede the placing of equipment on the market and the free circulation of such equipment in and between Member States.

2. Where provisions of this Directive can be implemented only by requiring specific technical features in electronic communications networks, Member States shall inform the Commission in accordance with the procedure provided for by Directive 98/34/EC of the European Parliament and of the Council of 22 June 1998 laying down a procedure for the provision of information in the field of technical standards and regulations and of rules on information society services(9) .

3. Where required, measures may be adopted to ensure that terminal equipment is constructed in a way that is compatible with the right of users to protect and control the use of their personal data, in accordance with Directive 1999/5/EC and Council Decision 87/95/EEC of 22 December 1986 on standardisation in the field of information technology and communications(10) .

For additional analytical, business and investment opportunities information, please contact Global Investment & Business Center, USA at (703) 370-8082. Fax: (703) 370-8083. E-mail: ibpusa3@gmail.com Global Business and Investment Info Databank - www.ibpus.com

ARTICLE 15 APPLICATION OF CERTAIN PROVISIONS OF DIRECTIVE 95/46/EC

1. Member States may adopt legislative measures to restrict the scope of the rights and obligations provided for in Article 5, Article 6, Article 8(1) , (2) , (3) and (4) , and Article 9 of this Directive when such restriction constitutes a necessary, appropriate and proportionate measure within a democratic society to safeguard national security (i.e. State security) , defence, public security, and the prevention, investigation, detection and prosecution of criminal offences or of unauthorised use of the electronic communication system, as referred to in Article 13(1) of Directive 95/46/EC. To this end, Member States may, inter alia, adopt legislative measures providing for the retention of data for a limited period justified on the grounds laid down in this paragraph. All the measures referred to in this paragraph shall be in accordance with the general principles of Community law, including those referred to in Article 6(1) and (2) of the Treaty on European Union.

2. The provisions of Chapter III on judicial remedies, liability and sanctions of Directive 95/46/EC shall apply with regard to national provisions adopted pursuant to this Directive and with regard to the individual rights derived from this Directive.

3. The Working Party on the Protection of Individuals with regard to the Processing of Personal Data instituted by Article 29 of Directive 95/46/EC shall also carry out the tasks laid down in Article 30 of that Directive with regard to matters covered by this Directive, namely the protection of fundamental rights and freedoms and of legitimate interests in the electronic communications sector.

ARTICLE 16 TRANSITIONAL ARRANGEMENTS

1. Article 12 shall not apply to editions of directories already produced or placed on the market in printed or off-line electronic form before the national provisions adopted pursuant to this Directive enter into force.

2. Where the personal data of subscribers to fixed or mobile public voice telephony services have been included in a public subscriber directory in conformity with the provisions of Directive 95/46/EC and of Article 11 of Directive 97/66/EC before the national provisions adopted in pursuance of this Directive enter into force, the personal data of such subscribers may remain included in this public directory in its printed or electronic versions, including versions with reverse search functions, unless subscribers indicate otherwise, after having received complete information about purposes and options in accordance with Article 12 of this Directive.

ARTICLE 17 TRANSPOSITION

1. Before 31 October 2003 Member States shall bring into force the provisions necessary to comply with this Directive. They shall forthwith inform the Commission thereof.

When Member States adopt those provisions, they shall contain a reference to this Directive or be accompanied by such a reference on the occasion of their official publication. The methods of making such reference shall be laid down by the Member States.

2. Member States shall communicate to the Commission the text of the provisions of national law which they adopt in the field governed by this Directive and of any subsequent amendments to those provisions.

ARTICLE 18 REVIEW

The Commission shall submit to the European Parliament and the Council, not later than three years after the date referred to in Article 17(1) , a report on the application of this Directive and its impact on economic operators and consumers, in particular as regards the provisions on

For additional analytical, business and investment opportunities information, please contact Global Investment & Business Center, USA at (703) 370-8082. Fax: (703) 370-8083. E-mail: ibpusa3@gmail.com Global Business and Investment Info Databank - www.ibpus.com

unsolicited communications, taking into account the international environment. For this purpose, the Commission may request information from the Member States, which shall be supplied without undue delay. Where appropriate, the Commission shall submit proposals to amend this Directive, taking account of the results of that report, any changes in the sector and any other proposal it may deem necessary in order to improve the effectiveness of this Directive.

ARTICLE 19 REPEAL

Directive 97/66/EC is hereby repealed with effect from the date referred to in Article 17(1) .

References made to the repealed Directive shall be construed as being made to this Directive.

ARTICLE 20 ENTRY INTO FORCE

This Directive shall enter into force on the day of its publication in the Official Journal of the European Communities.

DIRECTIVE OF THE EUROPEAN PARLIAMENT AND OF THE COUNCIL CONCERNING MEASURES TO ENSURE A HIGH COMMON LEVEL OF NETWORK AND INFORMATION SECURITY ACROSS THE UNION

EXPLANATORY MEMORANDUM

The aim of the proposed Directive is to ensure a high common level of network and information security (NIS) . This means improving the security of the Internet and the private networks and information systems underpinning the functioning of our societies and economies. This will be achieved by requiring the Member States to increase their preparedness and improve their cooperation with each other, and by requiring operators of critical infrastructures, such as energy, transport, and key providers of information society services (e-commerce platforms, social networks, etc) , as well as public administrations to adopt appropriate steps to manage security risks and report serious incidents to the national competent authorities.

This proposal is presented in connection with the joint Communication of the Commission and High Representative of the Union for Foreign Affairs and Security Policy on a European Cybersecurity Strategy. The objective of the Strategy is to ensure a secure and trustworthy digital environment, while promoting and protecting fundamental rights and other EU core values. This proposal is the main action of the Strategy. Further actions under the Strategy in this area focus on raising awareness, developing an internal market for cybersecurity products and services, and fostering R&D investment. These actions will be complemented by others aimed at stepping up the fight against cybercrime and building an international cybersecurity policy for the EU.

1.1. REASONS FOR AND OBJECTIVES OF THE PROPOSAL

NIS is increasingly important to our economy and society. NIS is also an important precondition to create a reliable environment for worldwide trade in services. However, information systems can be affected by security incidents, such as human mistakes, natural events, technical failures or malicious attacks. These incidents are becoming bigger, more frequent, and more complex. The Commission's online public consultation on 'Improving network and information security in the EU[1]' found that 57% of respondents had experienced NIS incidents over the previous year that had a serious impact on their activities. Lack of NIS can compromise vital services depending on the integrity of network and information systems. This can stop businesses functioning, generate substantial financial losses for the EU economy and negatively affect societal welfare.

1 The online public consultation on 'Improving network and information security in the EU' ran from 23 July to 15 October 2012.

Moreover, as a borderless communication instrument, digital information systems, in particular the internet, are interconnected across Member States and play an essential role in facilitating the cross-border movement of goods, services and people. Substantial disruption of these systems in one Member State can affect other Member States and the EU as a whole. The resilience and stability of network and information systems is therefore essential to the completion of the Digital Single Market and the smooth functioning of the Internal Market. The likelihood and frequency of incidents and the inability to ensure efficient protection also undermine public trust and confidence in network and information services: for example, the 2012 Eurobarometer on Cybersecurity found that 38% of EU internet users are concerned about the safety of online payments and have changed their behaviour because of concerns with security issues: 18% are less likely to buy goods online and 15% are less likely to use online banking[2].

The current situation in the EU, reflecting the purely voluntary approach followed so far, does not provide sufficient protection against NIS incidents and risks across the EU. Existing NIS capabilities and mechanisms are simply insufficient to keep pace with the fast-changing landscape of threats and to ensure a common high level of protection in all the Member States.

Despite the initiatives undertaken, the Member States have very different levels of capabilities and preparedness, leading to fragmented approaches across the EU. Given the fact that networks and systems are interconnected, the overall NIS of the EU is weakened by those Member States with an insufficient level of protection. This situation also hinders the creation of trust among peers, which is a prerequisite for cooperation and information sharing. As a result, there is cooperation only among a minority of Member States with a high level of capabilities.

Therefore, there is currently no effective mechanism at EU level for effective cooperation and collaboration and for trusted information sharing on NIS incidents and risks among the Member States. This may result in uncoordinated regulatory interventions, incoherent strategies and divergent standards, leading to insufficient protection against NIS across the EU. Internal Market barriers may also arise, generating compliance costs for companies operating in more than one Member State.

2Eurobarometer 390/2012.

Finally, the players managing critical infrastructure or providing services essential to the functioning of our societies are not under appropriate obligations to adopt risk management measures and exchange information with relevant authorities. On the one hand, therefore, businesses lack effective incentives to conduct serious risk management, involving risk assessment and taking appropriate steps to ensure NIS. On the other hand, a large proportion of incidents does not reach the competent authorities and go unnoticed. However, information on incidents is essential for public authorities to react, take appropriate mitigating measures, and set adequate strategic priorities for NIS.

The current regulatory framework requires only telecommunication companies to adopt risk management steps and to report serious NIS incidents. However, many other sectors rely on ICT as an enabler and should therefore be concerned about NIS as well. A number of specific infrastructure and service providers are particularly vulnerable, due to their high dependence on correctly functioning network and information systems. These sectors play an essential role in providing key support services for our economy and society, and the security of their systems is of particular importance to the functioning of the Internal Market. These sectors include banking, stock exchanges, energy generation, transmission and distribution, transport (air, rail, maritime) , health, internet services and public administrations.

A step-change is therefore needed in the way NIS is dealt with in the EU. Regulatory obligations are required to create a level playing field and close existing legislative loopholes. To address these problems and increase the level of NIS within the European Union, the objectives of the proposed Directive are as follows.

First, the proposal requires all the Member States to ensure that they have in place a minimum level of national capabilities by establishing competent authorities for NIS, setting up Computer Emergency Response Teams (CERTs) , and adopting national NIS strategies and national NIS cooperation plans.

Secondly, the national competent authorities should cooperate within a network enabling secure and effective coordination, including coordinated information exchange as well as detection and response at EU level. Through this network, Member States should exchange information and cooperate to counter NIS threats and incidents on the basis of the European NIS cooperation plan.

Thirdly, based on the model of the Framework Directive for electronic communications, the proposal aims to ensure that a culture of risk management develops and that information is shared between the private and public sectors. Companies in the specific critical sectors outlined above and public administrations will be required to assess the risks they face and adopt appropriate and proportionate measures to ensure NIS. These entities will be required to report to the competent authorities any incidents seriously compromising their networks and information systems and significantly affecting the continuity of critical services and supply of goods.

1.2. General context

Already in 2001, in its Communication Network and Information Security: Proposal for A European Policy Approach', the Commission outlined the increasing importance of NIS[3]. This was followed by the adoption in 2006 of a Strategy for a Secure Information Society[4], aiming to develop a culture of NIS in Europe. Its main elements were endorsed in a Council Resolution[5].

The Commission further adopted, on 30 March 2009, a Communication on Critical Information Infrastructure protection (CIIP) [6] focusing on the protection of Europe from cyber disruptions by enhancing security. The Communication launched an action plan to support Member States' efforts to ensure prevention and response. The Action Plan was endorsed in the Presidency Conclusions of the Ministerial Conference on CIIP in Tallinn in 2009. On 18 December 2009 the Council adopted a Resolution on 'A collaborative European approach to network and information security'[7].

The Digital Agenda for Europe[8] (DAE) , adopted in May 2010, and the related Council Conclusions[9] highlighted the shared understanding that trust and security are fundamental preconditions for the wide uptake of ICT and thus for achieving the objectives of the 'smart growth' dimension of the Europe 2020 Strategy[10]. Under its Trust and Security chapter, the DAE emphasised the need for all stakeholders to join forces in a holistic effort to ensure the security and resilience of ICT infrastructure, by focusing on prevention, preparedness and awareness, as well as to develop effective and coordinated security mechanisms. In particular, key action 6 of the Digital Agenda for Europe calls for measures aimed at a reinforced and high-level NIS policy.

In its Communication on CIIP of March 2011 on 'Achievements and next steps: towards global cyber-security'[11], the Commission took stock of the results achieved since the adoption of the

CIIP action plan in 2009, concluding that the implementation of the plan showed that purely national approaches to tackling the security and resilience challenges are not sufficient, and that Europe should continue its efforts to build a coherent and cooperative approach across the EU. The 2011 CIIP Communication announced a number of actions, with the Commission calling upon the Member States to set up NIS capabilities and cross-border cooperation. Most of these actions should have been completed by 2012, but have not yet been implemented.

In its Conclusions of 27 May 2011 on CIIP, the Council of the European Union stressed the pressing need to make ICT systems and networks resilient and secure against all possible disruptions, whether accidental or intentional, to develop across the EU a high level of preparedness, security and resilience capabilities, to upgrade technical competences to allow Europe to meet the challenge of network and information infrastructure protection, and to foster cooperation between the Member States by developing incident cooperation mechanisms between the Member States.

1.3. Existing European Union and international provisions in this area

Under Regulation (EC) No 460/2004, the European Community established in 2004 the European Network and Information Security Agency (ENISA) [12], with the aim of contributing to ensuring a high level and developing a culture of NIS within the EU.A proposal to modernise the mandate of ENISA was adopted on 30 September 2010[13] and is under discussion in the Council and the European Parliament. The revised regulatory framework for electronic communications[14], in force since November 2009, imposes security obligations on electronic communication providers[15]. These obligations had to be transposed at national level by May 2011.

All players that are data controllers (for example banks or hospitals) are obliged by the data protection regulatory framework[16] to put in place security measures to protect personal data. Also, under the 2012 Commission proposal for a General Data Protection Regulation[17], data controllers would have to report breaches of personal data to the national supervisory authorities. This means that, for example, a NIS security breach affecting the provision of a service without compromising personal data (e.g. an ICT outage at a power company resulting in a blackout) would not have to be notified.

Under Directive 2008/114 on the identification and designation of European Critical Infrastructures and the assessment of the need to improve their protection, the 'European Programme for Critical Infrastructure Protection (EPCIP) '[18] sets out the overall 'umbrella' approach to the protection of critical infrastructures in the EU. The objectives of EPCIP are fully consistent with this proposal and the Directive should apply without prejudice to Directive 2008/114. EPCIP does not oblige operators to report significant breaches of security and does not set up mechanisms for the Member States to cooperate and respond to incidents.

The co-legislators are currently discussing the Commission proposal for a Directive on attacks against information systems[19], which aims to harmonise the criminalisation of specific types of conduct. It covers only the criminalisation of specific types of conduct and does not address the prevention of NIS risks and incidents, the response to NIS incidents and the mitigation of their impact. The present Directive should apply without prejudice to the Directive on attacks against information systems.

On 28 March 2012, the Commission adopted a Communication on the establishment of a European Cybercrime Centre (EC3) [20]. This Centre, established on 11 January 2013, is part of the European Police Office (EUROPOL) and act as the focal point in the fight against cybercrime in the EU. EC3 is intended to pool European cybercrime expertise to support the Member States in capacity building, provide support to Member States' cybercrime investigations and, in close cooperation with Eurojust, become the collective voice of European cybercrime investigators across law enforcement and the judiciary.

The European Institutions, agencies and bodies have set up their own Computer Emergency Response Team, called CERT-EU.

At international level, the EU works on cybersecurity at both bilateral and multilateral level. The 2010 EU-US Summit[21] saw the establishment of the EU-US Working Group on Cybersecurity and Cybercrime. The EU is also active in other relevant multilateral fora, such as the Organisation for Economic Co-operation and Development (OECD) , the United Nations General Assembly (UNGA) , the International Telecommunication Union (ITU) , the Organisation for Security and Co-operation in Europe (OSCE) , the World Summit on the Information Society (WSIS) and the Internet Governance Forum (IGF) .

2. RESULTS OF CONSULTATIONS WITH THE INTERESTED PARTIES AND IMPACT ASSESSMENTS

2.1. Consultation with interested parties and use of expertise

An online public consultation on 'Improving NIS in the EU' ran between 23 July and 15 October 2012. In total, the Commission received 160 responses to the online questionnaire. The key outcome was that stakeholders showed general support for the need to improve NIS across the EU. In particular: 82.8% of respondents expressed the view that governments in the EU should do more to ensure a high level of NIS; 82.8% were of the opinion that users of information and systems were unaware of existing NIS threats and incidents; 66.3% would in principle be in favour of introducing a regulatory requirement to manage NIS risks; and

84.8 % said that such requirements should be set at EU level. A high number of respondents thought that it would be important to adopt NIS requirements in the following sectors in particular: banking and finance (91.1%) , energy (89.4%) , transport (81.7%) , health (89.4%) , internet services (89.1%) , and public administrations (87.5%) . Respondents also considered that if a requirement to report NIS security breaches to the national competent authority were introduced, it should be set at EU level (65.1%) and affirmed that public administrations should also be subject to it (93.5%) . Finally, respondents affirmed that a requirement to implement NIS risk management in line with the state of the art would entail for them no significant additional costs (63.4%) , and that a requirement to report security breaches would cause no significant additional costs (72.3%) .

Member States were consulted in a number of relevant Council configurations, in the context of the European Forum for Member States (EFMS) , at the Conference on Cybersecurity organised by the Commission and the European External Action Service on 6 July 2012, and in dedicated bilateral meetings convened at the request of individual Member States.

Discussions with the private sector were also held within the European Public-Private Partnership for Resilience[22] and through bilateral meetings. As for the public sector, the Commission held discussions with ENISA and the CERT for the EU institutions.

2.2. IMPACT ASSESSMENT

The Commission has carried out an impact assessment of three policy options:

Option 1: Business as usual (baseline scenario) : maintaining the current approach;

Option 2: Regulatory approach, consisting of a legislative proposal establishing a common EU legal framework for NIS regarding Member State capabilities, mechanisms for EU-level cooperation, and requirements for key private players and public administrations;

Option 3: Mixed approach, combining voluntary initiatives for Member State NIS capabilities and mechanisms for EU-level cooperation with regulatory requirements for key private players and public administrations.

The Commission concluded that Option 2 would have the strongest positive impacts, as it would considerably improve the protection of EU consumers, business and governments against NIS incidents. In particular, the obligations placed on the Member States would ensure adequate preparedness at national level and would contribute to a climate of mutual trust, which is a precondition for effective cooperation at EU level. The setting up of mechanisms for cooperation at EU level via the network would deliver coherent and coordinated prevention and response to cross-border NIS incidents and risks. The introduction of requirements to implement NIS risk management for public administrations and key private players would create a strong incentive to manage security risks effectively. The obligation to report NIS incidents with a significant impact would enhance the ability to respond to incidents and foster transparency. Moreover, by putting its own house in order, the EU would be able to extend its international reach and become an even more credible partner for cooperation at bilateral and multilateral level. The EU would hence also be better placed to promote fundamental rights and EU core values abroad.

The quantitative assessment showed that Option 2 would not impose a disproportionate burden on Member States. The costs for the private sector would also be limited since many of the entities concerned are already supposed to comply with existing security requirements (namely the obligation for data controllers to take technical and organisational measures to secure personal data, including NIS measures) . Existing spending on security in the private sector has also been taken into account.

This proposal observes the principles recognised by the Charter of Fundamental Rights of the European Union notably, the right to respect for private life and communications. the protection for personal data, the freedom to conduct a business, the right to property, the right to an effective remedy before a court and the right to be heard. This Directive must be implemented according to these rights and principles.

3. LEGAL ELEMENTS OF THE PROPOSAL

3.1. Legal basis

The European Union is empowered to adopt measures with the aim of establishing or ensuring the functioning of the Internal Market, in accordance with the relevant provisions of the Treaties (Article 26 of the Treaty on the Functioning of the European Union — TFEU) . Under Article 114 TFEU, the EU can adopt 'measures for the *approximation of the provisions laid down by law, regulation or administrative action in Member States* which have as their object the establishment and functioning of the internal market'.

As indicated above, network and information systems play an essential role in facilitating the cross-border movement of goods, services and people. They are often interconnected, and the internet is global in nature. Given this intrinsic transnational dimension, a disruption in one Member State can also affect other Member States and the EU as a whole. The resilience and stability of network and information systems is therefore essential to the smooth functioning of the Internal Market.

For additional analytical, business and investment opportunities information, please contact Global Investment & Business Center, USA at (703) 370-8082. Fax: (703) 370-8083. E-mail: ibpusa3@gmail.com Global Business and Investment Info Databank - www.ibpus.com

The EU legislator has already recognised the need to harmonise NIS rules to ensure the development of the Internal Market. In particular, this was the case for Regulation 460/2004 establishing ENISA[23], which is based on Article 114 TFEU.

The disparities resulting from uneven NIS national capabilities, policies and level of protection across the Member States lead to barriers to the Internal Market and justify EU action.

3.2. Subsidiarity

European intervention in the area of NIS is justified by the subsidiarity principle.

Firstly, considering the cross-border nature of NIS, non-intervention at EU level would lead to a situation where each Member State would act alone, disregarding the interdependencies among EU network and information systems. An appropriate degree of coordination among the Member States would ensure that NIS risks could be well managed in the cross-border context in which they arise. Divergences in NIS regulations represent a barrier to companies wanting to operate in several countries and to the achievement of global economies of scale.

Secondly, regulatory obligations at EU level are needed to create a level playing field and close legislative loopholes. A purely voluntary approach has resulted in cooperation only among a minority of Member States with a high level of capabilities. In order to involve all the Member States, it is necessary to ensure that they all have the required minimum level of capability. NIS measures adopted by governments need to be consistent with one other and be coordinated to contain and minimise the consequences of NIS incidents. Within the network, through exchange of best practices and continuous involvement of ENISA, the competent authorities and the Commission will cooperate to facilitate a convergent implementation of the Directive across the EU. In addition, concerted NIS policy actions can have a strong positive impact for the effective protection of fundamental rights, and specifically the right to the protection of personal data and privacy. Action at EU level would therefore improve the effectiveness of existing national policies and facilitate their development.

The proposed measures are also justified on grounds of proportionality. The requirements for the Member States are set at the minimum level necessary to achieve adequate preparedness and to enable cooperation based on trust. This also enables Member States to take due account of national specificities and ensures that the common EU principles are applied in a proportionate manner. The wide scope of application will allow the Member States to implement the Directive in light of the actual risks faced at national level as identified in the national NIS strategy. The requirements to implement risk management target only critical entities and impose measures that are proportionate to the risks. The public consultation underlined the importance of ensuring the security of these critical entities. The reporting requirements would concern only incidents with a significant impact. As indicated above, the measures would not impose disproportionate costs, as many of these entities as data controllers are already required by the current data protection rules to secure the protection of personal data.

To avoid imposing a disproportionate burden on small operators, in particular on SMEs, the requirements are proportionate to the risk presented by the network or information system concerned and should not apply to micro enterprises. The risks will have to be identified in the first place by the entities subject to these obligations, which will have to decide on the measures to be adopted to mitigate such risks.

The stated objectives can be better achieved at EU level, rather than by the Member States alone, in view of the cross-border aspects of NIS incidents and risks. Therefore, the EU may adopt measures in accordance with the principle of subsidiarity as set out in Article 5 of the

Treaty on European Union. In accordance with the principle of proportionality, the proposed Directive does not go beyond what is necessary in order to achieve those objectives.

To achieve the objectives, the Commission should be empowered to adopt delegated acts in accordance with Article 290 of the Treaty on the Functioning of the European Union, in order to supplement or amend certain non-essential elements of the basic act. The Commission's proposal also strives to support a process of proportionality in the implementation of the obligations placed upon private and public operators.

In order to ensure uniform conditions for the implementation of the basic act, the Commission should be empowered to adopt implementing acts in accordance with Article 291 of the Treaty on the Functioning of the European Union.

Considering in particular the broad scope of the proposed Directive, the fact that it tackles heavily regulated domains, and the legal obligations deriving from its Chapter IV, Explanatory Documents should accompany the notification of transposition measures. In accordance with the Joint Political Declaration of Member States and the Commission on explanatory documents of 28 September 2011, Member States have undertaken to accompany, in justified cases, the notification of their transposition measures with one or more documents explaining the relationship between the components of a Directive and the corresponding parts of national transposition instruments. With regard to this Directive, the legislator considers the transmission of such documents to be justified.

4. BUDGETARY IMPLICATIONS

Cooperation and exchange of information between Member States should be supported by a secure infrastructure. The proposal will have EU budgetary implications only if Member States choose to adapt an existing infrastructure (e.g. sTESTA) and task the Commission to implement this under the MFF 2014-2020. The one-off cost is estimated to be EUR 1250000 and would be borne by the EU budget, budget line 09.03.02 (to promote the interconnection and interoperability of national public services online as well as access to such networks — Chapter 09.03, Connecting Europe Facility — telecommunications networks) on condition that sufficient funds are available under CEF. Alternatively, Member States can either share the one-off cost of adapting an existing infrastructure or decide to set up a new infrastructure and bear the costs, which are estimated to be approximately EUR 10 million per year.

Proposal for a DIRECTIVE OF THE EUROPEAN PARLIAMENT AND OF THE COUNCIL concerning measures to ensure a high common level of network and information security across the Union

THE EUROPEAN PARLIAMENT AND THE COUNCIL OF THE EUROPEAN UNION,

Having regard to the Treaty on the Functioning of the European Union, and in particular Article 114 thereof,
Having regard to the proposal from the European Commission,
After transmission of the draft legislative act to the national Parliaments,
Having regard to the opinion of the European Economic and Social Committee[1],
After consulting the European Data Protection Supervisor,
Acting in accordance with the ordinary legislative procedure,

Whereas:

(1) Network and information systems and services play a vital role in the society. Their reliability and security are essential to economic activities and social welfare, and in particular to the functioning of the internal market.

(2) The magnitude and frequency of deliberate or accidental security incidents is increasing and represents a major threat to the functioning of networks and information systems. Such incidents can impede the pursuit of economic activities, generate substantial financial losses, undermine user confidence and cause major damage to the economy of the Union.

(3) As a communication instrument without frontiers, digital information systems, and primarily the Internet play an essential role in facilitating the cross-border movement of goods, services and people. Due to that transnational nature, substantial disruption of those systems in one Member State can also affect other Member States and the Union as a whole. The resilience and stability of network and information systems is therefore essential to the smooth functioning of the internal market.

(4) A cooperation mechanism should be established at Union level to allow for information exchange and coordinated detection and response regarding network and information security ("NIS") . For that mechanism to be effective and inclusive, it is essential that all Member States have minimum capabilities and a strategy ensuring a high level of NIS in their territory. Minimum security requirements should also apply to public administrations and operators of critical information infrastructure to promote a culture of risk management and ensure that the most serious incidents are reported.

(5) To cover all relevant incidents and risks, this Directive should apply to all network and information systems. The obligations on public administrations and market operators should however not apply to undertakings providing public communication networks or publicly available electronic communication services within the meaning of Directive 2002/21/EC of the European Parliament and of the Council of 7 March 2002 on a common regulatory framework for electronic communications networks and services (Framework Directive) [2], which are subject to the specific security and integrity requirements laid down in Article 13a of that Directive nor should they apply to trust service providers.

(6) The existing capabilities are not sufficient enough to ensure a high level of NIS within the Union. Member States have very different levels of preparedness leading to fragmented approaches across the Union. This leads to an unequal level of protection of consumers and businesses, and undermines the overall level of NIS within the Union. Lack of common minimum requirements on public administrations and market operators in turn makes it impossible to set up a global and effective mechanism for cooperation at Union level.

(7) Responding effectively to the challlenges of the security of network and information systems therefore requires a global approach at Union level covering common minimum capacity building and planning requirements, exchange of information and coordination of actions, and common minimum security requirements for all market operators concerned and public administrations.

(8) The provisions of this Directive should be without prejudice to the possibility for each Member State to take the necessary measures to ensure the protection of its essential security interests, to safeguard public policy and public security, and to permit the investigation, detection and prosecution of criminal offences. In accordance with Article 346 TFEU, no Member State is to be obliged to supply information the disclosure of which it considers contrary to the essential interests of its security.

For additional analytical, business and investment opportunities information, please contact Global Investment & Business Center, USA at (703) 370-8082. Fax: (703) 370-8083. E-mail: ibpusa3@gmail.com Global Business and Investment Info Databank - www.ibpus.com

(9) To achieve and maintain a common high level of security of network and information systems, each Member State should have a national NIS strategy defining the strategic objectives and concrete policy actions to be implemented. NIS cooperation plans complying with essential requirements need to be developed at national level in order to reach capacity response levels allowing for effective and efficient cooperation at national and Union level in case of incidents.

(10) To allow for the effective implementation of the provisions adopted pursuant to this Directive, a body responsible for coordinating NIS issues and acting as a focal point for cross-border cooperation at Union level should be established or identified in each Member State. These bodies should be given the adequate technical, financial and human resources to ensure that they can carry out in an effective and efficient manner the tasks assigned to them and thus achieve the objectives of this Directive.

(11) All Member States should be adequately equipped, both in terms of technical and organisational capabilities, to prevent, detect, respond to and mitigate network and information systems' incidents and risks. Well-functioning Computer Emergency Response Teams complying with essential requirements should therefore be established in all Member States to guarantee effective and compatible capabilities to deal with incidents and risks and ensure efficient cooperation at Union level.

(12) Building upon the significant progress within the European Forum of Member States ("EFMS") in fostering discussions and exchanges on good policy practices including the development of principles for European cyber crisis cooperation, the Member States and the Commission should form a network to bring them into permanent communication and support their cooperation. This secure and effective cooperation mechanism should enable structured and coordinated information exchange, detection and response at Union level.

(13) The European Network and Information Security Agency ("ENISA") should assist the Member States and the Commission by providing its expertise and advice and by facilitating exchange of best practices. In particular, in the application of this Directive, the Commission should consult ENISA. To ensure effective and timely information to the Member States and the Commission, early warnings on incidents and risks should be notified within the cooperation network. To build capacity and knowledge among Member States, the cooperation network should also serve as an instrument for the exchange of best practices, assisting its members in building capacity, steering the organisation of peer reviews and NIS exercises.

(14) A secure information-sharing infrastructure should be put in place to allow for the exchange of sensitive and confidential information within the cooperation network. Without prejudice to their obligation to notify incidents and risks of Union dimension to the cooperation network, access to confidential information from other Member States should only be granted to Members States upon demonstration that their technical, financial and human resources and processes, as well as their communication infrastructure, guarantee their effective, efficient and secure participation in the network.

(15) As most network and information systems are privately operated, cooperation between the public and private sector is essential. Market operators should be encouraged to pursue their own informal cooperation mechanisms to ensure NIS. They should also cooperate with the public sector and share information and best practices in exchange of operational support in case of incidents.

For additional analytical, business and investment opportunities information, please contact Global Investment & Business Center, USA at (703) 370-8082. Fax: (703) 370-8083. E-mail: ibpusa3@gmail.com
Global Business and Investment Info Databank - www.ibpus.com

(16) To ensure transparency and properly inform EU citizens and market operators, the competent authorities should set up a common website to publish non confidential information on the incidents and risks.

(17) Where information is considered confidential in accordance with Union and national rules on business confidentiality, such confidentiality shall be ensured when carrying out the activities and fulfilling the objectives set by this Directive.

(18) On the basis in particular of national crisis management experiences and in cooperation with ENISA, the Commission and the Member States should develop a Union NIS cooperation plan defining cooperation mechanisms to counter risks and incidents. That plan should be duly taken into account in the operation of early warnings within the cooperation network.

(19) Notification of an early warning within the network should be required only where the scale and severity of the incident or risk concerned are or may become so significant that information or coordination of the response at Union level is necessary. Early warnings should therefore be limited to actual or potential incidents or risks that grow rapidly, exceed national response capacity or affect more than one Member State. To allow for a proper evaluation, all information relevant for the assessment of the risk or incident should be communicated to the cooperation network.

(20) Upon receipt of an early warning and its assessment, the competent authorities should agree on a coordinated response under the Union NIS cooperation plan. Competent authorities as well as the Commission should be informed about the measures adopted at national level as a result of the coordinated response.

(21) Given the global nature of NIS problems, there is a need for closer international cooperation to improve security standards and information exchange, and promote a common global approach to NIS issues.

(22) Responsibilities in ensuring NIS lie to a great extent on public administrations and market operators. A culture of risk management, involving risk assessment and the implementation of security measures appropriate to the risks faced should be promoted and developed through appropriate regulatory requirements and voluntary industry practices. Establishing a level playing field is also essential to the effective functioning of the cooperation network to ensure effective cooperation from all Member States.

(23) Directive 2002/21/EC requires that undertakings providing public electronic communications networks or publicly available electronic communications services take appropriate measures to safeguard their integrity and security and introduces security breach and integrity loss notification requirements. Directive 2002/58/EC of the European Parliament and of the Council of 12 July 2002 concerning the processing of personal data and the protection of privacy in the electronic communications sector (Directive on privacy and electronic communications) 3 requires a provider of a publicly available electronic communications service to take appropriate technical and organisational measures to safeguard the security of its services.

(24) Those obligations should be extended beyond the electronic communications sector to key providers of information society services, as defined in Directive 98/34/EC of the European Parliament and of the Council of 22 June 1998 laying down a procedure for the provision of information in the field of technical standards and regulations and of rules on Information Society services4, which underpin

downstream information society services or on-line activities, such as e-commerce platforms, Internet payment gateways, social networks, search engines, cloud computing services, application stores. Disruption of these enabling information society services prevents the provision of other information society services which rely on them as key inputs. Software developers and hardware manufacturers are not providers of information society services and are therefore excluded. Those obligations should also be extended to public administrations, and operators of critical infrastructure which rely heavily on information and communications technology and are essential to the maintenance of vital economical or societal functions such as electricity and gas, transport, credit institutions, stock exchange and health. Disruption of those network and information systems would affect the internal market.

(25) Technical and organisational measures imposed to public administrations and market operators should not require that a particular commercial information and communications technology product be designed, developed or manufactured in a particular manner.

(26) The public administrations and market operators should ensure security of the networks and systems which are under their control. These would be primarily private networks and systems managed either by their internal IT staff or the security of which has been outsourced. The security and notification obligations should apply to the relevant market operators and public administrations regardless of whether they perform the maintenance of their network and information systems internally or outsource it.

(27) To avoid imposing a disproportionate financial and administrative burden on small operators and users, the requirements should be proportionate to the risk presented by the network or information system concerned, taking into account the state of the art of such measures. These requirements should not apply to micro enterprises.

(28) Competent authorities should pay due attention to preserving informal and trusted channels of information-sharing between market operators and between the public and the private sectors. Publicity of incidents reported to the competent authorities should duly balance the interest of the public in being informed about threats with possible reputational and commercial damages for the public administrations and market operators reporting incidents. In the implementation of the notification obligations, competent authorities should pay particular attention to the need to maintain information about product vulnerabilities strictly confidential prior to the release of appropriate security fixes.

(29) Competent authorities should have the necessary means to perform their duties, including powers to obtain sufficient information from market operators and public administrations in order to assess the level of security of network and information systems as well as reliable and comprehensive data about actual incidents that have had an impact on the operation of network and information systems.

(30) Criminal activities are in many cases underlying an incident. The criminal nature of incidents can be suspected even if the evidence to support it may not be sufficiently clear from the start. In this context, appropriate co-operation between competent authorities and law enforcement authorities should form part of an effective and comprehensive response to the threat of security incidents. In particular, promoting a safe, secure and more resilient environment requires a systematic reporting of incidents of a suspected serious criminal nature to law enforcement authorities. The serious criminal nature of incidents should be assessed in the light of EU laws on cybercrime.

For additional analytical, business and investment opportunities information, please contact Global Investment & Business Center, USA at (703) 370-8082. Fax: (703) 370-8083. E-mail: ibpusa3@gmail.com Global Business and Investment Info Databank - www.ibpus.com

(31) Personal data are in many cases compromised as a result of incidents. In this context, competent authorities and data protection authorities should cooperate and exchange information on all relevant matters to tackle the personal data breaches resulting from incidents. Member states shall implement the obligation to notify security incidents in a way that minimises the administrative burden in case the security incident is also a personal data breach in line with the Regulation of the European Parliament and of the Council on the protection of individuals with regard to the processing of personal data and on the free movement of such data[5]. Liaising with the competent authorities and the data protection authorities, ENISA could assist by developing information exchange mechanisms and templates avoiding the need for two notification templates. This single notification template would facilitate the reporting of incidents compromising personal data thereby easing the administrative burden on businesses and public administrations.

(32) Standardisation of security requirements is a market-driven process. To ensure a convergent application of security standards, Member States should encourage compliance or conformity with specified standards to ensure a high level of security at Union level. To this end, it might be necessary to draft harmonised standards, which should be done in accordance with Regulation (EU) No 1025/2012 of the European Parliament and of the Council of 25 October 2012 on European standardisation, amending Council Directives 89/686/EEC and 93/15/EEC and Directives 94/9/EC, 94/25/EC, 95/16/EC, 97/23/EC, 98/34/EC, 2004/22/EC, 2007/23/EC, 2009/23/EC and 2009/105/EC of the European Parliament and of the Council and repealing Council Decision 87/95/EEC and Decision No 1673/2006/EC of the European Parliament and of the Council[6].

(33) The Commission should periodically review this Directive, in particular with a view to determining the need for modification in the light of changing technological or market conditions.

(34) In order to allow for the proper functioning of the cooperation network, the power to adopt acts in accordance with Article 290 of the Treaty on the Functioning of the European Union should be delegated to the Commission in respect of the definition of the criteria to be fulfilled for a Member State to be authorized to participate to the secure information-sharing system, of the further specification of the triggering events for early warning, and of the definition of the circumstances in which market operators and public administrations are required to notify incidents.

(35) It is of particular importance that the Commission carry out appropriate consultations during its preparatory work, including at expert level. The Commission, when preparing and drawing up delegated acts, should ensure a simultaneous, timely and appropriate transmission of relevant documents to the European Parliament and to the Council.

(36) In order to ensure uniform conditions for the implementation of this Directive, implementing powers should be conferred on the Commission as regards the cooperation between competent authorities and the Commission within the cooperation network, the access to the secure information-sharing infrastructure, the Union NIS cooperation plan, the formats and procedures applicable to informing the public about incidents, and the standards and/or technical specifications relevant to NIS. Those powers should be exercised in accordance with Regulation (EU) No 182/2011 of the European Parliament and of the Council of 16 February 2011 laying down the rules and general principles concerning mechanisms for control by Member States of the Commission's exercise of implementing powers[7].

(37) In the application of this Directive, the Commission should liaise as appropriate with relevant sectoral committees and relevant bodies set up at EU level in particular in the field of energy, transport and health.

For additional analytical, business and investment opportunities information, please contact Global Investment & Business Center, USA at (703) 370-8082. Fax: (703) 370-8083. E-mail: ibpusa3@gmail.com Global Business and Investment Info Databank - www.ibpus.com

(38) Information that is considered confidential by a competent authority, in accordance with Union and national rules on business confidentiality, should be exchanged with the Commission and other competent authorities only where such exchange is strictly necessary for the application of this Directive. The information exchanged should be limited to that which is relevant and proportionate to the purpose of such exchange.

(39) The sharing of information on risks and incidents within the cooperation network and compliance with the requirements to notify incidents to the national competent authorities may require the processing of personal data. Such a processing of personal data is necessary to meet the objectives of public interest pursued by this Directive and is thus legitimate under Article 7 of Directive 95/46/EC. It does not constitute, in relation to these legitimate aims, a disproportionate and intolerable interference impairing the very substance of the right to the protection of personal data guaranteed by Article 8 of the Charter of fundamental rights. In the application of this Directive, Regulation (EC) No 1049/2001 of the European Parliament and of the Council of 30 May 2001 regarding public access to European Parliament, Council and Commission documents[8] should apply as appropriate. When data are processed by Union institutions and bodies, such processing for the purpose of implementing this Directive should comply with Regulation (EC) No 45/2001 of the European Parliament and of the Council of 18 December 2000 on the protection of individuals with regard to the processing of personal data by the Community institutions and bodies and on the free movement of such data.

(40) Since the objectives of this Directive, namely to ensure a high level of NIS in the Union, cannot be sufficiently achieved by the Member States alone and can therefore, by reason of the effects of the action, be better achieved at Union level, the Union may adopt measures, in accordance with the principle of subsidiarity as set out in Article 5 of the Treaty on European Union. In accordance with the principle of proportionality, as set out in that Article, this Directive does not go beyond what is necessary in order to achieve those objectives.

(41) This Directive respects the fundamental rights, and observes the principles, recognised by the Charter of Fundamental Rights of the European Union notably, the right to respect for private life and communications, the protection for personal data, the freedom to conduct a business, the right to property, the right to an effective remedy before a court and the right to be heard. This Directive must be implemented according to these rights and principles

HAVE ADOPTED THIS DIRECTIVE:

CHAPTER I GENERAL PROVISIONS

Article 1 Subject matter and scope

This Directive lays down measures to ensure a high common level of network and information security (hereinafter referred to as "NIS") within the Union.

To that end, this Directive:

(a) lays down obligations for all Member States concerning the prevention, the handling of and the response to risks and incidents affecting networks and information systems;

(b) creates a cooperation mechanism between Member States in order to ensure a uniform application of this Directive within the Union and, where necessary, a coordinated and efficient handling of and response to risks and incidents affecting network and information systems;

For additional analytical, business and investment opportunities information, please contact Global Investment & Business Center, USA at (703) 370-8082. Fax: (703) 370-8083. E-mail: ibpusa3@gmail.com Global Business and Investment Info Databank - www.ibpus.com

(c) establishes security requirements for market operators and public administrations.

The security requirements provided for in Article 14 shall apply neither to undertakings providing public communication networks or publicly available electronic communication services within the meaning of Directive 2002/21/EC, which shall comply with the specific security and integrity requirements laid down in Articles 13a and 13b of that Directive, nor to trust service providers.

This Directive shall be without prejudice to EU laws on cybercrime and Council Directive 2008/114/EC of 8 December 2008 on the identification and designation of European critical infrastructures and the assessment of the need to improve their protection[9]

This Directive shall also be without prejudice to Directive 95/46/CE of the European Parliament and of the Council of 24 October 1995 on the protection of individuals with regard to the processing of personal data and on the free movement of such data[10], and to Directive 2002/58/EC of the European Parliament and of the Council of 12 July 2002 concerning the processing of personal data and the protection of privacy in the electronic communications sector and to the Regulation of the European Parliament and of the Council on the protection of individuals with regard to the processing of personal data and on the free movement of such data[11].

The sharing of information within the cooperation network under Chapter III and the notifications of NIS incidents under Article 14 may require the processing of personal data. Such processing, which is necessary to meet the objectives of public interest pursued by this Directive, shall be authorised by the Member State pursuant to Article 7 of Directive 95/46/EC and Directive 2002/58/EC, as implemented in national law.

Article 2 Minimum harmonisation

Member States shall not be prevented from adopting or maintaining provisions ensuring a higher level of security, without prejudice to their obligations under Union law.

Article 3 Definitions

For the purpose of this Directive, the following definitions shall apply:

(1) "network and information system" means:

(a) an electronic communications network within the meaning of Directive 2002/21/EC, and

(b) any device or group of inter-connected or related devices, one or more of which, pursuant to a program, perform automatic processing of computer data, as well as

(c) computer data stored, processed, retrieved or transmitted by elements covered under point (a) and (b) for the purposes of their operation, use, protection and maintenance.

(2) "security" means the ability of a network and information system to resist, at a given level of confidence, accident or malicious action that compromise the availability, authenticity, integrity and confidentiality of stored or transmitted data or the related services offered by or accessible via that network and information system;

For additional analytical, business and investment opportunities information, please contact Global Investment & Business Center, USA at (703) 370-8082. Fax: (703) 370-8083. E-mail: ibpusa3@gmail.com Global Business and Investment Info Databank - www.ibpus.com

(3) "risk" means any circumstance or event having a potential adverse effect on security;

(4) "incident" means any circumstance or event having an actual adverse effect on security;

(5) "information society service" mean service within the meaning of point (2) of Article 1 of Directive 98/34/EC;

(6) "NIS cooperation plan" means a plan establishing the framework for organisational roles, responsibilities and procedures to maintain or restore the operation of networks and information systems, in the event of a risk or an incident affecting them;

(7) "incident handling" means all procedures supporting the analysis, containment and response to an incident;

(8) "market operator" means:

(a) provider of information society services which enable the provision of other information society services, a non exhaustive list of which is set out in Annex II;

(b) operator of critical infrastructure that are essential for the maintenance of vital economic and societal activities in the fields of energy, transport, banking, stock exchanges and health, a non exhaustive list of which is set out in Annex II.

(9) "standard" means a standard referred to in Regulation (EU) No 1025/2012;

(10) "specification" means a specification referred to in Regulation (EU) No 1025/2012;

(11) "Trust service provider" means a natural or legal person who provides any electronic service consisting in the creation, verification, validation, handling and preservation of electronic signatures, electronic seals, electronic time stamps, electronic documents, electronic delivery services, website authentication, and electronic certificates, including certificates for electronic signature and for electronic seals.

CHAPTER II NATIONAL FRAMEWORKS ON NETWORK AND INFORMATION SECURITY

Article 4 Principle

Member States shall ensure a high level of security of the network and information systems in their territories in accordance with this Directive.

Article 5

National NIS strategy and national NIS cooperation plan

1. Each Member State shall adopt a national NIS strategy defining the strategic objectives and concrete policy and regulatory measures to achieve and maintain a high level of network and information security. The national NIS strategy shall address in particular the following issues:

(a) The definition of the objectives and priorities of the strategy based on an up-to-date risk and incident analysis;

(b) A governance framework to achieve the strategy objectives and priorities, including a clear definition of the roles and responsibilities of the government bodies and the other relevant actors;

(c) The identification of the general measures on preparedness, response and recovery, including cooperation mechanisms between the public and private sectors;

(d) An indication of the education, awareness raising and training programmes;

(e) Research and development plans and a description of how these plans reflect the identified priorities.

2. The national NIS strategy shall include a national NIS cooperation plan complying at least with the following requirements

(a) A risk assessment plan to identify risks and assess the impacts of potential incidents;

(b) The definition of the roles and responsibilities of the various actors involved in the implementation of the plan;

(c) The definition of cooperation and communication processes ensuring prevention, detection, response, repair and recovery, and modulated according to the alert level;

(d) A roadmap for NIS exercises and training to reinforce, validate, and test the plan. Lessons learned to be documented and incorporated into updates to the plan.

3. The national NIS strategy and the national NIS cooperation plan shall be communicated to the Commission within one month from their adoption.

Article 6 National competent authority on the security of network and information systems

Each Member State shall designate a national competent authority on the security of network and information systems (the "competent authority") .

The competent authorities shall monitor the application of this Directive at national level and contribute to its consistent application throughout the Union.

Member States shall ensure that the competent authorities have adequate technical, financial and human resources to carry out in an effective and efficient manner the tasks assigned to them and thereby to fulfil the objectives of this Directive. Member States shall ensure the effective, efficient and secure cooperation of the competent authorities via the network referred to in Article 8.

Member States shall ensure that the competent authorities receive the notifications of incidents from public administrations and market operators as specified under Article 14(2) and are granted the implementation and enforcement powers referred to under Article 15.

The competent authorities shall consult and cooperate, whenever appropriate, with the relevant law enforcement national authorities and data protection authorities.

For additional analytical, business and investment opportunities information, please contact Global Investment & Business Center, USA at (703) 370-8082. Fax: (703) 370-8083. E-mail: ibpusa3@gmail.com Global Business and Investment Info Databank - www.ibpus.com

Each Member State shall notify to the Commission without delay the designation of the competent authority, its tasks, and any subsequent change thereto. Each Member State shall make public its designation of the competent authority.

Article 7 Computer Emergency Response Team

Each Member State shall set up a Computer Emergency Response Team (hereinafter: "CERT") responsible for handling incidents and risks according to a well-defined process, which shall comply with the requirements set out in point (1) of Annex I. A CERT may be established within the competent authority.

Member States shall ensure that CERTs have adequate technical, financial and human resources to effectively carry out their tasks set out in point (2) of Annex I.

Member States shall ensure that CERTs rely on a secure and resilient communication and information infrastructure at national level, which shall be compatible and interoperable with the secure information-sharing system referred to in Article 9.

Member States shall inform the Commission about the resources and mandate as well as the incident handling process of the CERTs.

The CERT shall act under the supervision of the competent authority, which shall regularly review the adequacy of its resources, its mandate and the effectiveness of its incident-handling process.

CHAPTER III COOPERATION BETWEEN COMPETENT AUTHORITIES

Article 8 Cooperation network

The competent authorities and the Commission shall form a network ("cooperation network") to cooperate against risks and incidents affecting network and information systems.

The cooperation network shall bring into permanent communication the Commission and the competent authorities. When requested, the European Network and Information Security Agency ("ENISA") shall assist the cooperation network by providing its expertise and advice.

Within the cooperation network the competent authorities shall:

circulate early warnings on risks and incidents in accordance with Article 10;

ensure a coordinated response in accordance with Article 11;

publish on a regular basis non-confidential information on on-going early warnings and coordinated response on a common website;

jointly discuss and assess, at the request of one Member State or of the Commission, one or more national NIS strategies and national NIS cooperation plans referred to in Article 5, within the scope of this Directive.

For additional analytical, business and investment opportunities information, please contact Global Investment & Business Center, USA at (703) 370-8082. Fax: (703) 370-8083. E-mail: ibpusa3@gmail.com Global Business and Investment Info Databank - www.ibpus.com

jointly discuss and assess, at the request of a Member State or the Commission, the effectiveness of the CERTs, in particular when NIS exercises are performed at Union level;

cooperate and exchange information on all relevant matters with the EuropeanCybercrime Center within Europol, and with other relevant European bodies in particular in the fields of data protection, energy, transport, banking, stock exchanges and health;

(g) exchange information and best practices between themselves and the Commission, and assist each other in building capacity on NIS;

(h) organise regular peer reviews on capabilities and preparedness;

(i) organise NIS exercises at Union level and participate, as appropriate, in international NIS exercises.

4. The Commission shall establish, by means of implementing acts, the necessary modalities to facilitate the cooperation between competent authorities and the Commission referred to in paragraphs 2 and 3. Those implementing acts shall be adopted in accordance with the consultation procedure referred to in Article 19(2) .

Article 9 Secure information-sharing system

The exchange of sensitive and confidential information within the cooperation network shall take place through a secure infrastructure.

The Commission shall be empowered to adopt delegated acts in accordance with Article 18 concerning the definition of the criteria to be fulfilled for a Member State to be authorized to participate to the secure information-sharing system, regarding:

the availability of a secure and resilient communication and information infrastructure at national level, compatible and interoperable with the secure infrastructure of the cooperation network in compliance with Article 7(3) , and

the existence of adequate technical, financial and human resources and processes for their competent authority and CERT allowing an effective, efficient and secure participation in the secure information-sharing system under Article 6(3) , Article 7(2) and Article 7(3) .

The Commission shall adopt, by means of implementing acts, decisions on the access of the Member States to this secure infrastructure, pursuant to the criteria referred to in paragraph 2 and 3. Those implementing acts shall be adopted in accordance with the examination procedure referred to in Article 19(3) .

Article 10 Early warnings

1. The competent authorities or the Commission shall provide early warnings within the cooperation network on those risks and incidents that fulfil at least one of the following conditions:

(a) they grow rapidly or may grow rapidly in scale;

For additional analytical, business and investment opportunities information, please contact Global Investment & Business Center, USA at (703) 370-8082. Fax: (703) 370-8083. E-mail: ibpusa3@gmail.com Global Business and Investment Info Databank - www.ibpus.com

(b) they exceed or may exceed national response capacity;

(c) they affect or may affect more than one Member State.

2. In the early warnings, the competent authorities and the Commission shall communicate any relevant information in their possession that may be useful for assessing the risk or incident.

At the request of a Member State, or on its own initiative, the Commission may request a Member State to provide any relevant information on a specific risk or incident.

Where the risk or incident subject to an early warning is of a suspected criminal nature, the competent authorities or the Commission shall inform the European Cybercrime Centre within Europol.

The Commission shall be empowered to adopt delegated acts in accordance with Article 18, concerning the further specification of the risks and incidents triggering early warning referred to in paragraph 1.

Article 11 Coordinated response

Following an early warning referred to in Article 10 the competent authorities shall, after assessing the relevant information, agree on a coordinated response in accordance with the Union NIS cooperation plan referred to in Article 12.

The various measures adopted at national level as a result of the coordinated response shall be communicated to the cooperation network.

Article 12 Union NIS cooperation plan

The Commission shall be empowered to adopt, by means of implementing acts, a Union NIS cooperation plan. Those implementing acts shall be adopted in accordance with the examination procedure referred to in Article 19(3) .

The Union NIS cooperation plan shall provide for:

for the purposes of Article 10:

a definition of the format and procedures for the collection and sharing of compatible and comparable information on risks and incidents by the competent authorities,

a definition of the procedures and the criteria for the assessment of the risks and incidents by the cooperation network.

the processes to be followed for the coordinated responses under Article 11, including identification of roles and responsibilities and cooperation procedures;

a roadmap for NIS exercises and training to reinforce, validate, and test the plan;

a programme for transfer of knowledge between the Member States in relation to capacity building and peer learning;

For additional analytical, business and investment opportunities information, please contact Global Investment & Business Center, USA at (703) 370-8082. Fax: (703) 370-8083. E-mail: ibpusa3@gmail.com Global Business and Investment Info Databank - www.ibpus.com

a programme for awareness raising and training between the Member States.

The Union NIS cooperation plan shall be adopted no later than one year following the entry into force of this Directive and shall be revised regularly.

Article 13 International cooperation

Without prejudice to the possibility for the cooperation network to have informal international cooperation, the Union may conclude international agreements with third countries or international organisations allowing and organizing their participation in some activities of the cooperation network. Such agreement shall take into account the need to ensure adequate protection of the personal data circulating on the cooperation network.

CHAPTER IV SECURITY OF THE NETWORKS AND INFORMATION SYSTEMS OF PUBLIC ADMINISTRATIONS AND MARKET OPERATORS

Article 14 Security requirements and incident notification

Member States shall ensure that public administrations and market operators take appropriate technical and organisational measures to manage the risks posed to the security of the networks and information systems which they control and use in their operations. Having regard to the state of the art, these measures shall guarantee a level of security appropriate to the risk presented. In particular, measures shall be taken to prevent and minimise the impact of incidents affecting their network and information system on the core services they provide and thus ensure the continuity of the services underpinned by those networks and information systems.

Member States shall ensure that public administrations and market operators notify to the competent authority incidents having a significant impact on the security of the core services they provide.

The requirements under paragraphs 1 and 2 apply to all market operators providing services within the European Union.

The competent authority may inform the public, or require the public administrations and market operators to do so, where it determines that disclosure of the incident is in the public interest. Once a year, the competent authority shall submit a summary report to the cooperation network on the notifications received and the action taken in accordance with this paragraph.

The Commission shall be empowered to adopt delegated acts in accordance with Article 18 concerning the definition of circumstances in which public administrations and market operators are required to notify incidents.

Subject to any delegated act adopted under paragraph 5, the competent authorities may adopt guidelines and, where necessary, issue instructions concerning the circumstances in which public administrations and market operators are required to notify incidents.

The Commission shall be empowered to define, by means of implementing acts, the formats and procedures applicable for the purpose of paragraph 2. Those implementing acts shall be adopted in accordance with the examination procedure referred to in Article 19(3) .

For additional analytical, business and investment opportunities information, please contact Global Investment & Business Center, USA at (703) 370-8082. Fax: (703) 370-8083. E-mail: ibpusa3@gmail.com Global Business and Investment Info Databank - www.ibpus.com

Paragraphs 1 and 2 shall not apply to microenterprises as defined in Commission Recommendation 2003/361/EC of 6 May 2003 concerning the definition of micro, small and medium-sized enterprises[12].

Article 15 Implementation and enforcement

Member States shall ensure that the competent authorities have all the powers necessary to investigate cases of non-compliance of public administrations or market operators with their obligations under Article 14 and the effects thereof on the security of networks and information systems.

Member States shall ensure that the competent authorities have the power to require market operators and public administrations to:

provide information needed to assess the security of their networks and information systems, including documented security policies;

undergo a security audit carried out by a qualified independent body or national authority and make the results thereof available to the competent authority.

Member States shall ensure that competent authorities have the power to issue binding instructions to market operators and public administrations.

The competent authorities shall notify incidents of a suspected serious criminal nature to law enforcement authorities.

The competent authorities shall work in close cooperation with personal data protection authorities when addressing incidents resulting in personal data breaches.

Member States shall ensure that any obligations imposed on public administrations and market operators under this Chapter may be subject to judicial review.

Article 16 Standardisation

To ensure convergent implementation of Article 14(1) , Member States shall encourage the use of standards and/or specifications relevant to networks and information security.

The Commission shall draw up, by means of implementing acts a list of the standards referred to in paragraph 1. The list shall be published in the Official Journal of the European Union.

CHAPTER V FINAL PROVISIONS

Article 17 Sanctions

Member States shall lay down rules on sanctions applicable to infringements of the national provisions adopted pursuant to this Directive and shall take all measures necessary to ensure that they are implemented. The sanctions provided for must be effective, proportionate and dissuasive. The Member States shall notify those provisions to the Commission by the date of transposition of this Directive at the latest and shall notify it without delay of any subsequent amendment affecting them.

Member states shall ensure that when a security incident involves personal data, the sanctions foreseen are consistent with the sanctions provided by the Regulation of

the European Parliament and of the Council on the protection of individuals with regard to the processing of personal data and on the free movement of such data[13].

Article 18 Exercise of the delegation

The power to adopt the delegated acts is conferred on the Commission subject to the conditions laid down in this Article.

The power to adopt delegated acts referred to in Articles 9(2) , 10(5) and 14(5) shall be conferred on the Commission. The Commission shall draw up a report in respect of the delegation of power not later than nine months before the end of the five-year period. The delegation of power shall be tacitly extended for periods of an identical duration, unless the European Parliament or the Council opposes such extension not later than three months before the end of each period.

The delegation of powers referred to in Articles 9(2) , 10(5) and 14(5) may be revoked at any time by the European Parliament or by the Council. A decision to revoke shall put an end to the delegation of the powers specified in that decision. It shall take effect the day following the publication of the decision in the *Official Journal of the European Union* or at a later date specified therein. It shall not affect the validity of any delegated act already in force.

As soon as it adopts a delegated act, the Commission shall notify it simultaneously to the European Parliament and to the Council.

A delegated act adopted pursuant to Articles 9(2) , 10(5) and 14(5) shall enter into force only if no objection has been expressed either by the European Parliament or the Council within a period of two months of notification of that act to the European Parliament and the Council or if, before the expiry of that period, the European Parliament and the Council have both informed the Commission that they will not object. That period shall be extended by two months at the initiative of the European Parliament or of the Council.

Article 19 Committee procedure

The Commission shall be assisted by a committee (the Network and Information Security Committee) . That committee shall be a committee within the meaning of Regulation (EU) No 182/2011.

Where reference is made to this paragraph, Article 4 of Regulation (EU) No 182/2011 shall apply.

Where reference is made to this paragraph, Article 5 of Regulation (EU) No 182/2011 shall apply.

Article 20 Review

The Commission shall periodically review the functioning of this Directive and report to the European Parliament and the Council. The first report shall be submitted no later than three years after the date of transposition referred to in Article 21. For this purpose, the Commission may request Member States to provide information without undue delay.

For additional analytical, business and investment opportunities information, please contact Global Investment & Business Center, USA at (703) 370-8082. Fax: (703) 370-8083. E-mail: ibpusa3@gmail.com Global Business and Investment Info Databank - www.ibpus.com

Article 21

Transposition

4. Member States shall adopt and publish, by [one year and a half after adoption] at the latest, the laws, regulations and administrative provisions necessary to comply with this Directive. They shall forthwith communicate to the Commission the text of such provisions.

They shall apply those measures from [one year and a half after adoption].

When Member States adopt those measures, they shall contain a reference to this Directive or be accompanied by such a reference on the occasion of their official publication. Member States shall determine how such reference is to be made.

5. Member States shall communicate to the Commission the text of the main provisions of national law which they adopt in the field covered by this Directive.

Article 22 Entry into force

This Directive shall enter into force on the [twentieth] day following that of its publication in the *Official Journal of the European Union.*

Article 23 Addressees This Directive is addressed to the Member States. Done at Brussels,

For the European Parliament For the Council The President The President

ANNEX I REQUIREMENTS AND TASKS OF THE COMPUTER EMERGENCY RESPONSE TEAM (CERT)

The requirements and tasks of the CERT shall be adequately and clearly defined and supported by national policy and/or regulation. They shall include the following elements:

(1) Requirements for the CERT

(a) The CERT shall ensure high availability of its communications services by avoiding single points of failure and have several means for being contacted and for contacting others. Furthermore, the communication channels shall be clearly specified and well known to the constituency and cooperative partners.

(b) The CERT shall implement and manage security measures to ensure the confidentiality, integrity, availability and authenticity of information it receives and treats.

(c) The offices of the CERT and the supporting information systems shall be located in secure sites.

(d) A service management quality system shall be created to follow-up on the performance of the CERT and ensure a steady process of improvement. It shall be based on clearly defined metrics that include formal service levels and key performance indicators.

(e) Business continuity:

For additional analytical, business and investment opportunities information, please contact Global Investment & Business Center, USA at (703) 370-8082. Fax: (703) 370-8083. E-mail: ibpusa3@gmail.com Global Business and Investment Info Databank - www.ibpus.com

– The CERT shall be equipped with an appropriate system for managing and routing requests, in order to facilitate handovers,

– The CERT shall be adequately staffed to ensure availability at all times,

– The CERT shall rely on an infrastructure whose continuity is ensured. To this end, redundant systems and backup working space shall be set up for the CERT to ensure permanent access to the means of communication.

(2) Tasks of the CERT

(a) Tasks of the CERT shall include at least the following:

– Monitoring incidents at a national level,

– Providing early warning, alerts, announcements and dissemination of information to relevant stakeholders about risks and incidents,

– Responding to incidents,

– Providing dynamic risk and incident analysis and situational awareness,

– Building broad public awareness of the risks associated with online activities,

– Organising campaigns on NIS;

(b) The CERT shall establish cooperative relationships with private sector.

(c) To facilitate cooperation, the CERT shall promote the adoption and use of common or standardised practises for:

– incident and risk handling procedures,

– incident, risk and information classification schemes,

– taxonomies for metrics,

– information exchange formats on risks, incidents, and system naming conventions.

ANNEX II LIST OF MARKET OPERATORS REFERRED TO IN ARTICLE 3(8) A) :

e-commerce platforms

Internet payment gateways

Social networks

Search engines

Cloud computing services

Application stores

Referred to in Article (3(8) b) :

1. Energy

– Electricity and gas suppliers

– Electricity and/or gas distribution system operators and retailers for final consumers

– Natural gas transmission system operators, storage operators and LNG operators

– Transmission system operators in electricity

– Oil transmission pipelines and oil storage

– Electricity and gas market operators

– Operators of oil and natural gas production, refining and treatment facilities

2. Transport

– Air carriers (freight and passenger air transport)

– Maritime carriers (sea and coastal passenger water transport companies and sea and coastal freight water transport companies)

– Railways (infrastructure managers, integrated companies and railway transport operators)

– Airports

– Ports

– Traffic management control operators

– Auxiliary logistics services (a) warehousing and storage, b) cargo handling and c) other transportation support activities)

Banking: credit institutions in accordance with Article 4.1 of Directive 2006/48/CE.

Financial market infrastructures: stock exchanges and central counterparty clearing houses

Health sector: health care settings (including hospitals and private clinics) and other entities involved in health care provisions

LEGISLATIVE FINANCIAL STATEMENT

FRAMEWORK OF THE PROPOSAL/INITIATIVE

For additional analytical, business and investment opportunities information, please contact Global Investment & Business Center, USA at (703) 370-8082. Fax: (703) 370-8083. E-mail: ibpusa3@gmail.com Global Business and Investment Info Databank - www.ibpus.com

1.1. Title of the proposal/initiative

1.2. Policy area(s) concerned in the ABM/ABB structure

1.3. Nature of the proposal/initiative

1.4. Objectives

1.5. Grounds for the proposal/initiative

1.6. Duration and financial impact

1.7. Management method(s) envisaged

MANAGEMENT MEASURES

2.1. Monitoring and reporting rules

2.2. Management and control system

2.3. Measures to prevent fraud and irregularities

ESTIMATED FINANCIAL IMPACT OF THE PROPOSAL/INITIATIVE

3.1. Heading(s) of the multiannual financial framework and expenditure budget line(s) affected

3.2. Estimated impact on expenditure

3.2.1. Summary of estimated impact on expenditure

3.2.2. Estimated impact on operational appropriations

3.2.3. Estimated impact on appropriations of an administrative nature

3.2.4. Compatibility with the current multiannual financial framework

3.2.5. Third-party contributions

3.3. Estimated impact on revenue

LEGISLATIVE FINANCIAL STATEMENT

1. FRAMEWORK OF THE PROPOSAL/INITIATIVE

1.1. Title of the proposal/initiative

Proposal for a Directive of the European Parliament and of the Council concerning measures to ensure a high level of network and information security across the Union.

1.2. Policy area concerned in the ABM/ABB structure37

- 09 – Communications Networks, Content and Technology

1.3. Nature of the proposal/initiative

- The proposal/initiative relates to a new action
- The proposal/initiative relates to a new action following a pilot project/preparatory action38
- The proposal/initiative relates to the extension of an existing action
- The proposal/initiative relates to an action redirected towards a new action

1.4. Objectives

1.4.1. The Commission's multiannual strategic objective(s) targeted by the proposal/initiative

The aim of the proposed Directive is to ensure a high common level of network and information security (NIS) across the EU.

1.4.2. Specific objectives and ABM/ABB activities concerned

The proposal lays down measures to ensure a high common level of network and information systems security across the Union.

The specific objectives are:

To put in place a minimum level of NIS in the Member States and thus increase the overall level of preparedness and response.

To improve cooperation on NIS at EU level with a view to counter cross border incidents and threats effectively. A secure information-sharing infrastructure will be put in place to allow for the exchange of sensitive and confidential information among the competent authorities.

To create a culture of risk management and improve the sharing of information between the private and public sectors.

ABM/ABB activities concerned

The Directive covers entities (companies and organisations, including some SMEs) in a number of sectors (energy, transport, credit institutions and stock exchanges, healthcare and enablers of key Internet services) as well as public administrations. It addresses links with law enforcement and data protection and NIS aspects of external relations.

-09 – Communications Networks, Content and Technology

-02 - Enterprise

-32 - Energy

-06 - Mobility and Transport

37 ABM: Activity-Based Management – ABB: Activity-Based Budgeting.

38 As referred to in Article 49(6) (a) or (b) of the Financial Regulation.

EN EN

For additional analytical, business and investment opportunities information, please contact Global Investment & Business Center, USA at (703) 370-8082. Fax: (703) 370-8083. E-mail: ibpusa3@gmail.com Global Business and Investment Info Databank - www.ibpus.com

-17 - Health and consumer protection

- 18 – Home affairs

-19 – External relations

-33 - Justice

-12- Internal market

1.4.3. Expected result(s) and impact Specify the effects which the proposal/initiative should have on the beneficiaries/groups targeted.

The protection of EU consumers, business and Governments against NIS incidents, threats and risks would improve considerably.

Further details can be found in Section 8.2 (Impact of Option 2 – Regulatory approach) of the Commission Staff Working Document Impact Assessment accompanying this legislative proposal.

1.4.4. Indicators of results and impact Specify the indicators for monitoring implementation of the proposal/initiative.

The indicators for Monitoring and Evaluation can be found in Section 10 of the Impact Assessment.

1.5.

1.5.1. Grounds for the proposal/initiative *Requirements to be met in the short or long term*

Each Member State would be required to have:

-a national NIS strategy;

-a NIS cooperation plan;

a NIS competent national authority; and

-a Computer Emergency Response Team (CERT)

At EU level, the Member States would be required to cooperate via a network.

Public administrations and key private players would be required to carry out NIS risk management and to report to the competent authorities NIS incidents with a significant impact.

1.5.2. Added value of EU involvement

Considering the cross-border nature of NIS, divergences in relevant legislation and policy represent a barrier for companies to operate in multiple countries and to the achievement of global economies of scale. Lack of intervention at EU level would lead to a situation where each Member State would act alone disregarding the interdependences amongst network and information systems.

For additional analytical, business and investment opportunities information, please contact Global Investment & Business Center, USA at (703) 370-8082. Fax: (703) 370-8083. E-mail: ibpusa3@gmail.com Global Business and Investment Info Databank - www.ibpus.com

The stated objectives can hence be better achieved via EU level action, rather than by the Member States alone.

1.5.3. Lessons learned from similar experiences in the past

The proposal stems from the analysis that regulatory obligations are needed to create a level playing field and close some legislative loopholes. In this field, a purely voluntarily approach has resulted in cooperation taking place only amongst a minority of Member States with a high level of capabilities.

1.5.4. Compatibility and possible synergy with other appropriate instruments

The proposal is fully consistent with the Digital Agenda for Europe and therefore with the EU2020 Strategy. It is also consistent with and complements the EU electronic communications regulatory framework, the EU Directive on European Critical Infrastructure and the EU data protection Directive.

The proposal accompanies and is an essential part of the Communication of the Commission and the High Representative of the Union for Foreign Affairs and Security Policy on the European Cybersecurity Strategy.

1.6. Duration and financial impact

– … Proposal/initiative of limited duration – • Proposal/initiative in effect from [DD/MM]YYYY to [DD/MM]YYYY – • Financial impact from YYYY to YYYY – : Proposal/initiative of unlimited duration

– Transposition period will start immediately after adoption (esimated in 2015) and run for 18 months. Implementation of the Directive will, however, start after adoption and will entail setting up the secure infrastructure that will support Member State cooperation.

– followed by full-scale operation.

1.7. Management modes envisaged[39]

– : Centralised direct management by the Commission – : Centralised indirect management with the delegation of implementation tasks to: – … executive agencies – • bodies set up by the Communities[40] – … national public-sector bodies/bodies with public-service mission – • persons entrusted with the implementation of specific actions pursuant to Title V of

the Treaty on European Union and identified in the relevant basic act within the meaning of Article 49 of the Financial Regulation – … Shared management with the Member States – … Decentralised management with third countries – … Joint management with international organisations, including the European Space Agency

If more than one management mode is indicated, please provide details in the "Comments" section.

Comments:

ENISA, a decentralised Agency created by the Communities, may assist the Member States and the Commission in the implementation of the Directive on the basis of its mandate and by the redeploiment of resources foreseen under the MFF 2014-2020 for this agency.

Details of management modes and references to the Financial Regulation may be found on the BudgWeb site:

http://www.cc.cec/budg/man/budgmanag/budgmanag_en.htm
lhttp://www.cc.cec/budg/man/budgmanag/budgmanag_en.ht ml

40

As referred to in Article 185 of the Financial Regulation.

2. MANAGEMENT MEASURES

2.1. Monitoring and reporting rules

Specify frequency and conditions.

The Commission willl periodically review the functioning of the Directive and report to the European Parliament and the Council.

The Commission will also assess the correct transposition of the Directive by the Member States.

The CEF proposal also provides for the possibility to undertake an evaluation of the methods of carrying out projects as well as the impact of their implementation, in order to assess whether the objectives, including those relating to environmental protection, have been attained.

2.2. Management and control system

2.2.1. Risk identified

- project implementation delays in building the secure infrastructure

2.2.2. Control methods envisaged

The agreements and decisions for implementing the actions under CEF will provide for supervision and financial control by the Commission, or any representative authorised by the Commission, as well as audits by the Court of Auditors and on-thespot checks carried out by the European Anti-Fraud Office (OLAF) .

2.2.3. Costs and benefits of controls and probable non-compliance rate

Risk based ex-ante and ex-post controls and the possibility of on-site audits will ensure that the costs of the controls are reasonable.

2.3. Measures to prevent fraud and irregularities *Specify existing or envisaged prevention and protection measures.*

The Commission shall take appropriate measures ensuring that when the action financed under this Directive is implemented, the financial interests of the Union are protected by the application of preventive measures against fraud, corruption and any other illegal activities by effective

For additional analytical, business and investment opportunities information, please contact Global Investment & Business Center, USA at (703) 370-8082. Fax: (703) 370-8083. E-mail: ibpusa3@gmail.com Global Business and Investment Info Databank - www.ibpus.com

checks and, if irregularities are detected, by the recovery of the amounts wrongly paid and, where appropriate, by effective, proportionate and deterrent penalties.

The Commission or its representatives and the Court of Auditors shall have the power of audit, on the basis of documents and on-the-spot, over all grant beneficiaries, contractors and subcontractors who have received Union funds under the Programme.

The European Anti-fraud Office (OLAF) may carry out on-the-spot checks and inspections on economic operators concerned directly or indirectly by such funding in accordance with the procedures laid down in Regulation (Euratom, EC) No 2185/96 with a view to establishing whether there has been fraud, corruption or any other illegal activity affecting the financial interests of the Union in connection with a grant agreement or grant decision or a contract concerning Union funding.

Without prejudice to the paragraphs above, cooperation agreements with third countries and international organisations and grant agreements and grant decisions and contracts resulting from the implementation of this Regulation shall expressly empower the Commission, the Court of Auditors and OLAF to conduct such audits, on-the-spot checks and inspections.

The CEF provides for contracts for grants and procurement to be based on standard models, which will set out the generally applicable anti-fraud measures.

EUROPEAN UNION AGENCY FOR NETWORK AND INFORMATION SECURITY (ENISA) [5]

THE EUROPEAN PARLIAMENT AND THE COUNCIL OF THE EUROPEAN UNION,
Having regard to the Treaty on the Functioning of the European Union, and in particular Article 114 thereof,
Having regard to the proposal from the European Commission,
After transmission of the draft legislative act to the national parliaments,
Having regard to the opinion of the European Economic and Social Committee (1) ,
Acting in accordance with the ordinary legislative procedure (2) ,

Whereas:

(1)

Electronic communications, infrastructure and services are essential factors, both directly and indirectly, in economic and societal development. They play a vital role for society and have in themselves become ubiquitous utilities in the same way as electricity or water supplies, and also constitute vital factors in the delivery of electricity, water and other critical services. Communications networks function as social and innovation catalysts, multiplying the impact of technology and shaping consumer behaviours, business models, industries, as well as citizenship and political participation. Their disruption has the potential to cause considerable physical, social and economic damage, underlining the importance of measures to increase protection and resilience aimed at ensuring continuity of critical services. The security of electronic communications, infrastructure and services, in particular their integrity, availability and confidentiality, faces continuously expanding challenges which relate, inter alia, to the individual components of the communications infrastructure and the software controlling those components, the infrastructure overall and the services provided through that infrastructure. This is of

[5] REGLATION (EU) No 526/2013 OF THE EUROPEAN PARLIAMENT AND OF THE COUNCIL of 21 May 2013

increasing concern to society not least because of the possibility of problems due to system complexity, malfunctions, systemic failures, accidents, mistakes and attacks that may have consequences for the electronic and physical infrastructure which delivers services critical to the well-being of European citizens.

(2)

The threat landscape is continuously changing and security incidents can undermine the trust that users have in technology, networks and services, thereby affecting their ability to exploit the full potential of the internal market and widespread use of information and communications technologies (ICT) .

(3)

Regular assessment of the state of network and information security in the Union, based on reliable Union data, as well as systematic forecast of future developments, challenges and threats, both at Union and global level, is therefore important for policy makers, industry and users.

(4)

By Decision 2004/97/EC, Euratom (3) , adopted at the meeting of the European Council on 13 December 2003, the representatives of the Member States decided that the European Network and Information Security Agency (ENISA) , that was to be established on the basis of the proposal submitted by the Commission, would have its seat in a town in Greece to be determined by the Greek Government. Following that Decision, the Greek Government determined that ENISA should have its seat in Heraklion, Crete.

(5)

On 1 April 2005, a Headquarters Agreement ('Seat Agreement') was concluded between the Agency and the host Member State.

(6)

The Agency's host Member State should ensure the best possible conditions for the smooth and efficient operation of the Agency. It is imperative for the proper and efficient performance of its tasks, for staff recruitment and retention and to enhance the efficiency of networking activities that the Agency be based in an appropriate location, among other things providing appropriate transport connections and facilities for spouses and children accompanying members of staff of the Agency. The necessary arrangements should be laid down in an agreement between the Agency and the host Member State concluded after obtaining the approval of the Management Board of the Agency.

(7)

In order to improve the operational efficiency of the Agency, the Agency has established a branch office in the metropolitan area of Athens, which should be maintained with the agreement and support of the host Member State, and where the operational staff of the Agency should be located. Staff primarily engaged in the administration of the Agency (including the Executive Director) , finance, desk research and analysis, IT and facilities management, human resources, training, and communications and public affairs, should be based in Heraklion.

For additional analytical, business and investment opportunities information, please contact Global Investment & Business Center, USA at (703) 370-8082. Fax: (703) 370-8083. E-mail: ibpusa3@gmail.com Global Business and Investment Info Databank - www.ibpus.com

(8)

The Agency has the right to determine its own organisation in order to ensure the proper and efficient performance of its tasks, while respecting the provisions on the seat and Athens branch office laid down in this Regulation. In particular, in order to carry out tasks involving interaction with key stakeholders such as the Union institutions, the Agency should make the necessary practical arrangements to enhance such operational efficiency.

(9)

In 2004 the European Parliament and the Council adopted Regulation (EC) No 460/2004 (4) establishing ENISA with the purpose of contributing to the goals of ensuring a high level of network and information security within the Union and developing a culture of network and information security for the benefit of citizens, consumers, enterprises and public administrations. In 2008, the European Parliament and the Council adopted Regulation (EC) No 1007/2008 (5) extending the mandate of the Agency until March 2012. Regulation (EC) No 580/2011 (6) extends the mandate of the Agency until 13 September 2013.

(10)

The Agency should succeed ENISA as established by Regulation (EC) No 460/2004. Within the framework of the Decision of the Representatives of the Member States, meeting in the European Council of 13 December 2003, the host Member State should maintain and further develop the current practical arrangements in order to ensure the smooth and efficient operation of the Agency, including its Athens branch office, and facilitate the recruitment and retention of highly qualified staff.

(11)

Since ENISA was set up, the challenges of network and information security have changed with technology, market and socioeconomic developments and have been the subject of further reflection and debate. In response to the changing challenges, the Union has updated its priorities for network and information security policy. This Regulation aims to strengthen the Agency to successfully contribute to the efforts of the Union institutions and the Member States to develop a European capacity to cope with network and information security challenges.

(12)

Internal market measures in the field of security of electronic communications and, more generally, network and information security require different forms of technical and organisational applications by the Union institutions and the Member States. The heterogeneous application of those requirements can lead to inefficiencies and can create obstacles to the internal market. This makes a centre of expertise at Union level necessary, providing guidance, advice and assistance on issues related to network and information security, which may be relied upon by the Union institutions and the Member States. The Agency can respond to those needs by developing and maintaining a high level of expertise and assisting the Union institutions, the Member States, and the business community in order to help them meet the legal and regulatory requirements of network and information security and to determine and address network and information security issues, thereby contributing to the proper functioning of the internal market.

(13)

For additional analytical, business and investment opportunities information, please contact Global Investment & Business Center, USA at (703) 370-8082. Fax: (703) 370-8083. E-mail: ibpusa3@gmail.com Global Business and Investment Info Databank - www.ibpus.com

The Agency should carry out the tasks conferred on it by legal acts of the Union in the field of electronic communications and, in general, contribute to an enhanced level of security of electronic communications as well as of privacy and personal data protection by, among other things, providing expertise and advice, and promoting the exchange of best practices, and offering policy suggestions.

(14)

Directive 2002/21/EC of the European Parliament and of the Council of 7 March 2002 on a common regulatory framework for electronic communications networks and services (Framework Directive) (7) requires that providers of public electronic communications networks or publicly available electronic communications services take appropriate measures to safeguard the integrity and security thereof, and introduces an obligation for the national regulatory authorities, where appropriate, to inform, inter alia, the Agency about any security breach or integrity loss that has had a significant impact on the operation of networks or services and to submit to the Commission and to the Agency an annual summary report on the notifications received and the action taken. Directive 2002/21/EC further calls on the Agency, by providing opinions, to contribute to the harmonisation of appropriate technical and organisational security measures.

(15)

Directive 2002/58/EC of the European Parliament and of the Council of 12 July 2002 concerning the processing of personal data and the protection of privacy in the electronic communications sector (Directive on privacy and electronic communications) (8) requires a provider of a publicly available electronic communications service to take appropriate technical and organisational measures to safeguard the security of its services and also requires that the confidentiality of the communications and related traffic data be maintained. Directive 2002/58/EC introduces personal data breach information and notification requirements for electronic communication services providers. It also requires the Commission to consult the Agency on any technical implementing measures to be adopted concerning the circumstances or format of and procedures applicable to information and notification requirements. Directive 95/46/EC of the European Parliament and of the Council of 24 October 1995 on the protection of individuals with regard to the processing of personal data and on the free movement of such data (9) requires Member States to provide that the controller must implement appropriate technical and organisational measures to protect personal data against accidental or unlawful destruction or accidental loss, alteration, unauthorised disclosure or access, in particular where the processing involves the transmission of data over a network and against all other unlawful forms of processing.

(16)

The Agency should contribute to a high level of network and information security, to better protection of privacy and personal data, and to the development and promotion of a culture of network and information security for the benefit of citizens, consumers, businesses and public sector organisations in the Union, thus contributing to the proper functioning of the internal market. In order to achieve this, the necessary budgetary funds should be allocated to the Agency.

(17)

Given the increasing significance of electronic networks and communications, which now constitute the backbone of the European economy, and the actual size of the digital economy, the financial and human resources allocated to the Agency should be increased to reflect its enhanced role and tasks, and its critical position in defending the European digital ecosystem.

(18)

The Agency should operate as a point of reference establishing trust and confidence by virtue of its independence, the quality of the advice it delivers and the information it disseminates, the transparency of its procedures and methods of operation, and its diligence in carrying out its tasks. The Agency should build on national and Union efforts and therefore carry out its tasks in full cooperation with the Union institutions, bodies, offices and agencies and the Member States, and be open to contacts with industry and other relevant stakeholders. In addition, the Agency should build on input from and cooperation with the private sector, which plays an important role in securing electronic communications, infrastructures and services.

(19)

A set of tasks should indicate how the Agency is to accomplish its objectives while allowing flexibility in its operations. The tasks carried out by the Agency should include the collection of appropriate information and data needed to carry out analyses of the risks to the security and resilience of electronic communications, infrastructure and services and to assess, in cooperation with Member States, the Commission and, where appropriate, with relevant stakeholders, the state of network and information security in the Union. The Agency should ensure coordination and collaboration with the Union institutions, bodies, offices and agencies and Member States, and enhance cooperation between stakeholders in Europe, in particular by involving in its activities competent national and Union bodies and high-level private sector experts in relevant areas, in particular providers of electronic communications networks and services, network equipment manufacturers and software vendors, taking into account that network and information systems comprise combinations of hardware, software and services. The Agency should provide assistance to the Union institutions and to the Member States in their dialogue with industry to address security-related problems in hardware and software products, thereby contributing to a collaborative approach to network and information security.

(20)

Network and information security strategies made public by a Union institution, body, office or agency or a Member State should be provided to the Agency for its information and to avoid duplication of effort. The Agency should analyse the strategies and promote their presentation in a format that facilitates comparability. It should make the strategies and its analyses available to the public through electronic means.

(21)

The Agency should assist the Commission by means of advice, opinions and analyses on all the Union matters related to policy development in the area of network and information security, including Critical Information Infrastructure Protection and resilience. The Agency should also assist the Union institutions, bodies, offices and agencies and where relevant, the Member States, at their request, in their efforts to develop network and information security policy and capability.

(22)

The Agency should take full account of the ongoing research, development, and technological assessment activities, in particular those carried out by the various Union research initiatives to advise the Union institutions, bodies, offices and agencies and where relevant, the Member States, at their request, on research needs in the area of network and information security.

(23)

The Agency should assist the Union institutions, bodies, offices and agencies as well as the Member States in their efforts to build and enhance cross-border capability and preparedness to prevent, detect and respond to network and information security problems and incidents. In this regard, the Agency should facilitate cooperation among the Member States and between the Commission and other Union institutions, bodies, offices and agencies and the Member States. To this end, the Agency should support the Member States in their continuous efforts to improve their response capability and to organise and run European exercises on security incidents and, at the request of a Member State, national exercises.

(24)

To understand better the challenges in the network and information security field, the Agency needs to analyse current and emerging risks. For that purpose the Agency should, in cooperation with Member States and, as appropriate, with statistical bodies and others, collect relevant information. Furthermore, the Agency should assist the Union institutions, bodies, offices and agencies and the Member States and in their efforts to collect, analyse and disseminate network and information security data. The collection of appropriate statistical information and data needed to carry out analyses of the risks to the security and resilience of electronic communications, infrastructure and services should take place on the basis of the information provided by the Member States and the Agency's insight to the Union institutions' ICT infrastructures in accordance with Union provisions and national provisions in compliance with Union law. On the basis of that information, the Agency should maintain awareness of the latest state of network and information security and related trends in the Union for the benefit of Union institutions, bodies, offices and agencies and the Member States.

(25)

In performing its tasks, the Agency should facilitate cooperation between the Union and the Member States to improve awareness of the state of network and information security in the Union.

(26)

The Agency should facilitate cooperation among the Member States' competent independent regulatory authorities, in particular supporting the development, promotion and exchange of best practices and standards for education programmes and awareness-raising schemes. Increased information exchange between Member States will facilitate such action. The Agency should contribute towards raising the awareness of individual users of electronic communications, infrastructure and services, including by assisting Member States, where they have chosen to use the public interest information platform provided for in Directive 2002/22/EC of the European Parliament and of the Council of 7 March 2002 on universal service and users' rights relating to electronic communications networks and services (Universal Service Directive) (10) , to produce relevant public interest information regarding network and information security, and also by assisting in the development of such information to be included with the supply of new devices intended for use on public communications networks. The Agency should also support cooperation between stakeholders at Union level, partly by promoting information sharing, awareness-raising campaigns and education and training programmes.

(27)

For additional analytical, business and investment opportunities information, please contact Global Investment & Business Center, USA at (703) 370-8082. Fax: (703) 370-8083. E-mail: ibpusa3@gmail.com Global Business and Investment Info Databank - www.ibpus.com

The Agency should, inter alia, assist the relevant Union institutions, bodies, offices and agencies and the Member States in public education campaigns to end users, aiming at promoting safer individual online behaviour and raising awareness of potential threats in cyberspace, including cybercrimes such as phishing attacks, botnets, financial and banking fraud, as well as promoting basic authentication and data protection advice.

(28)

To ensure that it fully achieves its objectives, the Agency should liaise with relevant bodies, including those dealing with cybercrime such as Europol, and privacy protection authorities to exchange know-how and best practices and provide advice on network and information security aspects that might have an impact on their work. The Agency should aim to achieve synergies between the efforts of those bodies and its own efforts to promote advanced network and information security. Representatives of national and Union law enforcement and privacy protection authorities should be eligible to be represented in the Agency's Permanent Stakeholders Group. In liaising with law enforcement bodies regarding network and information security aspects that might have an impact on their work, the Agency should respect existing channels of information and established networks.

(29)

The Commission has launched a European Public-Private Partnership for Resilience as a flexible Union-wide cooperation platform for resilience of ICT infrastructure, in which the Agency should play a facilitating role, bringing together stakeholders to discuss public policy priorities, economic and market dimensions of challenges and measures for the resilience of ICT.

(30)

In order to promote network and information security and its visibility, the Agency should facilitate cooperation among the Member States' competent public bodies, in particular by supporting the development and exchange of best practices and awareness-raising schemes and by enhancing their outreach activities. The Agency should also support cooperation between stakeholders and the Union institutions, partly by promoting information sharing and awareness-raising activities.

(31)

In order to enhance an advanced level of network and information security in the Union, the Agency should promote cooperation and the exchange of information and best practices between relevant organisations, such as Computer Security Incident Response Teams (CSIRTs) and Computer Emergency Response Teams (CERTs) .

(32)

A Union system of properly functioning CERTs should constitute a cornerstone of the Union's network and information security infrastructure. The Agency should support Member State CERTs and the Union CERT in the operation of a network of CERTs, including the members of the European Governmental CERTs Group. In order to assist in ensuring that each of the CERTs has sufficiently advanced capabilities and that those capabilities correspond as far as possible to the capabilities of the most developed CERTs, the Agency should promote the establishment and operation of a peer-review system. Furthermore, the Agency should promote and support cooperation between the relevant CERTs in the event of incidents, attacks on or disruptions of

For additional analytical, business and investment opportunities information, please contact Global Investment & Business Center, USA at (703) 370-8082. Fax: (703) 370-8083. E-mail: ibpusa3@gmail.com Global Business and Investment Info Databank - www.ibpus.com

networks or infrastructure managed or protected by the CERTs and involving or potentially involving at least two CERTs.

(33)

Efficient network and information security policies should be based on well-developed risk assessment methods, both in the public and private sector. Risk assessment methods and procedures are used at different levels with no common practice regarding how to apply them efficiently. Promoting and developing best practices for risk assessment and for interoperable risk management solutions in public- and private-sector organisations will increase the security level of networks and information systems in the Union. To this end, the Agency should support cooperation between stakeholders at Union level, facilitating their efforts relating to the establishment and take-up of European and international standards for risk management and for measurable security of electronic products, systems, networks and services which, together with software, comprise the network and information systems.

(34)

Where appropriate and useful for fulfilling its objectives and tasks, the Agency should share experience and general information with Union institutions, bodies, offices and agencies dealing with network and information security. The Agency should contribute to identifying research priorities, at Union level, in the areas of network resilience and network and information security, and should convey knowledge of industry needs to relevant research institutions.

(35)

The Agency should encourage Member States and service providers to raise their general security standards so that all internet users take the necessary steps to ensure their own personal cyber security.

(36)

Network and information security problems are global issues. There is a need for closer international cooperation to improve security standards, including the definition of common norms of behaviour and codes of conduct, and information sharing, promoting swifter international collaboration in response to, as well as a common global approach to, network and information security issues. To that end, the Agency should support further Union involvement and cooperation with third countries and international organisations by providing, where appropriate, the necessary expertise and analysis to the relevant Union institutions, bodies, offices and agencies.

(37)

The Agency should operate in accordance with the principle of subsidiarity, ensuring an appropriate degree of coordination between the Member States on matters relating to network and information security and improving the effectiveness of national policies, thus adding value to them and in accordance with the principle of proportionality, not going beyond what is necessary in order to achieve the objectives set out by this Regulation. The exercise of the Agency's tasks should reinforce, but not interfere with, the competences, nor should it pre-empt, impede or overlap with the relevant powers and tasks, of the national regulatory authorities as set out in the Directives relating to electronic communications networks and services, as well as those of the Body of European Regulators for Electronic Communications (BEREC) established by

Regulation (EC) No 1211/2009 (11) and the Communications Committee referred to in Directive 2002/21/EC, of the European standardisation bodies, the national standardisation bodies and the Standing Committee as set out in Directive 98/34/EC (12) and the independent supervisory authorities of the Member States as set out in Directive 95/46/EC.

(38)

It is necessary to implement certain principles regarding the governance of the Agency in order to comply with the Joint Statement and Common Approach agreed upon in July 2012 by the Inter-Institutional Working Group on EU decentralised agencies, the purpose of which statement and approach is to streamline the activities of agencies and improve their performance.

(39)

The Joint Statement and Common Approach should also be reflected, as appropriate, in the Agency's Work Programmes, evaluations of the Agency, and the Agency's reporting and administrative practice.

(40)

In order for the Agency to function properly, the Commission and the Member States should ensure that persons to be appointed to the Management Board have appropriate professional expertise. The Commission and the Member States should also make efforts to limit the turnover of their respective Representatives on the Management Board, in order to ensure continuity in its work.

(41)

It is essential that the Agency establish and maintain a reputation for impartiality, integrity and high professional standards. Accordingly, the Management Board should adopt comprehensive rules covering the entire Agency for the prevention and management of conflicts of interest.

(42)

Given the unique circumstances of the Agency and the difficult challenges facing it, the organisational structure of the Agency should be simplified and strengthened to ensure greater efficiency and effectiveness. Therefore, among other things, an Executive Board should be established in order to enable the Management Board to focus on issues of strategic importance.

(43)

The Management Board should appoint an Accounting Officer in accordance with rules adopted under Regulation (EU, Euratom) No 966/2012 (13) (the 'Financial Regulation') .

(44)

In order to ensure that the Agency is effective, the Member States and the Commission should be represented on the Management Board, which should define the general direction of the Agency's operations and ensure that it carries out its tasks in accordance with this Regulation. The Management Board should be entrusted with the powers necessary to establish the budget, verify its execution, adopt the appropriate financial rules, establish transparent working procedures for decision making by the Agency, adopt the Agency's work programme, adopt its own rules of procedure and the Agency's internal rules of operation, appoint the Executive Director, decide on the extension of the Executive Director's term of office after obtaining the views of the European Parliament, and decide on the termination thereof. The Management Board should set up an Executive Board to assist it with its administrative and budgetary tasks.

(45)

The smooth functioning of the Agency requires that its Executive Director be appointed on grounds of merit and documented administrative and managerial skills, as well as competence and experience relevant for network and information security, and that the duties of the Executive Director be carried out with complete independence as to the organisation of the internal functioning of the Agency. To this end, the Executive Director should prepare a proposal for the Agency's work programme, after prior consultation with the Commission, and take all necessary steps to ensure the proper execution of the work programme of the Agency. The Executive Director should prepare an annual report to be submitted to the Management Board, draw up a draft statement of estimates of revenue and expenditure for the Agency, and implement the budget.

(46)

The Executive Director should have the option of setting up ad hoc Working Groups to address specific matters, in particular of a scientific, technical or legal or socioeconomic nature. In setting up ad hoc Working Groups the Executive Director should seek input from and draw on the relevant external expertise needed to enable the Agency to have access to the most up-to-date information available regarding security challenges posed by the developing information society. The Executive Director should ensure that the ad hoc Working Groups' members are selected according to the highest standards of expertise, taking due account of a representative balance, as appropriate according to the specific issues in question, between the public administrations of the Member States, the Union institutions and the private sector, including industry, users, and academic experts in network and information security. The Executive Director should be able, as appropriate, to invite individual experts recognised as competent in the relevant field to participate in the Working Groups' proceedings, on a case-by-case basis. Their expenses should be met by the Agency in accordance with its internal rules and in accordance with rules adopted under the Financial Regulation.

(47)

The Agency should have a Permanent Stakeholders' Group as an advisory body, to ensure regular dialogue with the private sector, consumers' organisations and other relevant stakeholders. The Permanent Stakeholders' Group, set up by the Management Board on a proposal by the Executive Director, should focus on issues relevant to stakeholders and bring them to the attention of the Agency. The Executive Director should, where appropriate and according to the agenda of the meetings, be able to invite representatives of the European Parliament and other relevant bodies to take part in meetings of the Group.

(48)

Since there is provision for ample representation of stakeholders in the Permanent Stakeholders Group, and that group is to be consulted in particular regarding the draft Work Programme, there is no longer any need to provide for representation of stakeholders in the Management Board.

(49)

The Agency should apply the relevant Union provisions concerning public access to documents as set out in Regulation (EC) No 1049/2001 of the European Parliament and of the Council (14) . The information processed by the Agency for purposes relating to its internal functioning as well as the information processed in carrying out its tasks should be subject to Regulation (EC) No 45/2001 of the European Parliament and of the Council of 18 December 2000 on the protection of individuals with regard to the processing of personal data by the Community institutions and bodies and on the free movement of such data (15) .

(50)

The Agency should comply with the provisions applicable to the Union institutions, and with national legislation regarding the treatment of sensitive documents.

(51)

In order to guarantee the full autonomy and independence of the Agency and to enable it to perform additional and new tasks, including unforeseen emergency tasks, the Agency should be granted a sufficient and autonomous budget whose revenue comes primarily from a contribution from the Union and contributions from third countries participating in the Agency's work. The majority of the Agency staff should be directly engaged in the operational implementation of the Agency's mandate. The host Member State, or any other Member State, should be allowed to make voluntary contributions to the revenue of the Agency. The Union's budgetary procedure should remain applicable as far as any subsidies chargeable to the general budget of the European Union are concerned. Moreover, the Court of Auditors should audit the Agency's accounts to ensure transparency and accountability.

(52)

In view of the continually changing threat landscape and the evolution of Union policy on network and information security, and in order to align to the multiannual financial framework, the duration of the mandate of the Agency should be set to a limited period of seven years with a possibility of extending the duration.

(53)

The Agency's operations should be evaluated independently. The evaluation should have regard to the Agency's effectiveness in achieving its objectives, its working practices and the relevance of its tasks, in order to determine the continuing validity, or otherwise, of the objectives of the Agency and, based thereon, whether and for what period the duration of its mandate should be further extended.

(54)

If, towards the end of the duration of the mandate of the Agency, the Commission has not introduced a proposal for an extension of the mandate, the Agency and the Commission should take the relevant measures, addressing in particular issues relating to staff contracts and budget arrangements.

(55)

Since the objective of this Regulation, namely to establish a European Union Agency for Network and Information Security for the purpose of contributing to a high level of network and information

For additional analytical, business and investment opportunities information, please contact Global Investment & Business Center, USA at (703) 370-8082. Fax: (703) 370-8083. E-mail: ibpusa3@gmail.com Global Business and Investment Info Databank - www.ibpus.com

security within the Union and in order to raise awareness and develop and promote a culture of network and information security in society for the benefit of citizens, consumers, enterprises and public sector organisations in the Union, thus contributing to the establishment and proper functioning of the internal market, cannot be sufficiently achieved by the Member States and can therefore be better achieved at Union level, the Union may adopt measures, in accordance with the principle of subsidiarity as set out in Article 5 of the Treaty on European Union. In accordance with the principle of proportionality, as set out in that Article, this Regulation does not go beyond what is necessary in order to achieve that objective.

(56)

Regulation (EC) No 460/2004 should be repealed.

(57)

The European Data Protection Supervisor was consulted in accordance with Article 28(2) of Regulation (EC) No 45/2001 and adopted his opinion on 20 December 2010 (16) ,

HAVE ADOPTED THIS REGULATION:

SECTION 1 SCOPE OBJECTIVES AND TASKS

Article 1 Subject matter and Scope

1. This Regulation establishes a European Union Agency for Network and Information Security (ENISA, hereinafter 'the Agency') to undertake the tasks assigned to it for the purpose of contributing to a high level of network and information security within the Union and in order to raise awareness of network and information security and to develop and promote a culture, of network and information security in society for the benefit of citizens, consumers, enterprises and public sector organisations in the Union, thus contributing to the establishment and proper functioning of the internal market.

2. The objectives and the tasks of the Agency shall be without prejudice to the competences of the Member States regarding network and information security and in any case to activities concerning public security, defence, national security (including the economic well-being of the state when the issues relate to national security matters) and the activities of the state in areas of criminal law.

3. For the purposes of this Regulation 'network and information security' means the ability of a network or an information system to resist, at a given level of confidence, accidental events or unlawful or malicious actions that compromise the availability, authenticity, integrity and confidentiality of stored or transmitted data and the related services offered by or accessible via those networks and systems.

Article 2 Objectives

1. The Agency shall develop and maintain a high level of expertise.

2. The Agency shall assist the Union institutions, bodies, offices and agencies in developing policies in network and information security.

For additional analytical, business and investment opportunities information, please contact Global Investment & Business Center, USA at (703) 370-8082. Fax: (703) 370-8083. E-mail: ibpusa3@gmail.com Global Business and Investment Info Databank - www.ibpus.com

3. The Agency shall assist the Union institutions, bodies, offices and agencies and the Member States in implementing the policies necessary to meet the legal and regulatory requirements of network and information security under existing and future legal acts of the Union, thus contributing to the proper functioning of the internal market.

4. The Agency shall assist the Union and the Member States in enhancing and strengthening their capability and preparedness to prevent, detect and respond to network and information security problems and incidents.

5. The Agency shall use its expertise to stimulate broad cooperation between actors from the public and private sectors.

Article 3 Tasks

1. Within the purpose set out in Article 1, and in order to attain the objectives set out in Article 2, whilst respecting Article 1(2) , the Agency shall perform the following tasks:

(a) support the development of Union policy and law, by:

(i) assisting and advising on all matters relating to Union network and information security policy and law;

(ii) providing preparatory work, advice and analyses relating to the development and update of Union network and information security policy and law;

(iii) analysing publicly available network and information security strategies and promoting their publication;

(b) support capability building by:

(i) supporting Member States, at their request, in their efforts to develop and improve the prevention, detection and analysis of and the capability to respond to network and information security problems and incidents, and providing them with the necessary knowledge;

(ii) promoting and facilitating voluntary cooperation among the Member States and between the Union institutions, bodies, offices and agencies and the Member States in their efforts to prevent, detect and respond to network and information security problems and incidents where these have an impact across borders;

(iii) assisting the Union institutions, bodies, offices and agencies in their efforts to develop the prevention, detection and analysis of and the capability to respond to network and information security problems and incidents, in particular by supporting the operation of a Computer Emergency Response Team (CERT) for them;

(iv) supporting the raising of the level of capabilities of national/governmental and Union CERTs, including by promoting dialogue and exchange of information, with a view to ensuring that, with regard to the state of the art, each CERT meets a common set of minimum capabilities and operates according to best practices;

(v) supporting the organisation and running of Union network and information security exercises, and, at their request, advising Member States on national exercises;

For additional analytical, business and investment opportunities information, please contact Global Investment & Business Center, USA at (703) 370-8082. Fax: (703) 370-8083. E-mail: ibpusa3@gmail.com Global Business and Investment Info Databank - www.ibpus.com

(vi) assisting the Union institutions, bodies, offices and agencies and the Member States in their efforts to collect, analyse and, in line with Member States' security requirements, disseminate relevant network and information security data; and on the basis of information provided by the Union institutions, bodies, offices and agencies and the Member States in accordance with provisions of Union law and national provisions in compliance with Union law, maintaining the awareness, on the part of the Union institutions, bodies, offices and agencies as well as the Member States of the latest state of network and information security in the Union for their benefit;

(vii) supporting the development of a Union early warning mechanism that is complementary to Member States' mechanisms;

(viii) offering network and information security training for relevant public bodies, where appropriate in cooperation with stakeholders;

(c) support voluntary cooperation among competent public bodies, and between stakeholders, including universities and research centres in the Union, and support awareness raising, inter alia, by:

(i) promoting cooperation between national and governmental CERTs or Computer Security Incident Response Teams (CSIRTs) , including the CERT for the Union institutions, bodies, offices and agencies;

(ii) promoting the development and sharing of best practices with the aim of attaining an advanced level of network and information security;

(iii) facilitating dialogue and efforts to develop and exchange best practices;

(iv) promoting best practices in information sharing and awareness raising;

(v) supporting the Union institutions, bodies, offices and agencies and, at their request, the Member States and their relevant bodies in organising awareness raising, including at the level of individual users, and other outreach activities to increase network and information security and its visibility by providing best practices and guidelines;

(d) support research and development and standardisation, by:

(i) facilitating the establishment and take-up of European and international standards for risk management and for the security of electronic products, networks and services;

(ii) advising the Union and the Member States on research needs in the area of network and information security with a view to enabling effective responses to current and emerging network and information security risks and threats, including with respect to new and emerging information and communications technologies, and to using risk-prevention technologies effectively;

(e) cooperate with Union institutions, bodies, offices and agencies, including those dealing with cybercrime and the protection of privacy and personal data, with a view to addressing issues of common concern, including by:

(i) exchanging know-how and best practices;

For additional analytical, business and investment opportunities information, please contact Global Investment & Business Center, USA at (703) 370-8082. Fax: (703) 370-8083. E-mail: ibpusa3@gmail.com Global Business and Investment Info Databank - www.ibpus.com

(ii) providing advice on relevant network and information security aspects in order to develop synergies;

(f) contribute to the Union's efforts to cooperate with third countries and international organisations to promote international cooperation on network and information security issues, including by:

(i) being engaged, where appropriate, as an observer and in the organisation of international exercises, and analysing and reporting on the outcome of such exercises;

(ii) facilitating exchange of best practices of relevant organisations;

(iii) providing the Union institutions with expertise.

2. Union institutions, bodies, offices and agencies and Member State bodies may request advice from the Agency in the event of breach of security or loss of integrity with a significant impact on the operation of networks and services.

3. The Agency shall carry out tasks conferred on it by legal acts of the Union.

4. The Agency shall express independently its own conclusions, guidance and advice on matters within the scope and objectives of this Regulation.

SECTION 2 ORGANISATION

Article 4 Composition of the Agency

1. The Agency shall comprise:

(a) a Management Board;

(b) an Executive Director and staff; and

(c) a Permanent Stakeholders' Group.

2. In order to contribute to enhancing effectiveness and efficiency of the operation of the Agency, the Management Board shall establish an Executive Board.

Article 5 Management Board

1. The Management Board shall define the general direction of the operation of the Agency and ensure that the Agency works in accordance with the rules and principles laid down in this Regulation. It shall also ensure consistency of the Agency's work with activities conducted by the Member States as well as at Union level.

2. The Management Board shall adopt the Agency's annual and multiannual work programme.

3. The Management Board shall adopt an annual report on the Agency's activities and send it, by 1 July of the following year, to the European Parliament, the Council, the Commission and the Court of Auditors. The annual report shall include the accounts and describe how the Agency has met its performance indicators. The annual report shall be made public.

For additional analytical, business and investment opportunities information, please contact Global Investment & Business Center, USA at (703) 370-8082. Fax: (703) 370-8083. E-mail: ibpusa3@gmail.com Global Business and Investment Info Databank - www.ibpus.com

4. The Management Board shall adopt an anti-fraud strategy that is proportionate to the fraud risks having regard to a cost-benefit analysis of the measures to be implemented.

5. The Management Board shall ensure adequate follow-up to the findings and recommendations resulting from investigations of the European Anti-fraud Office (OLAF) and the various internal or external audit reports and evaluations.

6. The Management Board shall adopt rules for the prevention and management of conflicts of interest.

7. The Management Board shall exercise, with respect to the staff of the Agency, the powers conferred by the Staff Regulations of Officials and the Conditions of Employment of Other Servants of the European Union (the 'Staff Regulations' and the 'Conditions of Employment of Other Servants') , laid down in Regulation (EEC, Euratom, ECSC) No 259/68 (17) on the Appointing Authority and on the Authority Empowered to Conclude Contract of Employment, respectively.

The Management Board shall adopt, in accordance with the procedure under Article 110 of the Staff Regulations, a decision based on Article 2(1) of the Staff Regulations and on Article 6 of the Conditions of Employment of Other Servants delegating the relevant Appointing Authority powers to the Executive Director. The Executive Director may sub-delegate those powers.

Where exceptional circumstances so require, the Management Board may revoke the delegation of the powers of the Appointing Authority to the Executive Director and those sub-delegated by the Executive Director. In such a case, the Management Board may delegate them, for a limited period to one of its members or to a staff member other than the Executive Director.

8. The Management board shall adopt appropriate rules implementing the Staff Regulations and the Conditions of Employment of Other Servants in accordance with the procedure provided for in Article 110 of the Staff Regulations.

9. The Management Board shall appoint the Executive Director and may extend his term of office or remove him from office in accordance with Article 24 of this Regulation.

10. The Management Board shall adopt the rules of procedure for itself and for the Executive Board after consulting the Commission. The rules of procedure shall provide for expedited decisions through either written procedure or by remote conferencing.

11. The Management Board shall adopt the Agency's internal rules of operation after consulting the Commission services. Those rules shall be made public.

12. The Management Board shall adopt the financial rules applicable to the Agency. They may not depart from Commission Regulation (EC, Euratom) No 2343/2002 of 19 November 2002 on the framework Financial Regulation for the bodies referred to in Article 185 of Council Regulation (EC, Euratom) No 1605/2002 on the Financial Regulation applicable to the general budget of the European Communities (18) , unless such departure is specifically required for the Agency's operation and the Commission has given its prior consent.

13. The Management Board shall adopt a Multiannual Staff Policy Plan, after consulting the Commission services and having duly informed the European Parliament and the Council.

Article 6 Composition of the Management Board

For additional analytical, business and investment opportunities information, please contact Global Investment & Business Center, USA at (703) 370-8082. Fax: (703) 370-8083. E-mail: ibpusa3@gmail.com Global Business and Investment Info Databank - www.ibpus.com

1. The Management Board shall be composed of one representative of each Member State, and two representatives appointed by the Commission. All representatives shall have voting rights.

2. Each member of the Management Board shall have an alternate to represent the member in their absence.

3. Members of the Management Board and their alternates shall be appointed in light of their knowledge of the Agency's tasks and objectives, taking into account the managerial, administrative and budgetary skills relevant to fulfil the tasks listed in Article 5. The Commission and the Member States should make efforts to limit turnover of their representatives in the Management Board, in order to ensure continuity of that board's work. The Commission and the Member States shall aim to achieve a balanced representation between men and women on the Management Board.

4. The term of office of members of the Management Board and of their alternates shall be four years. That term shall be renewable.

Article 7 Chairperson of the Management Board

1. The Management Board shall elect its Chairperson and a Deputy Chairperson from among its members for a period of three years, which shall be renewable. The Deputy Chairperson shall ex officio replace the Chairperson if the latter is unable to attend to his or her duties.

2. The Chairperson may be invited to make a statement before the relevant committee(s) of the European Parliament and answer Members' questions.

Article 8 Meetings

1. Meetings of the Management Board shall be convened by its Chairperson.

2. The Management Board shall hold an ordinary meeting at least once a year. It shall also hold extraordinary meetings at the request of the Chairperson or of at least a third of its members.

3. The Executive Director shall take part, without voting rights, in the meetings of the Management Board.

Article 9 Voting

1. The Management Board shall take its decisions by an absolute majority of its members.

2. A two-thirds majority of all Management Board members shall be required for the adoption of the Management Board's rules of procedure, the Agency's internal rules of operation, the budget, the annual and multiannual work programme, the appointment, extension of the term of office or removal of the Executive Director, and the designation of the Chairperson of the Management Board.

Article 10 Executive Board

1. The Management Board shall be assisted by an Executive Board.

For additional analytical, business and investment opportunities information, please contact Global Investment & Business Center, USA at (703) 370-8082. Fax: (703) 370-8083. E-mail: ibpusa3@gmail.com Global Business and Investment Info Databank - www.ibpus.com

2. The Executive Board shall prepare decisions to be adopted by the Management Board on administrative and budgetary matters only.

Together with the Management Board, it shall ensure adequate follow-up to the findings and recommendations stemming from investigations of OLAF and the various internal or external audit reports and evaluations.

Without prejudice to the responsibilities of the Executive Director, as set out in Article 11, the Executive Board shall assist and advise the Executive Director in implementing the decisions of the Management Board on administrative and budgetary matters.

3. The Executive Board shall be made up of five members appointed from among the members of the Management Board amongst whom the Chairperson of the Management Board, who may also chair the Executive Board, and one of the representatives of the Commission.

4. The term of office of members of the Executive Board shall be the same as that of members of the Management Board set out in Article 6(4) .

5. The Executive Board shall meet at least once every three months. The chairperson of the Executive Board shall convene additional meetings at the request of its members.

Article 11 Duties of the Executive Director

1. The Agency shall be managed by its Executive Director, who shall be independent in the performance of his/her duties.

2. The Executive Director shall be responsible for:

(a) the day-to-day administration of the Agency;

(b) implementing the decisions adopted by the Management Board;

(c) after consultation with the Management Board, preparing the annual work programme and the multiannual work programme and submitting them to the Management Board after consulting the Commission;

(d) implementing the annual work programme and the multiannual work programme and reporting to the Management Board thereon;

(e) preparing the annual report on the Agency's activities and presenting it to the Management Board for approval;

(f) preparing an action plan following-up on the conclusions of the retrospective evaluations and reporting on progress every two years to the Commission;

(g) protecting the financial interests of the Union by the application of preventive measures against fraud, corruption and any other illegal activities, by effective checks and, if irregularities are detected, by the recovery of the amounts wrongly paid and, where appropriate, by effective, proportionate and dissuasive administrative and financial penalties;

For additional analytical, business and investment opportunities information, please contact Global Investment & Business Center, USA at (703) 370-8082. Fax: (703) 370-8083. E-mail: ibpusa3@gmail.com Global Business and Investment Info Databank - www.ibpus.com

(h) preparing an anti-fraud strategy for the Agency and presenting it to the Management Board for approval;

(i) ensuring that the Agency performs its activities in accordance with the requirements of those using its services, in particular with regard to the adequacy of the services provided;

(j) developing and maintaining contact with the Union institutions, bodies, offices and agencies;

(k) developing and maintaining contact with the business community and consumers' organisations to ensure regular dialogue with relevant stakeholders;

(l) other tasks assigned to the Executive Director by this Regulation.

3. Where necessary and within the Agency's objectives and tasks, the Executive Director may set up ad hoc Working Groups composed of experts, including from the Member States' competent authorities. The Management Board shall be informed in advance. The procedures regarding in particular the composition, the appointment of the experts by the Executive Director and the operation of the ad hoc Working Groups shall be specified in the Agency's internal rules of operation.

4. The Executive Director shall make administrative support staff and other resources available to the Management Board and the Executive Board whenever necessary.

Article 12 Permanent Stakeholders' Group

1. The Management Board, acting on a proposal by the Executive Director, shall set up a Permanent Stakeholders' Group composed of recognised experts representing the relevant stakeholders, such as the ICT industry, providers of electronic communications networks or services available to the public, consumer groups, academic experts in network and information security, and representatives of national regulatory authorities notified under Directive 2002/21/EC as well as of law enforcement and privacy protection authorities.

2. Procedures for, in particular, the number, composition, and the appointment of the members of the Permanent Stakeholders' Group by the Management Board, the proposal by the Executive Director and the operation of the Group shall be specified in the Agency's internal rules of operation and shall be made public.

3. The Permanent Stakeholders' Group shall be chaired by the Executive Director or by any person the Executive Director appoints on a case-by-case basis.

4. The term of office of the Permanent Stakeholders' Group's members shall be two-and-a-half years. Members of the Management Board may not be members of the Permanent Stakeholders' Group. Experts from the Commission and the Member States shall be entitled to be present at the meetings of the Permanent Stakeholders' Group and to participate in its work. Representatives of other bodies deemed relevant by the Executive Director, who are not members of the Permanent Stakeholders' Group, may be invited to be present at the meetings of the Permanent Stakeholders' Group and to participate in its work.

5. The Permanent Stakeholders' Group shall advise the Agency in respect of the performance of its activities. It shall in particular advise the Executive Director on drawing up a proposal for the Agency's work programme, and on ensuring communication with the relevant stakeholders on all issues related to the work programme.

For additional analytical, business and investment opportunities information, please contact Global Investment & Business Center, USA at (703) 370-8082. Fax: (703) 370-8083. E-mail: ibpusa3@gmail.com Global Business and Investment Info Databank - www.ibpus.com

SECTION 3 OPERATION

Article 13 Work Programme

1. The Agency shall carry out its operations in accordance with its annual and multiannual work programme, which shall contain all of its planned activities.

2. The work programme shall include tailored performance indicators allowing for effective assessment of the results achieved in terms of objectives.

3. The Executive Director shall be responsible for drawing up the Agency's draft work programme after prior consultation with the Commission services. By 15 March each year the Executive Director shall submit the draft work programme for the following year to the Management Board.

4. By 30 November each year, the Management Board shall adopt the Agency's work programme for the following year, after having received the opinion of the Commission. The work programme shall include a multiannual outlook. The Management Board shall ensure that the work programme is consistent with the Agency's objectives and with the Union's legislative and policy priorities in the area of network and information security.

5. The work programme shall be organised in accordance with the activity-based management principle. The work programme shall be in line with the statement of estimates of the Agency's revenue and expenditure and the Agency's budget for the same financial year.

6. The Executive Director shall, following adoption by the Management Board, forward the work programme to the European Parliament, the Council, the Commission and the Member States and shall publish it. At the invitation of the relevant committee of the European Parliament, the Executive Director shall present and hold an exchange of views on the adopted annual work programme.

Article 14 Requests to the Agency

1. Requests for advice and assistance falling within the Agency's objectives and tasks shall be addressed to the Executive Director and accompanied by background information explaining the issue to be addressed. The Executive Director shall inform the Management Board and Executive Board of the requests received, the potential resource implications, and, in due course, of the follow-up to the requests. If the Agency refuses a request, it shall give a justification.

2. Requests referred to in paragraph 1 may be made by:

(a) the European Parliament;

(b) the Council;

(c) the Commission;

(d) any competent body appointed by a Member State, such as a national regulatory authority defined in Article 2 of Directive 2002/21/EC.

For additional analytical, business and investment opportunities information, please contact Global Investment & Business Center, USA at (703) 370-8082. Fax: (703) 370-8083. E-mail: ibpusa3@gmail.com Global Business and Investment Info Databank - www.ibpus.com

3. The practical arrangements for applying paragraphs 1 and 2, regarding in particular submission, prioritisation, follow-up and information to the Management and Executive Board on the requests to the Agency, shall be laid down by the Management Board in the Agency's internal rules of operation.

Article 15 Declaration of interest

1. Members of the Management Board, the Executive Director and officials seconded by Member States on a temporary basis shall each make a declaration of commitments and a declaration indicating the absence or presence of any direct or indirect interest which might be considered prejudicial to their independence. The declarations shall be accurate and complete, made annually in writing and updated whenever necessary.

2. Members of the Management Board, the Executive Director, and external experts participating in ad hoc Working Groups shall each accurately and completely declare, at the latest at the start of each meeting, any interest which might be considered prejudicial to their independence in relation to the items on the agenda, and shall abstain from participating in the discussion of and voting upon such points.

3. The Agency shall lay down, in its internal rules of operation, the practical arrangements for the rules on declarations of interest referred to in paragraphs 1 and 2.

Article 16 Transparency

1. The Agency shall ensure that it carries out its activities with a high level of transparency and in accordance with Articles 17 and 18.

2. The Agency shall ensure that the public and any interested parties are given appropriate, objective, reliable and easily accessible information, in particular with regard to the results of its work. It shall also make public the declarations of interest made in accordance with Article 15.

3. The Management Board, acting on a proposal from the Executive Director, may authorise interested parties to observe the proceedings of some of the Agency's activities.

4. The Agency shall lay down, in its internal rules of operation, the practical arrangements for implementing the transparency rules referred to in paragraphs 1 and 2.

Article 17 Confidentiality

1. Without prejudice to Article 18, the Agency shall not divulge to third parties information that it processes or receives in relation to which a reasoned request for confidential treatment, in whole or in part, has been made.

2. Members of the Management Board, the Executive Director, the members of the Permanent Stakeholders Group, external experts participating in ad hoc Working Groups, and members of the staff of the Agency including officials seconded by Member States on a temporary basis shall comply with the confidentiality requirements under Article 339 of the Treaty on the Functioning of the European Union (TFEU) , even after their duties have ceased.

3. The Agency shall lay down, in its internal rules of operation, the practical arrangements for implementing the confidentiality rules referred to in paragraphs 1 and 2.

For additional analytical, business and investment opportunities information, please contact Global Investment & Business Center, USA at (703) 370-8082. Fax: (703) 370-8083. E-mail: ibpusa3@gmail.com Global Business and Investment Info Databank - www.ibpus.com

4. If required for the performance of the Agency's tasks, the Management Board shall decide to allow the Agency to handle classified information. In that case the Management Board shall, in agreement with the Commission services, adopt internal rules of operation applying the security principles set out in Commission Decision 2001/844/EC, ECSC, Euratom of 29 November 2001 amending its internal rules of procedure (19) . Those rules shall cover, inter alia, provisions for the exchange, processing and storage of classified information.

Article 18 Access to documents

1. Regulation (EC) No 1049/2001 shall apply to documents held by the Agency.

2. The Management Board shall adopt arrangements for implementing Regulation (EC) No 1049/2001 within six months of the establishment of the Agency.

3. Decisions taken by the Agency pursuant to Article 8 of Regulation (EC) No 1049/2001 may be the subject of a complaint to the Ombudsman under Article 228 TFEU or of an action before the Court of Justice of the European Union under Article 263 TFEU.

SECTION 4 FINANCIAL PROVISIONS

Article 19 Adoption of the budget

1. The revenues of the Agency shall consist of a contribution from the Union budget, contributions from third countries participating in the work of the Agency as provided for in Article 30, and voluntary contributions from Member States in money or in kind. Member States that provide voluntary contributions may not claim any specific right or service as a result thereof.

2. The expenditure of the Agency shall include staff, administrative and technical support, infrastructure and operational expenses, and expenses resulting from contracts entered into with third parties.

3. By 1 March each year, the Executive Director shall draw up a draft statement of estimates of the Agency's revenue and expenditure for the following financial year, and shall forward it to the Management Board, together with a draft establishment plan.

4. Revenue and expenditure shall be in balance.

5. Each year, the Management Board shall, on the basis of a draft statement of estimates of revenue and expenditure drawn up by the Executive Director, produce a statement of estimates of revenue and expenditure for the Agency for the following financial year.

6. The Management Board shall, by 31 March each year, send that statement of estimates, which shall include a draft establishment plan together with the draft work programme, to the Commission and the third countries with which the Union has concluded agreements in accordance with Article 30.

7. The Commission shall forward that statement of estimates to the European Parliament and the Council together with the draft general budget of the Union.

8. On the basis of that statement of estimates, the Commission shall enter in the draft budget of the Union the estimates it deems necessary for the establishment plan and the amount of the

subsidy to be charged to the general budget, which it shall submit to the European Parliament and the Council in accordance with Article 314 TFEU.

9. The European Parliament and the Council shall authorise the appropriations for the subsidy to the Agency.

10. The European Parliament and the Council shall adopt the establishment plan for the Agency.

11. Together with the work programme, the Management Board shall adopt the Agency's budget. It shall become final following definitive adoption of the general budget of the Union. Where appropriate, the Management Board shall adjust the Agency's budget and work programme in accordance with the general budget of the Union. The Management Board shall forward the budget without delay to the European Parliament, the Council and the Commission.

Article 20 Combating fraud

1. In order to facilitate the combating of fraud, corruption and other unlawful activities under Regulation (EC) No 1073/1999 (20) , the Agency shall, within six months from the day it becomes operational, accede to the Interinstitutional Agreement of 25 May 1999 concerning internal investigations by the European Anti-fraud Office (OLAF) (21) and shall adopt the appropriate provisions applicable to all the employees of the Agency, using the template set out in the Annex to that Agreement.

2. The Court of Auditors shall have the power of audit, on the basis of documents and on the spot, over all grant beneficiaries, contractors and subcontractors who have received Union funds from the Agency.

3. OLAF may carry out investigations, including on-the-spot checks and inspections, in accordance with the provisions and procedures laid down in Regulation (EC) No 1073/1999 and Council Regulation (Euratom, EC) No 2185/96 of 11 November 1996 concerning on-the-spot checks and inspections carried out by the Commission in order to protect the European Communities' financial interests against fraud and other irregularities (22) with a view to establishing whether there has been fraud, corruption or any other illegal activity affecting the financial interests of the Union in connection with a grant or a contract funded by the Agency.

4. Without prejudice to paragraphs 1, 2 and 3, cooperation agreements with third countries and international organisations, contracts, grant agreements and grant decisions of the Agency shall contain provisions expressly empowering the Court of Auditors and OLAF to conduct such audits and investigations, according to their respective competences.

Article 21 Implementation of the budget

1. The Executive Director shall be responsible for the implementation of the Agency's budget.

2. The Commission's internal auditor shall exercise the same powers over the Agency as over Commission departments.

3. By 1 March following each financial year (1 March of year N + 1) , the Agency's accounting officer shall send the provisional accounts to the Commission's accounting officer together with a report on the budgetary and financial management for that financial year. The Commission's

accounting officer shall consolidate the provisional accounts of the institutions and decentralised bodies in accordance with Article 147 of the Financial Regulation.

4. By 31 March of year N + 1, the Commission's accounting officer shall send the Agency's provisional accounts to the Court of Auditors, together with a report on the budgetary and financial management for that financial year. The report on the budgetary and financial management for the financial year shall also be sent to the European Parliament and the Council.

5. On receipt of the Court of Auditor's observations on the Agency's provisional accounts, pursuant to Article 148 of the Financial Regulation, the Executive Director shall draw up the Agency's final accounts under his/her own responsibility and send them to the Management Board for an opinion.

6. The Management Board shall deliver an opinion on the Agency's final accounts.

7. The Executive Director shall, by 1 July of year N + 1, transmit the final accounts, including the report on the budgetary and financial management for that financial year and the Court of Auditor's observations, to the European Parliament, the Council, the Commission and the Court of Auditors, together with the Management Board's opinion.

8. The Executive Director shall publish the final accounts.

9. The Executive Director shall send the Court of Auditors a reply to its observations by 30 September of year N + 1 and shall also send to the Management Board a copy of that reply.

10. The Executive Director shall submit to the European Parliament, at the latter's request, all the information necessary for the smooth application of the discharge procedure for the financial year in question, as laid down in Article 165(3) of the Financial Regulation.

11. The European Parliament, acting on a recommendation from the Council, shall, before 15 May of year N + 2, give a discharge to the Executive Director in respect of the implementation of the budget for the year N.

SECTION 5 STAFF

Article 22 General provisions

The Staff Regulations and the Conditions of Employment of Other Servants and the rules adopted by agreement between the Union institutions for giving effect to those Staff Regulations shall apply to the staff of the Agency.

Article 23 Privileges and immunity

Protocol No 7 on the Privileges and Immunities of the European Union annexed to the Treaty on European Union and to the TFEU shall apply to the Agency and its staff.

Article 24 Executive Director

1. The Executive Director shall be engaged as a temporary agent of the Agency under Article 2(a) of the Conditions of Employment of Other Servants.

2. The Executive Director shall be appointed by the Management Board from a list of candidates proposed by the Commission, following an open and transparent selection procedure.

For the purpose of concluding the contract of the Executive Director, the Agency shall be represented by the Chairperson of the Management Board.

Before appointment, the candidate selected by the Management Board shall be invited to make a statement before the relevant committee of the European Parliament and to answer Members' questions.

3. The term of office of the Executive Director shall be five years. By the end of that period, the Commission shall undertake an assessment which takes into account the evaluation of the performance of the Executive Director and the Agency's future tasks and challenges.

4. The Management Board may, acting on a proposal from the Commission which takes into account the assessment referred to in paragraph 3 and after obtaining the views of the European Parliament, extend once the term of office of the Executive Director for no more than five years.

5. The Management Board shall inform the European Parliament about its intention to extend the Executive Director's term of office. Within three months before any such extension, the Executive Director shall, if invited, make a statement before the relevant committee of the European Parliament and answer Members' questions.

6. An Executive Director whose term of office has been extended may not participate in another selection procedure for the same post.

7. The Executive Director may be removed from office only by decision of the Management Board.

Article 25 Seconded national experts and other staff

1. The Agency may make use of seconded national experts or other staff not employed by the Agency. The Staff Regulations and the Conditions of Employment of Other Servants shall not apply to such staff.

2. The Management Board shall adopt a decision laying down rules on the secondment to the agency of national experts.

SECTION 6 GENERAL PROVISIONS

Article 26 Legal status

1. The Agency shall be a body of the Union. It shall have legal personality.

2. In each of the Member States the Agency shall enjoy the most extensive legal capacity accorded to legal persons under their laws. It may, in particular, acquire and dispose of movable and immovable property and be a party to legal proceedings.

3. The Agency shall be represented by its Executive Director.

4. A branch office established in the metropolitan area of Athens shall be maintained in order to improve the operational efficiency of the Agency.

Article 27 Liability

1. The contractual liability of the Agency shall be governed by the law applicable to the contract in question.

The Court of Justice of the European Union shall have jurisdiction to give judgment pursuant to any arbitration clause contained in a contract concluded by the Agency.

2. In the case of non-contractual liability, the Agency shall, in accordance with the general principles common to the laws of the Member States, make good any damage caused by it or its servants in the performance of their duties.

The Court of Justice of the European Union shall have jurisdiction in any dispute relating to compensation for such damage.

3. The personal liability of its servants towards the Agency shall be governed by the relevant conditions applying to the staff of the Agency.

Article 28 Languages

1. Regulation No 1 of 15 April 1958 determining the languages to be used in the European Economic Community (23) shall apply to the Agency. The Member States and the other bodies appointed by them may address the Agency and receive a reply in the official language of the institutions of the Union of their choice.

2. The translation services required for the functioning of the Agency shall be provided by the Translation Centre for the Bodies of the European Union.

Article 29 Protection of personal data

1. When processing data relating to individuals, in particular while performing its tasks, the Agency shall observe the principles of personal data protection in, and be subject to, the provisions of Regulation (EC) No 45/2001.

2. The Management Board shall adopt implementing measures referred to in Article 24(8) of Regulation (EC) No 45/2001. The Management Board may adopt additional measures necessary for the application of Regulation (EC) No 45/2001 by the Agency.

Article 30 Participation of third countries

1. The Agency shall be open to the participation of third countries which have concluded agreements with the European Union by virtue of which they have adopted and applied Union legal acts in the field covered by this Regulation.

2. Arrangements shall be made under the relevant provisions of those agreements, specifying in particular the nature, extent and manner in which those countries will participate in the Agency's work, including provisions relating to participation in the initiatives undertaken by the Agency, financial contributions and staff.

Article 31 Security Rules on the protection of classified information

For additional analytical, business and investment opportunities information, please contact Global Investment & Business Center, USA at (703) 370-8082. Fax: (703) 370-8083. E-mail: ibpusa3@gmail.com Global Business and Investment Info Databank - www.ibpus.com

The Agency shall apply the security principles contained in the Commission's security rules for protecting European Union Classified Information (EUCI) and sensitive non-classified information, as set out in the Annex to Decision 2001/844/EC, ECSC, Euratom. This shall cover, inter alia, provisions for the exchange, processing and storage of such information.

SECTION 7 FINAL PROVISIONS

Article 32 Evaluation and review

1. By 20 June 2018 the Commission shall commission an evaluation to assess, in particular, the impact, effectiveness and efficiency of the Agency and its working practices. The evaluation shall also address the possible need to modify the mandate of the Agency and the financial implications of any such modification.

2. The evaluation referred to in paragraph 1 shall take into account any feedback made to the Agency in response to its activities.

3. The Commission shall forward the evaluation report together with its conclusions to the European Parliament, the Council and the Management Board. The findings of the evaluation shall be made public.

4. As part of the evaluation, there shall also be an assessment of the results achieved by the Agency, having regard to its objectives, mandate and tasks. If the Commission considers that the continuation of the Agency is justified with regard to its assigned objectives, mandate and tasks, it may propose that the duration of the mandate of the Agency set out in Article 36 be extended.

Article 33

Cooperation of the host Member State

The Agency's host Member State shall provide the best possible conditions to ensure the proper functioning of the Agency, including the accessibility of the location, the existence of adequate education facilities for the children of staff members, appropriate access to the labour market, social security and medical care for both children and spouses.

Article 34

Administrative control

The operations of the Agency shall be supervised by the Ombudsman in accordance with Article 228 TFEU.

Article 35

For additional analytical, business and investment opportunities information, please contact Global Investment & Business Center, USA at (703) 370-8082. Fax: (703) 370-8083. E-mail: ibpusa3@gmail.com Global Business and Investment Info Databank - www.ibpus.com

Repeal and succession

1. Regulation (EC) No 460/2004 is repealed.

References to Regulation (EC) No 460/2004 and to ENISA shall be construed as references to this Regulation and to the Agency.

2. The Agency succeeds the Agency that was established by Regulation (EC) No 460/2004 as regards all ownership, agreements, legal obligations, employment contracts, financial commitments and liabilities.

Article 36

Duration

The Agency shall be established for a period of seven years from 19 June 2013.

Article 37

Entry into force

This Regulation shall enter into force on the day following that of its publication in the Official Journal of the European Union.

SUPPLEMENTS

EU CYBER SECRURITY PROGRAMS COORDINATORS IN MEMBER COUNTRIES

Member State	National Liaison Officer
Austria	Mr. Timo MISCHITZ Austrian Federal Chancellery Federal ICT Strategy Cyber Security Coordinator Tel.: + 43 1 53115 2545 timo.mischitz(AT) bka.gv.at
Belgium	Mr. Stéphane VAN ROY Belgian Institute for postal services and telecommunications Advisor Tel.: + 32 2 226 87 68 stephane.van.roy(AT) IBPT.BE
Bulgaria	Ms. Tsvetanka KIRILOVA Head of the Interoperability and Information Security Department Ministry of Transport, Information Technologies and Communications Tel.: + 359 2 949 20 60 tskirilova(AT) mtitc.government.bg
Cyprus	Mr. Neophytos PAPADOPOULOS Director of the Commissioners Office for the control of the Telecommunications and Postal services Tel.: + 357 22 69 31 06 neophytos.papadopoulos(AT) ocecpr.org.cy Mr. Antonis ANTONIADES Senior Officer of the Commissioners Office for the control of the Telecommunications and Postal services Tel.: + 357 22 69 31 15 antonis.antoniades(AT) ocecpr.org.cy
Czech Republic	Mr. Tomas FLIDR National Center for Cyber Security National Security Authority of the Czech Republic Tel.:+ 420 257 283 203 t.flidr(AT) nbu.cz
Member State	National Liaison Officer
Denmark	Mr. Flemming FABER Head of Division of the IT-Security Division National IT and Telecom Agency Tel.+45 3545 0364 ff(AT) itst.dk
Estonia	Mr. Luukas Kristjan ILVES International Cooperation Expert Estonian Information System's Authority Tel.: + 372 666 8810 luukas.ilves(AT) ria.ee
Finland	Mr. Pauli PULLINEN Policy Department Senior Officer Ministry of Transport and Communications Tel: + 358 295 342 680

	pauli.pullinen(AT) LVM.FI
France	Mr. Jean-Baptiste DEMAISON ANSSI, International Relations Tel.: + 33 1 71 75 82 63 rit.sr.eu(AT) ssi.gouv.fr
Germany	Fabienne MIDDEKE Bundesamt für Sicherheit in der Informationstechnik Referat B 24 - Internationale Beziehungen und Koordination mit den Sicherheitsbehörden Tel.: + 49 228 99 9582-5818 SIB(AT) bsi.bund.de
Greece	Mr. Panagiotis PAPASPILIOPOULOS General Directorate of Communications Ministry of Transport and Communications Tel.: +30 210 6508538 p.papaspil(AT) yme.gov.gr
Hungary	Mr. Ferenc SUBA Chairman of the Board of CERT-Hungary Tel.:+36 1 301 2080 ferenc.suba(AT) cert-hungary.hu
Member State	National Liaison Officer
Ireland	Mr. James CAFFREY Department of Communications, Energy and Natural Resources Cyber Unit Tel.: + 353 16782427 James.Caffrey(AT) dcenr.gov.ie
Italy	Ms Rita FORSI Director General Ministry of Economic Development Tel.: +39 6 54442360 rita.forsi(AT) sviluppoeconomico.gov.it
Latvia	Mr. Viktors LIPENITS Transport and Communications Security Division, Senior Expert Ministry of Transport and Communications Tel.: + 371 670 28 227 Viktors.Lipenits(AT) SAM.GOV.LV
Lithuania	Mr. Vaidotas RAMONAS Chief Specialist of Internet Surveillance Division Communications Regulatory Authority Tel.: +85 210 5676 vramonas (AT) rrt.lt
Luxembourg	Mr. Manuel SILVOSO Ministry of the Economy and Foreign Trade - Department for e-commerce and information security Tel.: + 352 247 88429 Fax: + 352 247 84311 manuel.silvoso(AT) eco.etat.lu
Malta	Mr. Martin CAMILLERI INFOSEC Authority, Cabinet Office, Office of the Prime Minister Tel.: +356 2200 1285 martin.d.camilleri(AT) gov.mt
The Netherlands	Mr. Edgar DE LANGE Ministry of Economic Affairs

For additional analytical, business and investment opportunities information, please contact Global Investment & Business Center, USA at (703) 370-8082. Fax: (703) 370-8083. E-mail: ibpusa3@gmail.com Global Business and Investment Info Databank - www.ibpus.com

	Directorate-General for Energy and Telecommunications ALP C/334 Tel.: + 31 70 379 8153 e.r.delange(AT) minez.nl
Member State	National Liaison Officer
Poland	Mr. Krzysztof SILICKI Technical Director Research and Academic Computer Network NASK Tel.: + 48 22 5231315 krzysztof.silicki(AT) nask.pl
Portugal	Mr. Lino SANTOS CERT.PT/FCCN, Director of security and users services Tel.: +351218440100 lino(AT) fccn.pt
Romania	Mr. Dan TOFAN CERT-RO Tel.: + 752188854 dan.tofan(AT) CERT-RO.EU
Slovakia	Mr. Rastislav MACHEL CISSP Tel.: + 421-905-622435 Rastislav.Machel(AT) machel-cs.eu
Slovenia	Mr. Radovan PAJNTAR Ministry of Higher Education, Science and Technology, Directorat Information Society Directorate Trg Tel.: + 386-1-478-46-47 Fax: + 386-1-478-46-65 radovan.pajntar(AT) gov.si
Spain	Mr. Ignacio GONZÁLEZ UBIERNA Deputy Director for Corporate Development Instituto Nacional de Tecnologías de la Comunicación (InTeCo) Tel.: + 34 987 877 189 ignacio.gonzalez(AT) inteco.es
Sweden	Mr. Björn SCHARIN Adviser National Post and Telecom Agency Network Security Department Tel. + 46-8-678 55 98 Bjorn.Scharin(AT) pts.se
Member State	National Liaison Officer
United Kingdom	Mr. Giles SMITH Information Economy - Security and Resilience Department for Business, Innovation and Skills Tel.: +44 20 7215 5757 giles.smith(AT) bis.gsi.gov.uk
EEA	National Liaison Officer
Iceland	Mr. Thorleifur JONASSON Director of Technical Division Post and Telecom Administration Tel.: + 354 510 1500 thorleifur(AT) pfs.is

For additional analytical, business and investment opportunities information, please contact Global Investment & Business Center, USA at (703) 370-8082. Fax: (703) 370-8083. E-mail: ibpusa3@gmail.com Global Business and Investment Info Databank - www.ibpus.com

Liechtenstein	Mr. Kurt BUEHLER Director Office for Communications Tel.: + 423 236 6488 Fax: + 423 236 6489 kurt.buehler(AT) ak.llv.li
Norway	Mr. Hans Einar NERHUS Postal Services and Telecommunications Senior Advise Ministry of Transport and Communications Department of Civil Aviation Tel.: + 47 2224 8156 Hen(AT) sd.dep.no
European Commission	Mr. Ivan BRINCAT Policy Officer Tel.: + 32 2 2965311 Ivan.Brincat(AT) ec.europa.eu
Council of the European Union	Mr. Anastassios PAPADOPOULOS Council of the European Union - General Secretariat anastassios.papadopoulos(AT) consilium.europa.eu

CYBER ATTACK THREAT TRENDS

TOP CYBER THREATS

A **list of cyber attack threat trends** is presented in the order of sophistication which generally corresponds to the chronology of computer network used between the 1990s and 2008.

1. Internet social engineering attacks
2. Network sniffers
3. Packet spoofing
4. Session-hijacking
5. Cyber-threats & bullying (not illegal in all jurisdictions)
6. Automated probes and scans
7. GUI intrusion tools
8. Automated widespread attacks
9. Widespread, distributed denial-of-service attacks
10. Industrial espionage
11. Executable code attacks (against browsers)
12. Analysis of vulnerabilities in compiled software without source code
13. Widespread attacks on DNS infrastructure
14. Widespread attacks using NNTP to distribute attack
15. "Stealth" and other advanced scanning techniques
16. Windows-based remote access trojans (Back Orifice)
17. Email propagation of malicious code
18. Wide-scale trojan distribution
19. Distributed attack tools
20. Targeting of specific users
21. Anti-forensic techniques
22. Wide-scale use of worms
23. Sophisticated botnet command and control attacks

1 DRIVE-BY DOWNLOADS

Web based attacks implementing drive-by downloads scores for one more year as the top cyber threat. This is quite natural as web browsers are the first level of user interaction with the Internet. As such, web pages, web servers and web services have become the most important attack surface: attackers target web sites with the aim to infect them with malicious code, usually exploit kits (see corresponding threat below). Infected web sites are referred to as malicious URLs and are "door openers" for other threats such as exploit kits and malicious code infections (i.e. Worms/Trojans). Visitors of these web sites are automatically scanned through the maliciously installed exploit kits for weaknesses/vulnerabilities. Once vulnerabilities have been found in the device of the visitor, exploit kits automatically install the appropriate malware on the device. The installed malware may vary significantly according to the underlying user system/configuration and the vulnerabilities found. This threat belongs to the broad category of unauthorised software installation to the victim's device: starting from a victim web server and reaching the devices of visitors.

In the reporting period we have assessed that:

* Web based attacks remain as the number one threat. Malicious URLs are considered the main channel for malware installation. It has been observed that there is a shift from Botnets to URLs as means for malware distribution 56 .

* Java remains the most exploited software34,35 to infect a web site. In addition, attackers use code injection attacks (see threat below) to create malicious URLs 47 .

* As predicted in 2012, drive-by downloads have fully embraced mobile platforms. Just as any other device, mobile platforms are targeted by vulnerability scanning capabilities of exploit kits.

* As mentioned in the code injection threat below, manipulated CMSs are another source for the creation of malicious URLs36,37.

* Web based attacks are increasingly used within targeted attacks. Through the watering hole technique, attackers lure a specific group of victims to visit their malicious URLs. This technique has been increasingly used in 2013 with high infection rates38, 47 (see also threat below).

Observed current trend for this threat: *increasing*

Related threats: Code Injection, Exploit Kits, Worms/Trojans, Rogueware/Ransomware/Scareware, Targeted Attacks, Watering Hole.

2 MALICIOUS CODE: WORMS/TROJANS

In the reporting period, the threat of spreading malicious programs has been reported as very high in related reports. Malware and particularly trojans have been derived from previous versions in thousands of variants. This is due to the use of available toolkits allowing for the generation of user defined malware through variations of existing malware code. Due to functionality offered by toolkits, this activity can be performed by adversaries with moderate capabilities. The vast number of malware variations is deployed as an effective method to fool signature-based virus scanners: due to their large numbers, signatures of the created variants are not always available, leading thus to unnoticed infections. Mobile platforms supported the successful deployment of this threat. Mobile malware takes a significant part in malware statistics.

For additional analytical, business and investment opportunities information, please contact Global Investment & Business Center, USA at (703) 370-8082. Fax: (703) 370-8083. E-mail: ibpusa3@gmail.com Global Business and Investment Info Databank - www.ibpus.com

In the reporting period we have assessed that:

* Malware increasingly targets mobile platforms, with mobile trojans coming at the first position. This is due to the increasing use of mobile devices, the increased sophistication of attacks (see below) but also due to the weaker/immature security mechanisms implemented on these platforms.

* Available attack tools (see also exploit kits) allow for the creation of malware variants based on available malware code. This activity can be performed even from users with moderate capabilities. This phenomenon is called polymorphism of existing code and is a key trend in malware development.

* An increased sophistication in malware has been reported, especially on mobile platforms. Code obfuscation (i.e. code that bypasses vetting process of gated app stores) and use of multiple channels use are some characteristics of the complexity of malware39.

* Coordinated activities of developers have demonstrated their true potential in generating sophisticated malware by launching malware attacks against Mac computers40, 47 .

* There is a growing black/grey market for stolen user data41. This brings information stealing malware on the rise. Given the increased use mobile devices and the sophistication of attacks, information stealing malware is here to stay.

* Rogue certificates have been used to sign malicious code and thus distribute signed apps42. This has demonstrated that incidents with rogue certificates are still a serious risk that cannot be easily mitigated 109 ,43.

Observed current trend for this threat: *increasing*

Related threats: Drive-by Downloads, Code Injection, Exploit Kits, Botnets, Identity Theft/, Data Breaches, Rogueware/Ransomware/Scareware, Phishing, Targeted Attacks.

3 CODE INJECTION

In 2013, the mix of tools available to perform code injection attacks remained unchanged: Cross-Site Scripting (XSS), Directory Traversal, SQL injection (SQLi) and Cross-Site Request Forgery (CSRF). Within 2013 Code injection attacks are on sharp rise. The proliferation of automated attack tools impacted the frequency of this threat in the reporting period: hackers are in the position to launch large vulnerability scans in short time.

In the reporting period we have assessed that:

* A notable issue with regard to this threat is attacks against popular Content Management Systems (CMSs). Due to their wide use, popular CMSs make up a considerable attack surface that has drawn the attention of cyber-criminals44,45.

* Large scale automated attacks are being increasingly launched from within cloud service provider networks 61 .

For additional analytical, business and investment opportunities information, please contact Global Investment & Business Center, USA at (703) 370-8082. Fax: (703) 370-8083. E-mail: ibpusa3@gmail.com Global Business and Investment Info Databank - www.ibpus.com

* Code injections are combined with other threats to successfully infect victims 144 . A typical example in the reporting period is a series of incidents that have been caused by successful attacks combining SQLi together with spear-phishing and watering hole techniques46.

Observed current trend for this threat: *increasing*

Related threats: Drive-by Downloads, Exploit Kits, Data Breaches, Targeted Attacks.

4 EXPLOIT KITS

Exploit kits are the main tools in the hands of threat agents. These are ready-to-use software tools offering a large variety of functions, configuration options and automated means to launch attacks. Exploit kits search for vulnerabilities in order to abuse them and launch any applicable attack to take over an asset (also mentioned as Exploit attacks47). Exploit kits have been heavily used by hackers within the reporting period. Further, it has been reported that new business models emerge around such tools: developers of exploit kits maintain interaction with customers by offering support, customized configurations, etc48,49. The ability for updating, customization and the degree of automation provided is considered to be one of the main parameters for increase in all kinds of threats supported, such as malware, code injections, exploitation of vulnerabilities, etc.

In the reporting period we have assessed that:

* Exploit kits are entering a new era of higher maturity towards developer/user relationship. Additional “services”50,51 are developed and it seems that developers and users of exploit kits are two distinct types of cyber threat agents.

* Users are confronted to exploit kits mostly by accessing compromised URLs (see threat drive-by downloads above).

* Due to the popularity of exploit kits and the emerging need to feed them with known vulnerabilities, there is an increasing interest in zero-day vulnerabilities. This is a significant amplification effect for the market of exploits/vulnerabilities52. It is important to note that both hostile and friendly actors in cyber space show interest in purchasing zero-day vulnerabilities 47 .

* Efforts have been invested by exploit kit developers to encrypt their payloads, thus make them invisible from detection mechanisms53.

* Due to the existence of a market, it is expected that a developers instead of developing new malware, will concentrate on development of exploit kits 48 . Rather, exploit kits will be able to include new malware and available vulnerabilities.

* The developer and operator of Blackhole54, the most successful exploit kit has been arrested. It will be very interesting to observe future developments with this malicious tool. Are other threat agents going to take over development and operation of Blackhole or its derivates? Are other tools going to fill the possibly created gap? It is suggested to keep an eye on this issue, as it going to introduce significant impact to the threat landscape.

Observed current trend for this threat: *increasing*

Related threats: Drive-by Downloads, Code Injection, Worms/Trojans, Phishing, Rogueware/Ransomware/Scareware.

5 BOTNETS

Botnets, networks of compromised, remotely controlled computers, still pose a serious cyber threat. Being one of the oldest and more "mature" malicious infrastructures in cyber space, botnets currently undergo significant changes in their adaptation, reduction of traceability, business cases, channels used and technology usage. In the reporting period we have seen some of these changes become reality. The use of peer-to-peer technologies, not only increases the resilience of single nodes, it also enhances their ability to stay undetected. Although this development has been observed since 2012, the benefits of this technology have been demonstrated in 2013, as they can run on cloud infrastructures. Noticeable changes in the business models include a shift from botnets to URLs as means to install malware. Further, the botnet business model has concentrated on Bitcoin mining55. In addition, click fraud payloads have been deployed.

In the reporting period we have assessed that:

* Threat analysts see malicious URLs replacing botnets as the primary means for distribution malware (see also drive-by downloads above)56. Botnets are on decline with regard to this threat.

* Existing botnet infrastructure has been updated with P2P technology57. This increases resilience of botnet nodes when servers are taken down.

* Existing versions of botnet infrastructure are equipped with Bitcoin mining and click fraud functions. At the same time, they continue targeting social networks with spam.

* Botnets sometimes use the anonymizing network TOR. Lately malware families have been found using TOR as communication network58. It can be assumed that a considerable part of the vast increase of TOR traffic is caused by its use for malicious purposes59,60.

* Although botnet malware infections are on the decline 56 , it seems that botnets are still one of the most important cyber threats. The reasons for can be found in changes of malware infection strategies, use of P2P technology, use of anonymizing technologies etc.

* Within the current trend of cyber-crime-as-a-service, we see various "traditional" botnet functions to be offered as a service; similarly the availability of hosting services makes the use of cloud as a high performance botnet feasible61,62.

Observed current trend for this threat: *stable/slightly increasing*

Related threats: Drive-by Downloads, Worms/Trojans, Phishing, Spam, Denial of Service, Rogueware/Ransomware/Scareware.

6 PHYSICAL DAMAGE/THEFT/LOSS OF MEDIA

This threat has increased in 2013 due to the increasing number of mobile devices used and consequently stolen, lost or damaged. Taking reported percentages as a basis, one can conclude that some 70-80 million devices have been broken, stolen or lost63. Meanwhile, it is considered that hacking is not the main cause of data loss: ca. 36% of data breaches are attributed to theft/loss of devices

In the reporting period we have assessed that:

* Damage of devices seems to be the number one cause for losing data 63 . And although users are concerned about cyber-attacks, the awareness about the possibility of a damage/loss of device seems to be rather low. In this area there is a lot of space for improvements.

* As already assessed within the threat of data breach (see above), a significant part of data breaches is caused through physical access to the storage device. Theft/damage/loss seems to be the main cause for this65.

* Most of the data on damage, theft or loss are based on surveys/statistics and not on incidents. This is due to the fact that related incidents on physical damage, theft and loss are not always reported and gathered. Hence concluded damages (and costs 118) are just estimations that need to be validated.

* To reduce the impact of the damage/theft/loss threat, it is noticeable that the following factors play a significant role towards a reduction of incurred costs: "*strong security posture, incident response capabilities and appointment of a CISO*" 118 .

Observed current trend for this threat: *increasing*

Related threats: none

7 IDENTITY THEFT/FRAUD

Identity theft and identity fraud are threats that have led to some of the most impressive successful attacks in the reporting period 63 ,66. Identity theft is one of the core activities of many threat agent groups, as it gives access to a lot of data that bear potential for numerous malicious activities. Malware and trojans belong to the main tools to perform identity theft. In 2013, for example, financial trojans (e.g. Zeus, SpyEye, Citadel67) have been use to implement 2-factor authentication attack on mobile platforms68. The interest in identity theft, but also its importance in deploying multiple attacks has led to the creation of a market for this kind of data 96 . It is expected, that this threat will continue increasing, as the methods used increase in sophistication and spread.

In the reporting period we have assessed that:

* The inclusion of mobile platforms in identity hunting malware is a matter of fact and has demonstrated the potential behind successful attack on these platforms. As expected, data on financial and payment institutions are the most prominent ones for identity theft69,70.

* A significant source for applying this threat remains social media71. It is worth mentioning that an increase in malicious browser extensions has been registered, aimed at taking over social network accounts72,73. A market around social accounts has already been created74

* The use of Near Field Communication (NFC) capabilities for financial transactions, exchange of messages and interaction with other devices increases. This technology will provide an attack surface, especially with regard to eavesdropping75.

* Man-in-the-browser attacks are similar to man-in-the-middle attacks except that the intervention on an infected device happens over a Trojan that deviates traffic over a botnet (e.g. SpyEye v1.3 botnet76). Through these attacks, threat agents are stealing almost any information from the browser memory77.

* It is worth noticing how threat agents adapt to additional authentication mechanisms used for securing identity information, especially in financial transactions. SMS forwarding has been introduced to existing malware. This includes permissions linked with the SMS relay, whereas PC injection requests users to ender data that are also displayed on the handset. Hence a connection between these devices is established. Then the malware takes over SMS communication with the bank and misuses communicated credentials78 (i.e. man-in-the-mobile).

Observed current trend for this threat: *increasing*

Related threats: Drive-by Downloads, Exploit Kits, Code Injection, Botnets, Worms/Trojans, Phishing, Spam, Information Leakage, Data Breaches, Rogueware/Ransomware/Scareware.

8 DENIAL OF SERVICE

In the reporting period, a significant jump of Denial of Service attacks has been detected79. After the Spamhaus80 attack, DNS reflection attacks have gained in popularity81, 82 . DNS reflection amplification attacks target poorely configured DNS servers. Attackers seem to have adopted the DNS reflection technique to launch amplification attacks, an old technique that has made a come-back. Another reason for this increase is assumed in the availability of easy-to-use attack tools that embrace DoS capabilities82. Users with low skills can easily launch DoS attacks, and, when done in orchestration with other actors, significant striking power can be developed. Moreover, available high performance botnets contribute to the increased volume of DoS attacks83. Amplification, wide availability of tools/resources and coordination among threat agent groups seem to be the reason for the impressive DoS bandwidths achieved (2-10Gbps up to 300Gbps 85 , 86). The duration of attack has grown, indicating that attackers are risking detection of their resources (botnets, tools) in order to maximize impact on the attacked sites

In the reporting period we have assessed that:

* Sophistication of DoS attacks grows (multi-vendor and multi-layer attacks) making them difficult to defend84.

* Performance of available DoS attack infrastructure has grown. This includes both use of technology (amplification) and involved threat agents (coordination, orchestration).

* Features of attack infrastructure (see botnets above) such as resilience, clandestine communication and use of encryption lower detectability and allow for a longer duration of attacks.

* Attack bandwidths achieved have reached impressive levels: the rate of 2-10Gbps attacks has doubled85 and the level of 300Gbps attack was reached in 201386.

* While DoS targets mainly enterprise and commerce it seems that US and Asia Pacific are more targeted through DoS. Europe has lower attack rates87.

* A series of DDoS attacks to banks has drawn the attention of security professional in the reporting period88.

Observed current trend for this threat: *increasing*

Related threats: Botnets, Worms/Trojans.

9 PHISHING

The hunting of user credentials through phishing continues in 2013. Tools are e-mails, manipulated web pages, mobile apps and social media/social gaming. Through the proliferation of mobile devices, they constitute main targets/channels to obtain user credentials. In this context social engineering approaches target users over various channels supported in mobile devices such as voice, instant and short messages and rogue apps. These channels come to complement e-mail as common phishing delivery method89.

The complexity/sophistication of phishing methods varies as well. Fake websites is the simplest tool going up to infected web sites, malware and Pharming/DNS manipulations90. The range of complexity allows all threat agent groups, from novice to experts, to launch phishing attacks 47 . All in all, there has been an increase in phishing in 2013, with phishing sites targeting mainly Social Networking, Financial, Online Services, E-Commerce and Gaming 90 ,91(sequence according to number of phishing sites). Nevertheless, phishing targets vary from country to country

In the reporting period we have assessed that:

* Sophistication of phishing increases: in the reporting period we have seen phishing strategies to include methods that are difficult to spot 90 by end users. Moreover, phishing strategies seem to seek for tactics to fool users of multilevel security procedures introduced by targeted organisations.

* Phishing has a geographic component 90 , 91 . Phishing strategies are adapted to cultural, social and technological development of particular geographic areas. Therefore, phishing mitigation strategies have to take this dimension into account.

* As in other threats assessed, phishing can also be facilitated by easy-to-use tools 90 . This enables threat agents with low capabilities to launch phishing attacks.

* Phishing is heavily based on web site vulnerabilities 92 . This fact underlines the importance of in-depth web site/web application protection strategies.

* Powerful hosting environments (i.e. cloud computing), are an important target of phishing attacks. This is due to the multiplication effect of a successfully mounted attack. This strategy follows the same pattern as for botnets and DoS attacks, all using the power of virtual environments and the vast accumulation of data92.

* Threat agents will target end users of financial systems directly in order to obtain important information to perform fraud 90 and achieve profits. Hence, end user awareness, sensibilization and training are the key to protect against this threat.

For additional analytical, business and investment opportunities information, please contact Global Investment & Business Center, USA at (703) 370-8082. Fax: (703) 370-8083. E-mail: ibpusa3@gmail.com Global Business and Investment Info Databank - www.ibpus.com

Observed current trend for this threat: *increasing*

Related threats: Exploit Kits, Code Injection, Botnets, Worms/Trojans.

10 SPAM

With ca. 75% of the entire e-mail traffic, spam continues to constitute the major part of messages sent to bother security experts and end users 91 . Not only is filtering spam a resource consuming task; spam is one important channel to spread malware, attract user to malicious URLs, commit fraud, etc. Hence, defending against this threat is not all about filtering spam but also how to avoid the impact on end users with regard to fraud and malicious e-mail content. As originating mainly from botnets, spam has demonstrated an activity that is in analogy to the botnet activity: in the 1st quarter on 2013 we have experienced a dramatic increase 56 ,93, whereas the volume of spam dropped till the 1st half of the year 91 ,94. Finally, just like almost all other threats, spam has gone mobile: spam with Android malware has been on the rise95.

In the reporting period we have assessed that:

* Spam has a strong geographic component, with spam origin being on the focus 91 ,96: while in some areas spam traffic in on decline, there are countries with high/very high spam traffic.

* Spam content is related mainly (i.e. over 85%) to pharmacy, images, the so called "Nigerian scam"97, malware and non-pharmacy product ads 91 . Moreover, spam messages chose contemporary hot topics from the press to attract potential victims98 (e.g. Boston Marathon bombings, Pope Francis election, etc.). This might be an important piece of information for end users.

* Tricks used in spam/scam are identity theft targeting social accounts. This is being attempted either by means of luring potential victims through prizes/gifts, or by using fake websites to convince them to enter credential information99.

* It seems that spammers are checking regularly the capability/performance of existing spam filters. In the reporting period we have seen spams that have obviously no malicious background, have strange content and/or structure 98 ,100.

* The techniques of spammers evolve. For end users it is important to understand tricks101 and have basic sensitivity/awareness on this matter.

Observed current trend for this threat: *stable/flat increase*

Related threats: Drive-by Downloads, Exploit Kits, Code Injection, Botnets, Worms/Trojans.

ReconnaissanceWeaponisationDeliveryExploitationInstallationCommand andControlActions onObjectivesSpamStep of Attack WorkflowWidth of Purpose

Figure 14: Position of Spam in attack workflow

11 ROGUEWARE/RANSOMWARE/SCAREWARE

This threat is used to obtain profits from terrified end users. Rogue security software, ransomware and scareware are malicious pieces of software - distributed by threat agents - to terrify/blackmail users, thus demanding ransom payments. Although a decline has been reported regarding the number of fake Anti-Virus (AV) products in comparison to 2012, the overall numbers of rogueware/ransomeare/Scareware remain high 56 ,102,103. In particular, ransomware has reached high levels of infection104. Despite recent law enforcement advances105, the reports analysed provide strong evidence that there is an increase in ransomware threat 104 . One reason for the growth is the expansion of ransomware and fake Antivirus distribution to mobile platforms, such as Android106. Again, one significant component of the increase registered related to mobile platforms: ransomware (i.e. FakeAV) has hit this year Android 104 ,107,108.

In the reporting period we have assessed that:

* The availability of anonymous payment services to channel illegal profits obtained from this threat is a key enabler for this kind of fraud109.

* Rogueware, ransomware and scareware are distributed via exploit kits, while exploiting Java and Adobe vulnerabilities. The use of exploit kits (see also description of exploit kits threat above), is

concluded from the wide spread and the existence of variations/derivates of this malware, that is, alternations to some initial code performed by individual threat agents110.

* Just as it is the case with the rest of malware, the sophistication of ransomware increases111,112.

* In the reporting period a significant success of law enforcement led to arrest of members of cyber-criminal gang responsible for the "Police Virus" (statement of the Spanish Ministry of Interior113). This success demonstrates the importance of cooperation at international level114,115.

Observed current trend for this threat: *increasing*

Related threats: Drive-by Downloads, Exploit Kits, Code Injection, Botnets, Worms/Trojans, Phishing, Spam.

12 DATA BREACHES (COMPROMISING CONFIDENTIAL INFORMATION)

In cyber security, a lot of attention is being paid to data breaches. With this threat, we refer to loss of data occurring via intentional or unintentional information disclosure (i.e. through mistakes in managing information assets). This threat might originate from internal threat agents or external ones. In both cases there might have both hostile116 and non-hostile intentions (i.e. lack of knowledge or negligence). As regards intentional causes, this threat is rather a cumulative implication of other threats mentioned in this report on data. The unintentional part of it, however, is a threat that can materialize due to errors and mistakes of personnel. In all cases, data breaches are systematically reported in related publications. Data breaches are related to incidents from materialized threats, whereby information has been compromised. As such, data breach reporting is considered to be an important indicator of the protection level for company data, but also the effectiveness of malicious actions117. This information is useful for decision and policy makers, especially from the economic point of view118.

In the reporting period we have assessed that:

For additional analytical, business and investment opportunities information, please contact Global Investment & Business Center, USA at (703) 370-8082. Fax: (703) 370-8083. E-mail: ibpusa3@gmail.com Global Business and Investment Info Databank - www.ibpus.com

* Small organisations are more targeted by malware aiming at financial fraud. Larger organisations are targeted merely with the intention of espionage119. This might be indicative for the quality/quantity of protection measures. Eventually, larger organisations are better off in protecting themselves against more simple kinds of attacks, while they often become victims of highly skilled organised crime.

* As regards data breaches, internal actors are at the minority. The vast amount of data breaches are attributed to external threat agents 119 . This is reflected in a study on the costs of data breaches: malicious attacks are at the first position, while system failure and human factor score second and third respectively 118 .

* Data breach reporting is an important tool for the evaluation of effectiveness/maturity of existing controls. Data breach notification mechanisms are envisaged from policy makers as an instrument towards better cyber security governance120.

* Through the deployment of simple/low cost security controls organisations may drastically reduce data breaches: over 70% of incidents are based on simple/low difficulty attacks.

* Most of misuse actions are caused by physical access, either directly or indirectly to the asset targeted. LAN and remote access are following 119 .

Observed current trend for this threat: *increasing*

Related threats: Drive-by Downloads, Exploit Kits, Code Injection, Botnets, Worms/Trojans, Identity Theft/Fraud, Information Leakage, Physical Damage/Theft/Loss, Phishing, Spam, Rogueware/Ransomware/Scareware, Targeted Attacks, Watering Hole.

13 INFORMATION LEAKAGE

With information leakage we cover a set of threats related to the unintentional or maliciously triggered revelation of information of security related information to an unauthorised party. This threat is differentiated from data breaches, as it merely concerns technical or organisational information that might be interesting for threat agents in order to perform reconnaissance and delivery of their attacks; as opposed to data breach which is result of a successful attack targeting customers' data. In the reporting period aggressive adware collecting information has been encountered121,122. Moreover, unsecured file transfers might lead to severe information leakage, as well as poor encryption practices for mobile devices.

In the reporting period we have assessed that:

* Broken authentication and session management has the consequence that attackers may hijack user sessions, gain user credentials and obtain access to business transactions. This is based on leakage from bad session management123.

* Directory traversal is a threat that has been already mentioned in code injection (see above). Path manipulation124 and resource injection125 are attacks based on directory information leakage.

* Network reconnaissance126,127 is a known, yet very important information gaining method/attack to obtain system, network and other resources. Network reconnaissance is based on leakage of network structure and is an important part of targeted attacks.

Besides networks, availability of information on other resources may facilitate all kinds of attacks128.

* Due to user negligence but also maturity level of available apps, big parts of mobile communication take place unsecured, often over unsecured channels. This can lead to significant information leakage including personal and business information 65 .

* Research with support of social media can be a very effective way to obtain information on human resources. Widely available services on the web129 allow for identification of further personal details which, when combined with additional information may result in significant knowledge about targeted individuals.

* Although not explicitly a leakage issue, it is worth mentioning cloud services (e.g. cross VM side channels) as a potential to abuse computing power, data concentration and extract sensitive data130,131.

Observed current trend for this threat: *increasing*

Related threats: Drive-by Downloads, Exploit Kits, Code Injection, Botnets, Worms/Trojans, Identity Theft/Fraud, Information Leakage, Physical Damage/Theft/Loss, Phishing, Spam, Rogueware/Ransomware/Scareware, Targeted Attacks, Watering Hole.

14 TARGETED ATTACKS

Targeted attacks are characterized by their long endurance and specificity of the victim. Targeted attacks are further characterised by the capability level and dedication of the threat agent deploying the attack: all of the (successful) attacks reported in 2013 have been performed by threat agents with assumedly large resources132. Another important observation in the reporting period is a shift of APT targets from financial institutions to politically motivated targets such as NGOs, governmental organisations, politically active groups, etc133,134.

In the reporting period we have assessed that:

* 2013 has been characterised by numerous APT attakcs, whereas it has become clear that one should not assume only a few rogue states as main originators of targeted attacks. There are quite some nation states that have developed sufficient capabilities and infrastructure to successfully launch targeted attacks that can be used to infiltrate all kinds of targets.

* In 2013, targeted attacks demonstrated their true potential. In particular, cyber espionage attacks using targeted attack campaigns reached dimensions that went far beyond expectations135,136.

* With recent advances in mobile threats such as malware, code injection, scam/spam, etc., mobile platforms have become an important attack surface for targeted attacks 95 ,137. It is worth mentioning that mobile spyware applications might become strong tools for APTs targeting Bring Your Own Device environments138.

* Targeted attacks are applied as a pressure instrument at multiple levels. Concrete examples in the reporting period of successful attacks to notable social media accounts 96 ,139 have shown the potential towards the materialisation of risks similar to "Digital Wild Fires in a Hyper-connected World"140.

* Sophistication, complexity and stealthiness of targeted attacks are state-of-the-art in cyber-attack techniques141. Prevention from such attacks is a complex task that has to embrace all levels of organisational assets, from technology to processes to people. The defence has to be prepared and implemented as orchestrated as the attack itself.

Observed current trend for this threat: *increasing*

Related threats: Drive-by Downloads, Exploit Kits, Code Injection, Botnets, Worms/Trojans, Identity Theft/Fraud, Information Leakage, Physical Damage/Theft/Loss, Phishing, Spam, Rogueware/Ransomware/Scareware, Targeted Attacks, Watering Hole.

15 WATERING HOLE ATTACKS

Watering hole attacks consist of the attempt to attack a certain target group by manipulating web sites visited and trusted by members of this target group. When visiting a manipulated web site, devices of members of the target group get eventually infected142.

Although already mentioned in 2012, in the reporting period this threat has significantly increased and led to several successful attacks targeting high tech companies143,144, but also governmental organisations145. Though relatively low in number, these attacks have demonstrated the effectiveness of this threat as it has hit companies who are at the leading edge of technology. Hence, it is alarming that when targeting lower tech users, such attacks will be at least equally successful! This has created a lot of awareness in the threat analysts' community 47 , especially due to the fact that such attacks are usually launched within more extensive targeted attacks.

In the reporting period we have assessed that:

* Information about surfing habits are tracked via tracking services as the ones used by marketing companies to collect data. By tracking users of a specific company, it is possible to find web sites that are frequently used by groups of people. Obviously, these web sites are the best candidates to infect146.

* Watering hole attacks have some commonalities with search engine poisoning (SEP): attracting potential victims to visit an infected web site based on their interests. However, watering hole attacks are more effective especially when attackers want to focus to a specific user group.

* It is worth mentioning that watering hole attacks are more a method to downsize the effort of threat agents while being more successful: fewer web site infections do more effectively reach target victim group. Otherwise, the methods used for victim infection are the ones mentioned above (drive-by downloads, exploit kits, malware).

* It is expected that deployments of this type of threat will increase in the future147. It might be meaningful if owners of infected web sites inform their visitors. At the end, every web site is a "water hole" of some user group.

Observed current trend for this threat: *increasing*

Related threats: Drive-by Downloads, Exploit Kits, Code Injection, Worms/Trojans.

16 VISUALISING CHANGES IN THE CURRENT THREAT LANDSCAPE

For additional analytical, business and investment opportunities information, please contact Global Investment & Business Center, USA at (703) 370-8082. Fax: (703) 370-8083. E-mail: ibpusa3@gmail.com Global Business and Investment Info Databank - www.ibpus.com

As expected, in comparison with 2012 there have been changes in the current threat landscape. To facilitate comparability with the results of 2012, this section visualises changes between current threat landscape 2012 and 2013. In addition, changes in threat rankings of are also indicated in the table below.

Top Threats 2012	Top Threats 2013
1. Drive-by exploits (this threat has been renamed)	1. Drive-by downloads
2. Worms/Trojans	2. Worms/Trojans
3. Code Injection	3. Code Injection
4. Exploit Kits	4. Exploit Kits
5. Botnets	5. Botnets
6. Denial of Service	6. Physical Damage/Theft/Loss
7. Phishing	7. Identify Theft/Fraud
8. Compromising Confidential Information (this threat has been renamed to Data Breaches)	8. Denial of Service
9. Rogueware/ Ransomware/Scareware	9. Phishing
10. Spam	10. Spam
11. Targeted Attacks	11. Rogueware/Ransomware/ Scareware
12. Physical Theft/Loss/Damage	12. Data Breaches
13. Identity Theft	13. Information Leakage
14. Information Leakage	14. Targeted Attacks
15. Search Engine Poisoning (Threat dropped from list because no evidence	15. Watering Hole

For additional analytical, business and investment opportunities information, please contact Global Investment & Business Center, USA at (703) 370-8082. Fax: (703) 370-8083. E-mail: ibpusa3@gmail.com Global Business and Investment Info Databank - www.ibpus.com

BASIC TITLES ON EUROPEAN UNION (EU)

Title	ISBN
Euro-Mediterranean Free Trade Area Business Opportunities Handbook	9781577513445
European Aviation Industry Handbook - Important Regulations and Opportunities	1433015188
European Aviation Training System Handbook: Regulations, Programs and Procedures	1438716591
European Banking and Financial System Handbook Vol. 1 History and Functions	143301520X
European Banking and Financial System Handbook Vol. 2 Banking, Financial System and Regulations	1433015218
European Civil Aviation Flight Regulations Handbook: System and Procedures	1433015250
European Countries Antiterrorism Programs and Operations Handbook	1433015226
European Countries Antiterrorism Strategy and Regulations Handbook	1438716567
European Criminal Justice System and Police Cooperation Handbook	1433015293
European Defense and Military Strategy Handbook - Programs and Developments	1438716575
European Defense Policy Handbook: Basic Programs and Regulations	1438716583
European Defense Policy Handbook: Strategy & Cooperation	1433015242
European Defense Strategy Handbook: Programs, Activities Contacts	1433015234
European Financial and Foreign Investment Regulations Handbook	1433015277
European Free Trade System Handbook - Customs Regulations	1438716605
European Free Trade System Handbook - Important Regulations and Opportunities	1433015269
European International Financial Assistance to Developing Countries Handbook - Strategic Information and Programs Volume 1 Africa	1433015196
European International Financial Assistance to Developing Countries Handbook - Strategic Information and Programs Volume 2 Asia and Pacific	1438716559
European Investment Banks and Financial Markets Regulations Handbook	1438716613
European Police Cooperation Handbook - Important Programs and Regulations	143871663X
European Police Cooperation System Handbook - Coordination, Regulations, Contacts	1433015463
European Publishers and Book Distributors Directory	1433015307
European Publishing Industry Handbook - Important Regulations and Developments	1438716648
European Space Industry Regulations and Programs Handbook	1438716656
European Space Policy and Programs Handbook	1433015323
European Space Policy, Strategy and Agreements Handbook	1438716664
European Space Programs and Activities Handbook	1433015315
European Stock Exchanges and Financial Markets Opportunities Handbook	1433015285
European Stock Exchanges Handbook - Important Regulations and Opportunities	1438716621
European System for Military Cooperation Handbook	1438716672
European System for Security and Cooperation Handbook	1433015331
European Union - African Countries Trade and Economic Assistance Agreement - Strategic Information and Programs	1438748116
European Union - Caribbean Countries Trade and Economic Assistance Agreement - Strategic Information and Programs	1433049449

Title	ISBN
European Union - Eastern European Countries Trade and Economic Assistance Agreement - Strategic Information and Programs	1433049457
European Union - Pacific Countries Trade and Economic Assistance Agreement - Strategic Information and Programs	1438748124
European Union (EU) Government and Business Contacts Handbook	143301534X
EUROPEAN UNION Airlines Handbook	1438716524
European Union Airports Handbook - Basic Regulations and Contacts	1438716699
European Union Airports Handbook - Strategy for Development	1433015358
EUROPEAN UNION Anti Terrorism Activities, Cooperation an d Strategy Handbook	1433014904
European Union Anti Terrorism Activities, Cooperation an d Strategy Handbook	1438716265
EUROPEAN UNION Anti Terrorism Activities, Cooperation and Strategy Handbook	1433014912
EUROPEAN UNION Anti Terrorism Activities, Cooperation and Strategy Handbook	1438716273
EUROPEAN UNION Arms Export Policy and Control Procedures Handbook	1433014939
EUROPEAN UNION Arms Export Policy and Control Procedures Handbook	1433014920
EUROPEAN UNION Arms Export Policy and Control Procedures Handbook	143871629X
EUROPEAN UNION Arms Export Policy and Control Procedures Handbook	1438716281
European Union at the United Nations Cooperation Handbook	1433015366
European Union at the United Nations Joint Programs and Activities Handbook	1438716702
European Union Aviation & Aerospace Industry Handbook -	1438716710
European Union Aviation & Aerospace Industry Handbook - Basic Regulations	1433015374
EUROPEAN UNION Aviation and Aerospace Industry Handbook	1433014947
EUROPEAN UNION Aviation and Aerospace Industry Handbook	1438716303
EUROPEAN UNION Aviation Industry Strategy Handbook	1438716532
EUROPEAN UNION Aviation Safety Regulations Handbook	1438716540
EUROPEAN UNION Aviation Training and Psychology Handbook	143301517X
European Union Banking & Financial Market Handbook - Basic Regulations	1433015382
European Union Banking & Financial Market Handbook - Joint Programs	1438716729
European Union Business Law Handbook - Strategic Information and Basic Laws	1433015390
European Union Business Law Handbook - Strategic Information and Basic Laws	1438716737
EUROPEAN UNION -China Political and Economic Relations Handbook	1438716494
EUROPEAN UNION -China Political and Economic Relations Handbook	1433015137
EUROPEAN UNION Clothing & Textile Industry Handbook	143875843X
European Union Cosmetics Industry Handbook	1433015404
European Union Cosmetics Industry Handbook	1438716745
EUROPEAN UNION Counter Terrorism Strategy and Plans Handbook	1433065509
EUROPEAN UNION Customs and Trade Regulations Guide	1433014955
EUROPEAN UNION Customs and Trade Regulations Guide	1438716311
EUROPEAN UNION Defense Agency Handbook	1433014963
EUROPEAN UNION Defense Agency Handbook	143871632X
EUROPEAN UNION Defense and Military Cooperation Handbook	1433014971
EUROPEAN UNION Defense and Military Cooperation Handbook	1438716338

Title	ISBN
EUROPEAN UNION Defense Export Services Organization Handbook	143301498X
EUROPEAN UNION Defense Export Services Organization Handbook	1438716346
EUROPEAN UNION Defense Strategy and Armed Forces Handbook	1438716354
EUROPEAN UNION Defense Strategy and Armed Forces Handbook	1433014998
EUROPEAN UNION e Financial and Economic Development Handbook	1438716516
EUROPEAN UNION E-commerce Business Handbook	1433015153
EUROPEAN UNION E-commerce Business Handbook	1438716508
EUROPEAN UNION Emission Trading Laws, Regulations and Programs Handbook	9781577513421
EUROPEAN UNION Financial and Economic Development Handbook	1433008742
European Union HANDBOOK Volume 1 Strategic and Practical Information	1438716796
EUROPEAN UNION Healthcare Sector Organization, Management and Payment Systems Handbook - Strategic Information, Programs and Regulations	9781433085840
European Union Insolvency (Bankruptcy) Laws and Regulations Handbook - Strategic Information and Basic Laws	9781433085246
EUROPEAN UNION Intelligence and Security Policy and Cooperation Handbook	1433015005
EUROPEAN UNION Intelligence and Security Policy and Cooperation Handbook	1438716362
European Union Investment and Business Guide - Strategic and Practical Information	1438716753
European Union Investment and Business Guide - Strategic and Practical Information	1433015412
EUROPEAN UNION Mediterranean Partnership Handbook	1433065517
EUROPEAN UNION -Mexico Political and Economic Relations Handbook	1433015145
EUROPEAN UNION Military and Special Forces Handbook	1438716370
EUROPEAN UNION Military and Special Forces Handbook	1433015013
EUROPEAN UNION Monetary Financial Institutions Handbook	1433065525
EUROPEAN UNION Money Laundering Prevention Regulations Handbook	1433065533
EUROPEAN UNION n Airlines Handbook	1433015161
EUROPEAN UNION National Cyber Security Strategy and Programs Handbook - Strategic Information and Developments	9781577513438
EUROPEAN UNION Nuclear Energy Policy Handbook	1433065541
EUROPEAN UNION Pacific Region Countries Economic and Political Cooperation Handbook	1433015021
EUROPEAN UNION Pacific Region Countries Economic and Political Cooperation Handbook	1438716389
European Union Pharmaceutical Industry Handbook	1438716761
European Union Pharmaceutical Industry Handbook	1433015420
European Union Pharmaceutical Legislation Handbook	143871677X
European Union Pharmaceutical Legislation Handbook	1433015439
EUROPEAN UNION Pharmaceutical Legislation Handbook. Vol. 1. Legislation on Medicinal Products for Human Use	143301503X
EUROPEAN UNION Pharmaceutical Legislation Handbook. Vol. 1. Legislation on Medicinal Products for Human Use	1438716397
EUROPEAN UNION Pharmaceutical Legislation Handbook. Vol. 3 Legislation on Gene and Cell Therapy: see in particular Part IV of Annex I (Advanced therapy medicinal products)	1438716400

Title	ISBN
EUROPEAN UNION Pharmaceutical Legislation Handbook. Vol. 3 Legislation on Gene and Cell Therapy: see in particular Part IV of Annex I (Advanced therapy medicinal products)	1433015048
EUROPEAN UNION Pharmaceutical Legislation Handbook. Vol. 4 Legislation on Medical Devices	1438716419
EUROPEAN UNION Pharmaceutical Legislation Handbook. Vol. 4 Legislation on Medical Devices	1433015056
EUROPEAN UNION Pharmaceutical Legislation Handbook. Vol. 5 Legislation on the Quality and Safety of human tissues and cells	1433015064
EUROPEAN UNION Pharmaceutical Legislation Handbook. Vol. 5 Legislation on the Quality and Safety of human tissues and cells	1438716427
European Union Political and Government System Handbook	1438716680
EUROPEAN UNION Postal Service Handbook	1433015072
EUROPEAN UNION Postal Service Handbook	1438716435
European Union Privatization Programs and Regulations Handbook	1433015447
European Union Privatization Programs and Regulations Handbook	1438716788
EUROPEAN UNION Privatization Yearbook: Major Programs and Projects	143306555X
EUROPEAN UNION Security Strategy and Cooperation Handbook	1438716443
EUROPEAN UNION Security Strategy and Cooperation Handbook	1433015080
EUROPEAN UNION Shipbuilding Industry Handbook	1433015099
EUROPEAN UNION Shipbuilding Industry Handbook	1438716451
EUROPEAN UNION Shipbuilding Industry Investment and Business Guide - Strategic and Practical Information	143871646X
EUROPEAN UNION Shipbuilding Industry Investment and Business Guide - Strategic and Practical Information	1433015102
EUROPEAN UNION Shipbuilding Industry Law and Regulations Handbook	1433015110
EUROPEAN UNION Shipbuilding Industry Law and Regulations Handbook	1438716478
EUROPEAN UNION Terrorism Prevention Regulations Handbook	1433065568
EUROPEAN UNION Western European Armaments Organization Handbook	1438716486
EUROPEAN UNION Western European Armaments Organization Handbook	1433015129
European Union, The (EC) Handbook	1433015455
EUROPOL û European Police Office Handbook	143871680X
EU-Russia Political and Economic Relations Handbook	1433015471
EU-Russia Political and Economic Relations Handbook	1438716818

For additional analytical, business and investment opportunities information, please contact Global Investment & Business Center, USA at (703) 370-8082. Fax: (703) 370-8083. E-mail: ibpusa3@gmail.com Global Business and Investment Info Databank - www.ibpus.com

INTERNET AND CYBER SECURITY HANDBOOKS LIBRARY

Price: $99.95 Each

World Business Information Catalog: http://www.ibpus.com

Please contact ibpus3@gmail.com to request the latest ISBN numbers for each publcation

TITLE
Albania Internet and Cyner Security Laws and Regulations Handbook - Strategic Information, Programs, Regulations
Algeria Internet and Cyner Security Laws and Regulations Handbook - Strategic Information, Programs, Regulations
Angola Internet and Cyner Security Laws and Regulations Handbook - Strategic Information, Programs, Regulations
Argentina Internet and Cyner Security Laws and Regulations Handbook - Strategic Information, Programs, Regulations
Armenia Internet and Cyner Security Laws and Regulations Handbook - Strategic Information, Programs, Regulations
Australia Internet and Cyner Security Laws and Regulations Handbook - Strategic Information, Programs, Regulations
Austria Internet and Cyner Security Laws and Regulations Handbook - Strategic Information, Programs, Regulations
Azerbaijan Internet and Cyner Security Laws and Regulations Handbook - Strategic Information, Programs, Regulations
Bangladesh Internet and Cyner Security Laws and Regulations Handbook - Strategic Information, Programs, Regulations
Belarus Internet and Cyner Security Laws and Regulations Handbook - Strategic Information, Programs, Regulations
Belgium Internet and Cyner Security Laws and Regulations Handbook - Strategic Information, Programs, Regulations
Bolivia Internet and Cyner Security Laws and Regulations Handbook - Strategic Information, Programs, Regulations
Bosnia and Herzegovina Internet and Cyner Security Laws and Regulations Handbook - Strategic Information, Programs, Regulations
Botswana Internet and Cyner Security Laws and Regulations Handbook - Strategic Information, Programs, Regulations
Brazil Internet and Cyner Security Laws and Regulations Handbook - Strategic Information, Programs, Regulations
Bulgaria Internet and Cyner Security Laws and Regulations Handbook - Strategic Information, Programs, Regulations
Cambodia Internet and Cyner Security Laws and Regulations Handbook - Strategic Information, Programs, Regulations
Cameroon Internet and Cyner Security Laws and Regulations Handbook - Strategic Information, Programs, Regulations
Canada Internet and Cyner Security Laws and Regulations Handbook - Strategic Information, Programs, Regulations
Chile Internet and Cyner Security Laws and Regulations Handbook - Strategic Information, Programs, Regulations
China Internet and Cyner Security Laws and Regulations Handbook - Strategic Information, Programs, Regulations

TITLE
Colombia Internet and Cyner Security Laws and Regulations Handbook - Strategic Information, Programs, Regulations
Croatia Internet and Cyner Security Laws and Regulations Handbook - Strategic Information, Programs, Regulations
Cuba Internet and Cyner Security Laws and Regulations Handbook - Strategic Information, Programs, Regulations
Czech Republic Internet and Cyner Security Laws and Regulations Handbook - Strategic Information, Programs, Regulations
Denmark Internet and Cyner Security Laws and Regulations Handbook - Strategic Information, Programs, Regulations
Dominican Republic Internet and Cyner Security Laws and Regulations Handbook - Strategic Information, Programs, Regulations
Ecuador Internet and Cyner Security Laws and Regulations Handbook - Strategic Information, Programs, Regulations
Egypt Internet and Cyner Security Laws and Regulations Handbook - Strategic Information, Programs, Regulations
El Salvador Internet and Cyner Security Laws and Regulations Handbook - Strategic Information, Programs, Regulations
Equatorial Guinea Internet and Cyner Security Laws and Regulations Handbook - Strategic Information, Programs, Regulations
Estonia Internet and Cyner Security Laws and Regulations Handbook - Strategic Information, Programs, Regulations
Fiji Internet and Cyner Security Laws and Regulations Handbook - Strategic Information, Programs, Regulations
Finland Internet and Cyner Security Laws and Regulations Handbook - Strategic Information, Programs, Regulations
France Internet and Cyner Security Laws and Regulations Handbook - Strategic Information, Programs, Regulations
Germany Internet and Cyner Security Laws and Regulations Handbook - Strategic Information, Programs, Regulations
Greece Internet and Cyner Security Laws and Regulations Handbook - Strategic Information, Programs, Regulations
Guatemala Internet and Cyner Security Laws and Regulations Handbook - Strategic Information, Programs, Regulations
Guernsey Internet and Cyner Security Laws and Regulations Handbook - Strategic Information, Programs, Regulations
Honduras Internet and Cyner Security Laws and Regulations Handbook - Strategic Information, Programs, Regulations
Hungary Internet and Cyner Security Laws and Regulations Handbook - Strategic Information, Programs, Regulations
Iceland Internet and Cyner Security Laws and Regulations Handbook - Strategic Information, Programs, Regulations
India Internet and Cyner Security Laws and Regulations Handbook - Strategic Information, Programs, Regulations
Indonesia Internet and Cyner Security Laws and Regulations Handbook - Strategic Information, Programs, Regulations
Iran Internet and Cyner Security Laws and Regulations Handbook - Strategic Information, Programs, Regulations
Iraq Internet and Cyner Security Laws and Regulations Handbook - Strategic Information, Programs, Regulations
Ireland Internet and Cyner Security Laws and Regulations Handbook - Strategic Information, Programs, Regulations
Israel Internet and Cyner Security Laws and Regulations Handbook - Strategic Information, Programs, Regulations
Italy Internet and Cyner Security Laws and Regulations Handbook - Strategic Information, Programs, Regulations
Japan Internet and Cyner Security Laws and Regulations Handbook - Strategic Information, Programs, Regulations
Jordan Internet and Cyner Security Laws and Regulations Handbook - Strategic Information, Programs, Regulations
Kazakhstan Internet and Cyner Security Laws and Regulations Handbook - Strategic Information, Programs, Regulations
Kenya Internet and Cyner Security Laws and Regulations Handbook - Strategic Information, Programs, Regulations
Korea, South Internet and Cyner Security Laws and Regulations Handbook - Strategic Information, Programs,

TITLE
Regulations
Kuwait Internet and Cyner Security Laws and Regulations Handbook - Strategic Information, Programs, Regulations
Kyrgyzstan Internet and Cyner Security Laws and Regulations Handbook - Strategic Information, Programs, Regulations
Laos Internet and Cyner Security Laws and Regulations Handbook - Strategic Information, Programs, Regulations
Latvia Internet and Cyner Security Laws and Regulations Handbook - Strategic Information, Programs, Regulations
Lebanon Internet and Cyner Security Laws and Regulations Handbook - Strategic Information, Programs, Regulations
Libya Internet and Cyner Security Laws and Regulations Handbook - Strategic Information, Programs, Regulations
Lithuania Internet and Cyner Security Laws and Regulations Handbook - Strategic Information, Programs, Regulations
Macao Internet and Cyner Security Laws and Regulations Handbook - Strategic Information, Programs, Regulations
Macedonia, Republic Internet and Cyner Security Laws and Regulations Handbook - Strategic Information, Programs, Regulations
Madagascar Internet and Cyner Security Laws and Regulations Handbook - Strategic Information, Programs, Regulations
Malaysia Internet and Cyner Security Laws and Regulations Handbook - Strategic Information, Programs, Regulations
Malta Internet and Cyner Security Laws and Regulations Handbook - Strategic Information, Programs, Regulations
Mauritius Internet and Cyner Security Laws and Regulations Handbook - Strategic Information, Programs, Regulations
Mexico Internet and Cyner Security Laws and Regulations Handbook - Strategic Information, Programs, Regulations
Moldova Internet and Cyner Security Laws and Regulations Handbook - Strategic Information, Programs, Regulations
Mongolia Internet and Cyner Security Laws and Regulations Handbook - Strategic Information, Programs, Regulations
Morocco Internet and Cyner Security Laws and Regulations Handbook - Strategic Information, Programs, Regulations
Namibia Internet and Cyner Security Laws and Regulations Handbook - Strategic Information, Programs, Regulations
Netherlands Internet and Cyner Security Laws and Regulations Handbook - Strategic Information, Programs, Regulations
New Zealand Internet and Cyner Security Laws and Regulations Handbook - Strategic Information, Programs, Regulations
Nicaragua Internet and Cyner Security Laws and Regulations Handbook - Strategic Information, Programs, Regulations
Nigeria Internet and Cyner Security Laws and Regulations Handbook - Strategic Information, Programs, Regulations
Norway Internet and Cyner Security Laws and Regulations Handbook - Strategic Information, Programs, Regulations
Opportunities
Pakistan Internet and Cyner Security Laws and Regulations Handbook - Strategic Information, Programs, Regulations
Panama Internet and Cyner Security Laws and Regulations Handbook - Strategic Information, Programs, Regulations
Peru Internet and Cyner Security Laws and Regulations Handbook - Strategic Information, Programs, Regulations
Philippines Internet and Cyner Security Laws and Regulations Handbook - Strategic Information, Programs, Regulations
Poland Internet and Cyner Security Laws and Regulations Handbook - Strategic Information, Programs, Regulations
Portugal Internet and Cyner Security Laws and Regulations Handbook - Strategic Information, Programs, Regulations
Romania Internet and Cyner Security Laws and Regulations Handbook - Strategic Information, Programs, Regulations

TITLE
Russia Internet and Cyner Security Laws and Regulations Handbook - Strategic Information, Programs, Regulations
Saudi Arabia Internet and Cyner Security Laws and Regulations Handbook - Strategic Information, Programs, Regulations
Serbia Internet and Cyner Security Laws and Regulations Handbook - Strategic Information, Programs, Regulations
Singapore Internet and Cyner Security Laws and Regulations Handbook - Strategic Information, Programs, Regulations
Slovakia Internet and Cyner Security Laws and Regulations Handbook - Strategic Information, Programs, Regulations
Slovenia Internet and Cyner Security Laws and Regulations Handbook - Strategic Information, Programs, Regulations
South Africa Internet and Cyner Security Laws and Regulations Handbook - Strategic Information, Programs, Regulations
Spain Internet and Cyner Security Laws and Regulations Handbook - Strategic Information, Programs, Regulations
Sri Lanka Internet and Cyner Security Laws and Regulations Handbook - Strategic Information, Programs, Regulations
Suriname Internet and Cyner Security Laws and Regulations Handbook - Strategic Information, Programs, Regulations
Sweden Internet and Cyner Security Laws and Regulations Handbook - Strategic Information, Programs, Regulations
Switzerland Internet and Cyner Security Laws and Regulations Handbook - Strategic Information, Programs, Regulations
Taiwan Internet and Cyner Security Laws and Regulations Handbook - Strategic Information, Programs, Regulations
Tajikistan Internet and Cyner Security Laws and Regulations Handbook - Strategic Information, Programs, Regulations
Thailand Internet and Cyner Security Laws and Regulations Handbook - Strategic Information, Programs, Regulations
Tunisia Internet and Cyner Security Laws and Regulations Handbook - Strategic Information, Programs, Regulations
Turkey Internet and Cyner Security Laws and Regulations Handbook - Strategic Information, Programs, Regulations
Turkmenistan Internet and Cyner Security Laws and Regulations Handbook - Strategic Information, Programs, Regulations
Uganda Internet and Cyner Security Laws and Regulations Handbook - Strategic Information, Programs, Regulations
Ukraine Internet and Cyner Security Laws and Regulations Handbook - Strategic Information, Programs, Regulations
United Arab Emirates Internet and Cyner Security Laws and Regulations Handbook - Strategic Information, Programs, Regulations
United Kingdom Internet and Cyner Security Laws and Regulations Handbook - Strategic Information, Programs, Regulations
United States Internet and Cyner Security Laws and Regulations Handbook - Strategic Information, Programs, Regulations
Uruguay Internet and Cyner Security Laws and Regulations Handbook - Strategic Information, Programs, Regulations
US Internet and Cyner Security Laws and Regulations Handbook - Strategic Information, Programs, Regulations
Uzbekistan Internet and Cyner Security Laws and Regulations Handbook - Strategic Information, Programs, Regulations
Venezuela Internet and Cyner Security Laws and Regulations Handbook - Strategic Information, Programs, Regulations
Vietnam Internet and Cyner Security Laws and Regulations Handbook - Strategic Information, Programs, Regulations

INFORMATION STRATEGY, INTERNET AND E-COMMERCE DEVELOPMENT HANDBOOKS LIBRARY

Price: $99.95 Each

World Business Information Catalog: http://www.ibpus.com

TITLE
Albania Information Strategy, Internet and E-Commerce Development Handbook - Strategic Information, Programs, Regulations
Algeria Information Strategy, Internet and E-Commerce Development Handbook - Strategic Information, Programs, Regulations
Angola Information Strategy, Internet and E-Commerce Development Handbook - Strategic Information, Programs, Regulations
Argentina Information Strategy, Internet and E-Commerce Development Handbook - Strategic Information, Programs, Regulations
Armenia Information Strategy, Internet and E-Commerce Development Handbook - Strategic Information, Programs, Regulations
Australia Information Strategy, Internet and E-Commerce Development Handbook - Strategic Information, Programs, Regulations
Austria Information Strategy, Internet and E-Commerce Development Handbook - Strategic Information, Programs, Regulations
Azerbaijan Information Strategy, Internet and E-Commerce Development Handbook - Strategic Information, Programs, Regulations
Bangladesh Information Strategy, Internet and E-Commerce Development Handbook - Strategic Information, Programs, Regulations
Belarus Information Strategy, Internet and E-Commerce Development Handbook - Strategic Information, Programs, Regulations
Belgium Information Strategy, Internet and E-Commerce Development Handbook - Strategic Information, Programs, Regulations
Bermuda Information Strategy, Internet and E-Commerce Development Handbook - Strategic Information, Programs, Regulations
Bolivia Information Strategy, Internet and E-Commerce Development Handbook - Strategic Information, Programs, Regulations
Bosnia and Herzegovina Information Strategy, Internet and E-Commerce Development Handbook - Strategic Information, Programs, Regulations
Botswana Information Strategy, Internet and E-Commerce Development Handbook - Strategic Information, Programs, Regulations
Brazil Information Strategy, Internet and E-Commerce Development Handbook - Strategic Information, Programs, Regulations
Bulgaria Information Strategy, Internet and E-Commerce Development Handbook - Strategic Information, Programs, Regulations
Cambodia Information Strategy, Internet and E-Commerce Development Handbook - Strategic Information, Programs, Regulations
Cameroon Information Strategy, Internet and E-Commerce Development Handbook - Strategic Information, Programs, Regulations
Canada Information Strategy, Internet and E-Commerce Development Handbook - Strategic Information, Programs, Regulations
Chile Information Strategy, Internet and E-Commerce Development Handbook - Strategic Information, Programs,

TITLE
Regulations
China Information Strategy, Internet and E-Commerce Development Handbook - Strategic Information, Programs, Regulations
Colombia Information Strategy, Internet and E-Commerce Development Handbook - Strategic Information, Programs, Regulations
Cook Islands Information Strategy, Internet and E-Commerce Development Handbook - Strategic Information, Programs, Regulations
Costa Rica Information Strategy, Internet and E-Commerce Development Handbook - Strategic Information, Programs, Regulations
Croatia Information Strategy, Internet and E-Commerce Development Handbook - Strategic Information, Programs, Regulations
Cuba Information Strategy, Internet and E-Commerce Development Handbook - Strategic Information, Programs, Regulations
Cyprus Information Strategy, Internet and E-Commerce Development Handbook - Strategic Information, Programs, Regulations
Czech Republic Information Strategy, Internet and E-Commerce Development Handbook - Strategic Information, Programs, Regulations
Denmark Information Strategy, Internet and E-Commerce Development Handbook - Strategic Information, Programs, Regulations
Dominican Republic Information Strategy, Internet and E-Commerce Development Handbook - Strategic Information, Programs, Regulations
Dubai Information Strategy, Internet and E-Commerce Development Handbook - Strategic Information, Programs, Regulations
Ecuador Information Strategy, Internet and E-Commerce Development Handbook - Strategic Information, Programs, Regulations
Egypt Information Strategy, Internet and E-Commerce Development Handbook - Strategic Information, Programs, Regulations
El Salvador Information Strategy, Internet and E-Commerce Development Handbook - Strategic Information, Programs, Regulations
Equatorial Guinea Information Strategy, Internet and E-Commerce Development Handbook - Strategic Information, Programs, Regulations
Estonia Information Strategy, Internet and E-Commerce Development Handbook - Strategic Information, Programs, Regulations
Fiji Information Strategy, Internet and E-Commerce Development Handbook - Strategic Information, Programs, Regulations
Finland Information Strategy, Internet and E-Commerce Development Handbook - Strategic Information, Programs, Regulations
France Information Strategy, Internet and E-Commerce Development Handbook - Strategic Information, Programs, Regulations
Georgia Republic Information Strategy, Internet and E-Commerce Development Handbook - Strategic Information, Programs, Regulations
Germany Information Strategy, Internet and E-Commerce Development Handbook - Strategic Information, Programs, Regulations
Greece Information Strategy, Internet and E-Commerce Development Handbook - Strategic Information, Programs, Regulations
Guatemala Information Strategy, Internet and E-Commerce Development Handbook - Strategic Information, Programs, Regulations
Guernsey Information Strategy, Internet and E-Commerce Development Handbook - Strategic Information, Programs, Regulations
Guyana Information Strategy, Internet and E-Commerce Development Handbook - Strategic Information, Programs, Regulations
Haiti Information Strategy, Internet and E-Commerce Development Handbook - Strategic Information, Programs, Regulations
Honduras Information Strategy, Internet and E-Commerce Development Handbook - Strategic Information, Programs, Regulations
Hungary Information Strategy, Internet and E-Commerce Development Handbook - Strategic Information, Programs, Regulations
Iceland Information Strategy, Internet and E-Commerce Development Handbook - Strategic Information, Programs, Regulations
India Information Strategy, Internet and E-Commerce Development Handbook - Strategic Information, Programs, Regulations

TITLE
Indonesia Information Strategy, Internet and E-Commerce Development Handbook - Strategic Information, Programs, Regulations
Iran Information Strategy, Internet and E-Commerce Development Handbook - Strategic Information, Programs, Regulations
Iraq Information Strategy, Internet and E-Commerce Development Handbook - Strategic Information, Programs, Regulations
Ireland Information Strategy, Internet and E-Commerce Development Handbook - Strategic Information, Programs, Regulations
Israel Information Strategy, Internet and E-Commerce Development Handbook - Strategic Information, Programs, Regulations
Italy Information Strategy, Internet and E-Commerce Development Handbook - Strategic Information, Programs, Regulations
Jamaica Information Strategy, Internet and E-Commerce Development Handbook - Strategic Information, Programs, Regulations
Japan Information Strategy, Internet and E-Commerce Development Handbook - Strategic Information, Programs, Regulations
Jordan Information Strategy, Internet and E-Commerce Development Handbook - Strategic Information, Programs, Regulations
Kazakhstan Information Strategy, Internet and E-Commerce Development Handbook - Strategic Information, Programs, Regulations
Kenya Information Strategy, Internet and E-Commerce Development Handbook - Strategic Information, Programs, Regulations
Korea, North Information Strategy, Internet and E-Commerce Development Handbook - Strategic Information, Programs, Regulations
Korea, South Information Strategy, Internet and E-Commerce Development Handbook - Strategic Information, Programs, Regulations
Kuwait Information Strategy, Internet and E-Commerce Development Handbook - Strategic Information, Programs, Regulations
Kyrgyzstan Information Strategy, Internet and E-Commerce Development Handbook - Strategic Information, Programs, Regulations
Laos Information Strategy, Internet and E-Commerce Development Handbook - Strategic Information, Programs, Regulations
Latvia Information Strategy, Internet and E-Commerce Development Handbook - Strategic Information, Programs, Regulations
Lebanon Information Strategy, Internet and E-Commerce Development Handbook - Strategic Information, Programs, Regulations
Libya Information Strategy, Internet and E-Commerce Development Handbook - Strategic Information, Programs, Regulations
Lithuania Information Strategy, Internet and E-Commerce Development Handbook - Strategic Information, Programs, Regulations
Macao Information Strategy, Internet and E-Commerce Development Handbook - Strategic Information, Programs, Regulations
Macedonia, Republic Information Strategy, Internet and E-Commerce Development Handbook - Strategic Information, Programs, Regulations
Madagascar Information Strategy, Internet and E-Commerce Development Handbook - Strategic Information, Programs, Regulations
Malaysia Information Strategy, Internet and E-Commerce Development Handbook - Strategic Information, Programs, Regulations
Malta Information Strategy, Internet and E-Commerce Development Handbook - Strategic Information, Programs, Regulations
Mauritius Information Strategy, Internet and E-Commerce Development Handbook - Strategic Information, Programs, Regulations
Mauritius Information Strategy, Internet and E-Commerce Development Handbook - Strategic Information, Programs, Regulations
Mexico Information Strategy, Internet and E-Commerce Development Handbook - Strategic Information, Programs, Regulations
Micronesia Information Strategy, Internet and E-Commerce Development Handbook - Strategic Information, Programs, Regulations
Moldova Information Strategy, Internet and E-Commerce Development Handbook - Strategic Information, Programs, Regulations
Monaco Information Strategy, Internet and E-Commerce Development Handbook - Strategic Information,

TITLE
Programs, Regulations
Mongolia Information Strategy, Internet and E-Commerce Development Handbook - Strategic Information, Programs, Regulations
Morocco Information Strategy, Internet and E-Commerce Development Handbook - Strategic Information, Programs, Regulations
Myanmar Information Strategy, Internet and E-Commerce Development Handbook - Strategic Information, Programs, Regulations
Namibia Information Strategy, Internet and E-Commerce Development Handbook - Strategic Information, Programs, Regulations
Netherlands Information Strategy, Internet and E-Commerce Development Handbook - Strategic Information, Programs, Regulations
New Zealand Information Strategy, Internet and E-Commerce Development Handbook - Strategic Information, Programs, Regulations
Nicaragua Information Strategy, Internet and E-Commerce Development Handbook - Strategic Information, Programs, Regulations
Nigeria Information Strategy, Internet and E-Commerce Development Handbook - Strategic Information, Programs, Regulations
Norway Information Strategy, Internet and E-Commerce Development Handbook - Strategic Information, Programs, Regulations
Opportunities
Pakistan Information Strategy, Internet and E-Commerce Development Handbook - Strategic Information, Programs, Regulations
Panama Information Strategy, Internet and E-Commerce Development Handbook - Strategic Information, Programs, Regulations
Peru Information Strategy, Internet and E-Commerce Development Handbook - Strategic Information, Programs, Regulations
Philippines Information Strategy, Internet and E-Commerce Development Handbook - Strategic Information, Programs, Regulations
Poland Information Strategy, Internet and E-Commerce Development Handbook - Strategic Information, Programs, Regulations
Portugal Information Strategy, Internet and E-Commerce Development Handbook - Strategic Information, Programs, Regulations
Romania Information Strategy, Internet and E-Commerce Development Handbook - Strategic Information, Programs, Regulations
Russia Information Strategy, Internet and E-Commerce Development Handbook - Strategic Information, Programs, Regulations
Saudi Arabia Information Strategy, Internet and E-Commerce Development Handbook - Strategic Information, Programs, Regulations
Scotland Information Strategy, Internet and E-Commerce Development Handbook - Strategic Information, Programs, Regulations
Serbia Information Strategy, Internet and E-Commerce Development Handbook - Strategic Information, Programs, Regulations
Singapore Information Strategy, Internet and E-Commerce Development Handbook - Strategic Information, Programs, Regulations
Slovakia Information Strategy, Internet and E-Commerce Development Handbook - Strategic Information, Programs, Regulations
Slovenia Information Strategy, Internet and E-Commerce Development Handbook - Strategic Information, Programs, Regulations
South Africa Information Strategy, Internet and E-Commerce Development Handbook - Strategic Information, Programs, Regulations
Spain Information Strategy, Internet and E-Commerce Development Handbook - Strategic Information, Programs, Regulations
Sri Lanka Information Strategy, Internet and E-Commerce Development Handbook - Strategic Information, Programs, Regulations
Sudan Information Strategy, Internet and E-Commerce Development Handbook - Strategic Information, Programs, Regulations
Suriname Information Strategy, Internet and E-Commerce Development Handbook - Strategic Information, Programs, Regulations
Sweden Information Strategy, Internet and E-Commerce Development Handbook - Strategic Information, Programs, Regulations
Switzerland Information Strategy, Internet and E-Commerce Development Handbook - Strategic Information,

TITLE
Programs, Regulations
Syria Export Import &Business Directory
Taiwan Information Strategy, Internet and E-Commerce Development Handbook - Strategic Information, Programs, Regulations
Tajikistan Information Strategy, Internet and E-Commerce Development Handbook - Strategic Information, Programs, Regulations
Thailand Information Strategy, Internet and E-Commerce Development Handbook - Strategic Information, Programs, Regulations
Tunisia Information Strategy, Internet and E-Commerce Development Handbook - Strategic Information, Programs, Regulations
Turkey Information Strategy, Internet and E-Commerce Development Handbook - Strategic Information, Programs, Regulations
Turkmenistan Information Strategy, Internet and E-Commerce Development Handbook - Strategic Information, Programs, Regulations
Uganda Information Strategy, Internet and E-Commerce Development Handbook - Strategic Information, Programs, Regulations
Ukraine Information Strategy, Internet and E-Commerce Development Handbook - Strategic Information, Programs, Regulations
United Arab Emirates Information Strategy, Internet and E-Commerce Development Handbook - Strategic Information, Programs, Regulations
United Kingdom Information Strategy, Internet and E-Commerce Development Handbook - Strategic Information, Programs, Regulations
United States Information Strategy, Internet and E-Commerce Development Handbook - Strategic Information, Programs, Regulations
Uruguay Information Strategy, Internet and E-Commerce Development Handbook - Strategic Information, Programs, Regulations
US Information Strategy, Internet and E-Commerce Development Handbook - Strategic Information, Programs, Regulations
Uzbekistan Information Strategy, Internet and E-Commerce Development Handbook - Strategic Information, Programs, Regulations
Venezuela Information Strategy, Internet and E-Commerce Development Handbook - Strategic Information, Programs, Regulations
Vietnam Information Strategy, Internet and E-Commerce Development Handbook - Strategic Information, Programs, Regulations

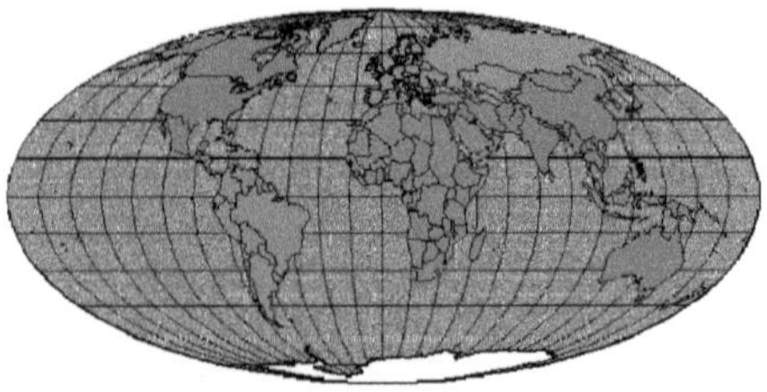

WORLD BUSINESS AND INVESTMENT OPPORTUNITIES YEARBOOK LIBRARY

World Business Information Catalog, USA: http://www.ibpus.com
Email: ibpusa3@gmail.com

Price: $99.95 Each

TITLE
Abkhazia (Republic of Abkhazia) Business and Investment Opportunities Yearbook Volume 1 Strategic, Practical Information and Opportunities
Afghanistan Business and Investment Opportunities Yearbook Volume 1 Strategic, Practical Information and Opportunities
Aland Business and Investment Opportunities Yearbook Volume 1 Strategic, Practical Information and Opportunities
Albania Business and Investment Opportunities Yearbook Volume 1 Strategic, Practical Information and Opportunities
Algeria Business and Investment Opportunities Yearbook Volume 1 Strategic, Practical Information and Opportunities
Andorra Business and Investment Opportunities Yearbook Volume 1 Strategic, Practical Information and Opportunities
Angola Business and Investment Opportunities Yearbook Volume 1 Strategic, Practical Information and Opportunities
Anguilla Business and Investment Opportunities Yearbook Volume 1 Strategic, Practical Information and Opportunities
Antigua and Barbuda Business and Investment Opportunities Yearbook Volume 1 Strategic, Practical Information and Opportunities
Antilles (Netherlands) Business and Investment Opportunities Yearbook Volume 1 Strategic, Practical Information and Opportunities
Argentina Business and Investment Opportunities Yearbook Volume 1 Strategic, Practical Information and Opportunities
Armenia Business and Investment Opportunities Yearbook Volume 1 Strategic, Practical Information and Opportunities
Aruba Business and Investment Opportunities Yearbook Volume 1 Strategic, Practical Information and Opportunities
Australia Business and Investment Opportunities Yearbook Volume 1 Strategic, Practical Information and Opportunities
Austria Business and Investment Opportunities Yearbook Volume 1 Strategic, Practical Information and Opportunities
Azerbaijan Business and Investment Opportunities Yearbook Volume 1 Strategic, Practical Information and Opportunities
Bahamas Business and Investment Opportunities Yearbook Volume 1 Strategic, Practical Information and Opportunities
Bahrain Business and Investment Opportunities Yearbook Volume 1 Strategic, Practical Information and Opportunities
Bangladesh Business and Investment Opportunities Yearbook Volume 1 Strategic, Practical Information and Opportunities
Barbados Business and Investment Opportunities Yearbook Volume 1 Strategic, Practical Information and Opportunities
Belarus Business and Investment Opportunities Yearbook Volume 1 Strategic, Practical Information and Opportunities

For additional analytical, business and investment opportunities information,
Please contact Global Investment & Business Center, USA
at (202) 546-2103. Fax: (202) 546-3275. E-mail: ibpusa3@gmail.com

TITLE
Belgium Business and Investment Opportunities Yearbook Volume 1 Strategic, Practical Information and Opportunities
Belize Business and Investment Opportunities Yearbook Volume 1 Strategic, Practical Information and Opportunities
Benin Business and Investment Opportunities Yearbook Volume 1 Strategic, Practical Information and Opportunities
Bermuda Business and Investment Opportunities Yearbook Volume 1 Strategic, Practical Information and Opportunities
Bhutan Business and Investment Opportunities Yearbook Volume 1 Strategic, Practical Information and Opportunities
Bolivia Business and Investment Opportunities Yearbook Volume 1 Strategic, Practical Information and Opportunities
Bosnia and Herzegovina Business and Investment Opportunities Yearbook Volume 1 Strategic, Practical Information and Opportunities
Botswana Business and Investment Opportunities Yearbook Volume 1 Strategic, Practical Information and Opportunities
Brazil Business and Investment Opportunities Yearbook Volume 1 Strategic, Practical Information and Opportunities
Brunei Business and Investment Opportunities Yearbook Volume 1 Strategic, Practical Information and Opportunities
Bulgaria Business and Investment Opportunities Yearbook Volume 1 Strategic, Practical Information and Opportunities
Burkina Faso Business and Investment Opportunities Yearbook Volume 1 Strategic, Practical Information and Opportunities
Burundi Business and Investment Opportunities Yearbook Volume 1 Strategic, Practical Information and Opportunities
Cambodia Business and Investment Opportunities Yearbook Volume 1 Strategic, Practical Information and Opportunities
Cameroon Business and Investment Opportunities Yearbook Volume 1 Strategic, Practical Information and Opportunities
Canada Business and Investment Opportunities Yearbook Volume 1 Strategic, Practical Information and Opportunities
Cape Verde Business and Investment Opportunities Yearbook Volume 1 Strategic, Practical Information and Opportunities
Cayman Islands Business and Investment Opportunities Yearbook Volume 1 Strategic, Practical Information and Opportunities
Central African Republic Business and Investment Opportunities Yearbook Volume 1 Strategic, Practical Information and Opportunities
Chad Business and Investment Opportunities Yearbook Volume 1 Strategic, Practical Information and Opportunities
Chile Business and Investment Opportunities Yearbook Volume 1 Strategic, Practical Information and Opportunities
China Business and Investment Opportunities Yearbook Volume 1 Strategic, Practical Information and Opportunities
Colombia Business and Investment Opportunities Yearbook Volume 1 Strategic, Practical Information and Opportunities
Comoros Business and Investment Opportunities Yearbook Volume 1 Strategic, Practical Information and Opportunities
Congo Business and Investment Opportunities Yearbook Volume 1 Strategic, Practical Information and Opportunities
Congo, Democratic Republic Business and Investment Opportunities Yearbook Volume 1 Strategic, Practical Information and Opportunities
Cook Islands Business and Investment Opportunities Yearbook Volume 1 Strategic, Practical Information and Opportunities
Costa Rica Business and Investment Opportunities Yearbook Volume 1 Strategic, Practical Information and Opportunities

TITLE
Cote d'Ivoire Business and Investment Opportunities Yearbook Volume 1 Strategic, Practical Information and Opportunities
Croatia Business and Investment Opportunities Yearbook Volume 1 Strategic, Practical Information and Opportunities
Cuba Business and Investment Opportunities Yearbook Volume 1 Strategic, Practical Information and Opportunities
Cyprus Business and Investment Opportunities Yearbook Volume 1 Strategic, Practical Information and Opportunities
Czech Republic Business and Investment Opportunities Yearbook Volume 1 Strategic, Practical Information and Opportunities
Denmark Business and Investment Opportunities Yearbook Volume 1 Strategic, Practical Information and Opportunities
Djibouti Business and Investment Opportunities Yearbook Volume 1 Strategic, Practical Information and Opportunities
Dominica Business and Investment Opportunities Yearbook Volume 1 Strategic, Practical Information and Opportunities
Dominican Republic Business and Investment Opportunities Yearbook Volume 1 Strategic, Practical Information and Opportunities
Ecuador Business and Investment Opportunities Yearbook Volume 1 Strategic, Practical Information and Opportunities
Egypt Business and Investment Opportunities Yearbook Volume 1 Strategic, Practical Information and Opportunities
El Salvador Business and Investment Opportunities Yearbook Volume 1 Strategic, Practical Information and Opportunities
Equatorial Guinea Business and Investment Opportunities Yearbook Volume 1 Strategic, Practical Information and Opportunities
Eritrea Business and Investment Opportunities Yearbook Volume 1 Strategic, Practical Information and Opportunities
Estonia Business and Investment Opportunities Yearbook Volume 1 Strategic, Practical Information and Opportunities
Ethiopia Business and Investment Opportunities Yearbook Volume 1 Strategic, Practical Information and Opportunities
Falkland Islands Business and Investment Opportunities Yearbook Volume 1 Strategic, Practical Information and Opportunities
Faroes Islands Business and Investment Opportunities Yearbook Volume 1 Strategic, Practical Information and Opportunities
Fiji Business and Investment Opportunities Yearbook Volume 1 Strategic, Practical Information and Opportunities
Finland Business and Investment Opportunities Yearbook Volume 1 Strategic, Practical Information and Opportunities
France Business and Investment Opportunities Yearbook Volume 1 Strategic, Practical Information and Opportunities
Gabon Business and Investment Opportunities Yearbook Volume 1 Strategic, Practical Information and Opportunities
Gambia Business and Investment Opportunities Yearbook Volume 1 Strategic, Practical Information and Opportunities
Georgia Business and Investment Opportunities Yearbook Volume 1 Strategic, Practical Information and Opportunities
Germany Business and Investment Opportunities Yearbook Volume 1 Strategic, Practical Information and Opportunities
Ghana Business and Investment Opportunities Yearbook Volume 1 Strategic, Practical Information and Opportunities
Gibraltar Business and Investment Opportunities Yearbook Volume 1 Strategic, Practical Information and Opportunities
Greece Business and Investment Opportunities Yearbook Volume 1 Strategic, Practical Information and Opportunities

TITLE
Greenland Business and Investment Opportunities Yearbook Volume 1 Strategic, Practical Information and Opportunities
Grenada Business and Investment Opportunities Yearbook Volume 1 Strategic, Practical Information and Opportunities
Guam Business and Investment Opportunities Yearbook Volume 1 Strategic, Practical Information and Opportunities
Guatemala Business and Investment Opportunities Yearbook Volume 1 Strategic, Practical Information and Opportunities
Guernsey Business and Investment Opportunities Yearbook Volume 1 Strategic, Practical Information and Opportunities
Guinea Business and Investment Opportunities Yearbook Volume 1 Strategic, Practical Information and Opportunities
Guinea-Bissau Business and Investment Opportunities Yearbook Volume 1 Strategic, Practical Information and Opportunities
Guyana Business and Investment Opportunities Yearbook Volume 1 Strategic, Practical Information and Opportunities
Haiti Business and Investment Opportunities Yearbook Volume 1 Strategic, Practical Information and Opportunities
Honduras Business and Investment Opportunities Yearbook Volume 1 Strategic, Practical Information and Opportunities
Hungary Business and Investment Opportunities Yearbook Volume 1 Strategic, Practical Information and Opportunities
Iceland Business and Investment Opportunities Yearbook Volume 1 Strategic, Practical Information and Opportunities
India Business and Investment Opportunities Yearbook Volume 1 Strategic, Practical Information and Opportunities
Indonesia Business and Investment Opportunities Yearbook Volume 1 Strategic, Practical Information and Opportunities
Iran Business and Investment Opportunities Yearbook Volume 1 Strategic, Practical Information and Opportunities
Iraq Business and Investment Opportunities Yearbook Volume 1 Strategic, Practical Information and Opportunities
Ireland Business and Investment Opportunities Yearbook Volume 1 Strategic, Practical Information and Opportunities
Israel Business and Investment Opportunities Yearbook Volume 1 Strategic, Practical Information and Opportunities
Italy Business and Investment Opportunities Yearbook Volume 1 Strategic, Practical Information and Opportunities
Jamaica Business and Investment Opportunities Yearbook Volume 1 Strategic, Practical Information and Opportunities
Japan Business and Investment Opportunities Yearbook Volume 1 Strategic, Practical Information and Opportunities
Jersey Business and Investment Opportunities Yearbook Volume 1 Strategic, Practical Information and Opportunities
Jordan Business and Investment Opportunities Yearbook Volume 1 Strategic, Practical Information and Opportunities
Kazakhstan Business and Investment Opportunities Yearbook Volume 1 Strategic, Practical Information and Opportunities
Kenya Business and Investment Opportunities Yearbook Volume 1 Strategic, Practical Information and Opportunities
Kiribati Business and Investment Opportunities Yearbook Volume 1 Strategic, Practical Information and Opportunities
Korea, North Business and Investment Opportunities Yearbook Volume 1 Strategic, Practical Information and Opportunities
Korea, South Business and Investment Opportunities Yearbook Volume 1 Strategic, Practical Information and Opportunities

TITLE
Kosovo Business and Investment Opportunities Yearbook Volume 1 Strategic, Practical Information and Opportunities
Kurdistan Business and Investment Opportunities Yearbook Volume 1 Strategic, Practical Information and Opportunities
Kuwait Business and Investment Opportunities Yearbook Volume 1 Strategic, Practical Information and Opportunities
Kyrgyzstan Business and Investment Opportunities Yearbook Volume 1 Strategic, Practical Information and Opportunities
Laos Business and Investment Opportunities Yearbook Volume 1 Strategic, Practical Information and Opportunities
Latvia Business and Investment Opportunities Yearbook Volume 1 Strategic, Practical Information and Opportunities
Lebanon Business and Investment Opportunities Yearbook Volume 1 Strategic, Practical Information and Opportunities
Lesotho Business and Investment Opportunities Yearbook Volume 1 Strategic, Practical Information and Opportunities
Liberia Business and Investment Opportunities Yearbook Volume 1 Strategic, Practical Information and Opportunities
Libya Business and Investment Opportunities Yearbook Volume 1 Strategic, Practical Information and Opportunities
Liechtenstein Business and Investment Opportunities Yearbook Volume 1 Strategic, Practical Information and Opportunities
Lithuania Business and Investment Opportunities Yearbook Volume 1 Strategic, Practical Information and Opportunities
Luxembourg Business and Investment Opportunities Yearbook Volume 1 Strategic, Practical Information and Opportunities
Macao Business and Investment Opportunities Yearbook Volume 1 Strategic, Practical Information and Opportunities
Macedonia Business and Investment Opportunities Yearbook Volume 1 Strategic, Practical Information and Opportunities
Madagascar Business and Investment Opportunities Yearbook Volume 1 Strategic, Practical Information and Opportunities
Madeira Business and Investment Opportunities Yearbook Volume 1 Strategic, Practical Information and Opportunities
Malawi Business and Investment Opportunities Yearbook Volume 1 Strategic, Practical Information and Opportunities
Malaysia Business and Investment Opportunities Yearbook Volume 1 Strategic, Practical Information and Opportunities
Maldives Business and Investment Opportunities Yearbook Volume 1 Strategic, Practical Information and Opportunities
Mali Business and Investment Opportunities Yearbook Volume 1 Strategic, Practical Information and Opportunities
Malta Business and Investment Opportunities Yearbook Volume 1 Strategic, Practical Information and Opportunities
Man Business and Investment Opportunities Yearbook Volume 1 Strategic, Practical Information and Opportunities
Marshall Islands Business and Investment Opportunities Yearbook Volume 1 Strategic, Practical Information and Opportunities
Mauritania Business and Investment Opportunities Yearbook Volume 1 Strategic, Practical Information and Opportunities
Mauritius Business and Investment Opportunities Yearbook Volume 1 Strategic, Practical Information and Opportunities
Mayotte Business and Investment Opportunities Yearbook Volume 1 Strategic, Practical Information and Opportunities
Mexico Business and Investment Opportunities Yearbook Volume 1 Strategic, Practical Information and Opportunities

**For additional analytical, business and investment opportunities information,
Please contact Global Investment & Business Center, USA
at (202) 546-2103. Fax: (202) 546-3275. E-mail: ibpusa3@gmail.com**

TITLE
Micronesia Business and Investment Opportunities Yearbook Volume 1 Strategic, Practical Information and Opportunities
Moldova Business and Investment Opportunities Yearbook Volume 1 Strategic, Practical Information and Opportunities
Monaco Business and Investment Opportunities Yearbook Volume 1 Strategic, Practical Information and Opportunities
Mongolia Business and Investment Opportunities Yearbook Volume 1 Strategic, Practical Information and Opportunities
Montserrat Business and Investment Opportunities Yearbook Volume 1 Strategic, Practical Information and Opportunities
Montenegro Business and Investment Opportunities Yearbook Volume 1 Strategic, Practical Information and Opportunities
Morocco Business and Investment Opportunities Yearbook Volume 1 Strategic, Practical Information and Opportunities
Mozambique Business and Investment Opportunities Yearbook Volume 1 Strategic, Practical Information and Opportunities
Myanmar Business and Investment Opportunities Yearbook Volume 1 Strategic, Practical Information and Opportunities
Nagorno-Karabakh Republic Business and Investment Opportunities Yearbook Volume 1 Strategic, Practical Information and Opportunities
Namibia Business and Investment Opportunities Yearbook Volume 1 Strategic, Practical Information and Opportunities
Nauru Business and Investment Opportunities Yearbook Volume 1 Strategic, Practical Information and Opportunities
Nepal Business and Investment Opportunities Yearbook Volume 1 Strategic, Practical Information and Opportunities
Netherlands Business and Investment Opportunities Yearbook Volume 1 Strategic, Practical Information and Opportunities
New Caledonia Business and Investment Opportunities Yearbook Volume 1 Strategic, Practical Information and Opportunities
New Zealand Business and Investment Opportunities Yearbook Volume 1 Strategic, Practical Information and Opportunities
Nicaragua Business and Investment Opportunities Yearbook Volume 1 Strategic, Practical Information and Opportunities
Niger Business and Investment Opportunities Yearbook Volume 1 Strategic, Practical Information and Opportunities
Nigeria Business and Investment Opportunities Yearbook Volume 1 Strategic, Practical Information and Opportunities
Niue Business and Investment Opportunities Yearbook Volume 1 Strategic, Practical Information and Opportunities
Northern Cyprus (Turkish Republic of Northern Cyprus) Business and Investment Opportunities Yearbook Volume 1 Strategic, Practical Information and Opportunities
Northern Mariana Islands Business and Investment Opportunities Yearbook Volume 1 Strategic, Practical Information and Opportunities
Norway Business and Investment Opportunities Yearbook Volume 1 Strategic, Practical Information and Opportunities
Oman Business and Investment Opportunities Yearbook Volume 1 Strategic, Practical Information and Opportunities
Pakistan Business and Investment Opportunities Yearbook Volume 1 Strategic, Practical Information and Opportunities
Palau Business and Investment Opportunities Yearbook Volume 1 Strategic, Practical Information and Opportunities
Palestine (West Bank & Gaza) Business and Investment Opportunities Yearbook Volume 1 Strategic, Practical Information and Opportunities
Panama Business and Investment Opportunities Yearbook Volume 1 Strategic, Practical Information and Opportunities

TITLE
Papua New Guinea Business and Investment Opportunities Yearbook Volume 1 Strategic, Practical Information and Opportunities
Paraguay Business and Investment Opportunities Yearbook Volume 1 Strategic, Practical Information and Opportunities
Peru Business and Investment Opportunities Yearbook Volume 1 Strategic, Practical Information and Opportunities
Philippines Business and Investment Opportunities Yearbook Volume 1 Strategic, Practical Information and Opportunities
Pitcairn Islands Business and Investment Opportunities Yearbook Volume 1 Strategic, Practical Information and Opportunities
Poland Business and Investment Opportunities Yearbook Volume 1 Strategic, Practical Information and Opportunities
Polynesia French Business and Investment Opportunities Yearbook Volume 1 Strategic, Practical Information and Opportunities
Portugal Business and Investment Opportunities Yearbook Volume 1 Strategic, Practical Information and Opportunities
Qatar Business and Investment Opportunities Yearbook Volume 1 Strategic, Practical Information and Opportunities
Romania Business and Investment Opportunities Yearbook Volume 1 Strategic, Practical Information and Opportunities
Russia Business and Investment Opportunities Yearbook Volume 1 Strategic, Practical Information and Opportunities
Rwanda Business and Investment Opportunities Yearbook Volume 1 Strategic, Practical Information and Opportunities
Sahrawi Arab Democratic Republic Volume 1 Strategic Information and Developments
Saint Kitts and Nevis Business and Investment Opportunities Yearbook Volume 1 Strategic, Practical Information and Opportunities
Saint Lucia Business and Investment Opportunities Yearbook Volume 1 Strategic, Practical Information and Opportunities
Saint Vincent and The Grenadines Business and Investment Opportunities Yearbook Volume 1 Strategic, Practical Information and Opportunities
Samoa (American) A Business and Investment Opportunities Yearbook Volume 1 Strategic, Practical Information and Opportunities
Samoa (Western) Business and Investment Opportunities Yearbook Volume 1 Strategic, Practical Information and Opportunities
San Marino Business and Investment Opportunities Yearbook Volume 1 Strategic, Practical Information and Opportunities
Sao Tome and Principe Business and Investment Opportunities Yearbook Volume 1 Strategic, Practical Information and Opportunities
Saudi Arabia Business and Investment Opportunities Yearbook Volume 1 Strategic, Practical Information and Opportunities
Scotland Business and Investment Opportunities Yearbook Volume 1 Strategic, Practical Information and Opportunities
Senegal Business and Investment Opportunities Yearbook Volume 1 Strategic, Practical Information and Opportunities
Serbia Business and Investment Opportunities Yearbook Volume 1 Strategic, Practical Information and Opportunities
Seychelles Business and Investment Opportunities Yearbook Volume 1 Strategic, Practical Information and Opportunities
Sierra Leone Business and Investment Opportunities Yearbook Volume 1 Strategic, Practical Information and Opportunities
Singapore Business and Investment Opportunities Yearbook Volume 1 Strategic, Practical Information and Opportunities
Slovakia Business and Investment Opportunities Yearbook Volume 1 Strategic, Practical Information and Opportunities

TITLE
Slovenia Business and Investment Opportunities Yearbook Volume 1 Strategic, Practical Information and Opportunities
Solomon Islands Business and Investment Opportunities Yearbook Volume 1 Strategic, Practical Information and Opportunities
Somalia Business and Investment Opportunities Yearbook Volume 1 Strategic, Practical Information and Opportunities
South Africa Business and Investment Opportunities Yearbook Volume 1 Strategic, Practical Information and Opportunities
Spain Business and Investment Opportunities Yearbook Volume 1 Strategic, Practical Information and Opportunities
Sri Lanka Business and Investment Opportunities Yearbook Volume 1 Strategic, Practical Information and Opportunities
St. Helena Business and Investment Opportunities Yearbook Volume 1 Strategic, Practical Information and Opportunities
St. Pierre & Miquelon Business and Investment Opportunities Yearbook Volume 1 Strategic, Practical Information and Opportunities
Sudan (Republic of the Sudan) Business and Investment Opportunities Yearbook Volume 1 Strategic, Practical Information and Opportunities
Sudan South Business and Investment Opportunities Yearbook Volume 1 Strategic, Practical Information and Opportunities
Suriname Business and Investment Opportunities Yearbook Volume 1 Strategic, Practical Information and Opportunities
Swaziland Business and Investment Opportunities Yearbook Volume 1 Strategic, Practical Information and Opportunities
Sweden Business and Investment Opportunities Yearbook Volume 1 Strategic, Practical Information and Opportunities
Switzerland Business and Investment Opportunities Yearbook Volume 1 Strategic, Practical Information and Opportunities
Syria Business and Investment Opportunities Yearbook Volume 1 Strategic, Practical Information and Opportunities
Taiwan Business and Investment Opportunities Yearbook Volume 1 Strategic, Practical Information and Opportunities
Tajikistan Business and Investment Opportunities Yearbook Volume 1 Strategic, Practical Information and Opportunities
Tanzania Business and Investment Opportunities Yearbook Volume 1 Strategic, Practical Information and Opportunities
Thailand Business and Investment Opportunities Yearbook Volume 1 Strategic, Practical Information and Opportunities
Timor Leste (Democratic Republic of Timor-Leste) Business and Investment Opportunities Yearbook Volume 1 Strategic, Practical Information and Opportunities
Togo Business and Investment Opportunities Yearbook Volume 1 Strategic, Practical Information and Opportunities
Tonga Business and Investment Opportunities Yearbook Volume 1 Strategic, Practical Information and Opportunities
Trinidad and Tobago Business and Investment Opportunities Yearbook Volume 1 Strategic, Practical Information and Opportunities
Tunisia Business and Investment Opportunities Yearbook Volume 1 Strategic, Practical Information and Opportunities
Turkey Business and Investment Opportunities Yearbook Volume 1 Strategic, Practical Information and Opportunities
Turkmenistan Business and Investment Opportunities Yearbook Volume 1 Strategic, Practical Information and Opportunities
Turks & Caicos Business and Investment Opportunities Yearbook Volume 1 Strategic, Practical Information and Opportunities
Tuvalu Business and Investment Opportunities Yearbook Volume 1 Strategic, Practical Information and Opportunities

TITLE
Uganda Business and Investment Opportunities Yearbook Volume 1 Strategic, Practical Information and Opportunities
Ukraine Business and Investment Opportunities Yearbook Volume 1 Strategic, Practical Information and Opportunities
United Arab Emirates Business and Investment Opportunities Yearbook Volume 1 Strategic, Practical Information and Opportunities
United Kingdom Business and Investment Opportunities Yearbook Volume 1 Strategic, Practical Information and Opportunities
United States Business and Investment Opportunities Yearbook Volume 1 Strategic, Practical Information and Opportunities
Uruguay Business and Investment Opportunities Yearbook Volume 1 Strategic, Practical Information and Opportunities
Uzbekistan Business and Investment Opportunities Yearbook Volume 1 Strategic, Practical Information and Opportunities
Vanuatu Business and Investment Opportunities Yearbook Volume 1 Strategic, Practical Information and Opportunities
Vatican City (Holy See) Business and Investment Opportunities Yearbook Volume 1 Strategic, Practical Information and Opportunities
Venezuela Business and Investment Opportunities Yearbook Volume 1 Strategic, Practical Information and Opportunities
Vietnam Business and Investment Opportunities Yearbook Volume 1 Strategic, Practical Information and Opportunities
Virgin Islands, British Business and Investment Opportunities Yearbook Volume 1 Strategic, Practical Information and Opportunities
Wake Atoll Business and Investment Opportunities Yearbook Volume 1 Strategic, Practical Information and Opportunities
Wallis & Futuna Business and Investment Opportunities Yearbook Volume 1 Strategic, Practical Information and Opportunities
Western Sahara Business and Investment Opportunities Yearbook Volume 1 Strategic, Practical Information and Opportunities
Yemen Business and Investment Opportunities Yearbook Volume 1 Strategic, Practical Information and Opportunities
Zambia Business and Investment Opportunities Yearbook Volume 1 Strategic, Practical Information and Opportunities
Zimbabwe Business and Investment Opportunities Yearbook Volume 1 Strategic, Practical Information and Opportunities

www.ingramcontent.com/pod-product-compliance
Ingram Content Group UK Ltd.
Pitfield, Milton Keynes, MK11 3LW, UK
UKHW051458290926
15471UKWH00008B/1277

9 781577 513438